2003
J.B.

RELIGION ON THE INTERNET: RESEARCH PROSPECTS AND PROMISES

RELIGION AND THE SOCIAL ORDER

Series Editor: David Bromley

RELIGION AND THE SOCIAL ORDER   VOLUME 8

RELIGION ON THE INTERNET: RESEARCH PROSPECTS AND PROMISES

EDITED BY

JEFFREY K. HADDEN
University of Virginia, USA

DOUGLAS E. COWAN
University of Missouri-Kansas City, USA

2000

JAI
An Imprint of Elsevier Science

Amsterdam – London – New York – Oxford – Paris – Shannon – Tokyo

ELSEVIER SCIENCE Inc.
655 Avenue of the Americas
New York, NY 10010, USA

First edition 2000

Library of Congress Cataloging in Publication Data
A catalog record from the Library of Congress has been applied for.

ISBN: 0-7623-0535-5
ISSN: 0161-5210

⊗ The paper used in this publication meets the requirements of ANSI/NISO Z39.48-1992 (Permanence of Paper).
Printed in The Netherlands.

CONTENTS

LIST OF CONTRIBUTORS

Matt Bahr

American Religion Data Archive
1365 Stone Hall
Purdue University
Lafayette, IN 47907-1365, USA
bahrm@purdue.edu

William Sims Bainbridge

National Science Foundation
4201 Wilson Boulevard
Arlington, Virginia 22230 USA
e-mail: wbainbri@nsf.gov

Kenneth B. Bedell

9515 Forest Dell Drive
Edmunds, WA 98020, USA
e-mail: kbedell@dnaco.net

Gary R. Bunt

Lecturer in Islamic Studies
University of Wales, Lampeter, U.K.
e-mail: g.bunt@lamp.ac.uk

Douglas E. Cowan

Department of Sociology/Criminal Justice
and Criminology
University of Missouri-Kansas City
208 Haag Hall, 5100 Rockhill Road,
Kansas City, Missouri 64110, USA
e-mail: dcowan@cadvision.com

Lorne L. Dawson

Department of Religious Studies
University of Waterloo
Waterloo, Ontario N2L3G1, Canada
e-mail: ldawson@watarts.uwaterloo.ca

Roger Finke

Professor of Sociology and Director of the
American Religion Data Archive
(www.thearda.com)
Pennsylvania State University
University Park, PA 16802, USA
e-mail: finke@purdue.edu

Jeffrey K. Hadden

Department of Sociology
539 Cabell Hall
University of Virginia, Charlottesville,
VA 22903, USA
e-mail: hadden@virginia.edu

Christopher Helland

Centre for the Study of Religion
University of Toronto,
123 St. George Street, Toronto, Ontario,
M5S 2E8, Canada
e-mail: c_hella@yahoo.com

Sara Horsfall

Department of Sociology
Texas Wesleyan University
Fort Worth, Texas, USA
e-mail: horsfals@txwes.edu;

Robert Glenn Howard

University of Oregon.
English Department and Folklore Program
Location: 461 PLC, Eugene, OR 97403,
USA
e-mail:rhoward@oregon.uoregon.edu

Massimo Introvigne

Center for Studies on New Religions
Torino, Italy (www.cesnur.org)
e-mail: censur@tin.it

Jean-François Mayer

Box 83 CH-1705 Fribourg, Switzerland
email: JFM@mcnet.ch

Jennifer McKinney

American Religion Data Archive
1365 Stone Hall, Purdue University
Lafayette, IN 47907-1365, USA
e-mail: mckinney@purdue.edu

Bruce A Robinson   473 Kingstondale Ave., Kingston, ON
K7M8A3, Canada
e-mail: ocrt@religioustolerance.org

Joanne Maguire Robinson   Department of Religious Studies
University of North Carolina at Charlotte
9201 University City Boulevard
Charlotte, NC 28223-0001, USA
e-mail: jmaguire@email.uncc.edu

1. INTRODUCTION

THE PROMISED LAND OR ELECTRONIC CHAOS? TOWARD UNDERSTANDING RELIGION ON THE INTERNET

Jeffrey K. Hadden and Douglas E. Cowan

> Is someone going to come to enlightenment on the Web? I doubt it, but you never can tell.
>
> John Daido Loori Roshi

E-PRESENCE: VIRTUALLY UNAVOIDABLE

In the early 1990s, the World Wide Web (WWW) hardly existed. Exchanging email and small files with what seem now like excruciatingly slow modems, a relative few technophiles and computer enthusiasts trudged their way along the information alleyway. While their path may only have been a dirt road at that point, the survey stakes for the coming information superhighway were already in place, and the roadbuilding equipment was poised just over the horizon. 1993 saw the advent of hypertext, and Web development gained speed and momentum. Now, less than a decade later, Web presence has established itself as one of the leading emblems of progressive engagement with culture. Only

Religion on the Internet, Volume 8, pages 3–21.
2000 by Elsevier Science Inc.
ISBN: 0-7623-0535-5

three decades after computer punch cards, technology has advanced to the point where silicon chips may soon be replaced by molecular electronics that measure their speed in terahertz (10^{12}, as opposed to megahertz, which is 10^6), their memory in the language of infinity, and their size in terms of how many of them can dance on the head of a pin (see Overton, 2000).

At the turn of the millennium, hardware availability and software evolution have rendered the virtual world virtually unvoidable.

Businesses which might otherwise have ignored the need for a Web site in the past now realize that such a presence is no longer a luxury, a flashy corporate extra. 'E-business', 'e-commerce', 'e-trade', and 'e-quests' to Top 40 radio stations have become standard additions to our North American discourse. University and public library holdings are now accessed through Web sites, reducing the venerable card catalogue to an historical footnote. More and more personal communication is done via email, and telephone service providers now regularly include the option for Internet access as part of their initial connection packages. Major – and not so major – newspapers and newsmagazines are readily available on-line. Real estate, complete with 'virtual tours' of selected homes; automobiles, organized according to make, model, price range, and distance from one's zip code; and the well-known 'E-bay', where vendors advertise everything from Duesenberg touring cars to the wartime letters of combat journalists, only begin to catalogue the commercial uses to which people have put this powerful cultural tool.

By 1998, the number of Web sites on-line was doubling every six months ('Pandora's Web', 1998). Virtual communities and alt. discussion forums had established themselves on the WWW to converse, debate, and flame, to buy, sell, and trade, and, according to Theodore Roszak, above all to advertise (Roszak, 1995, 1996). More and more powerful search engines evolved to help users navigate through a bewildering assortment of sites and pages devoted to everything from on-line support groups for those suffering from a variety of medical conditions to vacation planning and stock speculation, from UFO conspiracy theories to plasma physics. On-line activists carry out information and disinformation campaigns on the Net, and use its growing influence to pressure powers-that-be according to their particular agendas (Alam, 1996). And, of course, there is sex in all its myriad incarnations (see Lane III, 1999).

With the advent of WYSIWYG ("What you see is what you get") page editors, such as MS Frontpage, Claris Homeworks, and Dreamweaver, publishing on the Web became a domain no longer restricted to those conversant in the arcana of HTML or Java script. Point-and-click page construction has become the order of the day, and with Web page ease has come an e-space explosion. Personal Web sites abound. Family Web sites keep interested parties up-to-date on relatives flung far and wide around the globe. E-zines – electronic magazines devoted to poetry, short stories, music, and on-line multi-contributor novels – are born, live, and pass away at the whim of their creators, not their publishers. And, publication itself, long the Holy Grail for many a coffee table typist, is available to anyone with Internet access, server bandwidth, and thirty or forty dollars for the WYSIWYG software.

Who owns the data that populates the ever increasing number of Web sites, and who controls access to it, are questions of enormous importance (see Branscomb, 1994; Fisher, 1997; Garfinkel, 2000; Grossman, 1997). And data-bases, from library catalogue listings to the American Religion Data Archive (see Finke, McKinney and Bahr in this volume), from social survey data to the human genome project, offer unparalleled opportunities for researchers to broaden both their understanding and ability to do research. The various forms of data available on-line contribute to any number of educational endeavours, from freshman essays to the cutting edge of senior scholarship. Indeed, a recent article in a leading British Internet magazine declared: 'Instant Genius! Just add the Net'.

> Everyone hates a know-it-all. But who cares if you're the one with all the knowledge? Here are two resolutions for you. Don't be ignorant. And don't spend more time learning some-thing than you need to. Use the Net like Polyfilla and fill the gaps in your knowledge with ready-made, instant info bites. Just add a touch of brain power and mix until you dissolve the lumps. It's easy (Wright, 2000, p. 51).

This brief quote speaks to two important dynamics of the expansion of e-space into popular and professional culture: the compression of time, and the illusion of authority.

First, the compression of time. When letters were carried by railcar from their point-of-origin to destination sorting stations, then by hand to one's mailbox, a certain time lag in correspondence and communication was under-stood and accepted. We won't even discuss the years of the Pony Express. Aircraft changed the time frame for mail delivery and shortened the period of communication exchange, as did the advent of readily available private tele-phone lines. Beepers, cellular telephones, and faxes compressed it even further. Now, in many cases, there was no need for any appreciable time lag between contact and reply. The beeper goes off, and within a few minutes the reply is made. Without concern for geographical location, cell phones reduced that lag to precisely the number of rings it takes for the call recipient to answer.

Email, especially with the advent of free accounts and ready access to the Net, has generated an entire communication structure similar to surface mail, but with a very different time frame and discourse pattern. Instead of a second letter arriving, saying "I wrote you four months ago and have heard nothing in reply," email follow-ups measure that time in hours or even minutes. It is, however, still a written discourse. Thought must be organized according to the protocols of written communication and typed into the computer. But, because the time lag can be so short – replies coming in minutes, even seconds, from recipients who are on-line when the email arrives – the written discourse structure can follow a pattern more akin to a staggered and halting conversation than long, informative letters exchanged over a period of days or weeks.

With the Net, instead of a trip to the library to toil over the card catalogues, then perhaps request and wait for a book currently loaned out, *then* read through the inevitable irrelevancies before locating the data one requires, a search engine offers up in bare minutes a plethora of information choices. *With decreased time, though, comes increased expectation.* We are no longer willing to expend the time necessary to wade through piled-high back issues of *The New York Times* when a keyword search in the Lexis® – Nexis® Academic Universe returns in a few minutes all the stories related to our particular request. While these tools offer distinct and undeniable advantages in terms of a researcher's ability to prioritize and focus available time, there is the concomitant danger revealed in Wright's quote above. We will not take the time to *learn*; we will take only the time necessary to obtain the relevant facts, those 'ready-made, instant info bites' our information diet is perceived to lack. While hardly limited to the WWW, this phenomenon is exacerbated by the communications speed and the data search power offered by the Net. It encourages us to 'fill in the gaps' in such learning as we already possess, rather than take the time to gain a base of knowledge to which the information we acquire might contribute, and by which it can be evaluated.

Put differently, the problem is that we may not know enough to know that we really don't know anything at all. We have no foundation against which to measure that which we find on the Net. In e-space, there is no authoritative peer-review process, no editorial chain up which a potential article or book must be sold, no reliable mechanism by which information is vetted. And this is the Net's gift as well as its cost. While a greater amount of information is available on a wider basis than ever before, its quality spans the entire spectrum from the readily demonstrable to the unconditionally fabricated.

As Donath has pointed out, the community embodied in the virtual environment of the WWW is anchored in the person operating the keyboard – the one who conceptualizes, types, and uploads the message. It is, however, also disembodied in the manner of normal face-to-face communication because physical interpersonality and the attending social cues for communication are absent. The issue is not merely one of identity, but of the authority given the textual voice in the discourse. Donath gives the example of "a high school student [who] claims to be an expert on viruses" (Donath, 1999, p. 30). She continues that "patients desperate for a cure read the virtual virologist's pronouncements on new AIDS treatments, believing them to be backed by real world knowledge" (Donath, 1999, p. 30; cf. Foster, 1997).

Because there are less identity clues available in the virtual world, there appears at first glance, a levelling of the data playing field, an homogenization of the information available. This example, however, points out the danger of form over substance in the Net environment. The skill required to generate a very professional *looking* Web site pales in comparison with that required to produce the actual information, the content which will satisfy the visitor's need for knowledge. The Christian Apologetics and Resource Ministry (www.carm.org), for example, is a very impressively rendered Web site, devoted mainly to short essays about those religious groups its author considers 'cults'. The biographical information on CARM's author, however, reveals that "CARM is simply one man, me, Matt Slick. I write all the articles on the site" (Slick, 1999). At the time, Slick was an associate pastor at a fundamentalist Christian church, and while his site is impressive in its presentation, his M.Div. degree in no way guarantees either the veracity or accuracy of the information he provides.

Along with its vast commercial and scholarly possibilities, the democratization of Internet technology has opened the floodgates of potential both for inadvertent misinformation and for deliberate disinformation. How researchers learn from and study the Net must take both these factors into account.

RELIGION ON THE INTERNET: PROMISED LAND OR ELECTRONIC CHAOS?

It seems axiomatic that the easier the availability of production for such an obviously desirable commodity as Internet presence, the more that overall presence will expand. That religion would figure prominently in this expansion should not surprise; and as a number of contributors to this volume have pointed out, religion is one of the most popular items on the Net.

As that aspect of human relations that deals with issues of ultimate and transcendental concern, religion has a long history of employing new and innovative technology to promulgate its varied messages. Some of the oldest examples of written text are religious narratives. The first book off Gutenberg's famous printing press was the Bible. On Christmas Eve, 1906, the world's first radio broadcast was a religious service which included a violin solo of Gounod's 'O Holy Night' and readings from the Gospel of Luke. In fact, religious broadcasters, to a person, agree with broadcast historian J. Harold Ellens that "[it] is not without significance that the first voice broadcast was a Christian religious celebration.".

Indeed, perhaps no group was so quick to realize and embrace the potential of electronic communications as evangelical Christians (see Hadden & Shupe, 1988, Ch. 3). To those who take seriously Christ's commandment to go into all the world and preach the gospel to every creature (Mark, 16: 15), the revolution in electronic communications is not just one among many significant scientific advances in the 19th and early 20th centuries. Rather, since the coming of the Christ, it is perhaps the paramount event in human history. For the first time, the ability to transmit the voice and visual image of the preacher made it possible to fulfill the Great Commission, to reach all humankind with the Gospel message. The potential for realizing biblical eschatology became located in this wave of technological advance. While conservative Christian broadcasters have not rushed to embrace the Internet as quickly as they did radio and television, few now have not established their presence in e-space.

Although Christianity might have been the first to stake a claim on the audio and video airwaves, e-space is hardly limited to that religion. There is scarcely a religious tradition, movement, group, or phenomenon absent entirely from the Net. From the Norse neopaganism of Ásatrú to Christian countercult refutations of it, from Tibetan Buddhist prayer bowls and thangka paintings to Wiccan scrying bowls that come with easy-to-follow instructions, from a disenfranchised Catholic bishop exiled to a non-existent North African diocese to a cyber-monastery established exclusively for non-resident students of Zen, the only thing that seems crystal clear is that the presence of religion on the Internet will only expand as the Web technology and access availability increase.

That the information superhighway means *something* for religion, for religious adherents and communities, and for those who study them is undeniable. What that *something* might be is one of the agendas of this volume. Is the Net the promised land of discourse for religious supporters and scholars alike? Or is it more akin to an electronic chaos, a disorganized mass of information so diverse, so varied in its presentation, utility, and veracity, that it still awaits the hand of God to separate the dry land from the waters? Will it serve us on our long journey towards understanding, or drown us as unsurfable waves of information crest and crash over our heads?

E-FAITH: RELIGION ON-LINE OR ON-LINE RELIGION?

Modifying Christopher Helland's conceptualization somewhat (see Helland in this volume), one of the first differences to be identified on the WWW is that between 'religion on-line' and 'on-line religion'; both, however, are emerging as a presence in e-space. Essentially, *religion on-line* provides the interested web traveller with *information about* religion: doctrine, polity, organization, and belief; service and opportunities for service; religious books and articles; as well as other paraphernalia related to one's religious tradition or quest. On the other hand, *on-line religion* invites the visitor to *participate in* the religious dimension of life via the Web; liturgy, prayer, ritual, meditation, and homiletics come together and function with the e-space itself acting as church, temple, synagogue, mosque, and grove.

Three examples serve here to illustrate this difference: The Witch's Voice (www.witchvox.com), Partenia (www.partenia.fr), and Zen Mountain Monastery (www.zen-mtn.org).

WWW.WITCHVOX.COM

Begun in 1997, the project of Wren Walker and her partner Fritz Jung, The Witches' Voice is perhaps the most extensive Wiccan/Neopagan Web site on the Net. The mission statement on their homepage reads:

> The Witches' Voice is a proactive educational network dedicated to correcting misinformation about Witches and Witchcraft. Witchcraft-Wicca IS a legally recognized religion in the United States and it is our mission to protect that right through education and awareness. (http://www.witchvox.com)

Essentially a clearinghouse for information about the Craft, The Witches' Voice is *religion on-line*. They claim links to over three thousand other pagan Web sites, and over *31,000* total related links. Contained in these is a vast array of contact information for practitioners, URLs for Wiccan supply houses, chat rooms, and religious liberty forums. The sitemap comprises over thirty separate pages, each of which offers further layers of content. Some of the topics the site managers discuss are: the basics of witchcraft; covens, groups, and organizations; witches and pagans around the world ("Over 22,000 Witches, Wiccans and Pagans, Over 600 time-stamped Circles, Workshops, Gatherings and Events, over 1400 Covens and Groups and close to 879 Witch/ Metaphysical shops" [Walker & Jung, 2000]). Additional pages offer resources for teenage pagans, pagan parenting, gay and lesbian pagans, and pagans in the military.

One of the page layers that Walker and Jung consider the most important is the 'WVOX White Pages', printable versions of religious liberty documents related to Wicca and other Neopaganisms. These documents range from a sample letter that parents can send to elementary schools correcting misinformation about Wicca and Neopaganism in order to protect the rights of Wiccan/Neopagan children, to petitions asking for fairer treatment of non-traditional religious groups by the media. The authors are also endeavoring to survey the Neopagan community through their Web site. The first survey, on pagan working groups and run from September 12–27, 1999, drew nearly 2500 responses.

Religion on-line offers the widely varied and far flung Neopagan community an opportunity to connect, communicate, and share resources with other Neopagans in an environment which is considerably less hazardous than is often the case in real life.

WWW.PARTENIA.FR

January 1995 saw the evacuation of one Roman Catholic bishopric and the re-creation of another. However, while the former still includes the gothic cathedral at Evreux, France, the latter exists now only in e-space. It is Partenia, and its bishop is Jacques Gaillot. A Bishop without a diocese, he went onto the Internet in 1996 and declared Partenia "a diocese without borders" (www.partenia.fr).

On the official rolls of the Roman Catholic Church, the diocese of Partenia is in 'infidel hands', an ancient city in southern Algeria, buried beneath the Saharan desert since the Middle Ages. However, for his liberal views on birth control, celibacy, and homosexuality, Jacques Gaillot was stripped of his bishopric in the Normandy town of Evreux and given Partenia as punishment. Rather than simply submit to what he considered an unfair decision, Gaillot used this as an opportunity to reach beyond the borders of a traditional parish. Working also among the homeless and immigrant populations in France, he established Partenia as a witness to his vision of the Church and a testimony to its treatment of him. The gateway image into the site is a desert oasis, a globe, and Gaillot's smiling face.

Available in several languages, www.partenia.fr includes pastoral letters on a variety of social and religious issues, a 'log book' in which Gaillot reflects on significant events in the history of his unorthodox diocese, an electronic catechism which reflects his unorthodox theology, and a forum where inter ested visitors may post on any issue of interest to them. While providing information about the Catholic Church, in Gaillot's vision Partenia functions as a virtual diocese; it challenges the distinction of the border between *religion on-line* and *on-line religion.*

A Reuters report on Partenia the week it launched declared that, as "the first bishop in cyberspace," "Gaillot has become a media celebrity for his fight for greater rights for the homeless, the unemployed and those excluded from mainstream society. He says he wants Partenia to be a meeting place of all." However, *Le Figaro's* interpretation of Gaillot and his project highlights an issue often lost in the rhetoric of information and communication democratization: access is limited to those who can afford the tools of access. "It is a public place reserved for those who have computers, modems and subscriptions to the Internet. Not exactly what one would call social outcasts" (Bowen, 1995).

WWW.ZEN-MTN.ORG

Far from either Evreux or Partenia, in the mountains of upstate New York lies Zen Mountain Monastery. John Daido Loori Roshi, a Dharma heir of the late Hakuyu Taizen Maezumi Roshi, is the abbot. ZMM has maintained an active Web presence for some time. Their Web site includes *Mountain Record On-line*, the WWW version of ZMM's quarterly journal; an on-line archive of Daido Loori's dharma discourses; and 'Cybermonk', a senior student who is available on-line to answer questions of practitioners and interested visitors to the site. Additionally, Dharma Communications is ZMM's 'religious outreach' arm, providing resources to Buddhist practitioners over the Internet. Most of these resources are available through Dharma Communications' main vehicle, the Monastery Store On-line (www.zen-mtn.org/dc/store.shtml).

Since mid-1997, though, a number of Daido Loori's senior students have been working on a project called 'Cyber Monastery', "a Zen training program that will be accessible only on-line. On the screen appears a list of requirements. The first two point to the future: '1. zafu. 2. IBM Pentium (computer)' " (Zaleski, 1999, p. 53). Connecting the silicon chip with the traditional Zen sitting cushion, this is an example of the far edge of Buddhist *on-line religion*. Daido Loori explains how the process will work:

> People will register and go through the same screening process that any student who comes here to practice has to go through. If they are accepted, they will enter the program. They will receive in the mail an interactive CD-ROM and several video- and audiotapes. The CD-ROM will contain links to the chat room. They'll have an assigned training adviser who will be available for them in real time on-line for dialogues and discussions. There will be assignments, projects, and exams on-line, and the whole course will end with a traditional on-line Dharma combat with me (Daido Loori, in Zaleski, 1999, p. 53).

When asked whether the cyber monastery, while innovative, is not "a very poor substitute for the real thing," Daido Loori replied that it is "an extension of what we already do ... Is somebody going to come to enlightenment on the Web? I doubt it, but you never can tell" (Daido Loori, in Zaleski, 1999, p. 53). He is clear that, rather than replace the living, breathing relationship a Zen student has with his or her teacher, the cyber-monastery functions as an adjunct to the teacher. If it comes into being, however, it will offer one of the most fully-orbed examples of *on-line religion*.

Echoing communications scholars Harold Innes and Marshall McLuhan, Pavlik recalls Innes' theory that "the long-lasting social structure of ancient

Egypt was directly linked to the Egyptian's use of stone tablets as a medium of communication. When the Egyptians began to write on papyrus, a much less permanent and much more portable communication medium, their society began to undergo much more rapid social change" (Pavlik, 1998, pp. 286–7). How much less permanent is the unprinted email or on-line religious service, comprised of no more than electrons excited in a particular pattern, projected onto a screen, and subject to the caprice of power supply, server fortitude, and operator error? As we move towards a more virtually constructed environment, will the social controls established by the various religions decrease? On-line religion offers the freedom to participate from a remote location, but it invokes a reduction in the ability to enforce that participation. An email asking "Why didn't you log on for prayers this morning?" can be left unanswered for as long as one wants; it carries conceivably less relational weight than a face-to-face encounter with one's religious leader or peer asking the same question.

E-RESEARCH: AGENDAS AND ISSUES

If on-line religion and religion on-line are two facets of the issue for practitioners, two similar facets for researchers are: (a) studying religion as it exists on the WWW, and (b) using the WWW to study religion. Each of these raises particular questions: respectively, how can the Net be used to greatest advantage in religious research, and what are the ethical issues raised by research in an environment which allows such a high degree of camouflage and misrepresentation?

At its most basic level, a computer performs two tasks: it stores information, and it manipulates the information stored on it. Anything else – communication, web design, on-line gambling or pornography – derives from those two main functions. Databasing, then, archiving the kind of information useful for scholarship, and providing the tools to manipulate that information in useful ways, is one of the most exciting benefits of the WWW for researchers. Rather than requesting a time-consuming interlibrary loan for the 1993 Survey of American Catholic Priests, for example, the researcher simply accesses the ARDA website (www.thearda.com), selects the appropriate instrument, and downloads it complete with a modest version of the statistical software required to manipulate the data. What might have taken weeks can be accomplished in a matter of minutes.

Information retrieval is not the only advantage. The speed with which the Internet environment can *absorb* and *disseminate* information also contributes to the facility of its research function. In the normal course of print publication, the speed of absorption and dissemination is measured at least in months, often in years. By the time an article or book has been passed up the editorial chain, typeset, galleyed, printed, bound, and distributed, the information it contains or the argument it makes could be hopelessly out of date; thus, rather than a snapshot of the way things are, the time lag has rendered it an historical record of the way things were. In e-space, the absorption time of information is limited only by the proficiency of the producer with whatever Web-authoring tools he or she has at hand, and the speed with which his or her hardware and server connection can manage the upload.

For example, in March 2000, when a little-known religious group in southern Uganda appeared to have committed mass suicide in the face of failed prophetic expectations, there was no social scientific literature available on them. In the normal course of events, months would have passed before anything on the Restoration of the Ten Commandments of God Movement could have found its way into the traditional literature. The Internet, however, provided for the rapid dissemination of such information as was available to anyone who could access the appropriate URLs. Elaborate sites such as Introvigne's (www.cesnur.org; the Center for Study on New Religions in Torino, Italy), collected daily media reports on the tragedy from around the world, archiving them for retrieval and comparison. As well, commentaries and speculation were offered within hours by leading figures in the field.

The Net also offers intriguing possibilities for the production and deployment of social survey instruments. At this point, though, these appear to be most suited to studying interaction in the environment in which they are deployed; that is, surveys on the Net are most useful for studying human relations in e-space. The simple reason for this is that, despite their decreased cost and growing availability through schools, libraries, and Internet cafes, the technology is not available across the broad spectrum of human population, and is not likely to be in the near future. Economic realities render the technocratic dream of universal access to the Internet just that – a dream. A hierarchy of access still exists, determined by those who can afford the equipment and the connections; as a result of this, there is still a threshold below which access does not occur. There are people, perhaps millions (billions?) of people who have not and will not use a personal computer to access the Internet in their lifetimes. Researching the sociology of the Net takes place above this low water mark of e-space participation.

For example, survey instruments emailed to a particular discussion list, say alt.ufo.conspiracy, by definition go to those who operate above the threshold of Internet access; invitational surveys which are advertised for response either on the Net, or in print publications as available on the Net, likewise require that access in order to participate. Both exclude certain segments of the population which exist below the access threshold. It is not like a telephone survey, or a mail survey that includes pre-paid return envelopes, both of which require only the time and interest of the participant. In the case of the Internet, survey response requires the same tools as survey deployment. Until this reality can be accurately accounted for in the data manipulation process, researchers would do well to use the Web to its fullest, to push the limits of which the Web is capable as a research tool, but to recognize clearly that those limits exist.

Researching on the Net raises anew ethical issues which have generated debate in the social sciences for decades. While they may take various forms, these debates constellate around the concepts of coversion and disclosure in field research. Are we silent watchers from the jungle's edge or participant-observers in the life of the village? Alt.-style discussion groups, electronic bulletin boards which are open to all with neither moderation nor vetting, are the best e-space example of this. In these kind of forums, it is possible to 'lurk', to observe list content, traffic, participant factioning and alliance, authority declaration and acceptance (or rejection), and participant career with *no one* aware of the researcher's presence. The lack of requirement for identification, or even the indication of one's presence, makes the computer screen an almost perfect blind from which to watch. But is this ethical? Should disclosure of one's presence and purpose be an accepted protocol in this environment? As they have for real life ethnography, opinions vary (see, for example, Paccagnella, 1997). Some advocate full disclosure, others only in the event of publication that might identify the virtual community or its members. Still others seek the elusive purity of an 'untainted' observation and argue for non-disclosure.

The masking function of the Internet is not limited to non-disclosure, however; it also includes the possibility of outright deceit. While it would be physically impossible for a blond, Caucasian anthropologist to represent herself to the Bemba of East Africa as one of their own, such restrictions do not apply in e-space. Because few of the normal identity cues function in the virtual world, it is entirely possible to enter a discussion group and misrepresent oneself as a bona fide member of that group. How researchers monitor and regulate these kind of Internet research protocols will be another important aspect of this ethics discussion.

E-CLASSROOM: PEDAGOGY FACE-TO-FACE AND FAR AWAY

Virtual pedagogy offers two distinct lines of exploration as well, both essentially functions of distance: (a) using the Internet in a classroom environment to expand the range of resources available to both students and teachers, and (b) using the Internet to offer courses at distance for students who cannot be on site. In addition to regular computer labs and designated high-tech classrooms, more and more regular classrooms are being retrofitted with data jacks, docking stations for laptop computers, and computer carts. Calling up a particular URL, whether one prepared specifically for the course or another which illustrates the lesson for the class, could (and likely will) become as commonplace as operating a videocassette player or overhead projector. Software such as WebCT (Web Course Tools) brings the development and delivery of interactive course components within the range of more and more instructors.

Access to courses designed specifically for the Web both expands the potential student base for an institution and increases the ability of students to access higher education. Distance courses can be built on models as elementary as student papers posted to the registered group, with emailed critiques or threaded discussions sufficing to establish group discussion, participation, and evaluation. Courses can become as complex as instructors are willing to make them: prepared lectures on-line, with integrated audio and video; interactive CD-ROM assignments; real time CU-C-ME conferencing; discussion boards for course content and less formal student chat rooms (with or without instructor access); emailed course submissions and on-line examinations; as well as student homepages.

Encouraging students to use the Web in their own research adds another dimension to a standard pedagogical role: teaching students to conduct research thoughtfully and carefully. Hadden's Religious Movements Homepage project, for example, has contributions from many of his students in a sociology of religion class at the University of Virginia (see Hadden in this volume). Part of their course work for the term is to research a particular new religious movement and produce a Web page devoted to it. While they do use the standard primary and secondary scholarly resources – journals, books, etc. – the Internet is now added to that list as a fundamental resource. Because, in some cases, the Web provides a very broad range of primary and secondary sources, the latter often contradictory and disputative, depending on the group in question, the students gain experience in the evaluation and adjudication of evidence. Many of these pages have been vetted and reworked by Hadden, then uploaded to expand the Religious Movements homepage (www.religiousmovements.org).

VARIOUS VOICES: CONTRIBUTIONS TO THE CURRENT DISCUSSION

In this volume we have drawn together a number of different contributors, each offering insight into one of these three main aspects of religion on the Internet: e-faith, e-research, and e-teaching.

INTERNET RESEARCH:
STUDYING RELIGION ON THE WEB

The exploration of any new territory demands the production of accurate maps, useful concepts and terms to define and describe the terrain, and the dedication of men and women to the project of exploration. In 'Researching Religion in Cyberspace', University of Waterloo sociologist Lorne Dawson begins the navigation, arguing that the study of religion on the Internet cannot be separated from issues raised by the larger sociology of the Internet. Who are we when we are online? How are those identities formed and maintained? How do the various communities we form in e-space differ from those we participate in beyond the Net? Anchored in this larger understanding, Dawson outlines three specific research agendas particular to "the sociology of cyber-religion." What are the implications of the Internet for religious recruitment? How are religious conflicts and authority manifest, mediated, and resolved (if they are) on the Web? And, finally, how does the Internet function as a mediator of religious experience?

Senior science advisor to the Directorate for Social, Behavioral, and Economic Sciences of the National Science Foundation, William Sims Bainbridge continues the discussion, pushing the boundaries of our e-space cartography. 'Religious Ethnography on the World Wide Web' explores how the different forms of ethnography, the systematic documentation of a culture, can be employed when researching the very components of Internet sociology raised by Dawson. Using both informant interviews and participant-observation, Bainbridge illustrates these potentials through a theory-based exploration of religious Web sites and a report on a series of on-line questionnaires designed to create new survey items and measurement scales. Bainbridge's observational data generated a set of nine connected hypotheses about how Web sites might affect both the manner in which religious groups compete on the Web, and the manner in which they are challenged and contested by other groups. On the other hand, using The Question Factory, his private research Web site which creates and tests on-line surveys, ethnographic questionnaires collected material for 90 afterlife items and 100 future of religion items. These pilot projects demonstrate that the Web is ready to become a valuable channel for ethnographic research.

Accurate data that is readily available and easily comprehended is the lifeblood of any research enterprise. Using a grant from the Lilly Endowment, Pennsylvania State sociologist Roger Finke began the American Religion Data Archive at Purdue University in 1997, and is its current director. Gathering survey data from a wide variety of sources, the primary goal of the ARDA is as the subtitle to their contribution suggests, *democratizing data*. ARDA now holds over 150 data files on various aspects of American religion that are available to scholars and students. As Finke (with research associates Jennifer McKinney and Matt Bahr) notes, this archive comes equipped with an abundance of on-line features. From conducting basic analysis to reviewing codebooks, from constructing survey instruments to downloading data and software, the ARDA provides a wealth of data as well as the tools to use it. This chapter gives a brief overview of the kind of data archived at the ARDA, the users the ARDA serves, and the goals it seeks to achieve. As well, Finke, McKinney and Bahr illustrate how the ARDA can be used for teaching and research.

Once scholars are on-line, though, how do their discussions fare? Sometimes well; other times poorly. Internet discussion, whatever its form, presents its own unique set of opportunities and challenges. In the context of the academic discussion of religion, for example, how does one determine which threads are permissible on a particular list? How does one moderate on-line debates that often become acrimonious and quibbling when different participant agendas emerge? And, in the face of these problems, is it possible to manage who is allowed on discussion lists and how those discussions can maintain some semblance of academic integrity? Drawing primarily on the experience of Nurel-L, a list created by Irving Hexham for the academic discussion of new religious movements, University of Missouri-Kansas City MKC sociologist Douglas Cowan addresses these issues in 'Religion, Rhetoric, and Scholarship: Managing Vested Interest in E-Space'.

Internet Faith: Religions in Cyberspace

For a number of people, it may come as a surprise how significant a part of many Muslims' lives the Internet has become. From on-line copies of and commentaries on the Quran to virtual tours of the vicinity around the Kaba, from Shiism in cyberspace to Internet travel agencies specializing in the Hajj, University of Wales scholar Gary Bunt demonstrates how proactive many Muslims are in establishing a Web presence for Islam, what he calls *cyber Islamic environments*. As Bunt and others in this volume note, the Internet has raised the issue of authoritative perception. Groups which may be in the minority either numerically or influentially can operate on the Web with a presence that belies their actual power. 'Surfing Islam: Ayatollahs, Shayks and Hajjs on the Superhighway' is the result of several years' experience in teaching Islamic Studies, and draws on the writer's experience developing a guide to the Internet as an Islamic Studies resource.

In 'Online-Religion/Religion-Online and Virtual Communitas', Christopher Helland, a doctoral candidate at the Centre for the Study of Religion at the University of Toronto, uses the work of Victor Turner to develop a heuristic device for a general classification of religious and spiritually focused Web sites. He argues that religion on the Internet manifests itself in two basic forms. First, representing a direct reaction to institutionalized religion in the secular world, online-religion encourages a new manifestation of religious interaction, participation, and community. The Internet itself becomes the worship space, the prayer shawl, or the meditation bench. Conversely, though, harnessing the power of the Net as another means to maintain a traditional form of top-down, one-to-many communication, institutionalized religious structures characterize Helland's second form: Religion-Online.

Following on Helland's introduction to the topic, Texas Wesleyan sociologist Sara Horsfall looks at the various ways in which five different religious groups actually use the Internet. While each group has an active presence in the U.S., each is also an international movement. Interestingly, Horsfall found that individual Web pages often predated official Web sites. When they did enter cyberspace much of the official use was devoted to publicity and public relations. While for NRMs such as the Church of Scientology, the Internet has provided a means to counter its critics, other religious movements have used the Net to publish a wide variety of religious texts. From directories of churches and worship centers to the email and Web site addresses of individual members, a number of these international groups use e-space to keep their members informed of the latest policies and activities worldwide.

But how are other religious organizations using the Web to enhance their religious lives? Vice President of the Forum Foundation in Seattle, Ken Bedell spent nearly a year traversing the mainline Protestant religious territory on the Internet. He wanted to know whether and how these people were actively using the Web to support or enhance their spiritual lives or their participation in spiritual communities. 'Dispatches from the Electronic Frontier' is his report from ten months spent in cyberspace. Like other researchers, he found that people are eagerly adopting the Internet as a way of expanding their existing religious interest or commitments. That is, for those Bedell encountered, religion is one of countless topics that can be researched in cyberspace. However, while these same people expect that the Internet will play an important role in religious life in the future, Bedell found that, in the context of mainline Protestantism, there was little evidence that the Internet is being used to form new religious communities or to support new spiritual practices.

For the last few years, Robert Glenn Howard, a doctoral student in English at the University of Oregon, has been taking his own journey through e-space, this trip, though, in the domain of evangelical dispensationalism. Applying a mix of rhetorical criticism and ethnography, Howard set out to document and analyze this discrete community of Netizens. Because of the 'feverish rush' in which much of this community's discourse was carried out as the clock ticked down to the year 2000, Howard found that a rhetorical tension emerged in the on-line dispensationalist community. On the one hand, there were those who wanted to discuss events and their interpretations of them, that is, to *negotiate* about truth. On the other hand, many expressed the desire to expound an *experienced* or *revelatory* Truth, one which brooked neither discussion nor correction.

Simple deployment of resources and on-line worship does not exhaust the uses to which religious groups have put the Internet. Recalling part of Dawson's discussion, many have viewed the religious use of the Web with suspicion, seeing it as some new, powerful tool for emergent religious movements to proselytize and recruit. Swiss scholar Jean-François Mayer, however, argues that, because the Internet is a means of communication which even individuals are able to use efficiently and effectively, the Net has probably helped critics of religious movements more than the movements themselves. As 'The New Frontier of Cult Controversies', Mayer defines the various strategies which NRMs have adopted in relation to the Internet. Ranging from aggressive counter-attack to a strong official Web presence, from the multiplication of Web pages produced by members to the delegitimation of critics, Mayer uses the concept of 'cyberspace propaganda wars' in an attempt to identify some of these new battlegrounds.

The fear that cults would recruit via the Internet only increased in the wake of the 1997 Heaven's Gate suicides. Riding a wave of media conjecture and exaggeration, opponents of NRMs appear to have been more active and more aggressive in cyberspace than many of the movements themselves. Labelling this 'Anti-cult Terrorism via the Internet', Italian NRM scholar Massimo Introvigne uses emerging theoretical models of cyberspace to examine issues of violence and terrorism via the Internet. These models Introvigne then applies to the extreme fringe of anti-cultism, which he is clear is not to be confused with the more moderate cult awareness community. Rather, these are individuals and groups who use the Internet to disseminate religious hate propaganda. The activities of this 'lunatic fringe' focus on demonizing and dehumanizing the 'cults' and their alleged supporters; they promote increasingly wild conspiracy theories; and they target legitimate scholars of NRMs whom they have singled out as 'cult apologists'.

As both Mayer and Introvigne describe, one aspect of religious interaction – tolerance – is as lacking in virtual reality as in the other. Disturbed by what he saw as an increasing intolerance among the religious peoples of the world, Bruce Robinson, a retired software engineer, created the Ontario Consultants on Religious Tolerance, and its primary entity: www.religioustolerance.org, a site Hadden calls "probably the most magnificent religious Web page on the

Internet" (see Hadden in this volume). 'Evolution of a Religious Web Site Devoted to Tolerance' describes the site from its modest beginnings to the religious Web site visited by more people in a single day than any other in the world. Devoted to the reduction of religious tension and discrimination, the dissemination of accurate religious information, and the promotion of religious tolerance and respect, the OCRT Web site is a model of the way in which the Internet can function as a method of new media pedagogy. While much of the religious intolerance on the Net is spun from the webs of deceit both Mayer and Introvigne describe, Robinson has established www.religioustolerance.org as a way to break those strands and thereby weave a better world.

If the accurate understanding of a particular terrain is crucial to successfully and responsibly navigating that landscape, what happens when the maps we draw differ? How is a teacher to respond when the cognitive maps drawn by students to help them navigate class materials differ substantially from that of the teacher and those of fellow classmates? At the very least, it would be helpful to know when and how this occurs. In "Mapping a 'Cyberlimen', " University of North Carolina at Charlotte religious studies professor Joanne Maguire Robinson explores the benefits and limitations of integrating electronic class discussion boards into religious studies classes. Used experimentally in a class devoted to examining contentious theological, political, and ethical issues from the perspective of Christianity, Robinson learned how these maps differ and how, knowing that, she could better approach classes.

Finally, described as "a serendipitous by-product of my effort to learn how better to utilize multimedia resources in the classroom," University of Virginia sociologist Jeffrey K. Hadden's Religious Movements Homepage project has grown from a modest classroom Web site to an internationally recognized resource for scholars and students from around the world. 'Confessions of a Recovering Technophobe' is the personal story of how the particular problems Hadden encountered became avenues to even bigger opportunities.

CONCLUDING REMARKS

Any piece of written work is like a dye marker thrown into the ocean. It marks a particular spot at a particular time; its shape and duration is determined by sea state and weather. Occasionally, it allows for the location and relocation of that particular spot on the surface. This seems an apt metaphor for any book about the ocean of information that is the Internet, and the often bewildering fluidity of the e-space environment. It is our hope that the dye markers thrown into the sea by the contributors to this volume will offer both challenging descriptions of religion on the Net and substantial points of departure from which other researchers may proceed.

REFERENCES

Alam, S. (1996). On-line lifeline. *The New Internationalist,* (December): 14–15.

Bowen, C. (1995). The Power of One. Retrieved July 1, 2000, from the World Wide Web: http://www.socool.com/news/power.html.

Branscomb, A. W. (1994). *Who Owns Information? From Privacy to Public Access.* New York: HarperCollins Publishers, Basic Books.

Donath, J. S. (1999). Identity and deception in the virtual community. In: M. A. Smith, & P. Kollock, (Eds), *Communities in Cyberspace* (pp. 29–59). London and New York: Routledge.

Fisher, T. (1997). Intellectual Property On-line. In: O'Reilly & Associates (Eds.), *The Harvard Conference on the Internet and Society* (pp. 357–364). Sebastopol, CA: O'Reilly & Associates, Inc.

Foster, D. (1997). Community and Identity in the Electronic Village. In: D. Porter, (Ed.), *Internet Culture* (pp. 23–37). New York and London: Routledge.

Garfinkel, S. (2000). Welcome to Sealand. Now Bugger Off. *Wired,* (July): 230–239.

Grossman, L. K. (1997). Who Owns the Internet? In: O'Reilly & Associates (Eds), *The Harvard Conference on the Internet and Society* (pp. 449–463). Sebastopol, CA: O'Reilly & Associates, Inc.

Hadden, J. K., & Shupe, A. (1988). *Televangelism Power and Politics on God's Frontier.* New York: Henry Holt. Available online at
(http://cti.itc.virginia.edu/~jkh8x/relbroad/powerpolitics/home.html)

Lane III, F. S. (1999). *Obscene Profits: The Entrepreneurs of Pornography in the Cyber Age.* New York: Routledge.

Overton, R. (2000). Moletronics Will Change Everything. *Wired,* (July): 240–251.

Paccagnella, L. (1997). Getting the Seat of Your Pants Dirty: Strategies for Ethnographic Research on Virtual Communities. *Journal of Computer-Mediated Communication, 3*(1). Retrieved July 25, 1999, from the World Wide Web: http://jcmc.huji.ac.il/vol3/issue1/paccagnella.html.

Pandora's Web. (1998). *Web Techniques: Solutions for Internet and Web Developers,* 3:1 (January): 7.

Pavlik, J. V. (1998). *New Media Technology: Cultural and Commercial Perspectives,* 2nd ed. Boston: Allyn and Bacon.

Roszak, T. (1995). *The Cult of Information: A Neo-Luddite Treatise on High Tech, Artificial Intelligence and the True Art of Thinking.* Berkeley and Los Angeles: The University of California Press.

Roszak, T. (1996). Dumbing us down. *The New Internationalis*t, (December): 12–14.

Slick, M. (1999). *About CARM.* Retrieved July 21, 2000, from the World Wide Web: http://www.carm.og/aboutcarm.htm.

Walker, W., & Jung, F. (2000). *Witchvox Chapter Overviews.* Retrieved July 1, 2000, from the World Wide Web: http://www.witchvox.com/maps/map_chapters.html

Wright, S. (2000). Instant Genius! Just add the Net. *.net,* (June): 50–58.

Zaleski, J. (1999). Straight Ahead: Jeff Zaleski interviews John Daido Loori Roshi. *Tricycle: The Buddhist Review*, (Winter): 48–54.

2. INTERNET RESEARCH: STUDYING RELIGION ON THE WEB

RESEARCHING RELIGION IN CYBERSPACE: ISSUES AND STRATEGIES

Lorne L. Dawson

Computers have changed; times have changed; [we] have changed. But [one] could also write: Times have changed; [we] have changed; computers have changed. In fact, there are six possible sequences. We construct our technologies, and our technologies construct us and our times. Our times make us, we make our machines, our machines make our times. We become the objects we look upon but they become what we make of them (Turkle, 1995, p. 46).

ABSTRACT

This chapter argues that the emerging study of religion on-line and on-line religion needs to be anchored in an understanding of the issues raised by the larger sociology of the Internet. In particular the debates over the influence of the Internet on the processes of identity formation and the potential to establish virtual communities need to be examined. After providing an overview of these concerns, attention is turned to a discussion of three more specific concerns of the sociology of cyber-religion: the implication of the Internet for religious recruitment, religious conflicts and authority, and the mediation of religious experience. The chapter ends with a consideration of the possible synergistic links between the life in late modern society, the Internet, and the contemporary shift in religious sensibilities in the developed western societies.

Religion on the Internet, Volume 8, pages 25–54.
Copyright © 2000 by Elsevier Science Inc.
All rights of reproduction in any form reserved.
ISBN: 0-7623-0535-5

INTRODUCTION

Will the Internet change the nature and functioning of religion? Will the changes be significant? Will they be incremental, and in line with trends already in place? Or will the Internet foster more dramatic and immediate shifts in religious sensibilities and practices? Questions like these are just beginning to be asked, and the answers may be a long time in coming.

The creation and slow spread of the written word transformed the religious world, as did the invention of the printing press. Electronic mass media have been with us for less than a century and their impact on religion is still being assessed. Will the impact of the interactive Internet be in line with that of these broadcast media, or does it present us with an alternative situation? The Internet is less than a decade old, so it may be too early to tell. But in the wake of Marshal McLuhan (1965), few doubt that the Internet will change who we are as we use it, regardless of what we choose to transmit through it.

In the first flush of social commentary the Internet has been bathed in utopian and dystopian rhetoric (e.g. Barlow et al., 1995; Brooke, 1997; Mitchell, 1995; Ramo, 1996; Rheingold, 1993; Slouka, 1995; Stoll, 1995; Turkle, 1995; Zaleski, 1997). But more sober second thought is beginning to prevail as the social scientific study of the Internet begins in earnest (e.g. Gackenbach, 1998; Holmes, 1997; Jones 1995, 1998; Porter, 1997; Shields, 1996; Slevin, 2000; Smith & Kollock, 1999).

Both new and old religious groups have migrated to cyberspace with some enthusiasm. But the work done to date on religion on the Internet is quite limited, though promising. In fashioning a research agenda for this relatively new field of study we need to turn our attention to the issues being raised by the general sociology of the Internet. The ramifications of research into the social nature and consequences of the Internet have yet to be explored for the practice of religion.

Three kinds of research need to be undertaken in coming to grips with the new reality of religious life in a world increasingly geared to the forms and demands of computer mediated communication (Castells, 1996). The first research challenge is simply one of *identification and measurement.* What, with regard to religion, is on the Internet, and who is using it, how and why? The second challenge is the systematic *study of the key substantive concerns* raised by the initial studies of the social implications of the Internet, concerns about identity, community, authority, conflict, and simulated reality in general. The third challenge is the *theoretical and empirical exploration* of the speculated relationship between the Internet and an emerging new religious consciousness. This entails consideration of the complex connections between the Internet, postmodernist or late modernist society, globalization, and religious change.

Everything said about the social significance of the Internet is qualified, however, by the implicit phrase "in the developed world." It is all too easy to forget that we still live in a world where most people do not have regular access to a telephone, let alone a computer capable of surfing the World Wide Web. Even in the developed world, most of us are too preoccupied with the struggle to better our condition in conventional society to have much reason to feel the effects of participating in cybersociety. In the United Sates, by far the most 'wired' nation on the planet, the best estimates are that only about a third of the population has regular access to the Web (Kaye & Johnson, 1999, p. 324). But, as is widely recognized, the rate of growth of the Internet is staggering, and when the communication infrastructures of nations like Brazil and China are improved cyberspace will be flooded with new traffic (see Slevin, 2000, pp. 40–44 for some facts and figures). The speed with which the Internet may alter the world in which we live is likely to exceed that of the other electronic media. The Internet presents us with the subtlest combination of 'high' and 'low tech'. Minimal investment and knowledge is needed for any individual to reach out with rapidity to thousands of others around the world.

This said, let us begin by considering the need to get our bearings through the systematic empirical study of religion in cyberspace. We need to measure the phenomenon to supplant speculation with worthwhile analysis. This will be followed in the next section of the chapter by an overview of the two key substantive concerns of the existing sociology of the Internet: the role of cyber-life in the formation of identity and the possibility of virtual community. If the Internet is helping to change our conceptions and experiences of either identity or community, then scholars of religion need to take note, given the centrality of both concerns to religious life. The realities of life on line may well turn out to be more prosaic than anticipated, but in line with larger processes of change of consequence to religion.

The next section of the chapter briefly examines the possible impact of the Internet on three more specific aspects of religious life: recruitment, conflict and authority, and the inducement and communication of religious experiences.

Having thus examined the most pertinent aspects of social and religious life on-line, the last section of the chapter considers the wider social context of the Internet, and hence religion in cyberspace. The focus is James Slevin's (2000) analysis of the Internet in terms of sociological accounts of the conditions of late modernity. Such an analysis is imperative to a determination of the social and cultural significance of the Internet. Links are suggested with contemporaneous changes in the religious expectations of individuals seeking new forms of religious fulfilment.

MEASURING THE PHENOMENON

The first requirement of research into religion on the Internet is simply accurate data. To date piecemeal description and theoretical speculation has understandably dominated the social scientific study of the Internet (outside of commercial applications). With regard to religion there are roughly three different kinds of things we need to know.

- First, we need to know what is on the Internet, who has put it there, and for what purpose.
- Second, we need to know how many people are using these resources. How often are they using them? In what ways are they using them? We need to develop a social profile of those who use the Internet for religious purposes (or profiles of those who use different aspects of the Internet). We also need to compare that profile with data already available on the nature of net users in general (e.g. Johnson, 1998; Survey.net, 1999). Any notable differences might prove interesting.
- Third, we need to know what influence these activities are having on the religious beliefs and practices of users. Is participation in religion on-line invariably transformative or does it serve primarily to reinforced established orientations? Or, as is probably the case, is the impact variable? If so, then on what grounds does it vary? What are the salient correlations of independent and dependent variables? How are age, location, education, gender, ethnicity, income, and religious background related to usage and its consequences? This third concern touches on issues to be raised in the next section of this chapter, but the objective here is more rudimentary. We need statistically accurate responses to basic survey questions about people's use and perceptions of the religious aspects of the Internet.

This volume is part of the emerging scholarship that seeks to identify and describe what is on the net with regard to religion. Of course, the essays appearing in this volume address only a tiny fraction of the thousands of religious Web sites and Usenet discussion groups available at any one time. We see here case studies of some of the ways in which academics and others are seeking to use the Internet to inform and educate people about religions and religious issues. We see also how religious organizations are using the Internet to "get the message out," guide and assist members, and potentially win new converts. And we see how moral entrepreneurs are using the Internet to sway public opinion.

It is not an exaggeration to say that almost every religion, no matter how small or unusual has a presence on-line (e.g. see Dawson & Hennebry, 1999, pp. 22–23). Sara Horsfall (in this volume) introduces us to a sense of the nature and variety of the religious organizations on-line, ranging from mainline Christian denominations and other world religions (e.g. Buddhism) to such new religious movements as the Church of Scientology and Falun Gong. She also begins the process of shaping a descriptive typology of the ways in which religious groups are using the Internet.

These efforts need to be continued with reference to an even greater sampling of the religious organizations on-line. In *The Complete Idiot's Guide to Religions On-line* (2000), religious studies scholar Bruce Lawrence provides an even more comprehensive description of just what is out there. Together Horsfall and Lawrence provide us with helpful guides for surfing the Web for religious materials and they impress upon us the prolific character of religious life on the Internet. But a search of the database of any major bookseller will turn up a surprising number of other even more specialized guides to religion on the Internet, ranging from Baker's *Christian Cyberspace Companion: A Guide to the Internet and Christian On-line Resource*s (1997) through Zakar and Kaufmann's *Judaism On-line: Confronting Spirituality on the Internet* (1998) to Gold's *Mormons on the Internet, 2000–2001* (1999). More recently still, we have Gary Bunt's *Virtually Islamic*, a wonderfully comprehensive tour of Islam in cyberspace (2000; and see his chapter in this volume).

The bounty of materials on-line need some sorting, and like all typological tasks, the one begun by Horsfall needs to be extended. The highly flexible environment of the Web has spawned many sub-types of each type of religious use of the Internet, and these sub-types need to be mapped and analysed as well. To provide a blatant example, the net has given rise to a number of 'cyber-churches' and 'cyber-religions' (see discussions in Dawson, 2000; Dawson & Hennebry, 1999; Lawrence, 2000). These are religious organizations or groups that exist only in cyberspace, and their forms and functions are quite diverse.

Some sites, for example, offer computer-generated virtual spaces meant to function as substitutes for conventional churches and their services. Others offer sophisticated and extensive postmodern and comic religious writings designed to stimulate a new kind of spiritual awareness. A detailed study of the nature, origin, history, operation, and differences between these cyber-churches and these cyber-religions could reveal much about the possible impact of the Internet as a medium of religious expression.

In seeking to extend the initial task of describing the religious uses of the Internet, consideration must be given to the growing literature on the specific methodological challenges posed by using the Internet to do survey research in general, and surveys of net users in particular. On first appraisal the Internet appears to offer researchers a remarkable new tool for acquiring data. But matters have proved to be more complicated than anticipated. Without dwelling on the details, let me briefly discuss some of the seeming advantages and disadvantages of studying the net with the net (for more information see e.g. Cho & LaRose, 1999; Kaye & Johnson, 1999; Keeler, 1999; Schafer & Dillman, 1998).

"The World Wide Web and other new electronic technologies," Kaye and Johnson state (1999, p. 323), "might soon become the prime survey vehicles due to convenient, verifiable, low-cost delivery and return systems as well as easy access and feedback mechanisms" (see also Bainbridge in this volume). Internet surveys can be done by almost anyone, with little in the way of special equipment, personnel, or financial resources. Internet surveys eliminate the costs of postage, printing, telephone lines and time, and the training and payment of interviewers. They can be done faster than mailed surveys, the receipt of questionnaires can be verified, reminders can be issued more readily, and easy mechanisms exist to allow for more immediate questions or feedback from respondents. They provide the opportunity to access much larger and, if desired, cross-national survey samples. Or, through the use of search engines, on-line directories, and activity tracking programs, they allow more specific sub-populations, or even individuals, to be targeted with some accuracy.

Surveys administered through the Internet can be more complex as well. With the multimedia capacity of the Internet, people can be asked to respond to visual and auditory stimuli as well as written questions. Multi-part surveys can be more easily created and delivered. Possibilities for asynchronous responses are better suited to securing responses from an increasingly busy and mobile population. And finally, as Keeler (1999, pp. 7–8) observes, there is some evidence that the relative anonymity of the Internet, the absence of personal visual and auditory cues, may lead some respondents to be more open and sincere in discussing sensitive subjects (e.g. Locke & Gilbert, 1995; Walther, 1996; Walther, Anderson & Park, 1994). It may also help to reduce the tendency to provide 'socially desirable' responses.

In two key regards the results of Internet surveys to date have tended to be more problematic than anticipated: they suffer from lower response rates than more conventional surveys, and more sampling uncertainties. The very ease and anonymity of communicating by the Internet seems to have frequently induced higher rates of non-response, because respondents can more immediately and painlessly 'trash' email questionnaires or just lose them in the welter of messages received by heavy users. Moreover, the wide-open medium of the Internet is marked, curiously, by a higher demand for privacy than that customarily associated with the mail or the telephone. Unsolicited emails are often treated as 'spam'. On sensitive subjects, net users are also more suspicious, because of the increased possibility of deception on the Internet. In turn, researchers may have added reason to question whether the responses they receive to their questionnaires are genuine. People falling outside specified parameters of a survey (e.g. minors) can more readily respond on the Internet, and in the playful and still somewhat anarchistic atmosphere of cyberspace, where people often sustain several identities in different contexts, multiple responses may be submitted by the same person. In fact it remains to be determined who actually is most likely to respond to these surveys. Will there be a bias in favor of more, or less, active users? Either possibility could pose problems, and in surveying specific populations (e.g. religious), the net is of limited value since its regular use is still disproportionately restricted to young, white, well-educated, and relatively prosperous males.

All the same, steps are being taken to deal with these problems and to devise survey and interview formats better suited to the sensitivities of the Internet culture (see e.g. Cho & LaRose, 1999; Kaye & Johnson, 1999; Keeler, 1999; Schafer & Dillman, 1998). A process of methodological experimentation is underway and scholars interested in using the Net to acquire data on religion or the religious uses of the Internet will have to keep abreast of these developments.

KEY SUBSTANTIVE CONCERNS: IDENTITY AND COMMUNITY

The emerging sociology of the Internet has tended to gravitate around two closely intertwined issues: the formation of *personal identity* and the *formation of communities*. In both regards it is widely recognized that the Internet has ushered in new opportunities for experimentation in how identity and community are experienced. The initial task has been to document what these new opportunities might be and if a significant number of people are actually choosing to act on these opportunities. If people are, then the question is how are they doing so, and what are the consequences? The data is just beginning to emerge to sort reality from the rhetoric in these regards. The Internet seems clearly to not be revolutionizing or displacing conventional conceptions of identity or community, but it is probably facilitating or augmenting changes that are already underway in our societies.

In turning to the Internet to develop social ties something is gained and something is lost. This much is clear. The specific gains and losses will be the subject of research for some time to come, as the Internet expands in scope and complexity. Such research depends implicitly on a kind of social and cultural cost-benefit analysis, an analysis that necessitates grasping the Internet as a "contextualized social phenomenon" (Slevin, 2000, p. 8). The bulk of the research completed to date, however, is more preliminary in nature. The work is often still rather fragmentary, impressionistic, and speculative. It is still focussed, moreover, largely on the task of describing what Sherry Turkle (1995) calls "life on the screen."

Understanding the nature of computer-mediated social life is only one of the two necessary facets of the sociology of the Internet. It needs to be complemented with a second undertaking: understanding the impact of this new kind of social activity on the rest of our life-worlds (including religion). Pursuit of the latter concern has carried the sociology of the Internet into the debates over the nature and reality of postmodernity or what some prefer to call late modernity (or advanced capitalism). Life on the net is perceived to be consummately postmodern by some commentators (e.g. Turkle, 1995; Urban, 2000). Others disagree and have chosen to differentiate it, subtly, but significantly, as a typically late modern social development (e.g. Slevin, 2000).

Religion, as a mode of social life on the Internet, has yet to be integrated fully into these discussions. In fact, those who are specifically writing on the religious uses of the Internet have yet to significantly contextualize their findings in terms of the larger sociology of the Internet. Here I can only indicate some of the things that need to be taken into consideration in developing a proper sociological study of computer-mediated religiosity. The concerns of the sociology of religion and the sociology of the Internet converge naturally, however, on their common preoccupation with questions of identity and community.

Identity

Religion has always been wrapped-up with questions of identity, at both the personal and social levels (e.g. Durkheim, 1965; Mol, 1976; Weber, 1963). Religious activity and ideas have traditionally played a crucial role in the processes of socialization and social control that shape and maintain peoples' identities. Dialectically, a change in the way people conceive of their identities has serious implications for their religious life. And the sociology of the Internet is rife with claims that computer mediated communication is exerting a potentially transformative influence on the social construction of identity (e.g. see Jones, 1995; Rheingold, 1993; Turkle, 1995). In this regard, the literature repeatedly calls attention to a number of relevant aspects of life on the screen, like anonymity, plurality, risky behaviour, and gender bending. Let us briefly address each of these subjects.

An increasing number of people, hundreds of thousands, perhaps even millions, are spending part of their day engaged in extended (though sometimes sporadic) interactions with people they know only through typed messages on their computer screens. These interactions are happening in thousands of extremely diverse electronic bulletin boards, Usenet news groups, Internet Relay Chat sessions (allowing the synchronous exchange of messages), and MUDs (multiple user domains; originally called 'dungeons' because they were created for playing fantasy games). The focus of these interactions are as numerous and different as the interests of humankind. Religious subjects are amply represented.

A key feature of all these slightly different types of computer-mediated communication is the relative anonymity of the participation (Myers, 1987; Reid, 1995). With sufficient technical know-how, participants can be identified (at least to some degree). But by technical convention and social norm, postings are most often identified only by the 'name' (usually fictitious) that the participants choose for themselves. In MUDs and other closely related forms of simulated computer worlds (e.g. MOOs), participants actually create full character descriptions for themselves, along with descriptions of complete sub-worlds of places and things. Other players are invited to enter these environments, that are enmeshed in larger collective 'spaces' (ranging from space colonies on other planets to nineteenth century Parisian hotels) created by others, and to interact with these things and characters. As Turkle (1995, p. 11) says, they are invited to join in a collaborative and quite unpredictable act of collective writing or performance. At any one time, while some people are contributing to the enacted reality, many more are just watching; and since anyone can be as many characters in as many worlds as they wish, some may be acting and watching themselves at the same time (in the same or different worlds). It is common for heavy users of the Internet to have multiple presences, of diverse kinds, on the Net.

The plurality of social life on the Internet is multi-faceted. Users may craft several characters – sort of alter egos – that inhabit any one MUD or discussion group, or several different ones, simultaneously or serially (Donath, 1999; Turkle, 1995). The range and diversity of topics and worlds to which the user may be exposed represents another expression of plurality. As do the characters created and assumed by others. People have the opportunity to 'experience' worlds and 'associate' with people, real and fictitious, that may not have seemed likely, possible, or even desirable in their real lives. This experience is bound to have some feedback implications for their sense of self and society.

Observations of life in cyberspace suggest that the related features of anonymity and plurality often induce a process of self-reflection that encourages a more reflexive and playful, or performative (in the Goffmanian sense), conception of identity and of relationships (Turkle, 1995). This in turn can lead them to engage in more risky behavior than they would entertain in real life (Witmer, 1998), from simply talking to different kinds of people in different ways, to having intimate relations with a stranger or strange relations with an intimate. Suppressed, maybe even truly repressed, feelings may be expressed – from anger to love. People simply will say things they would not say otherwise. Rather virulent expressions of ridicule and hatred, for example, are commonly encountered on the Internet. So are statements that would probably be too embarrassing for most of us to say in other kinds of public forums.

Ironically, under conditions of technical anonymity, the sociality of the Internet offers an unparalleled opportunity for greater self-disclosure and exploration. A relatively common expression of this freedom is the adoption of the identity of the opposite sex (Danet, 1998; Fox & Roberts, 1999, p. 646; McRae, 1997; Slouka, 1995). In the male dominated confines of cyberspace, this most often means men pretending to be women. But it may also take the form of acting out some discredited or stigmatized identity. Or it may simply mean being the bold leader of a group for once, a flirt, a poet, or whatever. Turkle, an MIT psychologist, postulates that MUDs may have a psychotherapeutic function for some of their inhabitants (1995, pp. 196–206). Interviews of users led her to the notion that MUDs may offer individuals a 'moratorium' from some of the most distressing features of their real life; the Internet may provide "an outlet for people to work through personal issues in a productive way" (Turkle, 1995, pp. 196, 244).

Equally, however, some people may simply become lost in cyberspace. They may use the Internet merely to escape the real world and become dangerously 'addicted' to an endless play of diversions. Or they may just exploit the Internet to repetitiously 'act out' their maladaptive behavior with impunity. The psychological implications of heavy Internet use must be assessed on a case by case basis. But in the end, Turkle (1995, p. 263) believes the Internet holds the potential for considerable social betterment:

> Virtuality . . . can be the raft, the ladder, the transitional space, the moratorium, that is discarded after reaching greater freedom. We don't have to reject life on the screen, but we don't have to treat it as an alternative life either. We can use it as a space for growth. Having literally written our on-line personae into existence, we are in a position to be more aware of what we project into everyday life. Like the anthropologist returning home from a foreign culture, the voyager in virtuality can return to a real world better equipped to understand its artifices.

Turkle turns to the ideas of the French postmodernists (e.g. Lacan, Foucault, Derrida, Deluze & Guattair), as well as such fellow American psychologists as Robert Jay Lifton (1993) and Kenneth Gergen (1991), to develop an interpretive framework for grasping the possible cultural significance of life on the screen. In different but similar ways these thinkers point to the emergence of new patterns of self-conception. In the face of a social environment in which the boundaries between "the real and the virtual, the animate and the inanimate, and the unitary and the multiple self" (Turkle, 1995, p. 10) are being eroded. Turkle speaks provocatively of computer-mediated forms of communication as new 'objects-to-think-with' or 'test objects' (1995, pp. 22, 185) for experimenting with "the constructions and reconstructions of self" (1995, p. 180). The increasingly decentered sense of self that is emerging reflects renegotiations of our relationship with the world of machines, by means of computers and virtual realities. In our increasingly technologically mediated existence we are learning, she suggests, to "take things at interface value" (1995, p. 23). This means we are "increasingly comfortable with substituting representations of reality for the real" and are "explicitly turning to computers for experiences that [we] hope will change [our] ways of thinking or will affect [our] social and emotional lives" (1995, pp. 23–26).

As we become ever more accustomed to our technologically mediated social interactions, the multiple selves we are generating on screen are conditioning us to an increasingly fragmentary sense of self. Some people, Turkle proposes, are already beginning to envisioning themselves more as a composite of self-created characters than a set and unitary self. Personal identity is becoming ever more flexible as people 'cycle' in and out of virtual worlds on a daily basis, and on-line identities are being granted a surprising degree of equality with real life (1995, pp. 12–14).

The sheer popularity of Turkle's book suggests that her observations resonate with the experiences of those engaging in computer-mediated communications. But no one, to my knowledge, has attempted to replicate the extensive array of interviews undertaken by Turkle to probe her interpretations further. The precise impacts of things like MUDs on people's personalities, social relations, and their conceptions of identity have yet to be adequately investigated. Only a tiny percentage of the population is as yet fully immersed in these technologies anyway, and other studies of the less exotic uses of the Internet (e.g. email and Usenet groups), in which many more people are involved, suggest a more prosaic state of affairs.

People tend to either reveal their true identity on the Internet, in direct and indirect ways, or to adopt on-line identities that closely resemble who they are in real life (e.g. Baym, 1998, pp. 54–57; Brukhalter, 1999; Donath, 1999; O'Brien, 1999; Witmer & Katzman, 1998). The vaunted anonymity of the Internet is exaggerated. The innovative potential of cyberspace for social relations is circumscribed, it would appear, by a strong public desire to establish continuity between the experiences of on-line and off-line social relations (see Blanchard & Horan, 1998; Fox & Roberts, 1999; Parks & Roberts, 1998; Rheingold, 1993). Thus the implications of the Internet for the reformation of identity, and hence for the role of religion in shaping identity, and obversely the influence of alternative identity formations on the practice of religion, are minimal and speculative at present.

But we must be careful to recognize that a new set of possibilities has come into being that one day people may choose to act on in significant ways. Religions, as ideologies and social institutions, have traditionally played a strong role in moulding, managing, and maintaining peoples' personal and social identities. The emphasis has been on the integration and consolidation of those identities, with the use of myth and ritual to induce, guide and control any necessary changes (Mol, 1976). Of course religions have also traditionally introduced a measure of ecstasy and transcendence into human affairs (i.e. standing outside the normal state of affairs – psychologically, socially, and culturally), in dialectical balance with the demands for social order.

What happens to religion if a thoroughly technologically mediated social life begins to undermine the very idea that identity integration is an absolute good? Or alternatively, will the net, by making new kinds of community possible, become a new medium for identity creation and maintenance? Will these identities need religious legitimation? Can the kinds of ideological, ritualistic, and social functions of a traditional religious community – the means of fostering, legitimating, and effecting the controlled change of identities – be simulated in cyberspace? What of ecstasy? Is computer-mediated transcendence a possibility? What form would it take? Answers to all of these kinds of questions hinge on the related issue of whether alternative communities, in which identities may be formed, even exist on the Internet.

Community

In the widely read book *The Virtual Community*, Howard Rheingold argues that true communities have emerged in cyberspace when 'social aggregations' have discussed public issues on the Internet 'for long enough', and with 'sufficient human feeling', that "Webs of personal relationships" have formed (1993, p. 5). He grounds this claim largely in his own experience of an early computer conferencing system called the WELL (Whole Earth 'Lectronic Link) that allowed people from around the world to communicate by email and participate in a great variety of public discussion groups. Networks of sustained friendship and affiliation emerged from these discussions that often flowed over into real life. Certainly the literature on computer-mediated communication is replete with many stories of lasting connections made through the Internet, with people making friends, forming support and self-help groups, beginning business partnerships, and finding mates and starting families.

Most of the information available on these developments is anecdotal (e.g. Barlow et al., 1995; Foderaro, 1995, Turkle, 1995). But some limited academic studies have been done that support the claims (e.g. Furlong, 1989; King, 1994). From the beginning, however, it has been questioned whether virtual communities are anything more than pseudo-communities (e.g. Harasim, 1993; Lockhard, 1997; McLoughlin, Osborne & Smith 1995; Slouka, 1995; Stoll, 1995). Given the ambiguities of our conceptualization of community it is difficult to tell. And as Wellman and Guila (1999, p. 170) lament: "Unfortunately, there have been few detailed ethnographic studies of virtual communities, no surveys of who is connected to whom and about what, and no time-budget accounts of how many people spend what amount of hours virtually communing." All the same we have learned quite a bit about the net as a social phenomenon from the initial analyses that have been undertaken.

Thus if the notion of on-line religiosity is to be investigated seriously, the issues raised in the debate over virtual community have to be addressed. If real communities can exist on the Internet, then so can religions (as traditionally conceived). Identifying the limitations of community life will tell us a lot about the nature and prospects of religion on-line and on-line religions.

In times marked by the loss of the traditional sense of community, by the loss of the mediating structures and small public spaces that involve people in their societies (e.g. Bellah et al., 1985; Putnam, 1995; Riesman, 1950), it is clear why the opportunities raised by the Internet for new forms of association appear so enticing. Here is a means for bringing people together in dialogue and co-operation that can overcome the limitations of space, time, and mobility that plague modern life. People can reach out to others from around the world, twenty-four hours of the day, when it suits them. They can free themselves from the limited range of interactions and associations born of geographical happenstance and develop their true interests with others of like-mind in a virtual place. "Synchronously and asynchronously," as Dave Healy (1997, p. 60) states, "the sun never sets on the virtual community."

Moreover, these are happier communities, Rheingold argues, because they are voluntary and united by truly common interests. In fact, as Wellman and Gulia (1999, p. 185) propose: "people's allegiance to the Net's communities . . . may be more powerful than their allegiance to their neighborhood communities because those involved in the same virtual community may share more interests than those who live on the same block." These are communities in which the traditional social barriers to communication and association seem to be superseded as well. In the anonymous typed world of the net, distinctions of race, class, ethnicity, occupation, and gender are largely neutralized (Wellman & Gulia, 1999, p. 184).

Likewise the Internet facilitates, and to some extent may even structurally foster, 'boundary-breaking' interactions (Kinney, 1995, p. 770). People meet and enter into dialogue with others whom they might never encounter in their part of the world or culture. In general, Healy suggests, the Internet may also present Americans with an ideal way to cope with the traditional cultural dilemma of balancing the demands of community involvement and with an ideology of individualism. Like the physical frontier of the past, "the Internet is characteristically American in its forging a 'middle landscape' between isolation and connectedness" (1997, p. 65).

In response to these claims, sceptics ask the obvious: Can authentic community really be sustained by the attenuated kinds of communication available on the Internet? Isn't too much lost without bodily interactions or a shared time and location? Aren't most so-called virtual communities too specialized, largely ideational in content, and too intermittent or transitory to evoke the sense of we-ness commonly associated with the word community? People turn to the net to exchange information primarily. The limitations of the technology mean people are prone to fairly brief and succinct interactions. They can log-out or switch to another discussion group any time things get uncomfortable or simply boring.

Undoubtedly some strong relationships have formed through the Internet. But they are a tribute to the human capacity to overcome the low bandwidth of computer-mediated communications. They are not because of the Internet per se (see the summary discussions in Baym, 1998; Holmes, 1997; Wellman & Gulia, 1999). On the whole, as Clifford Stoll (1995, p. 24) worries, the bonds of the virtual community may be more illusion than fact: "Electronic communication is an instantaneous and illusory contact that creates a sense of intimacy without the emotional investment that leads to close friendships" (cited in Wellman & Gulia, 1999, p. 179).

Joseph Lockhard (1997, pp. 224–226) and others extol us to be wary of the commercial, and hence political, reasons for 'canonizing' what are essentially computer-mediated phone calls as a form of community. In fact, as I have argued (Dawson & Hennebry, 1999, p. 32): "The pitch for the creation of new virtual communities bears the hallmarks of the emergence of 'community' as a new commodity of advanced capitalism – a product which is marketed in ways that induce the felt need for a convenient substitute for an increasingly problematic reality."

The highly privatized and individually oriented structure of computer-mediated communications may favor ersatz communalism over the real thing. Can an individual seated before a screen in the comfort of his or her own home, or office, really have an experience of 'the other?' The appealing choice, control, and flexibility built into the Internet has led some commentators to wonder if on-line 'communities' are not more accurately characterized as extended selves, as exercises in solipsism (e.g. Foster, 1997; Lockhard, 1997; Willson, 1997). The connectivity that the technology confers, Foster proposes (1997, pp. 26–27), may blind us to the social dangers of the attenuated nature of the others we are encountering in cyberspace. The self is defined and develops in interaction with others, and by coping with true otherness. But computer-mediated interactions may embody "a situation in which 'the other is not really other, but is actually a moment in [one's] own self-becoming' " (Foster, 1997, p. 27).

This possibility is reinforced by the implicit cult of romantic individualism that pervades the computer sub-culture (Herman & Sloop, 1999), and even more by the probable homogeneity of most so-called virtual communities (Foster, 1997; Healy, 1997). The homogeneity in question is manifested in two ways. First, most virtual communities are specialized. They are essentially lifestyle or intellectual enclaves. Second, the Internet itself is still largely homogeneous – in terms of its class, race, and gender features. Lockhard (1997, p. 227) sums up the suspicions of these critics well:

> While [the] Internet's intercontinental breadth ensures its multi-racial character, its character as a totalizing medium denies the diversity of its users. This lack of correspondence between racial/ethnic presence and felt presence points, if not to the extinguishing of alterity, to its extreme marginalization. Such internalized on-line monoculturalism reiterates the external racisms prevalent in American social structures. Middle-class suburban America, confronted with its diversity on urban streets, has retreated to cyberspace to avoid the otherwise inescapable realities of diversity.

Paradoxically, at the most basic structural level, the medium of the Internet necessitates the physical isolation of us as a precondition for its form of togetherness (Willson, 1997). The promise of new community builds upon the "cellularization of the population by workstation" (Holmes, 1997, p. 16).[1]

Explicitly or implicitly these perceptive criticisms of the notion of virtual community rest upon some *Gemeinschaft-like* conception of traditional communities (Toennies, 1957). It is unclear, however, that such intensely integrated societies ever existed, and abundantly apparent that the continued belief in such communities in modern societies is nostalgic at best. I have to agree with Wellman and Gulia (1999, p. 187) when they conclude:

> Pundits worry that virtual community may not truly be community. These worriers are confusing the pastoralist myth of community for the reality. Communities are already geographically dispersed, sparsely knit, connected heavily by telecommunications (phone and fax), and specialized in content. There is so little community in most neighborhoods in western cities that it is more useful to think of each person as having a personal community: an individual's social network of informal interpersonal ties, ranging from a half-dozen intimates to hundreds of weaker ties.

In one of the best studies of the issue done to date, Wellman and Gulia argue that the jury is still out. There is a lack of adequate systematic studies on whether on-line relationships are narrowly specialized or broadly supportive, on whether there is reciprocity and attachment in virtual communities, and on the strength, degree of intimacy, and longevity of on-line relationships.

There is some interesting evidence in each case, however, that some broadly supportive, reciprocal, reasonably intimate and long-lived ties have developed between people in cyberspace. But on the whole there seem to be two important things to keep in mind. First, strong social ties on the net simply take longer to develop, given the reduced flows of information and more specialized reasons for interaction (Walther, 1995; see Wellman & Gulia, 1999, p. 180). Second, the ties people form through the Internet are largely of the intermediate-strength (or 'intimate secondary') and weak variety. The former type are "informal, frequent and supportive community ties that nevertheless operate only in one specialized domain" (Wellman & Gulia, 1999, p. 181), while the latter are the pervasive glue of modern societies with their advanced division of labor (Wellman & Gulia, 1999, pp. 181–186). We depend on a plethora of such weak ties everyday to acquire the information needed to thrive in our functionally interdependent environments. In other words, the "limited evidence available suggests that the relationships people develop and maintain in cyberspace are much like most of the ones they develop in their real-life communities" (Wellman & Gulia, 1999, p. 186).

Some support for this point of view comes from Parks and Roberts' (1998) study of the development of personal relationships amongst users of MOOs (multi-user domains, object oriented). Real relationships are regularly formed on-line, they discovered, relationships that frequently migrate to off-line interactions. But, on average, while MOO relationships "were found to be more developed than newsgroup relationships," they were "less developed than off-line relationships." Fox and Roberts (1999, p. 666) reach similar conclusions in their study of doctors on-line in Britain. Even these moderate relationships would seem more likely to evolve into a more extensive and sustained feeling of community when the on-line interaction is anchored in some common off-line context (e.g. an urban area, profession, cultural heritage) or regular off-line activity (Blanchard & Horan, 1998; Rheingold, 1993; Turkle, 1995).

A more realistic position is beginning to emerge, then, between the utopian and dystopian rhetoric of the debate on virtual community. A sense of community with real consequences for the behavior of participants can be created on-line. But the process is normally quite slow and depends on many contingencies. Moreover, the community in question is likely to be characterized by a moderate level of interaction and commitment with regard, in most cases, to a fairly specific set of concerns.

In the end, on-line communities are most likely to succeed, to truly effect peoples' lives, when they are paired with other off-line involvements. It seems plausible, then, that virtual religious communities are a real possibility – in this delimited sense. The features of virtual communalism, after all, fit the profile of most off-line religious communities in contemporary societies in the developed world. It remains an open question whether this means the Internet is best suited to these kinds of mainstream religious groups, as opposed to more totalistic organizations like such new religious movements as the Unification Church and The Family, or even such older groups as the Jehovah's Witnesses. It would appear to be quite well suited, however, for those new religious practices in which individuals continue to live their ordinary lives while engaging in a course of religious education, largely at their own pace (e.g. Eckankar, Soka Gakkai and Scientology).

Some virtual religious communities, or at least nascent communities, have already been addressed in the little literature that is available on religion on the Internet (e.g. Davis, 1995 and O'Leary, 1996 on the 'technopagans'; Schroeder, Heather & Lee, 1998 on a virtual Pentecostal group; and Dawson & Hennebry, 1999 on the postmodernist cyber-religion called The Church ov MOO; Helland, 2000). But we have only begun to scratch the surface.

As sociologists of the Internet begin to undertake the kinds of systematic ethnographic and survey analyses advocated by Wellman and Gulia (1999), sociologists of religion need to begin to do the same for religious interactions in cyberspace. In the process they need to delve additionally into the role religion itself may play as either a catalyst or impediment to the rise of genuine community. In fact, attention must be paid more specifically to how different kinds of religious foci (i.e. different beliefs and practices) affect the formation and operation of virtual communities.

These kinds of investigations can take their cue, once again, from what the sociology of the Internet has already learned about the factors influencing the character of computer-mediated communication, and hence the specific nature of virtual communities. Nancy Baym provides a good overview of these factors, and the relevant literature available, in her discussion of 'The Emergence of On-line Community' (1998, pp. 39–49).

First there are the external factors to consider. Baym isolates two such factors: the pre-existing cultural backgrounds of on-line interactants, and their more immediate situations, especially those affecting their access to the Internet (e.g. are the participants all employees of the same organization, or undergraduate students). "Participant perceptions . . . [are] important determinants of communicative outcomes" (1998, p. 47).

Second there is the influence of the temporal structure of the computer-mediated communication. Whether it is synchronistic or asynchronistic influences the content and the style of the interaction, and hence the relative sense of community. For instance, in synchronistic systems, the duration of time between replies will take on more normative significance.

Third, there is the influence of the system infrastructure of the computer network being used. The pattern of communication will be affected by such variables as the number of computers involved, how they are spatially dispersed, the speed of the system, the flexibility, programmability, and overall user-friendliness of the system.

Fourth, there is the impact of the assumed purpose of the group interaction (e.g. recreation versus work). It makes a great deal of difference whether a group believes it is required to "generate ideas or plans, choose amongst answers or solutions, negotiate conflicting views or conflicting interests, or execute performances in competition with opponents or external standards" (Baym, 1998, p. 46).

Fifth and lastly, there are the features of the participating group itself: its size, demographic composition, joint interactional history, degree of training in the medium, and organizational structure (e.g. group hierarchies).

In the end we are dealing with a complicated interaction of many variables and sub-variables, and as Baym (1998, p. 49) concludes, "[i]t may not be possible to specify the specific factors that will combine to affect . . . outcomes in a particular group in advance of actual interaction, let alone what the impact of those factors will be." But "[r]esearch on [computer-mediated communication] must attend to these factors if the findings are to be comparable with those of other studies and the complexities and differences of on-line communities understood." Few, if any, of these factors have been systematically examined with regard to religious developments on the Internet. Our work is cut out for us.

SOME MORE SPECIFIC CONCERNS FOR THE STUDY OF RELIGION ON THE INTERNET

The study of religion in cyberspace prioritizes a number of special concerns, all of which, have been discussed in some measure by the sociology of the Internet. These concerns need to be addressed in an equally systematic manner, and with an eye to what has been learned about the formation of identity and community on the Internet.

Without proceeding in any particular order, or seeking to be comprehensive, the first concern I have is _recruitment_ to religious organizations and movements. Like several other scholars I was first drawn to the study of religion in cyberspace by the controversy surrounding the use of the Internet by Heaven's

Gate (Dawson & Hennebry, 1999; Dawson 2000; see also Robinson, 1997; Herman & Sloop, 1999; Urban, 2000). Media reports suggested that the Internet was supplying dangerous 'cults' with an effective new tool for recruiting more potential 'victims' of abuse and violence.

Jenna Hennebry and I argued against the likelihood of this happening, given what is known about the importance of face-to-face interactions and pre-existing social networks in the recruitment of new religious movements. This conclusion is reinforced by the observation that social relationships on the Internet are more likely to blossom into lasting ties when the on-line interactions are grounded in some pre-existing or created off-line interaction. In addition, it remains unclear whether the Internet on its own can serve as an effective medium for mobilizing social movements. At present many observers are doubtful (e.g. Cox, 2000; Mele, 1999; Poster, 1997). Our limited study of the Web pages and Web-masters of thirty new religions suggested that the religious uses of the Internet had yet to evolve much beyond treating the Internet as another information delivery system. Interactive uses of the Internet are still minimal, if they exist at all, and they have yet to be effectively paired with any off-line activities. But the potential to form true virtual communities is there waiting to be exploited, so ongoing study of this issue is warranted.

A second concern for the study of religion in cyberspace is religious *conflict and authority*. As the essays of Robinson, Mayer and Introvigne in this volume address these matters, I will keep my comments to a minimum. A quick search of the World Wide Web using the word 'cult' reveals the merit of Mayer's supposition that the Internet has been a boon mostly to the opponents of various religious groups. We have returned to the heyday of religious pamphleteers, but with one marked difference. These poisonous tracts can be fashioned and distributed at little expense to potentially millions of readers (including children) with relative impunity. The trappings of religious conflict on the Internet, thus, constitute a prime illustration of one of the most lamented features of the World Wide Web: the proliferation of misinformation and disinformation (Dawson, 2000; O'Leary, 2000; Zaleski, 1997: 108). It is the price paid for the much-trumpeted freedom of the Internet.

A component part of this process that may prove a greater worry to religious organizations is the relative loss of control over religious materials. Attempts have been made to enforce copyright laws in cyberspace (e.g. Grossman, 1997; Peckham, 1998), but with limited success. The medium is just too fluid and dispersed in design to permit complete control, through the courts or otherwise. In the face of this fundamental fact of life on the net, the Canadian Radio, Television and Telecommunications Commission, for example, has declared that it has no intention of even trying to regulate the Internet (news report, May 17,

1999). This opens new opportunities for both the exposure and the manipulation of guarded secrets, or the fashioning of competing syncretic religious systems. It may also provide, I suppose, some people with new ways to more or less blackmail religious organizations for political or financial reasons.

On another front, the ease with which Web pages and discussion groups can be mounted offers new opportunities for grass roots forms of witnessing. Many adherents have launched their own confessional or pedagogical sites. In general, Zaleski (1997) speculates, the ease of computer-mediated communications may have "a demoncratizing effect on all religions and work against those religions that resist this consequence" (Dawson & Hennebry, 1999, p. 34).

Third, and rather crucially, we need to inquire into whether _religious experiences_ can be induced by or conveyed through the Internet (see the discussion in Dawson, 2000). Some attempt has already been made to perform rituals in cyberspace, and to hold church services – even Pentecostalist ones (e.g. Davis, 1995; O'Leary, 1996; Schroeder et al., 1998). These efforts are highly experimental and limited as yet, but as knowledge of the Internet spreads and more people become comfortable with operating in cyberspace, it is likely that truly interactive and elaborate virtual religious communities, parallel to such well established secular MOOs as LambhaMOO, will be created.

There is no technological reason why many of the ordinary functions of a religious organization cannot be replicated on the Internet (e.g. scripture studies, sermons, confessions, counselling). Can rituals, though, really be recreated in cyberspace? "Clearly a problem is posed by the complete substitution of typed words or computer-generated images and sounds for real bodies . . . in real-time" (Dawson, 2000). Much hinges, of course, on how much of this kind of religious experience is attributable to the full stimulation of our senses as opposed to the subjective processes of projection and interpretation.

To my knowledge no one has tried as yet to analyse a virtual ritual from the vantage point of a systematic theory of ritual. We have every reason to believe, in any case, that the results will vary between different kinds of rituals and religious traditions. A semiotic or rhetorical analysis of virtual rituals or services could prove most enlightening. An entire comparative field of study awaits exploration. In saying these things we must keep in mind that many of the most momentous events in religious history are the products of human encounters with words alone (e.g. the conversion experience of St. Augustine). That is part of the power and importance of scriptures, and the Internet, like the radio and television, can be the vehicle for the delivery of many moving words and images.

We need more work on the whole issue of technologically mediated religious experiences. Are they possible, and if so, how are they accomplished? In this regard the Internet has the marked advantage over the other broadcast media –

its interactive potential. Though televangelists have used telephones to seemingly great effect for years.

SOCIAL CHANGE, THE INTERNET, AND NEW RELIGIOUS SENSIBILITIES

To this point we have been discussing the technical structure and culture of the Internet as a mode of mediating identity, community and religion, and whether this mediation will have a transformative effect on our lives. That has been the dominant focus of the sociology of the Internet. It is preoccupied with describing and assessing what is happening on-line. As James Slevin argues in *The Internet and Society* (2000), however, we must extend our efforts to a consideration of the broader social context of the Internet. We must consider the ways in which the Internet is functioning as a medium of cultural transmission, as a dialectical partner in the transformation of late modern societies. As indicated, a stab in this direction has been made when scholars relate features of life on the screen to elements of postmodernism. But these discussions are largely philosophical and speculative in nature. Postmodernist ideas are being used to model and understand cyber-life. The reality of postmodernity as a social condition is not examined or questioned.

Favoring a less radical and more empirically grounded approach, Slevin (2000, pp. 11–26) alternatively begins the process of situating the rise, spread, and significance of the Internet in the conceptions of late modern society. His argument builds on the social theory of Jurgen Habermas (1987), Urlich Beck (1992), Anthony Giddens (1990, 1991, 1994) and John Thompson (1990; 1995) (see also Beck, Giddens & Lash, 1994). Within this framework, modernity itself is identified with the increased mediaziation of culture. Technological mediation is becoming increasingly characteristic of human relations with the world and each other. This mediation is part of the processes of globalization that are transcending the traditional barriers of space, time, and social distinction, and generating unprecedented levels of material wealth and power.

The price of this 'progress' is what Beck calls 'risk' and Giddens 'manufactured uncertainty'. In a world of such massive functional interdependencies no one can be certain anymore of the consequences of their actions, no matter how small or large. We live in perpetual and mounting moral ambiguity. This fact is being repeatedly driven home to us by another pervasive feature of our increasingly mediated experience, our extended and intensified 'social reflexivity'. We are being overburdened with an abundance of information and as a consequence we are ever more aware of the environment of risk in which we are operating and the telling uncertainties built into all that we may choose to do.

Knowledge is power, especially in our age of information. But we are experiencing an increasing disjunction between the amount of information available to us, and our sense of real control over our lives. We are having trouble relating the mass of mediated experiences to which we are exposed to the practical contexts of our day-to-day lives. This is so, in part, because these same processes are helping to effect a 'detraditionalization' of our societies.

Modernity overthrew the old order, but it substituted its own powerful traditions and social organizations. These institutions helped to define the truth, to legitimize action, and reduce the risk of decision-making. But the flood of information and reflexivity released by their own success has undermined their legitimacy. They have foster an unprecedented social and cultural pluralism that calls into question their own singularity and hence truth. This in turn has precipitated a new and more radical quest for identity (social and personal), a second great wave of modern subjectivism borne along by the extreme individualism facilitated by the increased technological mediaziation of our experience of the world and each other.

At the heart of this search for new understandings of identity is the need to deal with the new parameters of risk and uncertainty in late modern life. There is no turning back to a time of greater certainty, despite the best efforts of various fundamentalist movements. *The Internet is, simultaneously, a product of this age of uncertainty, a promoting agent of this uncertainty, and a cultural response to this uncertainty.* To understand its social significance we need to understand this complex state of affairs.

Slevin doubts that the Internet can effect some miraculous electronic reversal of history through the creation of virtual communities, as implied by Rheingold. While, on the other hand, he doubts that we are in the process of slipping into a comfortable postmodernist world of playfully decentered and multiple selves, as implied by Turkle (see Slevin, 2000, pp. 90–117). Instead, he suggests, we must think in terms of new forms of human association, congruent with developments on the Internet, that fall somewhere between these existing interpretative options. The world most of us inhabit is now too cosmopolitan and reflexive to support the old-style organic, teleological, exclusive, and spatially limited communities of the past – even as imagined entities (Anderson, 1983) – either on or off-line. Yet there is no doubting the drive towards a new 'tribalism', as many call it, as the processes of economic, social, and political globalization relativize modern institutions like the nation state and ironically intensify the ideology of individualism that comes with a global consumer culture.

What Slevin believes and hopes he sees emerging on the Internet are new patterns of association that conform to what Giddens calls 'intelligent relationships'. People are linked by choosing to live in the same 'discursive space' and 'discursive time'. They share interests and an investment in a shared social practice, with an interactional history. But they are not united by some greater common purpose or held in place by compulsory forces. Participants are knowledgeable agents, more aware than the average social actor of the constraints and capabilities the new social institutions they are constructing (though much of the knowledge is tacit and incomplete). They have entered into limited mutual commitments, against the backdrop of a system of association that structurally incorporates a respect for the autonomy of each participant.

This is a new and complex state of affairs that can only be captured fully by grasping the situated character of the social practices of so-called virtual communities. As an examination of these communal forms of on-line interaction reveals, but Rheingold, Turkle and others have failed to sufficiently appreciate, dialogue on the Internet is as messy and fragmentary as other forms of personal communication. It depends upon the development of shared and complex stocks of knowledge and trust in the integrity of others that can only come from participation in other forms of interaction, by email, letters, the phone, and face-to-face. Rheingold repeatedly notes this situation but fails to integrate it into his claims about virtual community. On-line forms of association, then, represent neither a simple alternative to nor replacement of real interaction and community, nor the development of some parallel universe that leads to the fragmentation of people's lives. Rather, users are involved in the "skilful splicing together of differential interactional situations" (Slevin, 2000, p. 113) to facilitate their practical exploitation of more flexible, sporadic, and delimited relationships.

In other words, Slevin suggests that the Internet is facilitating the formation and spread of the kind of intermediate strength social bonds postulated as a feature of modern life by Wellman and Gulia (1999). To this conclusion he adds, under the influence of Giddens' social theory, due consideration of the agency and reflexivity of Internet users. Through the Internet modern individuals are characteristically constructing identities for themselves in an open-ended institutional environment. They are less immersed than their predecessors in small circles of strong attachments. But they are being increasingly exposed to larger circles of weak to moderate social ties. Whether this is a desirable development or not is almost beside the point, because it seems to be ineluctably happening. Computer-mediated communication, then, is merely accelerating a process of social transformation that was initiated in the early modern period.

Seeking to counter a recent and much publicized negative assessment of the psychological and social consequences of Internet use (e.g. Kraut et al., 1998), Slevin argues that there are at least four ways in which the Internet empowers people in the face of the uncertainties of life in late modernity.

First he stresses: "Probably more than with any other medium, individuals using intranets and internets have to actively negotiate mediated experience and endow it with structures of relevance to the self" (2000, p. 175). Internet usage, we must remember is highly selective; it perpetually reinforces agency.

Second, the Internet "is vastly increasing the individual's ability to intervene in events that are not normally 'within reach' " (2000, p. 177). It allows people to be empowered by sharing knowledge with new people in novel circumstances, to safely compare and assess claims made by rival authorities, and "to bypass certain intermediaries or gatekeepers who once managed and limited their access to information and their channels of communication" (2000, p. 177).

Third, the diversity of the Internet can shatter parochialism. By accessing a broader social world people are prompted to better articulate the nature of their individual commitments and "assess their implications for others whose interests and outlook may be different" (2000, p. 178).

Fourth, this means that people are more likely to be exposed to conflicting dispositions, including conflicts that are quite foreign to their own day-to-day routines, and to learn how to manage or transcend these conflicts through dialogue and the acquisition of better information. In these regards, ironically, Slevin ends up returning to and reinforcing many of the positive attributes of the Internet first heralded by Rheingold and Turkle.

Certainly Slevin's analysis resonates with the findings of sociologists of religion when they dare to contemplate the future of religion in the developed world (e.g. Heelas, 1998; Roof, 1999). Religious questions continue to play a crucial role in guiding the modern quest for identity – in metaphysically anchoring the sub-cultural responses of those that are comfortable with the modernist project and those who reject it.

But, as I have discussed elsewhere (Dawson, 1998), many sociologists think a shift in religious sensibilities is underway (Lambert, 1999). This shift is rendering some forms of religion "more compatible with the new social order emerging around us, whether it is called advanced capitalism, late or high modernism, post-industrialism, or post-modernism" (Dawson, 1998, p. 141). I have argued that this shift can be identified in terms of six features, and at least five of them appear to be convergent with the mediated reality of doing religion on the Internet. Most briefly, contemporary religious life is "marked by a pronounced . . . individualism', and an 'emphasis . . . on experience and faith rather than doctrine and belief." This has resulted in the adoption of "a more pragmatic attitude to questions of religious authority and practice," and a remarkably more tolerant, even syncretistic, approach to other religious worldviews and systems (Dawson, 1998, pp. 138–139). Lastly, there is a preference for greater organizational openness. Overall this means, I conclude (Dawson, 1998, p. 140):

In Westley's Durkheimian turn of phrase (1978, p. 138), since new religions will be characterized increasingly "by the respect and awe accorded the sacred *within* each individual, we may expect that this will be ritually expressed by each individual's private preoccupation with the relationship of the divine within to the external, everyday personality. While people may gather in groups to celebrate the cult, the source of sacred power (and of group integration) will be acknowledged by each individual turning inward as opposed to joining together with others to worship an external symbol of group unity." Less effort will be made to attempt to address all aspects of followers' lives, to provide a truly encompassing worldview. More attention will be given to cultivating and serving crucial but socially segmented psychological and spiritual needs and desires. This will be done, moreover, within flexible organizational frameworks that allow for, maybe even foster, different ways of "doing the religion."

This new religious orientation fits the style of social and religious life encouraged by the culture, social life, and technical constraints and capabilities of computer-mediated communication. A synergistic linkage may well be established, then, between the Internet and the processes of religious change already underway in our societies. In saying this, however, we remain wandering in the realm of theoretical possibilities and educated hunches until some empirical studies of specific manifestations of religion in cyberspace – their nature and consequences – begin to blaze a trail out of the wilderness of speculation. These studies need to capitalize on the work underway on the most basic aspects of identity and community in cyberspace. But the sociology of cyberspace, let alone religion on-line, is still in its infancy.

NOTE

1. Of course the debate over virtual communities has sparked another more radical line of critique not discussed here, that of the so-called hyperrealists. Employing a postmodernist framework, these critics charge that the misconception of virtual community as a real community is reflective of the rise of a culture of simulation in which self-referential and closed symbolic systems have largely displaced reality (see e.g. Nunes, 1997; Rheingold, 1993, pp. 297–300; Turkle, 1995). For a fascinating application of these ideas to the study of religion in cyberspace see Urban's (2000) analysis of Heaven's Gate.

REFERENCES

Baker, J. D. (1997). *Christian Cyberspace Companion: A Guide to the Internet and Christian On-line Resources*. Grand Rapids, MI: Baker Books.

Barlow, J. P., Birkets, S., Kelly, K., & Sloula, M. (1995). What are we Doing On-Line? *Harper's*, (August): 35–46.

Baym, N. K. (1998). The Emergence of On-Line Community. In: S. Jones (Ed.), *Cybersociety 2.0: Revisiting Computer-Mediated Communication and Community* (pp. 35–68). Thousand Oaks, CA: Sage Publications.

Beck, U. (1992). *Risk Society: Towards a New Modernity*. London: Sage Publications.

Beck, U., Giddens, A., & Lash, S. (1994). *Reflexive Modernization: Politics, Tradition and Aesthetics in the Modern Social Order*. Cambridge: Polity Press.

Bellah, R., Madsen, R., Sullivan, W.M., Swidler, A., & Tipton, S. (1985). *Habits of the Heart: Individualism and Commitment in American Life*. New York: Harper and Row.

Blanchard, A., & Horan, T. (1998). Virtual Communities and Social Capital. *Social Science Computer Review, 16*(3) 293–307.

Brooke, T. (1997). *Virtual Gods: The Seduction of Power and Pleasure in Cyberspace*. Eugene, OR: Harvest House.

Brukhalter, B. (1999). Reading Race On-line: Discovering Racial Identity in Usenet Discussions. In: M. A. Smith, & P. Kollock (Eds), *Communities in Cyberspace* (pp. 60–75). New York: Routledge.

Bunt, G. (2000). *Virtually Islamic: Computer-Mediated Communication and Cyber Islamic Environments*. Cardiff: University of Wales Press.

Castells, M. (1996). *The Rise of the Network Society*. Oxford: Blackwell.

Cho, H., & LaRose R. (1999). Privacy Issues in Internet Surveys. *Social Science Computer Review, 17*(4), 421–434.

Cox, C. (2000). Plugged Into Protest? E-activists Rally on the Web, But Can They Build a Movement? *Utne Reader* (July-August): 14–15.

Danet, B. (1998). Text as Mask: Gender, Play, and Performance on the Internet. In: S. G. Jones (Ed.), *Cybersociety 2.0: Revisting Computer-Mediated Communication and Community* (pp. 129–158). Thousand Oakes, CA: Sage Publications.

Davis, E. (1995). Technopagans: May the Astral Plane be Reborn in Cyberspace. *Wired*. Retrieved January 1998 from the World Wide Web: http://www.wired.com:80/wired/archives/3.07/technopagans_pr.html.

Dawson, L. L. (2000). New Religions in Cyberspace: The Promise and the Perils of a New Public Space. In: P. Cote (Ed.), a forthcoming chapter *Chercheurs de dieux dans l'espace public/Frontier Religions in the Public Space*. Ottawa, Ontario: University of Ottawa Press.

Dawson, L. L., & Hennebry, J. (1999). New Religions and the Internet: Recruiting in a New Public Space. *Journal of Contemporary Religion, 14*(1), 17–39.

Donath, J. (1999). Identity and Deception in Virtual Community. In: M. A. Smith, & P. Kollock (Eds), *Communities in Cyberspace* (pp. 29–59). New York: Routledge.

Durkheim, E. (1965). *The Elementary Forms of Religious Life*. New York: Free Press.

Foderaro, L. (1995). Seekers of Self-Help Finding it On Line. *New York Times*, March 23.

Foster, D. (1997). Community and Identity in the Electronic Village. In: D. Porter (Ed.), *Internet Culture* (pp. 23–37). New York: Routledge.

Fox, N., & Roberts, C. (1999). GPs in Cyberspace: The Sociology of a 'Virtual Community'. *The Sociological Review, 47*(4) 643–671.

Frankel, R. (1987). *Televangelism: The Marketing of Popular Religion*. Carbondale, IL: Southern Illinois University Press.

Furlong, M. (1989). An Electronic Community for Older Adults: The SeniorNet Network. *Journal of Communication, 39*(3), 145–153.

Gachenbach, J. (Ed.) (1998). *Psychology and the Internet: Intrapersonal, Interpersonal, and Transpersonal Implications*. San Diego, CA: Academic Press.

Gergen, K. (1991). *The Saturated Self: Dilemmas of Identity in Contemporary Life*. New York: Basic Books.

Giddens, A. (1990). *The Consequences of Modernity*. Cambridge: Polity Press.

Giddens, A. (1991). *Modernity and Self-Identity: Self and Society in the Late Modern Age*. Cambridge: Polity Press.

Giddens, A. (1994). *Beyond Left and Right: The Future of Radical Politics*. Cambridge: Polity Press.

Gold, L. (1999). *Mormons on the Internet, 2000–2001*. New York: Random House.

Grossman, W. M. (1997). *net.wars*. New York: New York University Press.

Harasim, L. (1993). Networlds: Networks as Social Space. In: L. M. Harasim (Ed.), *Global Networks: Computers and International Communication* (pp. 3–14). Cambridge, Mass.: MIT Press.

Habermas, J. (1987). *The Theory of Communicative Action, vol. 2: The Lifeworld and System: A Critique of Functionalist Reason*. Cambridge: Polity Press.

Healy, D. (1997). Cyberspace and Place: The Internet as Middle Landscape on the Electronic Frontier. In: D. Porter (Ed.), *Internet Culture* (pp. 55–68). New York: Routledge.

Heelas, P. (Ed.), (1998) *Religion, Modernity and Postmodernity*. Oxford: Blackwell.

Helland, C. (2000). GroundCrew/Planetary Activation Organization. In: J. R. Lewis (Ed.). *Encyclopedia of UFO Folklore and Popular Culture*. Santa Barbara, CA: ABC-Clio Pub.

Herman, A., & Sloop J. H. (1999). 'Red Alert!' Heaven's gate and Friction Free Capitalism. Manuscript of forthcoming chapter. In: A. Herman, & J. H. Sloop (Eds), *The World Wide Web and Contemporary Cultural Studies*. New York: Routledge.

Holeton, R. (1998). *Composing Cyberspace: Identity, Community, and Knowledge in the Electronic Age*. Boston: McGraw-Hill.

Holmes, D., (1997). *Virtual Politics: Identity and Community in Cyberspace*. London: Sage Publications.

Hoover, S. M. (1988). *Mass Media Religion: The Social Sources of the Electronic Church*. Newbury Park, CA: Sage Publications.

Johnson, D. (1998). Whose on the Internet and Why? *The Futurist* (August-September) 32(6): 11.

Jones, S. G., (Ed.), (1995). *Cybersociety: Computer-Mediated Communication and Community*. Thousand Oaks, CA: Sage Publications.

Jones, S. G. (Ed.), (1998). *Cybersociety 2.0: Revisiting Computer-Mediated Communication and Community*. Thousand Oaks, CA: Sage Publications.

Kaye, B. K., & Johnson, T. J. (1999). Research Methodology: Taming the Cyber Frontier. *Social Science Computer Review, 17*(3) 323–337.

Keeler, J. D. (1999). Surveying the Internet Religious Landscape: Methodological and Ethical Challenges and Opportunities. Paper presented to the Society for the Scientific Study of Religion, Boston.

King, S. (1994). Analysis of Electronic Support Groups for recovering Addicts. *Interpersonal Computing and Technology, 2*(3), 47–56.

Kinney, J. (1995). Net Worth? Religion, Cyberspace and the Future. *Futures 27*(7): 763–776.

Kraut, R., Patterson, M., Lundmark, V., Kiesler, S., Mukophadhyay, T., & Scherlis, W. (1998). Internet Paradox: A Social Technology that Reduces Social Involvement and Psychological Well-Being? *American Psychologist, 53*(9): 1017–1031.

Lambert, Y. (1999). Secularization or New Religious Paradigms? *Sociology of Religion, 60*(3): 303–333.

Lawrence, B. B. (2000). *The Complete Idiot's Guide to Religions On-line*. Indianapolis, IN: Alpha Books.

Lifton, R. J. (1993). *The Protean Self: Human Resilience in the Age of Fragmentation*. New York: Basic Books.

Locke, S. D., & Gilbert B. O. (1995). Method of Psychological Assessment, Self-Disclosure, and Experiential Differences: A Study of Computer Questionnaire and Interview Assessment Formats. *Journal of Social Behavior and Personality*, 10, 255–263.

Lockhard, J. (1997). Progressive Politics, Electronic Individualism and the Myth of Virtual Community. In: D. Porter (Ed.), *Internet Culture* (pp. 219–231). New York: Routledge.

McLoughlin, M. L., Osbourne, K. K., & Smith, C. B. (1995). Standards of Conduct on Usenet. In: S. G. Jones, (Ed.), *Cybersociety: Computer-Mediated Communication and Community* (pp. 90–111). Thousand Oakes, CA: Sage.

McLuhan, M. (1965). *Understanding Media*. New York: McGraw-Hill.

McRae, S. (1997). Flesh Made Word: Sex, Text, and Virtual Body. In: D. Porter (Ed.), *Internet Culture* (pp. 73–86). New York: Routledge.

Mele, C. (1999). Cyberspace and Disadvantaged Communities: The Internet as a Tool for Collective Action. In: M. A. Smith, & P. Kollock (Eds), *Communities in Cyberspace* (pp. 290–310). New York: Routledge.

Mitchell, W. J. (1995). *City of Bits: Space, Place and the Infobahn*. Cambridge, MA: MIT Press.

Mol, H. J. (1976). *Identity and the Sacred*. New York: Free Press.

Myers, D. (1987). 'Anonymity is Part of the Magic': Individual Manipulation of Computer-Mediated Communication Contexts. *Qualitative Sociology, 19*(3) 251–266.

Nunes, M. (1997). What Space is Cyberspace? The Internet and Virtuality. In: D. Holmes (Ed.), *Virtual Politics: Identity and Community in Cyberspace* (pp. 163–178). London: Sage Publications.

O'Brien, J. (1999). Writng the Body: Gender (Re)production in On-line Interaction. In: M A. Smith, & P. Kollock (Eds), *Communities in Cyberspace* (pp. 76–104). New York: Routledge.

O'Leary, S. D. (1996). Cyberspace as Sacred Space: Communicating Religion on Computer Networks. *Journal of the American Academy of Religion, 64*(4) 781–808.

O'Leary, S. D. (2000). Falun Gong and the Internet. *OJR* (USC Annenberg On-line Journalism Review). Retrieved June 20, 2000, from the World Wide Web: http://ojr.usc.edu/content/print.cfm?print=390

Parks, M. R., & Roberts, L.D. (1998). 'Making MOOsic': The Development of Personal Relationships On Line and a Comparison to their Off-Line Counterparts. *Journal of Social and Personal Relationships, 15*(4) 517–537.

Peckham, M. (1998). New Dimension of Social Movement/Countermovement Interaction: The Case of Scientology and Its Internet Critics. *Canadian Journal of Sociology, 23*(4) 317–347.

Porter, D. (Ed.), (1997). *Internet Culture*. New York: Routledge.

Poster, M. (1997). Cyberdemocracy: The Internet and the Public Sphere. In: D. Holmes (Ed.), *Virtual Politics: Identity and Community in Cyberspace* (pp. 212–228). London: Sage Publications.

Putnam, R. (1995). Bowling Alone: America's Declining Social Capital. *Journal of Democracy, 6*(1) 65–78.

Ramo, J. C. (1996). Finding God on the Web. Cover story in December Time. Reprinted in Holeton, R. (Ed.), *Composing Cyberspace: Identity, Community, and Knowledge in the Electronic Age* (pp. 180–186). Boston: McGraw-Hill.

Reid, E. (1991). *Electropolis: Communication and Community on Internet Relay Chat*. Honours thesis for Department of History, University of Melbourne, widely distributed on the Internet.

Reid, E. (1995). Virtual Worlds: Culture and Imagination. In: S. G. Jones (Ed.), *Cybersociety: Computer-Mediated Communication and Community* (pp. 164–183). Thousand Oakes, CA: Sage Publications.

Rheingold, H. (1993). *The Virtual Community: Homesteading on the Electric Frontier*. New York: Addison-Wesley.

Riesman, D. (1950). *The Lonely Crowd: A Study of the Changing American Character*. New Haven, CT: Yale University Press.

Robinson, W. G. (1997). Heaven's Gate: The End? *Journal of Computer Mediated Communication*, 3(3) Retrieved in January 1998 from the World Wide Web: http://jcmc.huji.ac.il/vol3/issue3/robinson.html.

Roof, W. C. (1999). *Spiritual Marketplace: Baby Boomers and the Remaking of American Religion.* Princeton: Princeton University Press.

Schafer, D. R., & Dillman, D. A. (1998). Development of a Standard Email Methodology: Results of an Experiment. *Public Opinion Quarterly*, 62, 378–397.

Schroeder, R., Heather, N., & Lee, R. M. (1998). The Sacred and the Virtual: Religion in Multi-User Virtual Reality. *Journal of Computer Mediated Communication, 4*(2). Retrieved from the World Wide Web: http://www.ascusc.org/jcmc/vol4/issue2/schroeder.html.

Shields, R. (Ed.). (1996). *Cultures of the Internet: Virtual Spaces, Real Histories, Living Bodies.* London: Sage Publications.

Slevin, J. (2000). *The Internet and Society.* Cambridge: Polity Press.

Slouka, M. (1995). *War of the Worlds: Cyberspace and the High-Tech Assault on Reality.* New York: Basic Books.

Smith, M. A., & Kollack, P. (Eds). (1999). *Communities in Cyberspace.* New York: Routledge.

Stoll, C. (1995). *Silicon Snake Oil: Second Thoughts on the Information Highway.* New York: Doubleday.

Survey.net. (1999). Inter Commerce Corporation, March 21, 1999 Internet User Survey Results. Retrieved from the World Wide Web: http://www.survey.net/inet2r.html.

Thompson, J. B. (1990). *Ideology and Modern Culture: Theory in the Era of Mass Communication.* Cambridge: Polity Press.

Thompson, J. B. (1995). *The Media and Modernity: A Social Theory of Media.* Cambridge: Polity Press.

Toennies, F. (1957). *Community and Society.* New York: Michigan University Press.

Turkle, S. (1995). *Life on the Screen: Identity ion the Age of the Internet.* New York: Simon and Schuster.

Urban, H. B. (2000). The Devil at Heaven's Gate: Rethinking the Study of Religion in the Age of Cyber-space. *Nova Religio, 3*(2), 268–302.

Walther, J. B. (1996). Computer-Mediated Communication: Impersonal, Interpersonal and Hyperpersonal Interaction. *Communication Research, 23*(1), 3–43.

Walther, J. B., Anderson, J. F., & Park, D. W. (1994). Interpersonal Effects in Computer-Mediated Interaction: A Meta-Analysis of Social and Antisocial Communication. *Communication Research, 21*(4), 460–487.

Weber, M. (1963). *The Sociology of Religion. Trans. Ephraim Fischoff.* Boston: Beacon Press.

Wellman, B., & Guila, M. (1999). Virtual Communities as Communities: Net Surfers Don't Ride Alone. In: M. A. Smith & P. Kollock (Eds), *Communities in Cyberspace* (pp. 167–194). New York: Routledge.

Westley, F. (1978). The Cult of Man: Durkheim's Predictions and the New Religious Movements. *Sociological Analysis, 39*, 135–145.

Willson, M. (1997). Community in the Abstract: A Political and Ethical Dilemma? In: D. Holmes (Ed.), *Virtual Politics: Identity and Community in Cyberspace* (pp. 145–162). London: Sage Publications.

Witmer, D. (1998). Practicing Safe Computing: Why People Engage in Risky Computer-Mediated Communication. In: F. Sudweeks, M. McLoughlin, & S. Rafaeli (Eds), *Network and Netplay: Virtual Groups on the Internet* (pp. 147–156). Cambridge, MA: MIT Press.

Witmer, D., & Katzman, S. (1998). Smile When You Say That: Graphic Accents as Gender Markers in Computer-Mediated Communication. In: F. Sudweeks, M. McLoughlin, & S. Rafaeli (Eds), *Network and Netplay: Virtual Groups on the Internet* (pp. 3–11). Cambridge, MA: MIT Press.

Wolf, C. (1998). Going Virtual: The World Wide Web as a Market Place for Religious
    Organizations. Paper presented to the International Sociological Association.
Zakar, S. M., & Kaufmann, D. (1998). *Judaism On-line: Confronting Spirituality on the Internet*.
    New York: Jason Aronson Pub.
Zaleski, J. (1997). *The Soul of Cyberspace*. San Francisco, CA.: HarperCollins.

RELIGIOUS ETHNOGRAPHY ON THE WORLD WIDE WEB*

William Sims Bainbridge

ABSTRACT

Ethnography, the systematic documentation of a culture, can be carried out over the World Wide Web, employing either observation or informant techniques. This chapter illustrates these potentials through a theory-based exploration of religious Web sites and a report on a series of on-line questionnaires designed to create new survey items and measurement scales. Extensive on-line observation provided the insights for a set of nine connected hypotheses about how websites might have impact and thus serve as a medium through which religious groups compete with each other and by which other groups may attack religion. On-line ethnographic questionnaires, administered by The Question Factory, collected material for 90 afterlife items and 100 future of religion items. These pilot projects demonstrate that the Web is ready to become a valuable channel for ethnographic research.

INTRODUCTION

Social scientists have begun exploring the research promise of the World Wide Web, employing a range of methodologies. There is probably great potential

Religion on the Internet, Volume 8, pages 55–80.
2000 by Elsevier Science Inc.
ISBN: 0-7623-0535-5

for survey research, and computer techniques for administering questionnaires over the Internet are well developed. However, there is great concern in the survey research community that on-line questionnaires will be biased because they do not obtain anything like a random sample of the general population. Given time, survey research may find ways to deal with this problem, for example recruiting respondents carefully, using passwords or identification codes to control who responds, and employing statistical weighting procedures to compensate for any remaining sampling bias (Bainbridge, 1999; Witte, Amoroso & Howard, 2000).

When random samples are unavailable, experimental design is often a successful way to achieve objectivity of results, and many kinds of on-line experiment are currently being conducted, especially employing bargaining and auction techniques. However, experimental methods have been used only to a very limited extent in religious research, and it is not obvious how the Internet would help overcome the ethical and practical problems of studying faith through this intrusive methodology (Batson, 1977; Yeatts & Asher, 1979).

A traditional methodology that did not worry much about random samples or experimental manipulation is ethnography, the qualitative documentation of a relatively coherent culture. Religious movements and organizations are especially well suited for this general approach, because they do tend to be relatively well defined cultures, with particular beliefs and practices that can be documented reasonably accurately by qualitative methods such as participant observation or open-ended interviewing. This study will stress two ways in which qualitative ethnography can link to other methodologies and often is a necessary step prior to the use of quantitative techniques. First, ethnographic field research can provide a powerful stimulus to theory-building, and theories developed on qualitative data can be tested by more systematic methods. Second, observations, interviews, and qualitative questionnaires can provide the material needed to design surveys that then would be administered to random samples. Thus, for social-scientific research on religion, Internet ethnography is an especially attractive technique given the current level of development of Web-based methodologies.

I first browsed the World Wide Web in the spring of 1994, using a beta version of Mosaic which was developed at the National Center for Supercomputing Applications supported by the National Science Foundation. I switched to its successor, Netscape, early in 1995. In 1996 I became the webmaster for NSF's social and behavioral science division, creating the first Web site for its Sociology Program which became the template for the other programs, and in 1999 I took on similar responsibilities for the encompassing Directorate for Social, Behavioral and Economic Sciences. In May, 1997, I launched my private Web site oriented toward religious research, The Question Factory, which creates and tests on-line surveys.

This work is divided into two main sections. The first section reports results of the on-line ethnography, which I began as soon as I obtained Mosaic, examining ways in which religious movements seek to compete with each other on the Web. This might be termed *observation ethnography*, because it involves the relatively passive examination of Web sites, without full interaction with the people who created them. The second section examines how the Web can be used to blend ethnographic with survey methods, illustrating the approach with results from The Question Factory. This might be termed *informant ethnography*, because it involves a full active cycle of communication with human beings over the Web, asking questions and receiving answers in a manner analogous to interviews.

OBSERVATION ETHNOGRAPHY

Although not guided by a formal sampling frame, this exploration was informed by a well-developed theoretical agenda, which R. Stephen Warner (1993) calls the 'New Paradigm' of the sociology of religion. In the 'old paradigm' (e.g. Freud, 1927; Wallace, 1966), religion is described as the lingering residue of ancient superstitions, destined to fade away as the light of science blazes ever more brightly and societal institutions become rationalized. In contrast, the New Paradigm theorizes that religion is an inevitable human response to the inescapable limitations of human existence, including the universal threat of death and the relative deprivations suffered by many in stratified societies (Stark & Bainbridge, 1985, 1987). The modern dynamism of religion suggests that it may find entirely new arenas for its activity, such as the Web (Bainbridge, 1995b, 1997b, pp. 149–155; Wilson, 2000).

Perhaps the central body of work within the New Paradigm conceptualizes religious organizations and cultural traditions as competitors in a dynamic marketplace or ecological system (Finke & Stark, 1992; Bainbridge, 1997b). Thus, conflict is fundamental to religion, and we would expect it to appear in the vigorous electronic religious communication that sprang into being as soon as the Web was created. However, the dominant perspective on religious conversion asserts that impersonal communications are ineffective. The key factor causing an individual to join a particular religious group is the development of strong social attachments to individual members, with a concomitant loss of attachment to non-members (Lofland & Stark, 1965; Stark & Bainbridge, 1980; Stark, 1996). These social bonds are presumably created and sustained by frequent, rewarding face-to-face interactions between individuals. Thus, attempts to recruit via impersonal media like the Web should be ineffective (Shupe, 1976; Lofland, 1977).

The New Paradigm is often described in terms of economic metaphors and Rational Choice Theory (Collins, 1993; Iannaccone, 1998). However, largely unnoticed is its strong basis in communication and information theory. "Human action is directed by a complex but finite information-processing system that functions to identify problems and attempt solutions to them . . . In solving problems, the human mind must seek explanations . . . Explanations are statements about how and why rewards may be obtained and costs are incurred" (Stark & Bainbridge, 1987, pp. 29–30). In other words, humans need information about how to get rewards and avoid costs, in the form of practical instructions, directions, recipes, explanations, or as I prefer to call them: *algorithms*.

Much of the information on which human beings rely comes to them through verbal communication. There are two reasons why intimate personal relationships should be the most effective channel for religious messages. First, people commonly exchange all kinds of information with their friends through gossip, chatting, advice-giving and so forth. Second, because religious commitment depends so much upon faith, yet many mutually-contradictory belief systems exist, people are unlikely to heed a religious message unless it comes from someone they trust, especially someone who has provided information of many kinds in the past that proved to be valuable. The question of the Web's efficacy thus boils down to the issues of what kinds of information it can disseminate and what might lead people to give it credence.

Here I will offer a rough analysis of the ways that Web-communicated information might have impact and thus serve as a medium through which religious groups compete with each other and by which other groups may attack religion. The following list of nine qualities of communication, arranged in three groups, is a reasonable first typology:

A. Cultural Continuity
    1. Doctrines that build on existing beliefs
    2. Rhetoric that can strengthen one side in an existing debate
    3. Emotionally powerful impressions

B. Information Evaluation
    4. Information that fills a gap in the person's knowledge
    5. Secrets that have face validity once they are revealed
    6. Practical information that can be tested by the individual

C. Social Networks
    7. Information that facilitates development of social bonds
    8. Resources for opinion leaders
    9. Virtual community

A. Cultural Continuity

Doctrines that build on existing beliefs allow a religious movement to retain cultural continuity with the conventional faiths of the surrounding society (Stark, 1987), and thus to draw plausibility from the beliefs that people already have. For example, the Mexican schismatic Catholic 'Third Testament' movement distributes English translation excerpts of four modern books it believes should be added to the Bible. (Web sites are listed in the appendix.) It is plausible that a small fraction of Roman Catholics who discover this material might at first simply add it to the religious faith in which they were raised without even feeling that to do so was particularly deviant. Then the person would be well primed for recruitment to a Third Testament religious movement if he or she ever actually encountered it.

Societies are not uniform, and there always exist counter-cultures that themselves may provide plausibility structures that movements may exploit. Small population pools exist that are already culturally oriented toward exotic Asian religions (such as Tibetan Buddhism) and the dead religions of the classical past. Every educated person has heard of these religions and may have read books about them. A very large number of small groups are dedicated to the resurrection of dead religions (Adler, 1986; Luhrmann, 1989), and several networks of such groups have achieved a considerable presence on the Web: the Pagan Federation, the Cathars, the Ásatrú Alliance (Norse and German paganism), Ár nDraíocht Féin (Druidism), and the Covenant of the Goddess ('Wicca' or witchcraft). For centuries, rumors have spread throughout Western civilization about an ancient fraternity of spiritual adepts, variously called Ascended Masters, Illuminati, or Rosicrucians (McIntosh, 1992). A seeker can now find it easily on the Web, at either the Rosicrucian Fellowship or 'AMORC'.

Peter Blau (1964, p. 233) argues that "shared ideals are a source of social attraction, making it possible for strangers quickly to establish bonds of fellowship." Thus, Web information related to famous but exotic religious movements could prepare socially isolated and dissatisfied individuals to become serious members of a new religion. The next step would be making contact with a group of members, not in cyberspace but in the material world.

A second kind of cultural continuity gives plausibility to *rhetoric that can strengthen one side in an existing debate*. Conflict already exists along traditional religious cleavages, such as that between established churches and dissenting sects (Johnson, 1963; Stark & Bainbridge, 1985). Jehovah's Witnesses are among the best-known, large sects in the Adventist tradition (Bainbridge, 1997b, pp. 89–118), and a very large number of Web sites are critical of this movement, including Free Minds, the Watchtower Observer, and

New Light Ministries. Among the most vocal opponents of Jehovah's Witnesses are evangelical Christian groups that themselves are in relatively high tension with secular society but are in a very different tradition from Adventism. The Watchman Fellowship vigorously criticizes the Watchtower movement and offers many substantial written critiques of Witness theology and governance.

Often great conflict can break out between groups in the same tradition at almost the same level of tension if they are in direct competition with each other for membership, as is often the case for groups that originated together in the fragmentation of an earlier sect. The Nation of Islam, founded in 1934 by Elijah Muhammad, experienced many schisms (Fauset, 1944; Muhammad, 1965; Haley, 1965; Marsh, 1984; Evanzz, 1992; Friedly, 1992). In 1963 Clarence 13X broke with Elijah Muhammad's group and was assassinated, but not before founding the Five Percent Nation of Islam which has a Web site. After Elijah Muhammad's death, Louis Abdul Farrakhan and Silis Muhammad (no relation of Elijah) separately led schisms, creating the Nation of Islam and the Lost-Found Nation of Islam. In 1995, while Farrakhan's Web site was promoting his Million Man March, Muhammad's Web site was complaining that it proved Farrakhan had abandoned Black Muslim principles.

Emotionally powerful impressions can be transmitted over the Internet, despite the fact that this medium of communication was originally designed for the exchange of scientific data. A good example is the Waco Holocaust Electronic Museum which stirs up sympathy for the Branch Davidians and ire at the government by distributing photographs of terribly burned children's bodies, taken from the autopsy reports on the 80 members killed in the 1993 flames.

One of the most emotionally arousing battles raging on the Web is a multi-lateral struggle between anti-Semitic groups, Christian groups trying to evangelize Jews, and Jewish defense groups. Among the many Web sites offering anti-Semitic literature from a radical Protestant perspective are Kingdom Identity Ministries and International Christian Educational Services (cf. Glock & Stark, 1966). Both offer copies of the fraudulent Protocols of the Elders of Zion which alleges that a Jewish conspiracy seeks to dominate the world, and which has long fueled anti-Jewish hate propaganda in America (Lipset & Raab, 1970). To counter such activity, Congregation Emmanu-El in Victoria, British Columbia, supports the Nizkor Project on the Web.

Attempts to convert Jews to Christianity are not necessarily related to anti-Semitism, but they can rouse similar emotions. Web sites of the Messianic Jewish Alliance of America and the Association of Torah-Observant Messianics promote Hebrew Christianity. From the Jews for Jesus home page one can even download audio clips of Jewish gospel music. In reaction, the Jews for Judaism Web site attacks Christianity through essays exposing contradictions in the New Testament and claiming to refute the very basis of Christian faith. Essays on the Web site describe religious conversion of Jews in essentially genocidal terms, for example calling the Christian conversion of Russian Jews the 'silent Holocaust'.

B. Information Evaluation

Information that appears to fill a gap in a person's knowledge may be accepted if it does not conflict with what the person already believes, and many users value the information they obtain from strangers via electronic communications (Constant, Sproull & Kiesler, 1997). People who lack strong motivations to get information about a particular religious group may nonetheless feel some mild curiosity, and thus they will tend to accept information presented in an apparently responsible manner that satisfies that curiosity. This piece of data will be incorporated in their common fund of knowledge, may get passed on as reliable information to friends and family members in casual conversation, and may be of crucial importance at some later time when the religious group in question suddenly becomes salient in the person's life. Suppose, for example, that someone happened to be prejudiced against Mormons and noticed one day that their town had a branch of the Reorganized Church of Jesus Christ of Latter Day Saints. This person might leap to the assumption that this was a Mormon church, and (for instance) forbid a son or daughter to date a member, or might treat a member disrespectfully.

However, the Web pages of the Reorganized Church of Jesus Christ of Latter Day Saints explain that this 250,000-member denomination is quite distinct from the larger Utah-based group, although both consider *The Book of Mormon* to be scripture. Our hypothetical person who was prejudiced against Mormons might decide that members of the Reorganized Church were not really Mormons, but some kind of modest middle-west Protestants. Even though the information about the church came from an impersonal source, our hypothetical person who was prejudiced against Mormons might accept it because it fills an obvious gap in his or her knowledge of history, because the history of the group gives the person an interesting story to pass on to his or her friends, and because this new knowledge allows the person to have happy relations with members of a local church without changing his or her attitudes.

One potent category of gaps in knowledge is *secrets that can have face validity once they are revealed*. Information can be a valuable reward in social exchange, and exclusive possession of a valued reward confers power on the person or group that possesses it (Stark & Bainbridge, 1987, pp. 30–34; Blau, 1964). People like secrets and often go to great lengths to ferret them out, especially in the realm of the supernatural (Evans-Pritchard, 1937, pp. 150–152).

Thus, people may be open to believe exposés and revelations that purport to offer secrets about religious groups.

The most prominent Internet religious struggle has raged around Scientology, a technological religion originally founded as Dianetics in 1950 by science-fiction writer L. Ron Hubbard (Wallis, 1976; Bainbridge & Stark, 1980; Bainbridge, 1987a). An Internet usegroup called *alt.religion.scientology* began disseminating affidavits from court cases critical of the church and texts of Scientology scriptures that are usually provided only to members who have reached advanced levels of religious development (Grossman, 1995; Fearer, 1995; Post, 1996). Arguing that its copyrights and intellectual property rights were being violated, Scientology took legal action against some of those involved. A university website posted what it claimed were plans for making Scientology e-meters, electronic devices used in the church's confessional (Hubbard, 1967, 1968). The battle over Scientology became such a test case for Web norms that an archive of related legal actions was put on the Web by the Electronic Frontier Foundation.

Scientology describes itself as "an applied religious philosophy" (Church of Scientology, 1992, p. x) possessing precise mental technologies capable of elevating the individual to the high spiritual levels known as Clear and Operating Thetan (OT). Thus, Scientology belongs to a family of initiatory religions (Bainbridge, 1985). Western culture de-emphasizes the initiatory approach to the sacred, but anthropologists report that initiatory religions have been quite common around the world and throughout history (Eliade, 1958, 1962, 1969; van Gennep, 1959). An initiatory system would collapse if everybody had free access to all parts of the sacred culture, so it is entirely reasonable for Scientologists to resist the uncontrolled broadcasting of their secret doctrines.

In some cases, of course, *practical information can be tested by an individual*, indirectly establishing the credibility of other information from the same source. In personal relationships, individuals learn to trust each other on the basis of how rewarding the other is as an exchange partner and how well information provided by the other has checked out against experience. There are many kinds of moder-ately valuable, verifiable information that can be transmitted via the Internet. For example, a religious group could cite scripture for some of its theological claims, and the user could easily verify the biblical citations. The Bible Gateway offers an excellent on-line search by word or verse number in six English translations of the Bible plus versions in six other languages: German, Swedish, Latin, French, Spanish, and Tagalog. Once the user finds a passage in one of the English transla-tions, he or she can click a button to compare the same passage in another version.

Among the most valuable kinds of information on the Web is legal refer-ences, such as case citations or presentations concerning particular statutes.

The Religious Freedom Web site sponsored by Christian Science described the (now inoperative) Religious Freedom Restoration Act of 1993 in detail and provided a constantly updated list of court cases (358 as of August 13, 1996) and publications. Many organizations representing different political tendencies have gone on the Web to provide legal advice and stimulate court-based activism promoting particular views of the proper relationships between church and state. Among these are Liberty Counsel, The Freedom Forum's First Amendment Center, People for the American Way, The Rutherford Institute, and Americans United for Separation of Church and State. Other organizations, like the Baptist Joint Committee and the Anti-Defamation League, address a variety of religious freedom issues as well as promoting the social and theological views of the member denominations and groups. To the extent that one of these organizations provides valuable legal information over the Web, it strengthens its reputation among people who might become supporters or members.

C. Social Bonds

Information that facilitates development of social bonds can come in the simple form of instructions on how to get in touch with a particular group. The International Research Institute for Zen Buddhism, in Japan, offers a directory of Zen centers around the world, classified by nation. Outside Japan where Zen Buddhism is a traditional religious alternative, as of April 19, 2000, there were 33 centers in Asia, 642 in the United States, 62 in the rest of North and Central America, 48 in South America, 41 in Australia and New Zealand, 11 in Africa, and 540 in Europe.[1] A Scientology Web site displays a rotatable globe of the world, and clicking on a continent allows the user to zoom in on a nation and get the addresses of local Scientology centers, complete with a road map that shows how to reach them. Alternately, one can type the name of a city into a search engine that provides information about the nearest Scientology center.

Neopagan groups tend to be tiny and geographically dispersed, so the power of Web sites like the World Pagan Network to put individuals in touch with local cells must be a great advantage for them. The Military Pagan Network puts a member of the armed forces "in touch with Pagan, Neo-pagan, and occult organizations near their future duty station."

An operation called Webring recruits Web sites literally into a ring – each is linked to the next until the links come back around to the starting site – as a way of helping users find sites of a similar nature. Each of the many rings represents something like a solitary group that is distinct from the members of other rings. On May 15, 2000 there were 808 rings in the 'religion' area, with an average of 54 Web sites per ring.[2] The largest is the Christian Webring with

2,272 sites. Second place is held by the Witches WebRing with 1,034, and the largest ten webrings also include: The Southern Baptist Ring (963 sites), Roman Catholic WebRing (701), Christian Teens Webring (666), [Christian] Believer's Ring (566), Jesus Freak Ring (555), Freethought [Internet Infidels] Ring (554), The [Wicca and Neopagan] Goddess Circle (528), and the Christian Cybergrace Ring of Truth (490).

Little is required to belong to a webring, and at various times I have enrolled The Question Factory in a webring merely to have access to the other members as questionnaire respondents. Members of a webring often exchange email messages with each other, as a step toward meeting and developing conventional social bonds, so they can be a medium of recruitment. Small, obscure groups have largely been frozen out of traditional communication media, but the Internet is wide open. The entry cost is low, and a Web site literally broadcasts 'World Wide'. Research on electronic communication in corporations suggests that its introduction increases the influence of peripheral employees relative to those that were already central to the communication network (Sproull & Kiesler, 1991). Other research suggests that non-traditional political organizations may benefit more than traditional ones through attempts at Web-based political mobilization (Bimber 1998). Thus, we can plausibly extrapolate that the Web could benefit peripheral religions.

On May 9, 2000, the Yahoo 'faiths and practices' Web page had one link labeled 'Christianity' that went to 24,251 Web sites, and another link labeled 'International Raelian Movement' that led to only 3 Web sites. This illustrates the way that obscure little religions may achieve a kind of parity with the great world religions, not in terms of membership or even numbers of websites, but in terms of their prominence in the indexes and decision trees. Many radical religious movements draw upon population pools that are tiny fractions of the population (Fischer, 1975), but the Internet allows them to reach those populations effectively over a wide area.

Resources for opinion leaders can be distributed from a Web site, and individuals who are or who want to be leaders in their communities may employ them, thereby promoting both themselves and the movement from which they came. Recall the two-step model of mass media influence (Katz & Lazarsfeld, 1955). First, the communication goes impersonally to a small number of individuals who serve as opinion leaders for their communities. Second, if they are convinced, they transmit the message personally to other members of the population who play a more passive role.

Both conventional and unconventional groups have taken advantage of Web-based resource distribution. *The Book of Common Prayer* of the Anglican Church is on the Web, for example, and the World Prayer Network distributes a new set of prayers each month for world peace, guidance, healing, and prosperity. The Family (Children of God) has long published an annual book with a homily for each day of the year, called Daily Might, and it now offers the same over the Web with the user clicking on a calendar day to get the right homily. Zen@SunSite offers a random *koan*.

A spectacular example is the Chinese spiritual movement, Falun Gong. In 1992, Master Li Hongzhi introduced a system of spiritual cultivation based on traditional qigong principles, based on five exercises consisting of arm and body movements, associated with consciousness focusing. When the communist government of China began its fierce crackdown on Falun Gong and other independent religious movements in 1999, it burned the movement's books, but electronic copies remained available over the Web, along with downloadable movies of Master Li demonstrating his five qigong exercises.

Virtual communities can emerge from webrings, from scattered opinion leaders who obtain their religious resources over the web, and from informal Internet communications. When the Internet was created, the assumption was that people would use it as a tool for transmitting information, but in fact people turn to it as well for affiliation and emotional support (Sproull & Faraj, 1997). Some have suggested it is a sufficiently powerful medium to create and sustain social relationships, without the need for face-to-face interaction (Rheingold, 1993). However, social scientists debate whether electronic communication is effective enough to create new social relationships or merely to sustain existing ones (Carley & Wendt, 1991; Wellman et al., 1996; Wellman, 1997).

The Internet may be especially conducive for development of sacred communities, because a standard feature of religion is a sense of social attachment to persons (such as Jesus or Krishna) with whom one has interacted seldom if ever within the ordinary world of every-day life (Shinn, 1985). Television has already proven to be an effective medium for creating a sense of religious community (Hadden & Swann, 1981; Hadden & Shupe 1988), and the Internet may be even more effective because it gives the ordinary person an active role to play in communicating.

One tactic that has been successful in the past in recruiting followers rapidly without having to proceed with agonizing slowness through an existing network of social relationships, is fulfillment of messianic prophecy (Hobsbawm, 1959; Cohn, 1961). The preconditions are the existence of a traditional prophecy that a great leader will come, meeting certain cultural specifications, plus a frustrated segment of the population that has no objective way of improving its conditions other than seeking the aid of a savior. An individual appears out of nowhere, claiming to fulfill the prophecy, and very quickly a millenarian or revolutionary movement arises around him. Even before the advent of this messiah, the potential recruits may have a sense of belonging to a pseudocommunity (Cameron, 1959) of followers. Such movements need not be Christian, as illustrated by Web sites in the Buddhist millenarian Maitreya tradition.

Virtual spiritual contact is also offered by prayer sites such as Call to Prayer, the Greater Grace Prayer Chain, and Grace Notes Prayer Net. Web-based virtual communities often arise among defectors from intense religious movements, as in the case of the Peregrine Foundation of defectors from the Bruderhof religious communes (Zablocki, 1971; Whitworth, 1975). It remains to be seen whether the Internet can create really cohesive communities from scratch. In March 1997, the media reported the Heaven's Gate ritual suicide of 39 people in California, initially implying that the victims were members of a Web-based cult. In fact, it was a long-standing millenarian movement that had only recently launched a Web site (Hewes & Steiger, 1976; Balch & Taylor, 1977; Balch, 1980, 1985, 1995).

INFORMANT ETHNOGRAPHY

The methodological approach described in this section might be called the inductive method of questionnaire construction. It is a rigorous form of ethnography, that charts the beliefs and opinions that a group of people has about the particular topic, beginning and ending with their own thoughts.

Perhaps the best way to explain it is to begin by rooting it in the standard practices of traditional social psychology, and to use a well-known example, the development of the Machiavellianism scale by Richard Christie in the 1960s (Christie & Geis, 1970). Modern sociology and political science are still influenced by ideas enunciated by the 16th-century Italian political theorist Niccoló Machiavelli, who was infamous for conceptualizing human relationships in terms of guile, deceit and opportunism. Christie believed that it would be worth creating a questionnaire instrument that measured the degree to which respondents shared Machiavelli's world-view.

Christie read through Machiavelli's writings, copying out a number of statements that expressed his view of human nature. Naturally, he had to edit some of Machiavelli's sentences to turn them into declarative statements, to cut out unnecessary words, and to combine pieces of an idea that were separated in the original by other verbiage. With the help of other scholars, he augmented the set of statements with others from other sources that seemed to express the same idea, until he had fully 71 statements that he framed in a questionnaire as agree-disagree items.

Christie then administered this questionnaire to 1196 college students and used statistical analysis of the resulting data to identify a subset of 20 items that constituted a reliable measurement scale. The battery of 20 items and variants of it have been used in a very large number of empirical studies to identify the attitudinal and behavioral correlates of Machiavellianism.

In the sociology and psychology of religion, we could do the same thing with the writings of a leading religious figure such as St. Augustine or Norman Vincent Peale. But we can also obtain the material for our measurement scales from the rank-and-file members of a particular religious group, or from the general public.

On May 23, 1997, The Question Factory was launched on the Web to pilot on-line ethnographic methods for developing survey measurement scales and to achieve a particular set of religious goals. The fundamental idea is a two-stage process rather like that employed by Christie. In the first stage, a brief questionnaire is posted on the Web, consisting of a few open-ended questions soliciting ideas the respondents may have about a particular topic. At this point the researcher needs a practical way of recruiting respondents who have a range of views on the topic at hand. In actual practice, The Question Factory sought the help of professors teaching relevant courses to recruit their students, sent messages inviting the members of selected webrings to respond, placed a link on the Web site of a particular organization to recruit its members, and was able to include items in a massive survey being administered via the Web by the National Geographic Society.

Once anywhere from a hundred to several thousand people had responded, their verbiage was culled for phrases that could be made into questionnaire items. This is comparable to scanning the writings of Machiavelli in search of statements that express his key ideas. This leads to the second phase of the process, creating an on-line or disk-based questionnaire incorporating the items, in order to collect data to assess the intercorrelations among items and thus identify reliable measurement scales. The general process could be adopted for a wide range of goals in religious studies, and many of the questionnaire items developed by The Question Factory could be used in reliable measurement scales in a variety of pure research studies.

However, it is important to emphasize that the Web and associated new computing technologies are not merely fresh ways of accomplishing old tasks. They also open up entirely new possibilities, both scientific and religious. Therefore, a few words on the religious goals of The Question Factory are in order here (cf. Bainbridge, 1993).

Beginning perhaps a half-century ago, an entirely new approach to the fundamentally religious problem of immortality began to emerge, leading to considerable discussion today and the beginnings of practical accomplishments. In 1953, science-fiction writer Arthur C. Clarke imagined that human immortality might be achieved technologically through the creation of a vast computer which could store the information needed to re-create a society, including all of its members. The theme of cybernetic immortality has continued to fascinate science fiction writers, and it plays a central role in the *Neuromancer* series of novels by William Gibson, which also originated the concept of cyberspace. The influential television series *Babylon 5* frequently dramatized similar ideas, notably in the episodes 'Soul Hunter' and 'River of Souls'. But just as the science fiction idea of space travel has become reality, and Clarke's original concept of communication satellites has become a standard part of the world's infrastructure, technological immortality has recently become a topic of serious research and debate.

In his widely-read book, *The Age of Spiritual Machines,* Ray Kurzweil (1999) argues that the combination of brain scanning, neural implants, nanotechnology, and supercomputing will achieve the union of humans and machines within twenty or thirty years, leading to the transformation of humanity into a species no longer limited by mortal bodies. Kurzweil gains some credibility for his ideas from the fact that he is a highly successful pioneer in the practical fields of computer recognition of spoken language and computer-generated speech.

Already today, work has begun on some of the ancillary technologies that will be required to achieve cybernetic immortality. The National Aeronautics and Space Administration and the Defense Advanced Research Projects Agency have jointly launched the 'InterPlaNetary Internet' (IPN) initiative to work out the top level architecture to give interplanetary scope to Internet and thus to the cybernetic noosphere (cf. Teilhard de Chardin, 1964).

Elsewhere, movie producer Steven Spielberg has established the Survivors of the Shoah Visual History Foundation, which videotaped interviews with 50,000 Holocaust victims to be preserved in an advanced, hypermedia information system. The Informedia digital library at Carnegie Mellon University has been developing a system called 'Experience on Demand', with the goal of achieving a "complete, searchable record of personal memory and experience." Among the many small social movements oriented toward these ideas, especially notable is the Transhumanist Movement, a Web-based network of intellectuals who are developing new conceptions of human society commensurate with the technological potentials.

Skepticism about these possibilities can be rooted either in an awareness of the technical challenges that lie ahead or in commitment to the very different images of the human soul and of immortality offered by traditional religions. Thus it is worth noting that new religious movements have begun to arise that seek to spiritualize technology. For example, the Raelian Movement is promoting the religious benefits of biological cloning technologies.

The first really successful religious movement related to computing is probably Scientology. L. Ron Hubbard, founder of Scientology, spoke of the human mind as a perfect computer in his first Dianetics book (Hubbard, 1950), and he explained the spiritual technology he called *clearing* in terms of clearing false data from memory registers. To accelerate clearing processes, Scientology developed the electronic e-meter, and recent models are capable of downloading their data into computers.

In the mid-1980s, I experimented with adding circuitry to an e-meter that would transmit the spiritual data into a computer for analysis and long-term storage. A fully functioning system was demonstrated to a Harvard University colloquium at which a representative of the Church of Scientology was present. Subsequent demonstration to an editor at Wadsworth publishing company led to my publishing a series of textbook-software packages that were designed both to teach conventional social science and develop spiritual computing techniques. Some of these projects explored psychological and sociological methods for capturing aspects of a person's mind (Bainbridge, 1986, 1989), and others employed computerized neural networks for modeling religious faith (Bainbridge, 1987b, 1995a).

The Question Factory was the next logical step in this project, designed to assemble a corpus of more than 10,000 questionnaire items that would be incorporated in computer software designed to measure and record an individual's attitudes, beliefs and personality. But it is certainly not necessary to share the religious motives behind the work to benefit from the methodological developments or research findings. The example of a survey on beliefs about the afterlife will illustrate the utility of Web-based informant ethnography.

A. Web-Based Afterlife Surveys

A good example of the methodology is a qualitative Death questionnaire and the quantitative Afterlife questionnaire that was one of its results. First, a brief survey was placed on the Web including several open-ended items that asked people to express their beliefs about death and the afterlife. For example, three of these items were: "What do you BELIEVE will happen to you personally, after you die? What do you HOPE will happen to you personally, after you die? What do you FEAR will happen to you personally, after you die?" The respondent was given a space on the electronic form to write a response to each of these items, as long or short as he or she wished.

A total of 131 people responded to these 10 items, producing about 1,300 statements about death and the afterlife. Following grounded theory methods (Glaser & Strauss, 1967; Bainbridge, 1991), 270 distinct ideas were culled from this mass of material, writing them as phrases based as much as possible on the verbatim language of the respondents. A third of these phrases became a new 90-item fixed-choice survey on the afterlife, posted on the Question Factory website, asking people to rate each item on a 7-point scale: "How likely do you think it is that this will happen to you after you die?" Table 1 shows some results of an exploratory factor analysis of data from the first 198 respondents, employing varimax rotation and assigning each item to the factor on which it was most strongly loaded.

Table 1 quotes the most highly loaded item collected by each of the eleven meaningful factors, and each factor has a label that roughly communicates its general sense. The first factor was extremely powerful, collecting 33 items, more than a third of the total. Nine items, loaded from 0.89 to 0.80, clearly represent the Christian image of Heaven: "Spend eternity with God. Praise and worship God for all eternity. Be filled with awe and thankfulness at the goodness and mercy of God. Stand before your God and account for the life you led on Earth. Give and receive pure love. Relax in a perfect place with no crime, no violence, no war, just peace. Become pure and untouched by sin. Grow in spiritual understanding. Hear the voice of God say, Well done, my good and faithful servant." Another twenty items loaded from 0.75 down to 0.40 describe Heaven in greater detail, and four items that loaded strongly negatively (from –0.85 to –0.58) express disbelief in the Christian afterlife: "Not experience anything, because

Table 1. Factor Analysis of Afterlife Beliefs

Factor	Items	Label	Most Strongly Loaded Items
I	33	Heaven	Spend eternity with God. (0.89)
			Not experience anything, because there is no afterlife and death is final. (–0.85)
II	16	Hell	Enter a terrible place filled with never-ending fear, pain, torment, hate, anger, cruelty, and sadness. (0.94)
III	1?	Reincarnation	Be reborn into a new child or animal. (0.89)
IV	8	Powerlessness	Feel unendurable boredom, lacking challenges and creativity. (0.66)
V	3	Paradise I	See a beautiful sunset. (0.74)
VI	3	Paradise II	See many white clouds with little angels playing trumpets. (0.76)
VII	3	Oblivion	Just sleep forever. (0.50)
IX	3	Ascended Masters	Teach others about the plan, in a spirit world. (0.66)
X	2	Wish Fulfillment	Find a happy place where you may be whatever you want, go wherever you want, and have anything you want. (0.62)
XI	2	Grave	Be buried in the cold hard ground. (0.76)

there is no afterlife and death is final. Cease to exist, never thinking or feeling again. Feel nothing, and you will not even know that you are dead. Cease to exist except for the memories of you that remain in the hearts and minds of those who knew you and continue to live on Earth."

Focusing on Factor III, 'Reincarnation', will illustrate how these methods can create new measurement scales for use in future questionnaires. Table 2 lists the twelve items loaded above 0.40 on this factor and which were more strongly loaded on this factor than on any other. Each of these dozen items was based on one or more written responses to the open-ended items in the Web-based Death questionnaire. They were among the 90 fixed-choice items in the Afterlife questionnaire, and they are grouped into this factor by statistical analysis of responses to that second Web-based survey. Thus, in this process qualitative ethnography blends into quantitative ethnography.

Examination of Table 2 suggests that a narrowly-focused 'reincarnation' scale could be created out of the first six items, all loaded above 0.65. In fact, a measurement scale calculated simply by adding the scores from these six items together is highly reliable, achieving a Cronbach's alpha of 0.91. Generally speaking, an alpha of 0.70 is considered quite good, and this scale surpasses that criterion by a wide margin. An index composed of all 12 items obviously covers a broader conceptual territory than just reincarnation, but with twice as many items it also achieves an alpha of 0.91. Therefore, if one were creating

Table 2. The Reincarnation Factor

Loading	Item
0.89	Be reborn into a new child or animal.
0.86	Go through a series of many lives, eventually reaching Nirvana.
0.84	Be reincarnated in a form that you deserve, as a result of your behavior in this life.
0.81	Have another opportunity to choose a situation to be born into that will allow you to learn lessons you need to learn.
0.70	Exist as a spirit on the earth, inhabiting an animal, tree, or other part of nature.
0.66	Be reborn near the family you love so dearly in this lifetime.
0.59	Move on to the next realm of existence to learn the lessons you did not learn on earth.
0.59	Return to earth as a spirit guardian to guide people along the right path.
0.52	Become part of a huge network of energy connecting each dead person to all the other entities, making a vast web that encompasses the whole universe.
0.44	Feel free from individual ego identification and completely unified with all other forms of energy.
0.44	Stay on Earth for a while after the funeral, visiting loved ones to comfort them.
0.44	Have the same feelings you had before you were born.

a new questionnaire, one could employ either six or twelve of the items as a reliable measure either of reincarnation beliefs or of the wider cultural orientation in which they are embedded.

Clearly, the results of this pilot study of afterlife beliefs demonstrate that Web-based administration of qualitative and quantitative questionnaires can be used to create measurement scales for inclusion in scientific surveys, and each factor is the beginning of such a scale. Another example illustrates how this process can be use to develop religion-related items in the context of a broader study of people's views of the future.

B. The Future of Religion

One of the qualitative ethnographic surveys posted on The Question Factor concerned people's view about the future, including an open-ended item about possible religious events in the year 2000, several questions about the ethics of human cloning, plus some standard survey items categorizing the respondent's religious affiliation. Results indicated that the following open-ended item functioned well: "Imagine the future and try to predict how the world will change over the next century. Think about everyday life as well as major changes in society, culture, and technology." This item was then placed in *Survey 2000*, a complex Web-based questionnaire sponsored by the National Geographic Society and designed by a team led by James Witte.

Most of the 46,000 adult and 13,000 child respondents were recruited through advertisements in National Geographic publications and on the Society's popular Web site, but some were school children doing the survey in connection with Geography Awareness Week. There were many items on migration and regional culture, musical preferences, book reading, and the kinds of foods people in different regions like. About half of the adults who responded to the survey wrote in at least one idea about the future, from one sentence to as much as several paragraphs. The entire 15 megabytes of their responses was read through, and nearly 5,000 somewhat distinctive ideas were identified. The 5,000 were collated and edited down to a final 2,000 future-oriented ideas that were then incorporated in a Windows-based software module called *The Year 2100*, which was then placed on the Web site for anyone who wanted it to download.

The software asks the user to evaluate each idea in terms of two dimensions: (1) How GOOD versus BAD such a future would be, and (2) How LIKELY versus UNLIKELY it is that the idea will come true. The module measures the user's optimism versus pessimism in twenty areas of life, plus the user's priorities and values concerning the future. The software not only does the necessary statistical analysis but also produces word processing files collecting ideas the user rated in a similar way. For example, the user's personal Utopia consists of those ideas rated both very good and very unlikely. *The Year 2100* is a tool for self-analysis of goals, needs, and general personality, as well as part of a system for recording an individual for later technological resurrection.

One of the twenty areas of life was religion, and the software module thus contains 100 items about the possible future of faith. To illustrate, here are the three religion items that the first research subject to use the software module judged were most like to come true over the following century: "A major new religion will emerge, based on Pentecostal or Evangelical principles. Religious groups, including Islam and Christianity, will oppose dominance by American materialist culture. The spiritual deadness affecting prosperous societies will lead to a proliferation of strange cults and fanatic religious movements."

Naturally, other respondents would select a different group of items for their personal predictions of the future. The first research subject considered the following items to be especially unlikely to come true: "Angels will influence people's lives. God will wipe every tear from the eyes of believers, and they will see death no more. All good people who have died in the past 6,000 years will be resurrected and live forever on God's clean and beautiful Earth. Jesus Christ will return to Earth. Those who do not accept Jesus as their savior will perish in a time of terrible tribulation. God will rule over the Earth, destroy wickedness, and bring perfection to mankind. People will be living in an Earth-wide paradise, after God destroys all the wicked during the battle of Armageddon. God will bring an end to war, famine, and disease." Most of these items reflect a millenarian perspective, rejected by this respondent but reflecting the views of many other people. All we would need to create a millenarian measurement scale would be responses from a sufficient number of other respondents to identify which subset of items achieves a desirable level of statistical reliability.

Table 3 provides an overview of responses from two test subjects, 'WSB', a 59 year-old male, and 'WAB', a 12 year-old female, highlighting the religion category. The table covers half of the items, 1,000 statements arranged in 10 equal groups of 100. On average, the two research subjects gave almost identical 'good' ratings, 4.64 and 4.68 on the 1 to 8 scale. The difference was also narrow for the group of 100 religion items, 4.51 versus 4.46. But across all ten groups they differed by an average of 0.37. Their average ratings on the 'likely' scale were more different, 4.92 versus 4.49. This is a difference of 0.43, but the average difference across the ten groups is 0.59. Of course, the two respondents differ in their ratings of most of the 2,000 specific judgements (1,000 stimuli times 2 responses each).

Table 3. Comparison of Two Respondents (WSB and WAB) to The Year
2100

Category	Mean GOOD Rating		Mean LIKELY Rating		Optimism (r)	
	1=WSB	2=WAB	1=WSB	2=WAB	1=WSB	2=WAB
Art-entertainment	4.48	4.99	5.20	4.65	0.40	0.28
Business-economic	4.23	3.64	4.90	4.45	0.46	0.21
Domestic-food-urban	4.83	5.32	5.15	4.64	0.54	0.28
Education	4.48	4.76	4.98	4.44	0.26	0.13
Family	4.27	4.12	4.91	4.38	0.10	−0.03
Miscellaneous	4.51	4.85	5.07	4.23	0.51	−0.02
Outer space	6.13	5.99	4.74	5.55	−0.36	0.03
Population	4.20	3.54	4.90	4.63	−0.14	0.00
Religion	4.51	4.46	4.53	3.43	0.61	−0.04
Technology-transport	4.72	5.16	4.82	4.48	0.52	0.31
AVERAGE of 10	4.64	4.68	4.92	4.49	0.29	0.12

Because the 100 religion items were in the same format as hundreds of items
about other topics, and because the items were all drawn by the same process
from the same ethnographic survey, we can compare the ranking of religion
with those of other categories. On average, the first respondent rated religion
items as less good than just three of the other nine groups (outer space, tech-
nology-transport, and domestic-food-urban) and tied with the group of 100
miscellaneous items. The second respondent rated religion lower, in seventh
rank out of ten.

The last two columns in Table 3 show the average 'optimism' or 'pessimism'
scores of the two respondents. Optimism is measured by the correlation between
the 'good' and 'likely' ratings. That is, if a person tends to feel that good ideas
about the future are likely to come true – and bad ideas are unlikely to come
true – there will be a positive correlation between the two ratings.

Conversely, if the respondent feels that bad things are likely to happen in
the future, there will be a negative correlation between 'good' and 'likely'. For
example, in the religious area the first test subject is very optimistic (0.62), but
he is significantly pessimistic about the future of the space program (−0.36).
Also, he shows much wider swings of optimism or pessimism across the ten
topic areas, compared with the second test subject. Notably, the second test
subject shows no correlation between rating religious items 'good' and 'likely'.
The average difference between the optimism scores of the two subjects, across
the ten areas, is 0.28.

If one had responses from many research subjects, it would be possible to develop a large number of subscales from the 2,000 items in The Year 2100, and employ them in future scientific studies. But as the original goal of the software was to archive aspects of a personality, it is important to note that the software can give meaningful statistical results from a single subject, such as the optimism correlations for the full list of 20 topic areas.

CONCLUSION

The World Wide Web and the Internet are very promising realms in which to do scientific religious research. Observational ethnography can be carried out on some topics by visiting Web sites and viewing them in the light of a theoretical perspective. Here we have used that approach to develop a loosely connected list of nine hypotheses about how religious movements could compete on-line. Informant ethnography, in the form of Web-based qualitative questionnaires, can provide the material for new measurement scales that can be incorporated in conventional surveys or that in future may form the basis of on-line surveys as the problems of sampling bias are gradually served. The Question Factory has followed that approach to create several hundred religion-related questionnaire items, illustrated here by 90 afterlife items and 100 items concerning the future of religion. These techniques are ready to accomplish many practical tasks, whether the goal is to carry out academic research or to advance a religious agenda.

NOTES

*The views expressed in this essay do not necessarily represent the views of the National Science Foundation or the United States. An earlier draft was presented at the 1998 annual meetings of the American Sociological Association in San Francisco.

1. On March 17, 1996, there were eleven nations with more than ten centers. All of these showed substantial growth over the following four years: United States (306 to 642), Germany (89 to 135), Britain (50 to 81), France (34 to 74), Canada (19 to 50), Italy (19 to 45), Spain (16 to 34), Poland (14 to 23), Belgium (13 to 45), Switzerland (13 to 19), and Australia (12 to 31).

2. A website may belong to several rings, so the apparent total of 43,657 sites may represent possibly half this number. However, each site belongs to a ring only once.

REFERENCES

Adler, M. (1986). *Drawing Down the Moon*. Boston: Beacon.

Bainbridge, W. S. (1985). Cultural Genetics. In: R. Stark (Ed.), *Religious Movements* (pp. 157–198). New York: Paragon House.

Bainbridge, W. S. (1986). *Experiments in Psychology*. Belmont, California: Wadsworth.

Bainbridge, W. S. (1987a). Science and Religion: The Case of Scientology. In: D. G. Bromley, & P. E. Hammond (Eds), *The Future of New Religious Movements* (pp. 59–79). Macon, GA: Mercer University Press.

Bainbridge, W. S. (1987b). *Sociology Laboratory*. Belmont, California: Wadsworth.

Bainbridge, W. S. (1989). *Survey Research: A Computer-Assisted Introduction*. Belmont, California: Wadsworth.

Bainbridge, W. S. (1991). *Goals in Space*. Albany, NY: State University of New York Press.

Bainbridge, W. S. (1993). New Religions, Science and Secularization. In: D. G. Bromley, & J. K. Hadden (Eds), *Religion and the Social Order* (pp. 277–292). Greenwich, CT: JAI Press.

Bainbridge, W. S. (1995a). Neural Network Models of Religious Belief. *Sociological Perspectives, 38*, 483–495.

Bainbridge, W. S. (1995b). Sociology on the World Wide Web. *Social Science Computer Review, 13*, 508–523.

Bainbridge, W. S. (1997a). The Omicron Point. In: R. A. Eve, S. Horsfall, & M. E. Lee, (Eds), *Chaos, Complexity, and Sociology* (pp. 91–101). Thousand Oaks, CA: Sage Publications.

Bainbridge, W. S. (1997b). *The Sociology of Religious Movements*. New York: Routledge.

Bainbridge, W. S. (1999). International Network for Integrated Social Science. *Social Science Computer Review, 17*, 405–420.

Bainbridge, W. S., & Stark, R. (1980). Scientology: 'To Be Perfectly Clear'. *Sociological Analysis, 41*, 128–136.

Balch, R. W. (1980). Looking Behind the Scenes in a Religious Cult: Implications for the Study of Conversion. *Sociological Analysis, 41*, 137–143.

Balch, R. W. (1985). When the Light Goes Out, Darkness Comes. In: R. Stark (Ed.), *Religious Movements* (pp. 11–63). New York: Paragon House.

Balch, R. W. (1995). Waiting for the Ships: Disillusionment and the Revitalization of Faith in Bo and Peep's UFO Cult. In: J. R. Lewis (Ed.), *The Gods Have Landed: New Religions From Other Worlds* (pp. 137–166). Albany, NY: State University of New York Press.

Balch, R. W., & Taylor, D. (1977) . Seekers and Saucers: The Role of the Cultic Milieu in Joining a UFO Cult. *American Behavioral Scientist, 20*, 839–859.

Batson, C. D. (1977). Experimentation in Psychology of Religion. *Journal for the Scientific Study of Religion, 16*, 413–418.

Bimber, B. (1998). The Internet and Political Mobilization. *Social Science Computer Review, 16*, 391–401.

Blau, P. (1964). *Exchange and Power in Social Life*. New York: Wiley.

Cameron, N. (1959). The Paranoid Pseudo-Community Revisited. *American Journal of Sociology, 65*, 52–58.

Carley, K. M., & Wendt, K. (1991). Electronic Mail and Scientific Communication: A Study of the Soar Extended Research Group. *Knowledge: Creation, Diffusion, Utilization, 12*, 406–440.

Christie, R., & Geis, F. L. (1970). *Studies in Machiavellianism*. New York: Academic Press.

Church of Scientology. (1992). *What is Scientology?* Los Angeles: Bridge Publications.

Clarke, A. C. (1953). *The City and the Stars*. New York: Harcourt, Brace and Company.

Cohn, N. (1961). *The Pursuit of the Millennium*. New York: Harper and Row.

Collins, R. (1993). A Theory of Religion. *Journal for the Scientific Study of Religion, 32*, 402–406.

Constant, D., Sproull, L., & Kiesler, S. (1997). The Kindness of Strangers: On the Usefulness of Electronic Weak Ties for Technical Advice. In: S. Kiesler (Ed.), *Culture of the Internet* (pp. 303–322). Mahwah, NJ: Lawrence Erlbaum.

Eliade, M. (1958). *Rites and Symbols of Initiation*. New York: Harper and Row.

Eliade, M. (1962). *The Forge and the Crucible*. New York: Harper and Row.

Eliade, M. (1969). *Yoga: Immortality and Freedom*. Princeton, NJ: Princeton University Press.

Evans-Pritchard, E. E. (1937). *Witchcraft, Oracles and Magic among the Azande*. London: Oxford University Press.

Evanzz, K. (1992). *The Judas Factor: The Plot to Kill Malcolm X*. New York: Thunder's Mouth.

Fauset, A. H. (1944). *Black Gods of the Metropolis*. Philadelphia: University of Pennsylvania Press.

Fearer, M. (1995). Scientology's Secrets. *Internet World, 6*, 12.

Finke, R., & Stark, R. (1992). *The Churching of America, 1776–1990*. New Brunswick, NJ: Rutgers University Press.

Fischer, C. S. (1975). Toward a Subcultural Theory of Urbanism. *American Journal of Sociology, 80*, 1319–1341.

Freud, S. (1927). *The Future of an Illusion*. Garden City, NY: Doubleday [1961].

Friedly, M. (1992). *Malcolm X: The Assassination*. New York: Carroll and Graf.

Glaser, B. G., & Strauss, A. L. (1967). *The Discovery of Grounded Theory*. Chicago: Aldine de Gruyter.

Glock, C. Y., & Stark, R. (1966). *Christian Beliefs and Anti-Semitism*. New York: Harper and Row.

Grossman, W. M. (1995). 'alt.scientology.war'. *Wired*, December. Retrieved July 22, 2000, from the World Wide Web: http://www.wired.com/wired/archive/3.12/alt.scientology.war.html.

Hadden, J. K., & Shupe, A. (1988). *Televangelism: Power and Politics on God's Frontier*. New York: Henry Holt.

Hadden, J. K., & Swann, C. W. (1981). *Prime Time Preachers: The Rising Power of Televangelism*. Reading, MA: Addison-Wesley.

Haley, A. (1965). *The Autobiography of Malcolm X*. New York: Ballantine.

Hewes, H., & Steiger, B. (1976). *UFO Missionaries Extraordinary*. New York: Pocket Books.

Hobsbawm, E. J. (1959). *Primitive Rebels*. Manchester, England: Manchester University Press.

Hubbard, L. R. (1950). *Dianetics, the Modern Science of Mental Health*. New York: Paperback Library.

Hubbard, L. R. (1967). *E-Meter Essentials 1961*. Edinburgh, Scotland: Publications Organization World Wide.

Hubbard, L. R. (1968). *The Book Introducing the E-Meter*. Edinburgh, Scotland: Publications Organization World Wide.

Iannaccone, L. R. (1998). Introduction to the Economics of Religion. *Journal of Economic Literature, 36*, 1465–1496.

Johnson, B. (1963). On Church and Sect. *American Sociological Review, 28*, 539–549.

Katz, E., & Lazarsfeld, P. (1955). *Personal Influence*. New York: Free Press.

Kurzweil, R. (1999). *The Age of Spiritual Machines*. New York: Penguin Books.

Lipset, S. M., & Raab, E. (1970). *The Politics of Unreason: Right-Wing Extremism in America, 1790–1970*. New York: Harper.

Lofland, J. (1977). *Doomsday Cult*. New York: John Wiley.

Lofland, J., & Stark, R. (1965). Becoming a World-Saver: A Theory of Conversion to a Deviant Perspective. *American Sociological Review, 30*, 862–875.

Luhrmann, T. M. (1989). Persuasions of the Witch's Craft. Cambridge: Harvard University Press.

Marsh, C. (1984). From Black Muslims to Muslims: The Transition from Separatism to Islam, 1930–1980. Metuchen, NJ: Scarecrow.

McIntosh, C. (1992). The Rose Cross and the Age of Reason. Leiden: E. J. Brill.

Muhammad, E. (1965). Message to the Blackman in America. Chicago: Muhammad Mosque of Islam No. 2.

Post, D. G. (1996). New World War. Reason, April 27, 28–33.

Rheingold, H. (1993). The Virtual Community: Homesteading on the Electronic Frontier. Reading, MA: Addison-Wesley.

Shinn, L. D. (1985). Conflicting Networks: Guru and Friend in ISKCON. In: R. Stark (Ed.), Religious Movements (pp. 95–114). New York: Paragon House.

Shupe, A. D. (1976). 'Disembodied Access' and Technological Constraints on Organizational Development: A Study of Mail-Order Religions. Journal for the Scientific Study of Religion, 15, 177–185.

Sproull, L., & Faraj, S. (1997). Atheism, Sex, and Databases: The Net as a Social Technology. In: S. Kiesler (Ed.), Culture of the Internet (pp. 35–51). Mahwah, NJ: Lawrence Erlbaum.

Sproull, L., & Kiesler, S. (1991). Connections: New Ways of Working in the Networked Organization. Cambridge: MIT Press.

Stark, R. (1987). How New Religions Succeed: A Theoretical Model. In: D. G. Bromley, & P. E. Hammond (Eds), The Future of New Religious Movements (pp. 11–29). Macon, GA: Mercer University Press.

Stark, R. (1996). The Rise of Christianity. Princeton, NJ: Princeton University Press.

Stark, R., & Bainbridge, W. S. (1980). Networks of Faith. American Journal of Sociology, 86, 1376–1395.

Stark, R., & Bainbridge, W. S. (1985). The Future of Religion. Berkeley and Los Angeles: University of California Press.

Stark, R., & Bainbridge, W. S. (1987). A Theory of Religion. New York and Toronto: Lang.

Teilhard de Chardin, P. (1964). The Future of Man. New York: Harper.

Van Gennep, A. (1959). The Rites of Passage. Chicago: University of Chicago Press.

Wallace, A. F. C. (1966). Religion: An Anthropological View. New York: Random House.

Wallis, R. (1976). The Road to Total Freedom. New York: Columbia University Press.

Warner, R. S. (1993). Work in Progress toward a New Paradigm for the Sociological Study of Religion in the United States. American Journal of Sociology, 98, 1044–1093.

Wellman, B. (1997). An Electronic Group is Virtually a Social Network. In: S. Kiesler (Ed.), Culture of the Internet (pp. 179–205). Mahwah, NJ: Lawrence Erlbaum.

Wellman, B., et al. (1996). Computer Networks as Social Networks: Collaborative Work, Telework, and Virtual Community. Annual Review of Sociology, 22, 213–238.

Whitworth, J. M. (1975). God's Blueprints. London: Routledge and Kegan Paul.

Wilson, W. (2000). The Internet Church. Nashville: Word.

Witte, J. C., Amoroso, L. M., & Howard, P. E. N. (2000). Research Methodology: Method and Representation in Internet-Based Survey Tools. Social Science Computer Review, 18, 179–195.

Yeatts, J. R., & Asher, W. (1979). Can We Afford Not to Do True Experiments in Psychology of Religion? Journal for the Scientific Study of Religion, 18, 86–89.

Zablocki, B. D. (1971). The Joyful Community. Baltimore, MD: Penguin.

APPENDIX

Selected Web Addresses
(all operative as of May 22, 2000)

Americans United for Separation of Church and State: www.au.org/
AMORC: www.rosicrucian.org/
Anti-Defamation League: www.adl.org/
Ár nDraíocht Féin: www.adf.org/
Ásatrú: asatru.org/
Association of Torah Observant Messianics: www.teshuvah.com/
Baptist Joint Committee: www.bjcpa.org/
Bible Gateway: bible.gospelcom.net/
Book of Common Prayer: http://justus.anglican.org/resources/bcp/
Bruderhof: www.bruderhof.org/
Call to Prayer: www.gospelcom.net/ibs/ctp/
Cathars: www.cathar.net/
Covenant of the Goddess: www.cog.org/welcome.html
Electronic Frontier Foundation: www.eff.org/
E-Meters: www.cs.cmu.edu/~dst/Secrets/E-Meter/
Experience on Demand: www.informedia.cs.cmu.edu/eod_html/Eod7–10/sld001.htm
Falun Gong (Falun Dafa): falundafa.org/
Family (Children of God): www.thefamily.org/
Five Percent Nation of Islam: www.allahteam.com/
Free Minds: www.freeminds.org/
Freedom Forum: www.freedomforum.org/first/welcome.asp
General Social Survey: www.icpsr.umich.edu/GSS99/
General Social Survey (Creator): www.icpsr.umich.edu/GSS99/codebook/creator.htm
Grace Notes Prayer Net: www.realtime.net/~wdoud/prayernet.html
Greater Grace Prayer Chain: www.ggwo.org/prayer/
Heaven's Gate: www.heavensgate.com/
International Christian Educational Services: www.iahushua.com/BeWise/bewise.html
International Research Institute for Zen Buddhism: www.iijnet.or.jp/iriz/
Interplanetary Internet: www.ipnsig.org/
Jehovah's Witnesses: www.watchtower.org/
Jews for Jesus: www.jewsforjesus.org/
Jews for Judaism: www.jewsforjudaism.org/
Kingdom Identity Ministries: www.kingidentity.com/
Liberty Counsel: www.lc.org/
Lost-Found Nation of Islam: members.aol.com/akankem/Intro.htm
Maitreya (Benjamin Creme): www.wonp.org/
Maitreya (Margaret Birkin): www.lord-maitreya.org/default.htm
Messianic Jewish Alliance of America: www.mjaa.org/
Military Pagan Network: milpagan.org/
Nation of Islam: www.noi.org/
New Light Ministries: www.newlightministries.com/
Nizkor Project: www.nizkor.org/

Noosphere: www.technoetic.com/noosphere/
Pagan Federation: www.paganfed.demon.co.uk/
People for the American Way: www.pfaw.org/
Peregrine Foundation: www.perefound.org/
Question Factory: users.erols.com/bainbri/qf.htm
Raelian Movement: www.rael.org/
Religious Freedom Home Page: www.religious-freedom.org/welcome.html
Reorganized LDS: www.rlds.org/
Rosicrucian Fellowship: www.rosicrucian.com/
Rutherform Institute: www.rutherford.org/
Scientology: www.scientology.org/
Shoah Visual History Foundation: www.vhf.org/
Third Testament: euforia.com/book-of-life/temas.htm
Transhumanist Movement: http://www.transhumanist.org/
Waco Holocaust: www.mnsinc.com/SkyWriter/WacoMuseum/
Watchman Fellowship: www.watchman.org/
Watchtower Observer: watchtower.observer.org/
WebRing: www.webring.org/
World Pagan Network: www.geocities.com/Athens/Aegean/8773/wpntoc.html
World Prayer Network: worldprayer.org/
Yahoo: dir.yahoo.com/Society_and_Culture/Religion_and_Spirituality/Faiths_and_Practices/
Zen@SunSite: sunsite.unc.edu/zen/

DOING RESEARCH AND TEACHING WITH THE AMERICAN RELIGION DATA ARCHIVE: INITIAL EFFORTS TO DEMOCRATIZE ACCESS TO DATA

Roger Finke, Jennifer McKinney and Matt Bahr

ABSTRACT

The American Religion Data Archive (ARDA) strives to democratize access to data on American religion. Holding over 150 data files on American religion, this Internet-based archive is equipped with an abundance of useful on-line features: conducting basic analysis, reviewing codebooks, constructing a survey instrument, downloading data and software, and searching for variables, principal investigators or topics of interest. This chapter gives a brief overview of the data archived, the users served and the goals ARDA is trying to achieve. The majority of the essay, however, is devoted to explaining and illustrating how the ARDA can be used for teaching and research.

INTRODUCTION

The American Religion Data Archive (ARDA) was developed to provide immediate access to the best data on American religion at no charge. Beginning in

Religion on the Internet, Volume 8, pages 81–99.

1997, the Internet-based archive was designed to serve a highly diverse audience. Along with social scientists and their students, who typically use quantitative data sets on religion, the ARDA was intended for those holding a strong interest in American religion, but with little or no training in the social sciences. Seminarians, journalists, church leaders, and scholars beyond the social sciences were all part of the target audience. Serving this diverse audience required the ARDA to meet the rigorous methodological standards of the social science community, and still be easily used by those without a knowledge of statistics, research design or data management. The outcome has been increasing the ease of use for all.

Since its inception, the ARDA has attempted to democratize access to data, without compromising the integrity of the data being archived. This essay will review our efforts. We begin by giving a brief overview of the data we archive, the users we serve, and the goals we are trying to achieve. Although the goals are similar to other archives, we will highlight how we have developed features that allow us to achieve these goals in new and creative ways. We devote the majority of the chapter, however, to explain and illustrate how the ARDA can be used for teaching and research.

ABOUT THE ARDA

When the ARDA was initially conceived, the 1995–96 *ICPSR Guide to Resources and Services* reported on more than 40,000 data files from over 3,000 social research studies. Even a topic such as education, which had comparatively few entries, reported 119 data files from 65 studies, with 34 of these studies being conducted since 1980. By comparison, the subheading of religion reported only nine data files from nine studies, with only two of these being conducted after 1980. Yet, this paucity of archived data on religion does not mean that data are not being collected. Over the last 10 years alone, Lilly Endowment has funded over 150 grants with a data collection component, the Pew Charitable Trusts has funded several major national and international surveys, and many denominations support research divisions that collect large amounts of data each year. Unlike education, health care and other substantive areas, where most studies are funded by government sources, private endowments or religious organizations funded nearly all of the data collections on religion. Most funding sources have either wanted the data to remain 'in house' or have not required principal investigators to place the data files in a public archive.

In the mid-1990s, however, the Lilly Endowment began a major initiative for improving data dissemination. One component of this initiative was the American Religion Data Archive. After awarding a planning grant to Roger Finke in 1996, Lilly Endowment funded the start up and operation of the American Religion Data Archive in 1997. Although the funding source for the ARDA remains private, the data are now easily accessible to a wide audience.

ARDA DATA SOURCES

The ARDA holds over 150 data files and continues to grow. These studies include national samples of the United States and Canada, regional samples of selected communities or areas, and samples of selected religious groups or professionals. Here are a few of the surveys included:

Pew Center for the People and the Press' Survey on Religion and Politics in America, 1996
Bibby's Project Canada, 1975, 1980, 1985, 1990, 1995
Middletown Area Studies, 1978–1996
Educational Testing Services' Surveys of Entering and Exiting Seminarians, 1994–96
Davidson's National and Indiana Surveys of Catholics, 1995
Nygren and Ukeritis' National Survey of Religious Life Futures Project, 1990
The Presbyterian Panel Surveys, 1994–1996
Hunter's Survey of the Beliefs and Moral Values of America's Children, 1989
Queen's University Survey of Religion, Politics and Social Involvement in Canada and the United States, 1996

Although the majority of the ARDA collection is comprised of surveys on individuals, the archive also holds data collections on congregations, including selected annual congregational reports for the Church of the Nazarene and the Southern Baptist Convention, and Hoge, Zech, McNamara and Donahue's data on congregational giving. Additionally, the ARDA holds several files based on ecological units, such as the Church and Church Membership Surveys of 1952, 1971, 1980, and 1990.

Although the Lilly Endowment maintains the leading role in funding data collections on American religion, denominations, universities, professional organizations, other endowments and individual researchers have all contributed to the data archive. Moreover, these data collections were produced by a diverse source of principal investigators and represent a wide range of topics on American religion.

ARDA GOALS

ARDA goals are similar to those of many other archives. The ARDA was established to:

1. Preserve Data
2. Improve Access to Data
3. Increase the Use of Data
4. Allow Comparisons Across Data Files

To achieve these goals we combine proven archiving practices with new attempts to serve a diverse audience.

The first goal, *preserving data*, is the foundation of virtually all archives, and in the case of data on American religion, it was the most essential. Of the first 150 data files we received, only three were previously held in a public archive. But preserving data requires more than merely collecting data files, the data files must be verified and information must be assembled on how the research was completed.

Preparing the data for the ARDA follows many of the same procedures developed by other scholarly archives. Upon receiving electronic copies of the data files (as well as the original survey instrument and frequencies for each variable), we verify the accuracy of the data by comparing our variable frequencies with those from the principal investigator. Once accuracy of the data have been verified, we begin collecting 'metadata', or summary information for each study, including when, where and how the research was completed.

In our effort to democratize access to the data, however, we have gone beyond the standard procedures used by most scholarly archives. We have added features that make the data files more accessible, more efficient and easier to use. First, we recreate the original survey instrument within the data set. Using the original questionnaires, we attach the complete variable descriptions and response categories to each variable. This creates a data file that is also a codebook. No longer are users forced to keep a secondary codebook by their side to decipher truncated variable information.[1] Second, the ARDA web site is designed to promote responsible use of data files. Users are automatically directed to a *Description* page, reviewing summary information about the research study, before they download files. This information is also easily linked to from anywhere on the site. This is not only handy for experienced researchers, but is necessary for those with less experience.

Improving access to data, the second ARDA goal, was primarily achieved by adding an easy *Download* feature to the site. Thanks to the support of the Lilly Endowment, anyone with access to the Internet can download the data free of charge. Once users find a data file they want, they can easily download it to their own computer as an SPSS, ASCII, Excel or MicroCase file. They also have the option of downloading a codebook without the data, as well as downloading a simplified version of the MicroCase ExplorIt software.

We have also simplified the search process for the type of data desired. The *Search* feature allows for keyword searches of survey *Questions (Variables),* the *Study Abstracts* or the *Investigators/Institutions* completing and supporting the study – searches that can include all data files or selected groups of files (e.g. national, selected religious groups, etc.). Hence, the various *Search* options allow users to conduct general searches on topics of interest or search selected groups of studies. Our goal is to improve access to data by making it easy to find, easy to understand and easy to download.

For the third goal, *increasing the use of the data,* we allow users to conduct basic analyses of the data files on-line or off-line. Although experienced researchers will use the downloaded data in the statistical software of their choice, many others will have neither the software nor the expertise for analyzing the data. Teaming up with the educational software company, MicroCase Corporation, we developed options to provide statistical tools designed for those lacking expertise in statistics and software. For users who download data, we give them the option of downloading a simplified version of MicroCase's ExplorIt software.[2] This software is used by thousands of under-graduate social science students each year, and is remarkably easy to use. The software is free of charge and is fully compatible with the MicroCase data files available from our site, and allows users to run basic univariate and cross-tabular analyses.

A second tool for increasing data usage is our on-line *Analyze* feature. Again, working with MicroCase the auto-analyzer was added to the ARDA web site. Using a handful of pre-selected variables (often including sex, race, marital status, education, income and age), the auto-analyzer constructs and percent-ages tables. After a user selects a question of interest, the auto-analyzer compares responses by age, income groups or other pre-selected variables. Later in this chapter we will provide additional description and illustration on the use of this popular feature.

The fourth goal, *allowing comparisons across data files and over time,* is achieved through standard searches. Users can search for a topic of interest within a single data file, a selected group of data files or all ARDA data files. After locating questions of interest, users can quickly compare the results for each question by conducting on-line analysis, or they can compare the data files from which the questions were selected. They also have the option of using the *Search* and *Question Bank* features to save questions for designing new surveys.

Because the complete survey questions and response categories are added and stored in the data file, the ARDA serves as a complete archive of the questions used and the data received.

Achieving the goals outlined above has allowed us to democratize access to data. This ease of accessing and analyzing data has made the data available to new users and has opened up new avenues for using the data.

USING THE ARDA

When the ARDA was first established, one of our overriding goals was to serve as a repository for major data collections on American religion. At the outset, we were most aware of the social scientists using these data collections for research published in social science journals. This audience, often sophisticated in research methods and statistics, however, represents only a small portion of the total audience we wanted to target. Many of our users have little background in the social sciences and are not actively engaged in social science research. Instead, many are students, journalists and those in disciplines not directly associated with the social sciences. These are the people who previously have had the least access to data on American religion. In fact, based on our web site reports, seminaries have made more contacts and referrals to the ARDA site than any other type of educational institution. And, though we have no record of individual users, our most frequent e-mail and telephone inquiries come from journalists and students. Rather than limiting access to a small group of researchers, the ARDA has democratized access to data, and a disparate audience is taking advantage of this access.

The ARDA has been used for many purposes, from journalistic inquiries to personal curiosity, but below we will confine our attention to education and research. We will offer several examples of how the ARDA has been used by classroom teachers and by research scholars. We thank the many ARDA users who have shared their experiences, ideas and questions when using the archive.

TEACHING WITH THE ARDA

Educators have long acknowledged that active learning, the process of students participating in the learning and discovery of new information, is the foundation for effective teaching. Yet, in the social sciences, we have often failed to provide experiences that allow for active learning. While students are mixing chemicals in chemistry and collecting plants in botany, they have few laboratory experiences in the social sciences or religious studies. Visiting local churches or violating etiquette rules for riding elevators provide a few interesting field observations, but getting the students beyond the local community is a more difficult task. The ARDA is designed to allow students to explore American religion beyond their local community. Here they can embark on an exploration using the same top-quality data sources used by leading researchers.

The ARDA offers several avenues for student discovery. Below we review and illustrate three educational options for exploring the ARDA data: exploring data on-line, exploring downloaded data, and exploring data in the classroom.

Exploring Data On-line

Along with the absence of readily available and fully documented files on American religion, social science instruction has also been plagued (until recently) with a lack of software that was suitable for instruction. If a research exercise, using real data, were introduced, the instructor would devote extensive class time to teaching the statistical software and the appropriate techniques for constructing tables. From our own classroom experiences with undergraduates, we knew how confusing even the construction of tables can be. First, constructing the table requires students (or any user) to fill in boxes that ask for an independent and dependent variable – unfamiliar and unfriendly words for most. Second, they must select variables with an appropriate number of categories. For example, when a student tries to set up a table with age by income, the resulting table might offer an incomprehensible 70 columns and 20 rows. And, even if they are successful in constructing an appropriate table, they need to know which way to percentage the table. Choosing to percentage in the wrong direction leads to meaningless, or often misleading, results.

As mentioned previously, we have avoided this quagmire by working with MicroCase Corporation to develop a simplified version of their auto-analyzer for our web site. When users find a question of interest, they can click on the Analyze feature and tables are constructed using pre-selected variables. The tables are percentaged correctly and typically offer standard demographic variables like sex, race, marital status, education, income and age. This avoids the potential problems of choosing an independent and dependent variable or deciding which way to percentage.[3]

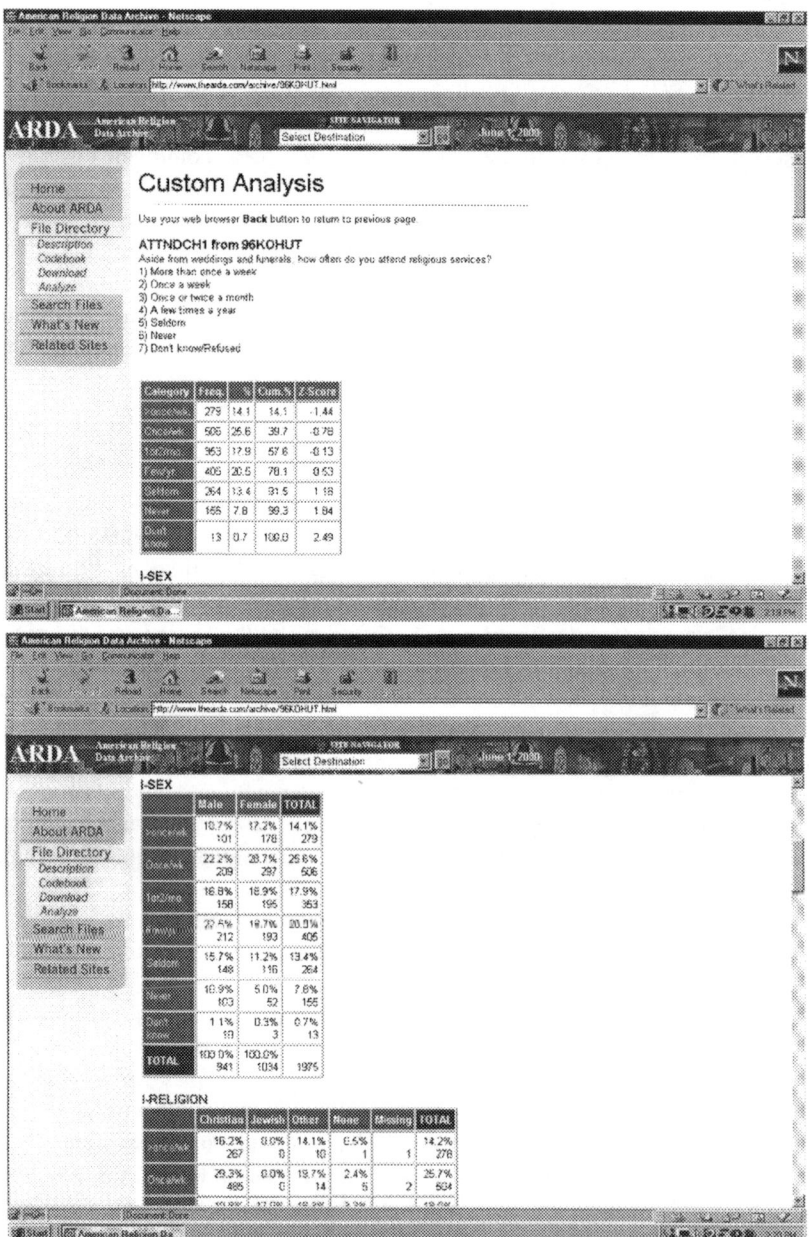

Fig. 1.

Figure 1 offers an example of the tables returned from auto-analyzer.[4] After the student selects a question of interest within a data file (e.g. Aside from weddings and funerals, how often do you attend religious services?) and presses the *Analyze* button, the ARDA site returns the page shown in Fig. 1. As the student scrolls down the page, she will receive the complete table showing attendance differences by sex and additional tables for attendance differences by religion, political party, age, marital status, education, race, income and region. Notice, the tables are percentaged correctly and the student was not forced to answer questions about independent and dependent variables. The student selected the variable or question that interested her, and the tables were constructed. Without learning about the language or conventions of social science research, the student can explore the variation in church attendance for several variables of interest.

The tables presented in Fig. 1 show the final product of the student's search, but instructors can vary in how much they limit or structure their students' search criteria. One option is a search with no restrictions. Here students are allowed to search for any topic of interest, from any data set they choose. For example, if they searched for 'vote', the *Search* feature would yield all questions that included the word 'vote' across the entire range of studies in the ARDA, from national, regional or local samples to samples of specific groups (e.g. Catholics or religious professionals). The results of the search, using the keyword 'vote', would yield a list of 227 questions from 70 different data files. This completely unstructured assignment is initially appealing, but for many students it fails to give them the direction they need.

A second option is to offer more restrictions to the students' search. For example, students might be asked to limit their search to data files using only a national sample. The above search using 'vote' would return 76 questions from 18 of the 20 national studies. This restriction assures the instructor that the questions returned from the *Search* feature will be from national samples, and helps to reduce the number of questions returned. But even these restrictions provide little structure or direction to the class assignment.

A third option, for on-line analysis, is to limit the search to a single data file in the ARDA. Here students can go directly to the *Data File Directory* and select the data file assigned. Once they have clicked on a single data set, they will receive a *Description* of the study and how the study was conducted. From here they click on *Codebook* to review a complete list of survey questions or they can use *Search* to find questions in the selected file. This approach has the advantage of giving the students a more focused and restricted area for their search.

Yet another option is to provide students with a written exercise or worksheet that asks them to explore the results for specific questions, from a specific data file. This allows the students to still discover and interpret the results, but gives the instructor more control over what is being explored and makes the grading of projects much easier. Although this approach might seem confining, when there is such a wealth of data available, we have found this to be the most effective strategy for the initial class project. As students develop skills in framing the research question and interpreting tables, we then allow them to expand their searches.

Exploring Downloaded Data

Having students use the on-line analyzer is perhaps the easiest to organize, but using the *Download* option offers many other pedagogical advantages and options. One advantage is that instructors can pare down the number of variables (or questions) available in a given data file. This allows the instructor to confine the data file to questions relating to the topics being studied. For example, the Queen's data file (God and Society in North America) contains questions covering topics ranging from religiosity and community involvement to political preferences, denominational affiliation and voting behavior. Downloading the file allows the instructor to save a second file that is tailored for the course at hand. The number of questions might be reduced from about 220 to a more manageable size of 50 to 75 variables directly relevant to the class projects assigned.

Downloading the files also allows instructors the option of expanding the analysis conducted by the students. If the instructor downloads the free ExplorIt software available from the ARDA *Download,* students can construct tables that go beyond the pre-selected variables. For instance, with the on-line example given earlier, the students can construct tables exploring the relationship between church attendance and denominational affiliation or beliefs, rather than being confined to the variables of age or gender. We should caution, however, that undergraduate students need instruction on how to create and percentage tables. This option also allows students to create colorful pie and bar charts, and allows them to view summary statistics for the tables.

Finally, because the ARDA *Download* feature offers several options, the data can be imported into any statistical package or spreadsheet. Our options for downloading data files include SPSS portable, ASCII, MicroCase, and Excel. If instructors want their students to have more statistical options, or want them to work with selected data files on a local network, they can download selected files and analyze them with the statistical software of their choice. This option is especially attractive for more advanced students, who will be working with advanced statistics or are familiar with other statistical packages.

Classroom Explorations

Yet another teaching option is to allow the students to explore the data with you in the classroom. Using a notebook computer and an LCD projector, instructors can offer classroom presentations that allow students to see the results for themselves. These presentations also allow one to illustrate the skills they will need for later class projects. By keeping presentations focused on interesting substantive questions, students gradually learn about reading tables and statistics without warning – a method of learning that is far less painful for all.

When we state that the students will join you in an exploration, however, we are not suggesting that the exploration should be unplanned. Watching a professor wander aimlessly through an archive will not enhance the students' learning experience. Like any lecture, the exploration should address the teaching objectives and should be prepared in advance. Still, this method of presentation promotes serendipitous learning, energizes discussions and engages students in the research process. As you give the presentation, students will want to try their own questions for explaining church attendance, voting behavior, or whatever the topic might be. Once again, it offers a pedagogical tool that allows students to become actively engaged in the learning process.

DOING RESEARCH WITH THE ARDA

Because the use of data archives is nothing new for experienced researchers, many features of the ARDA require little explanation. In fact, many of the procedures we follow replicate long established archiving conventions. But the ARDA also offers relatively new archiving features that might easily be overlooked by researchers familiar with other archives. Below we review a few of the new features that are most useful for researchers.

An Archive of Questions: Using the Question Bank

As we noted earlier, the ARDA is an archive of both data and survey questions. Along with providing the quantitative data from surveys and other collections, the site also provides the complete wording of all survey questions and their responses. By including the entire question, the archive becomes a rich resource of questions and question responses, as well as a tool for designing new surveys. The ARDA site has combined keyword searches for finding questions, with a *Question Bank* for saving, editing and printing the questions.

Fig. 2.

Using the ARDA's archive of questions begins with the *Search Files* page. Like all ARDA searches, the researcher can choose the search parameters for the keywords entered and can search all files or within a selected group of files. After entering the word(s) in the search box, the researcher receives a list of questions that hold a match to the key word(s) entered. For example, after searching for the phrase 'financial contribution' in all archived data files, Fig. 2 shows four questions with exact matches. The researcher can now choose to analyze any of the questions listed or enter any (or all) questions into the *Question Bank*. After getting the question(s) needed from the first search, the researcher can continue to conduct additional searches, adding additional questions whenever a desired question is found. If the researcher forgets which questions have been entered, clicking on the *View Question Bank* lists the entire contents of the *Question Bank*. After adding all of the desired questions, the items can now be copied directly into an existing word processing file or saved as a new text file.[5] Researchers can also look more closely at files that contain questions of interest. When the *Search* feature returns the questions matching the keyword(s), the file from which the question was taken is highlighted in hypertext next to the variable name. Clicking on this file name will take the researcher to the file, where additional questions can be reviewed. Drawing on the resources of well over 100 surveys, and without ever typing a complete question, the researcher has saved items for designing a new questionnaire.

Auto-analyzer: Previewing results

After using the *Search* or *Codebook* to find questions of interest, users also have the option to use the Analyze feature. Here the auto-analyzer provides a list of responses for the selected variable and constructs a table for this variable with pre-selected independent variables. An example of the tables constructed was shown earlier in Fig. 1. This feature was designed to construct tables for those with little or no research background, yet it is equally useful for experienced researchers. For the experienced researcher this *Analyze* feature offers an ideal way of previewing data. For example, when considering questions for the *Question Bank*, a researcher can examine the variation in responses. Did the question capture the variation desired, or were the responses primarily limited to only one category? Or, before downloading a data file, the researcher might review variation in the dependent variable of interest. The *Analyze* feature will never provide a complete analysis, but it does offer a useful preview.

MetaData: Information on the Study

Because information on a research study is critical for responsibly using the data, we place the *Description* page, which offers the research information (or metadata) on the study, at a virtual crossroads of the site. This allows users to access the study information from several locations. For example, whenever users click on the file name, whether it is located on the *Data File Directory* page, the *What's New* page, or the *Search* pages, they are immediately directed to the *Description* page. Indeed, before users are ever allowed to download data, they are taken to the *Description* page where they are given the options to *Search, Analyze*, review the *Codebook*, or *Download* the research study selected. In an effort to increase the responsible use of secondary data, the site was intentionally designed to offer users a description of the data file before they download the data.

The information that is provided on the *Description* page is similar to the metadata of most other archives. We try to include the following information for each file.

Abstract (project summary)
Data file information (number of cases, variables)
Funding agency
Data collection (collection and sampling procedures)
Principal Investigator
Publications using the data
Supplementary information regarding weighting techniques, indexes, etc.

In addition, we follow the conventions of other archives by making the appropriate 'weight' variables available in the file, however, following archiving convention, all downloaded files are unweighted (the 'weight' variable is not invoked).

Multiple Searches: Searching abstracts, investigators, and questions

When initiating the ARDA, the *Search* feature was limited to variable descriptions. Users could select a topic of interest, enter the keywords, and get a list of variables containing any or all of the keywords entered. Because the archive collection was initially small, finding files of interest, or a specific principal investigator, was relatively easy. As the archive has grown, however, we have tried to increase the sophistication of our search engine, without adding needless complexity.

Here is a brief overview of our current *Search* page, as shown in Fig. 3. Like most search features, users can enter a single word or multiple words in the

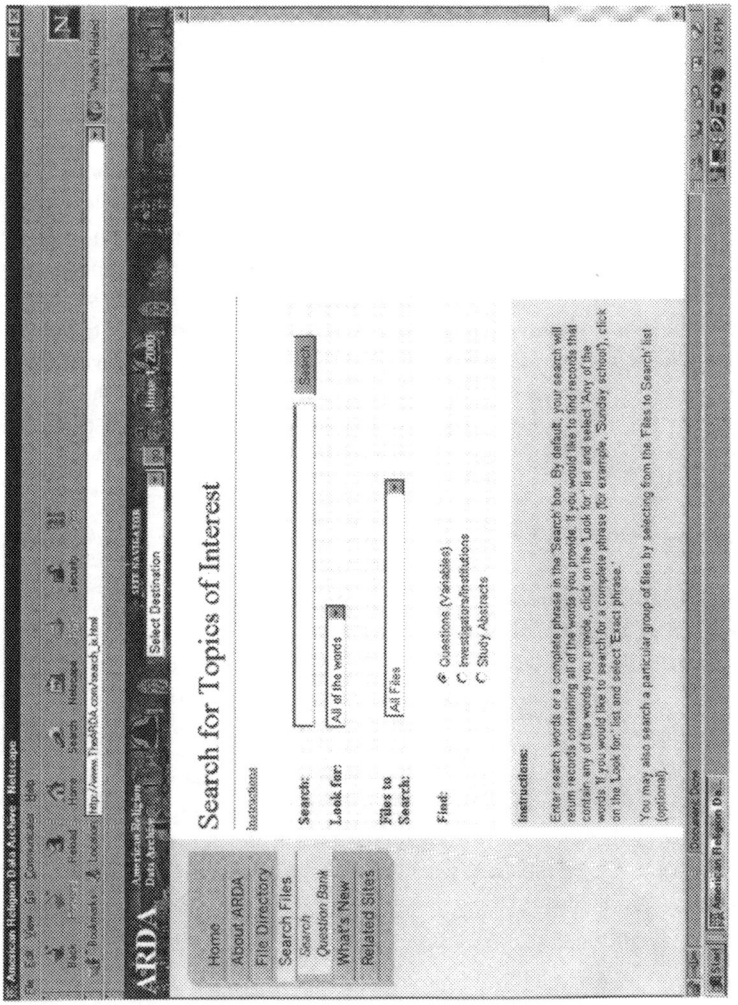

Fig. 3.

keyword box. Here they are given the choice of searching for all of the words entered, any of the words entered or the exact phrase entered, with the default being *All of the words*. Below this selection, they can choose to search all files or a selected group of files, such as *National Surveys*. Here the default is *All Files*. Finally, they can choose to search three different sources. The default, *Questions (Variables)*, allows them to search all questions in the ARDA. As noted earlier, the results of this search allow users to *Analyze* any of the questions listed or to save the questions to their own *Question Bank*. A second choice is to search by *Investigators/Institutions*. This option allows users to search for all studies completed by a specific principal investigator or receiving support from a specific institution (e.g. the Lilly Endowment). For example, when the *Investigators/Institutions* option is selected, a search for 'Hoge' will list seven data files where Dean Hoge served as a principal investigator. A third option is to search the *Study Abstracts*. When interested in an overview of the study, rather than a specific question, this option is especially attractive. For all of the searches, when the results list the name of the data file for a question, investigator or abstract, the file's name serves as a link to the *Description* page of the file. Thus, after locating the information of interest, additional information on the research study is close at hand.

Download Options: SPSS, MicroCase, Excel, ASCII, and Codebooks

For the *Download* feature, we have tried to select download formats that are most frequently used by researchers, teachers and general users. Because the various formats differ in the restrictions they place on variable descriptions and the number of variables included, users should be aware of the limitations of each download format. Here is a brief review of the data formats available:

MicroCase: The advantage of MicroCase files is that they will retain the complete variable descriptions and the complete response categories for all variables in the file. The disadvantage is that the file format is only used by the MicroCase statistical package and the ExplorIt educational software for the social sciences.

SPSS portable file: The advantage of SPSS portable files is that they are easily imported by all versions of SPSS and most major statistical packages. The disadvantage is that the SPSS character limitations truncate many of the variable descriptions and the response categories.

Excel: The advantage is that Excel is a widely used spreadsheet and can be imported by many other software programs. The disadvantage is that

Excel does not accept over 256 variables and keeps only the variable name intact, requiring the user to print a separate codebook for full variable descriptions and response categories.[6]

ASCII: The advantage is that ASCII files can be read by almost any program. The disadvantage is that they are much harder to import. Users should be aware that when the ASCII option is selected, two files are included in the download. One file contains the data and the second file contains the column specifications.

Codebook: Because many software packages will truncate long variable descriptions and response categories, we also offer an option for downloading a codebook with the complete variable descriptions and labels.

ExplorIt: As explained earlier, this is a simplified version of MicroCase's ExplorIt software, allowing users to conduct univariate analysis and construct crosstabs.

Finally, users should be aware that all files are downloaded as executable files (they have an .exe extension) beginning with the letters 'ard'. After double clicking on the executable file, the downloaded file is saved under the filename listed on the ARDA (e.g. 96Kohut) and is ready for use.

REQUIREMENTS: USING THE DATA RESPONSIBLY

When using data from the American Religion Data Archive, the obligations are relatively few and, thanks to the support of the Lilly Endowment, the costs are none. We do ask users, however, to acknowledge the American Religion Data Archive and the original collector(s) of the data. For example, they might explain that 'The data used in this publication were made available by the American Religion Data Archive and were originally collected by [name of principal investigator(s)]. And, of course, we ask all users to make responsible use of all data, software and documentation obtained from the American Religion Data Archive.

SUMMARY

Internet technologies have broken down many of the barriers for easily accessing data. Yet, the technology is useless unless the data are collected and available for access in an easy to use format. The ARDA has taken the initial steps in democratizing access to data on American religion.

We recognize that there are far more steps to be taken, yet we are encouraged by our initial progress. The support of the Lilly Endowment has made the archive possible and has eliminated the barrier of financial cost for using the data. The availability of downloading MicroCase's ExplorIt software and using their on-line analysis tool has greatly reduced the barrier of data analysis for a larger audience. Providing data files that offer complete question wording, detailed metadata, verified data and multiple download formats, renders a rich resource to the experienced and inexperienced user alike. Reducing each of these barriers, and extending the services offered, has helped to increase the use of the data and expand the diversity of the audience using the ARDA.

This essay has reviewed and illustrated how the reduction of these barriers has contributed to teaching and research on American religion. For research, the new steps were incremental, building on the work of past archives. Along with preserving data for future use, the ARDA also allows users to preview the data on-line, search for desired data sources, and download the data in a variety of formats. Perhaps the most creative new feature, however, is the *Question Bank*. Combining the *Search* feature with the *Question Bank,* users can easily search, access and save the complete wording of questions for a new survey. This allows the ARDA to serve as an archive of questions as well as data.

While the changes for research have been incremental, the ARDA offers completely new opportunities for teaching. The ARDA allows students to become actively engaged in the learning process by allowing them to explore high quality data on American religion. Instructors can now have their students conduct analysis on-line, using the tables constructed by the auto-analyzer. Or, instructors can download software and data sets, allowing students to conduct analysis using software and data sets on their local network.

We want to close with a reminder and a thank you. Developing an archive that democratizes access to data is, in part, made possible by recent advances in technology. The most significant contribution, however, is still made by the many principal investigators who make their data available to others. We would like to thank all of the principal investigators who have generously placed their data in the ARDA.[7]

NOTES

1. When data sets are downloaded using the MicroCase software, full descriptions and labels are retained. Due to the character limitations of SPSS, however, some of the questions will be truncated when SPSS portable files are downloaded.

2. The simplified version of the ExplorIt software, downloaded from the ARDA web site, provides univariate statistics with the appropriate bar graphs and pie charts, crosstabs

with the appropriate statistics, and a complete list of survey questions that can be searched for a topic of interest.

3. Users receive a message indicating if/when a variable has too many categories for constructing a table.

4. Figure 1 is a capture of two screens. Other pre-selected variables not shown include political party, age, marital status, education, race, income and region.

5. Each session allows users to store questions in the ARDA Question Bank. Exiting the Web site or a browser resets the bank.

6. When ARDA files exceed 256 variables, the Excel download is not offered as an option.

7. If you have data on American religion to submit, or you know of data that should be submitted, contact the ARDA (arda@pop.psu.edu) or download a submission form from our Web site (www.TheARDA.com).

RELIGION, RHETORIC, AND SCHOLARSHIP: MANAGING VESTED INTEREST IN E-SPACE

Douglas E. Cowan

ABSTRACT

When employed as vehicles for scholarly discourse, Internet discussion lists present their own unique set of opportunities and challenges. Several questions emerge about how this discourse is and ought to be carried out. How does one, for example: (a) determine which threads of discussion are permissible within a particular list? (b) moderate on-line debates that can (and often do) become acrimonious and quibbling? and (c) manage list membership and discussions to maintain the academic integrity of list content? Using primarily the experience of Nurel-L, a list opened for the academic discussion of new religious movements, the author concludes that two particular aspects of list management can seriously affect list participation, and offers two suggestions for their resolution.

INTRODUCTION

How many times a day do you check your email? Simply stopping to think about it points to the enormous shift in consciousness that has taken place in

Religion on the Internet, Volume 8, pages 101–124.

Western culture in the past decade. Many of us now regularly split our affairs between actual and virtual worlds, between real and on-line consciousnesses. Whether by email, synchronous chat environments such as IRCs or MUDs (Multi-User Dimensions, or 'Dungeons', depending with whom one talks), or asynchronous exchange media such as newsgroups and topic-specific listservs, myriad forms of computer-mediated communication (CMC) take place every day. And each brings with it its own unique package of problems and promises.

Text-based communication (as opposed to video and CU-C-ME) in e-space is something of a more delicate balance than in real life. For those who seek to communicate effectively in this environment, the disrupted order in which messages often appear, the specialized experience and demands of text-only communication, the absence of normal interaction cues, the primitive nature of comment-and-reply structures, and the management of discussion topics all contribute to that balance.

This chapter considers one particular experience of academic discussion in the virtual world: Nurel-L, a discussion list devoted to the academic study of new religious movements. As an investigation of the listserv experience as a medium for the management and facilitation of scholarly discussion of religious phenomena, groups, movements, and personalities, I address two basic questions: (a) What is Nurel-L and how does it function? And (b) what are some of the specific problems and prospects for discussion forums of this kind?

Turoff and his colleagues note that "the current state of the art of Computer Mediated Communications is limited mainly by the fairly primitive discourse structures underlying most current asynchronous conference systems" (Turoff et al., 1999). Put differently, if we could only improve the technology of these systems, render them less primitive, a number of problems which arise in such media as listservs and threaded discussion lists would disappear. What the Nurel-L experience (and to some extent that of a cognate list, SSREL-L) demonstrates is that, while technology does indeed hamper the effectiveness with which communication takes place, it is far from being the only obstacle. In many cases, the quirks and quibbles, the agendas and the acrimony, the ego and the obstinacy of the human factor in the equation renders the technological problems pale by comparison. In short, we quarrel as often in VR as IRL.

Following a brief description of Nurel-L, these problems are discussed with reference to two issues which seriously affected its list constituency and participation: (a) the ban on discussion of or related to the Church of Scientology, and (b) the shift to Majordomo and its accompanying H-Net list membership protocols. From these experiences, two general propositions about message volume and diversity become clear. These are:

- The greater the restrictions placed on the nature or tenor of discussion on a listserv, the more the message traffic and diversity will decline.
- The greater the restrictions placed on list membership, the narrower the list constituency will become as potential and actual stakeholders are excluded; and the more the message traffic and diversity will decline.

While these negative correlations may seem obvious, their force is, in fact, masked by much of the rhetoric of openness and democratization that pervades discourse about the Net. Despite some industry and enthusiast claims to the contrary (see, for example, Shirky, 1995), the reality is that there *are* hierarchies in place in the virtual world (Kim, 1998; Gutstein, 1999). Some are technological in nature; others evolve out of the e-space environment and its fundamental dramaturgy, including the masks and identities it allows participants to create and assume. The propositions considered here illustrate only two of these hierarchies. What is clear is that there are consequences to discussion environments such as listservs when such hierarchies are identified and enforced.

NUREL-L HISTORY

In 1993, religious studies professor Irving Hexham saw the Internet as a "wonderful opportunity" to bring scholars and other interested parties into a common discussion around new religious movements (I. Hexham, personal conversation, June 20, 1999). Prior to that, if there was extra-conference collaboration between colleagues, it took place on a relatively small scale (in terms of aggregate participants); it excluded vast numbers of others simply by virtue of distance, the resulting difficulty of communication, and the fact that many scholars may simply be unknown to one another. And, when it did happen, such discussions were hardly open to the informed public.

The increased accessibility of the Internet and the availability of point-to-multipoint 'mail exploder' software such as Listserv allowed Hexham to open Nurel-L in September 1993. By January 1994, the list had about fifty subscribers and posted an average of 1–2 messages per day (I. Hexham, personal conversation, June 20, 1999). Two years later, while Hexham was on sabbatical and the list moderated by a colleague, message traffic climbed to 3–5 posts per day, and the subscription list grew to over one hundred. Participation continued to expand, both in depth and in scope, well into 1998 when, with around 250 members, message traffic often exceeded ten posts per day on a wide variety of topics.

While Nurel-L discussion is often quite free-ranging, moving with sometimes amazing rapidity from NRM description and inquiry to research methodology and ethics, from list protocol and dynamics to acrimony and apologetics, the academic field of NRM study is the anchor to which all posts are expected to tie in some fashion. Nurel-L's statement of purpose reads:

> Nurel-L is a public forum for the discussion of cults, sects, and new religions. It is open to anyone provided they are seriously interested in the study of religion. The tone of the group is academic. Irving Hexham moderates the group and rejects petty, libelous or other postings which may prove problematic or distract from serious dialogue (Hexham, 1999).[1]

While, in practice, for most of its history the potential for libel was the main criterion employed in moderation of the list, eventual choices with respect to permissible discussion did affect both list traffic and membership.

In its discourse structure, Nurel-L is similar to most newsgroups, with two important exceptions. Unlike newsgroups, access to Nurel-L discussions is regulated in that participants must be approved by the listowner before they are granted privileges on the list. Until the shift to H-Net protocols (see below), this approval was a pro forma technical requirement. The prospective list member contacted the listserv and sent a message requesting subscription to the list. Once received, Listserv automatically forwarded the request to the listowner (or moderator) for approval. As well, as a moderated list, all posts are approved by the listowner prior to general distribution.

In April 1999, Listserv was abandoned as the server suite for the list by the University of Calgary. Nurel-L was switched over to the Majordomo suite and its accompanying H-Net protocols.[2] While the only reason given to listowners was that this change offered 'many advantages', Hexham noted that he has yet to see any (I. Hexham, personal communication, April 3, 1999). Indeed, experience indicates that this was one of two turning points in the career of Nurel-L.

NUREL-L CONSTITUENCY

From the beginning of 1998 to April 1999, the period from which the majority of data for this study was drawn, Nurel-L had around 250 subscribers. About half that number had identifiable academic account names – .edu in the United States, u***.ca in Canada, .ac in Great Britain; the others were various commercial account, including Netcom, America Online, Delphi, and Compuserve. In addition to the countries just mentioned, list membership included participants from: Germany, Finland, Holland, Italy, France, Australia, South Africa, and Israel.

Religious composition was similarly varied. Some list members were Christian – Roman Catholic, Protestant, and Orthodox; liberal, evangelical, and fundamentalist. Others were Neopagan, or members/ex-members of various NRMs; and still others were very clear that they professed no religious faith whatsoever (and, indeed, some of these maintained that this made them more credible researchers in or commentators on the field).

In terms of expertise and education in the field of NRMs, however, the Nurel-L constituency was a mixed bag at best. Many of the list members were well-known scholars in the fields of religious studies, history, sociology, psychology, philosophy, and anthropology. Others were informed and interested lay people. These are what I term 'generalist participants'; that is, while acknowledging their disciplinary variety, their contributions to the list were defined by a broader interest in the field of religious studies and a more specific regard for the academic study of new religious movements.

A different group I have designated 'issue-oriented participants'. These are list members who brought to the discussion very particular and clearly identifiable agendas. Many, for example, were ex-members of different religious groups who, as occasionally happens, have dedicated part or all of their lives to 'exposing' the group to which they belonged. While it became apparent that many of those who posted regularly to the list did so to engage in meaningful discussion of NRM phenomena, most of these 'issue-oriented participants' joined the list explicitly to challenge the legitimacy of one NRM or another (e.g. those who joined to attack the Church of Scientology). Indeed, one such member often appended to his posts and later chose as his email address name 'le secticide' (loosely translated 'The Sect-Killer'). Others participants joined to defend the integrity of their own tradition against any and all criticism (e.g. those who found themselves defending the Church of Scientology against all manner of reproach). Conversely, a few joined to challenge the legitimacy of *any* tradition *other than* their own (e.g. countercult Christians who perceived Nurel-L as another vehicle to denounce NRMs in favor of evangelical/fundamentalist Christianity). While the former two tended to have an admirable tenacity in the face of often quite blunt criticism of their viewpoints, the latter inclined towards short careers on Nurel-L.

How do these myriad participants in Nurel-L perceive their membership in the 'complex social structure' (Donath, 1999, p. 30) that evolved in the e-space environment? Opinions and perceptions vary. During the debate over list parameters, for example, one member – who admitted lurking on the list prior to this discussion (that is, reading posts and observing discussions without contributing) – wrote:

> I like the idea of being in a little city, or little nation full of people interested enough in the issue of NRM's to apply for citizenship. Some hate NRM's some are in NRM's and so forth . . . I like the idea of this community being big enough so that just like in real life I gravitate towards those with whom I resonate, but also enjoy the abundant context for these friendships by having other groups and other types around ('G', April 16, 1998).

Responding to the same discussion thread, another member reiterated (and emphasized) the nature of Nurel-L as a 'community' – that is, something socially constructed and in which people participate relationally, something other than merely lines of text that scroll up a computer screen.

> I consider threatening to unsubscribe because one does not particularly like a
> discussion thread 'whining'.

As someone who has posted to indicate that I was almost ready to unsubscribe, I feel that this allegation is unfair [name deleted]! This list *is* a community, even if not everyone posts all the time ('SM', April 21, 1998).

Both these posts raise the issue of *actualized presence* versus *perceived absence*, a particular difficulty in many aspects of the virtual environment.

E-PRESENCE: ACTUALIZED OR PERCEIVED

Any message posted to any discussion list does two things: (a) it contributes content to the discussion, whatever that content is and however well or poorly it is received; and at least as importantly (b), it announces "the fact of the participant's presence" (Donath, Karahalios & Viégas, 1999). As these researchers note: "In a text-based chat, presence is manifest only when actively messaging: silence is indistinguishable from absence" (Donath, Karahalios & Viégas, 1999). Even in synchronous MUDs, MOOs, and chat rooms, this principle applies. While a search of the participants currently on-line may reveal that <Wolfman> or <Lady Gray> are still technically in the environment, there is no way of knowing whether these individuals are still physically in front of their computer, that is, still active in their engagement with the environment.

By way of analogy, consider a cocktail party. Whether everyone is speaking or not, a brief glance around the room will determine who is actually in the room, who is listening to and/or participating in which conversation cluster, and possibly even who was in the room but has now left. These social cues are absent in much of the virtual community of e-space. Many times, for example, during periods of slow list traffic on Nurel-L, a message would come through asking: "Hey, is anyone out there? Has the list shut down?" An almost existential angst underpinned these posts: Am I the only one left? Has this (albeit virtual) world ceased to exist?

Often, these kind of messages contained questions about sender/receiver technical problems. Were messages going out to the list, but being rejected by one's local server? Was there a problem at the point of origin which was preventing messages from going out at all? In face-to-face communication, both technical and conventional aspects of interrupted conversation are readily apparent – one can easily tell when the discussion has been disrupted by the time taken either to collect one's thoughts or to clear one's throat after swallowing a bug. Because silence in the virtual world is perceived as absence, though, these problems often lead to no little anxiety on the part of list members who fear they have either been dropped from the list inadvertently or that their equipment is not functioning properly.

E-DENTITY: ESTABLISHING THE AUTHORITATIVE VOICE

A not uncommon experience for Nurel-L members was misunderstanding the purpose of the list itself. Over the years, because of this confusion, several threads were closed by the moderator and participants were asked to move them to more appropriate venues. Often, these were threads that had derived from ones that were appropriate to the list, but had gone off in directions such as Christian history, theology, or veracity. While a number of discussion lists exist for these topics, one such closure prompted a member to write:

> Apparently we disagree theologically on the matter of Gods omnipotence and human free will. But although I would love to pursue this thread, Irving has asked us to conclude.

> I received the same message and was puzzled by it. Perhaps I am not understanding the purpose of this list. I was under the impression that it was a forum to discuss issues regarding religion ('FG', January 8, 1998).

Following up on this post, another member contributed:

> As I originally understood it, the purpose of the list is to discuss so-called 'new' religions from a variety of viewpoints. So far I've only noticed conservative monotheist and conservative Secular Humanist viewpoints showing up very often ('JC', January 9, 1998).

One of the dynamics of any list, whether newsgroup or moderated listserv, is the element of correction which members bring to the common discourse. As Aycock (1996) has noted in his study of Internet newsgroups, correction, whether in the form of factual information or derogatory flaming, is a recurring means by which identity and voice (i.e. authority) are established in an environment where most conventional indicators are absent. That one member is uncertain about the purpose of the list, and another is able to provide information which fills that gap establishes, at least for the moment, a particular hierarchy of voice and authority. The following example in the same discussion thread came not from the moderator, but from another list member.

> The purpose of this list is not to discuss religion in general, but new religious movements, that is, those that have arisen in the last 200 hundred years or so.

Because these new religious movements (and the members of the list) have widely varying theologies, any form of theological advocacy would soon get the list bogged down.

My personal opinion (which I offer to Irving as the list owner as an indication of what at least one member of the list wants to see here) is that theological input into the list should be descriptive rather than hortatory. One could described the theology of an NRM, and say how it differs from others NRMs, or an ORM from which it sprang, but one should not use the list to advocate the superiority of one theology or philosophy over another ('TI', January 9, 1998).

In this post, 'TI' accurately described much of what had been happening on the list with respect to discussions around the Church of Scientology, the ability of scholars to study NRMs, and religious conservatism and fundamentalism.

At first blush, these discussions appear to be taking place on a level field of discourse. The embodiment of on-line voice and authority, however, quickly establishes the agendas of many participants – that is, is their participation generalist or issue-oriented? As Donath has pointed out, the community *embodied* in e-space is anchored to the person operating the keyboard – the one who conceptualizes, types, and uploads the message. It is, however, also *disembodied* because the physical interpersonality of normal face-to-face communication is not available. The issue of authority, then – how credible is the textual voice? – is of considerable importance in the virtual world. Donath uses the trenchant example of "a high school student who claims to be an expert on viruses" (Donath, 1999, p. 30). She notes that "patients desperate for a cure read the virtual virologist's pronouncements on new AIDS treatments, believing them to be backed by real world knowledge" (Donath, 1999, p. 30).

Most prevalent in its Listserv incarnation, this same dynamic obtains in the Nurel-L environment. How much does one credence the information contained in a particular post? How does one determine who is 'talking', and how much authority ought to be granted that person? As I have noted elsewhere, with specific reference to the Christian countercult and secular anticult movements, the Internet has provided an opportunity unparalleled in communications history for the establishment of authoritative voice. It is in the nature of e-space to allow for the creation of authoritative identities even when no other accepted criteria for authority have been met.

Put differently, the ability to function as 'significant others', to use Berger and Luckmann's phrase (cf. Berger & Luckmann, 1966, pp. 169–172), has been manufactured through a technology which has stripped the environment of normal social cues. Those who would participate are no longer subject to the commercial mandates of editors, publishers, and book retailers (many office suites now come loaded with the software required to construct quite an elaborate website)[3]; neither are they bound by the academic gatekeeping functions of higher education (the process of peer-review, for example, in both doctoral and post-doctoral milieus). Yet, initial participation in e-space discussion occurs as though a level playing field exists for and among all participants.

In Nurel-L, this perceived democratization often manifested in the debate over the academic study of NRMs *versus* the lived experience of former members as primary indicators of authority. In this it revisited an ongoing debate among NRM scholars over the weight which ought to be granted apostate testimony. While the playing field in e-space may have been entered level, different voices quickly moved to shift weight from one end to the other. In response to a request from Hexham for references supporting several statements made about a particular NRM, for example, and informing the member that potentially libelous statements would be edited out of his posts, the reply came:

> Okay, no problem . . . I suppose that scholars have to find out as well the insider's truths; one of the reasons I asked to be on your group was that: saying what I know because I've lived it. I'm very often surprised (but, confidentially, not in the case of some scholars which I don't consider honestly working, like [name deleted]) to see that both sides of this extremely controversial topic of cults are not always used ('SH', July 17, 1998).

The issue of academic discourse vs. apostate testimony haunted the career of Nurel-L, as it does the larger field of NRM studies. Hexham tried to strike a balance between those who feel their voices are bounded out of academic discussion because of perceived or actual antagonism towards the group in question (i.e. apostate testimony), and those who feel that the information provided by apostates is often less credible by virtue of that antagonism. Unfortunately, because of the intractable positions often taken by each side, the level of discussion on a number of occasions descended perilously close to a flame war.

PROHIBITED SPEECH:
THE CASE OF SCIENTOLOGY ON NUREL-L

When asked what the most difficult part of managing Nurel-L has been, Hexham replied without hesitation: "the antagonism from both sides of a thread" (I. Hexham, personal communication, June 20, 1999). That is, when one side of a discussion thread was asked to tone down its rhetoric, substantiate its claims, or had posts refused, Hexham was accused – sometimes privately, sometimes in a list post – of "being partisan to the other side" (I. Hexham, personal communication, June 20, 1999). Upon reflection, there appeared to be no clear delineation between sides in this and the experience manifest itself across several subject areas.

"I tried to remain neutral when I moderate," Hexham said, "but I found myself attacked for being biased" (I. Hexham, personal communication, June

20, 1999). Sometimes, list members who were not interested in a particular thread that had captured the attention of the list (or the few people on the list for whom it was a burning issue), emailed Hexham demanding that the discussion be curtailed. In many cases, their posts read as though there was limited space available for discussion, and that the offending thread was using more than its fair share. This, of course, was not the case. To others, however, the issue was not taking up space available for discussion, but the intrusion into their mail boxes of material they were not interested in receiving. Because many members did not use the subject line of their message with care – i.e. to clearly identify what the post was about – many posts had to be opened and read, when they might otherwise have been deleted immediately.

As he responded in a 1998 message, though: "Complaining about the posts is not too helpful if no one posts anything better" ('IH', April 15, 1998). Many members regretted the time (and bandwidth) apparently devoted to issues surrounding the Church of Scientology, but at least one was unwilling to unsubscribe from the list because he didn't "know of any other that offers new material on NRMs" ('QP', April 16, 1998).

Without doubt, the most vigorous – some would say 'relentless' – discussion thread in the career of Nurel-L has been the Church of Scientology and the multiplicity of issues it draws into its orbit (on Scientology, see also Horsfall, Introvigne, and Mayer in this volume). Over the years, these issues have included, among others: the Scientological view of sexuality; the influence the Church of Scientology allegedly attempted to wield in the White House over John Travolta's portrayal of the President Clinton character in *Primary Colors;* the German Enquete-Kommision report and that country's treatment of religious minorities including Scientology; the allegations of brainwashing made by Stephen Kent in his 1997 SSSR presentation; and freedom of speech and the 'fair use' of copyrighted materials (especially as they pertain to the Internet). Some of these threads drew considerable response and continued for many weeks; others generated only three or four replies.

It was this perceived monopoly of the list by discussion devoted to the Church of Scientology, though, and the resultant clash of authoritative claimsmakers that brought about what might be called the first crisis in Nurel-L list management. The member 'SH' quoted above, an 'issue-oriented' participant and one of those who eventually precipitated Hexham's decision to ban list discussion of the Church of Scientology, sought with others to shift the agenda of debate on Nurel-L from scholarly to polemic based on the primacy of his authority as a former member, "an ex-high level scieno" ('SH', July 16, 1998).

One thing that makes discussion of Scientology unique in the Nurel-L experience is that *no post* in the available archive of messages went unchallenged or unanswered entirely. Very often, in the normal discourse pattern, messages would be posted to the list asking for information on a certain group or individual, commenting on a current situation, or picking up a tangent from another thread – all of which are attempts to start a new thread. Sometimes, these threads were simply ignored; no follow-up messages were posted and, rather than the ordinary process of topic decay, the thread was 'snapped', as it were, from the beginning. In all the available archives, this was never the case with Scientology.

While a number of reasons suggest why Scientology was such a vigorous subject cluster on the list, two in particular stand out. First, it is a new religious movement which has experienced a not-insignificant media presence both in North America and in Europe; this includes both reportage[4] and self-generated promotional materials. Since much of the discussion on Nurel-L originates from media portrayals of one NRM or another, that Scientology appeared with some regularity is hardly surprising. For example, the thread about the so-called 'Cultgate', – Travolta, Clinton, *Primary Colors,* and the Church of Scientology – began as a post from Irving Hexham:

> I picked up part of a broadcast where someone was talking about 'Cultgate'. This seems to be something to do with 'The Color Purple', and an alleged attempt by Scientology to influence Clinton. It is also supposed to be all the buzz in Washington. Has anyone heard anything about it? ('IH', 07 March 1998).

While Hexham was quickly corrected as to the title of the film, the thread continued for two weeks. It diverged into sub-threads as varied as allegations of Scientological influence on the leader of the South African Inkatha Freedom Party to consideration of the religious conversion requirements implicit in the Church's 501.c.3 application.

A second reason for the tenacity of the topic was the presence of vested interest and conflicting claimsmakers on the list. Prior to the Majordomo shift, Nurel-L membership included at least one highly placed official from the Canadian branch of the Church, as well as at least two members who joined Nurel-L specifically to expand their Internet attacks on Scientology beyond their own personal webpages, unmoderated newsgroups such as alt.religion.scientology, and other moderated discussion groups such as 'Cultwatch' (e.g. http://www.cultwatch.com/christian-issues). Since each of these individuals brought these primary interests and concerns to their participation on Nurel-L, again it is hardly surprising that little to do with Scientology passed without comment from either side.

In terms of a sociology of knowledge, Nurel-L became another forum for the contest of divergent and incompatible constructions of reality; it became another venue for therapeutic reality-maintenance and repair on the part of both sides. When it appeared as though the discussion supported some aspect of

Scientology, those 'issue-oriented participants' opposed to the Church would question the validity of the thread, the academic or personal integrity of those participating, or attempt to shift the thread onto more contentious ground. In similar fashion, when a post critical of Scientology came through to the list, others rose to its defense. Although, as Hexham pointed out in one post, while Scientologists "are defensive and sensitive to criticism," in all his interaction with them, "they have been perfectly respectful and polite even though Karla Poewe and I describe Scientology as one of many 'Manipulationist sects' in our book 'Understanding Cults and New Religions' " ('IH', March 19, 1998).[5]

On 15 April 1998, in response to a number of private and public messages, Hexham posted the following to the list:

> If the majority of list members believe that the ongoing discussion about Scientology and theology is irrelevant and non-academic I am prepared to close the thread. But, before I do so I would like to know (a) that this is a general feeling; and (b) the others have issues they would like to discuss. Complaining about the posts is not too helpful if no one posts anything better ('IH', April 15, 1998).

Two issues became clear from answers generated by Hexham's question: (a) the fear of limitation or control placed on discussion, and (b) the reality that few others chose to begin alternative discussion threads. Responses to his challenge came quickly, registering all points on the discursive spectrum.

> If freedom of speech is limited the discussion might tend to be limited or controlled. I wonder if the academics/scholars on the list care about questions like that with reference to whatever is being looked at. Seems like examining what actually occurs should be an important part of the research picture ('K', April 16, 1998).

> For my part, my active participation has been hitting the delete key. I find this entire discussion to be so far outside the realms of the academic study of religion, and the academic discussion of the filed of New Religious Movements that I am seriously considering de-listing ('SM', April 16, 1998).

> I vote to allow discussion to be as open, free-wheeling, and far-ranging as possible. Ignore the whiners, please. Thanks ('SFP', April 16, 1998).

> Please count me in as one who feels so annoyed by the conglomerate of evangelicals and scientologists that I was on the point of unsubscribing. I look forward to your reining this discussion in. The only function of a list like this is to study new religious movements and their context. Theological assessment of nrm's benefits/drawbacks can be explored in the pages of CHRISTIAN CENTURY and numerous other magazines. How could Chen Tao's unfulfilled prophecies and UFO-preparations have gone completely undiscussed, for example? Is anyone out there? ('EUG', April 16, 1998).

Numerous posts of a similar nature continued for several days, devolving into a few derivative threads. In the end, the only thing that was clear was that there was no clear consensus on the question Hexham proposed.

By late summer of 1998, though, due in large measure to the increasingly inflammatory nature of the postings, discussion of Scientology was banned from the list.[6] The reality was that discussion of Scientology, while it may have annoyed some list members, *did* involve a good many list members and *did* represent a large proportion of the traffic volume on Nurel-L. With this source of message volume eliminated, list traffic thinned; fewer and fewer posts came through on a daily basis, and those threads which were established did not prove themselves nearly as robust as anything dealing with Scientology. Occasional posts came through referring obliquely to Scientology as, for example, 'an un-named cult' ('SH', November 4, 1998), and a number were rejected by Hexham when they sought to resurrect discussion.

By early 1999, however, some posts began coming through referring to police raids on Scientology offices in Russia. When questioned whether this was a change in list policy, Hexham replied that it wasn't, but that this news deserved to be reported on the list. A new debate blossomed on the propriety of a ban on discussion of Scientology. One member argued that since "standard news sources such as the New York Times and Washington Post regularly fall for Scientology's propaganda tricks," the academic freedom of those participating on Nurel-L was at stake. "What you are doing now is to support Scientology's propaganda and to curtail academic freedom by ruling out any discussion on the topic. If you want NUREL to be an academic discussion list, you should better revise your list policy" ('CT', March 10, 1999).

Once again, Hexham came under severe criticism for his policy. A former Scientologist and 'issue-oriented participant' accused him of being 'pro-cult' and afraid of Scientology. This member argued that "as scientology is really accumulating every and all characters of coercive cults, it's quite interesting to study in such a list!" ('SH', March 14, 1999). A sociologist of religion acknowledged the intent behind the policy, but felt that it was "just not working." "Although I think the motivations behind the policy were sincere, the policy itself has been inconsistently and arbitrarily enforced. It smells of censorship (rightly or wrongly) and it serves mainly to cast a shadow of doubt over how free all of the other discussions on this list may be" ('CA', March 15, 1999). Another member agreed, declaring, "I know that I have lost most of my interest in participating here due to the 'rules' that have been imposed" ('SFP', March 17, 1999).

Once again, though, still others rose in defense of Hexham's policy. Some argued that because there are other well-established venues for the discussion of Scientology, and the threads on Nurel-L "very tiresome and repetitive," that Hexham should maintain his position ('QI', March 15, 1999). Another posted: "I support the list policy on Scientology. If the list is devoted to discussing NRMs, then Scientology should be left out" ('CCI', March 19, 1999).

The consensus of opinion was no clearer in the second round of discussion than the first. And, on April 3, 1999, Hexham closed the book on Nurel-L's consideration of Scientology with the post:

> Discussion of Scientology, and related issues, such as CAN, the Cult Awareness Network, has been banished from this list because it causes too many problems. Anyone wishing to discuss this issue should join Christine Norstrand's Psychology of Religion discussion list ('IH', April 3, 1999).

In the face of the renewed policy, list traffic declined dramatically.

CLOSING THE VALVE:
THE SHIFT TO MAJORDOMO AND H-NET

The same week that Hexham announced the final decision with regards to Scientology also saw what might be called the second crisis for Nurel-L. He was informed that the University listserv on which Nurel-L operated would be closed and discussion forums would be moved to a Majordomo server. Because the Majordomo server functions with H-Net membership protocols, this would result in a serious decline in list membership. Prior to the shift, Hexham posted this message to the entire list.

> Practically, it means a short break in service plus the application of H-Net standards. Consequently, only people with a clearly identified university or college e-mail address and academic positions will be allowed to remain on the list. Effectively, this removes about half our members including a number of regular contributors.
>
> The only exception to this rule are people who can prove that although they do not use an academic e-mail they are qualified to participate by holding at least a master's degree or its equivalent in a relevant academic discipline. Initially, everyone who cannot be clearly shown to meet these requirements will be removed from the list ('IH', April 3, 1999).

In fact, this shift removed some of Nurel-L's most prodigious posters. In one week, list membership dropped by roughly one-half. Message traffic slowed even further, and some weeks existed not at all. Discussion revived sporadically over the treatment of Falun Gong in China, occasional bulletins and announcements from CESNUR (The Center for Studies on New Religions), and the mass deaths of the Restoration of the Ten Commandments of God movement in March 2000. However, it has never recovered, either in aggregate posts or message volume related to particular issues. If the closure of threads related to Scientology threatened the health of Nurel-L, the removal of half the list members placed it on the critical list.

SSREL-L: BY WAY OF COMPARISON

In late 1991, Donald Ploch began SSREL-L, a list devoted to the scientific study of religion and intended to follow the fashion of leading academic journals in the field. The SSREL-L experience provides an interesting counterpoint to Nurel-L in that, like Hexham, Ploch recognized the tremendous opportunities afforded by the Internet to increase communication among scholars. Never designed to replace conference interaction or the professional journal, the listserv would add yet another venue through which scholars could discuss the work they deemed important. However, while it has always operated using ostensibly similar criteria to H-Net (though not a Majordomo list) and has been understood as a place to discuss the phenomenon of religion from a social scientific standpoint, similar debates as occurred on Nurel-L did blossom and when tighter monitoring of list content began, similar reductions in list traffic did ensue.

Shortly after its beginning, SSREL-L had twenty-three members. A somewhat novel experiment in scholarly discourse, given the state of CMC technology at the time, the exact manner in which the list would evolve was still to be determined. Hoping that it would "identify threads of conversation to follow-up," Ploch, for example, invited members to introduce themselves and say something about their interests and research specialities ('DP', 18 November 1991). Another member suggested that the list could serve as a forum "to exchange papers before and/or after meetings," an idea Ploch thought 'delightful' ('DP', 19 November 1991), and which did in fact occur at several points in its history. In this way, SSREL-L continued normal modes of scholarly discourse.

Six months later, though, Ploch noted that traffic to that point had consisted of a few introductions, the tables of contents from various journals posted for information, and a few brief exchanges questioning the appropriateness of certain discussion threads. Gradually, different threads began to evolve, enjoy some manner of lifespan, and decay, occasionally being directed elsewhere, other times fading through lack of interest or challenges to their appropriateness (whether made publicly or privately). A review of SSREL-L digests from 1991–1998, however, reveals that: (a) no discussion cluster enjoyed the robustness of Scientology on Nurel-L, and (b) the overall message volume did not reach the aggregate levels of Nurel-L.

In the early stages of SSREL-L's career, membership was not actively limited to scholars of religion, and participants with a variety of agendas descended on the list. Wanting to open the discussion as widely as possible, and uncertain how a forum such as this might evolve, that Ploch did not regulate list membership as tightly as the H-Net protocols might demand is hardly surprising. A greater variety of voices means the potential for more stimulating discussion. However, where Nurel-L had its academic discourse disrupted on numerous occasions by anticultists and countercultists (those I have termed 'issue-oriented participants'), a similar category of participants who did not fit the expectations of social scientists also found its way to SSREL-L. In the words of one former member, these others included "skeptics, atheists who were amused by the idea of scholars studying religion, a few fundamentalists, and a few naive and lonely souls who just wanted to talk," (J.K. Hadden, personal communication, July 14, 2000).

For example, in 1992, a number of posts came through extolling the virtues of Josh McDowell and his books, *Evidence that demands a verdict, and More evidence that demands a verdict.* McDowell, a fundamentalist Christian long associated with Campus Crusade for Christ, wrote the books as "irrefutable apologetic evidence" of the truth of "historic Christianity" (e.g. the Mosaic authorship of the the the Pentateuch, historical veracity of the Virgin Birth, literal inspiration of the Bible). After a flurry of messages, in response to a question about the appropriateness of the McDowell material for discussion on the list Ploch responded: "Don't know the McDowell work. If it is a scientific study of religion, it does [belong]. If it is religion, but not the study of religion, then probably not. If you have doubts, why not raises issues from it or about it. The rest of us can decide relevance" ('DP', 31 January 1992). Since McDowell's books are entirely about establishing the primacy and veracity of his particular version of Christianity over all other religious traditions, it clearly contravened the purpose of the list, and the thread quickly dwindled away.

Whatever the formal rules for list admission, in the early years contributors posted on all manner of topics in a free-wheeling and often haphazard way. In response to messages which were clearly outside the parameters of the venue as understood by social scientists, a number of members undertook to email contributors privately and correct them. As with Nurel-L, though, the list still became clogged with message traffic many believed clearly outside the domain of SSREL-L's stated purpose, and therefore of little interest to the scholars for whom it had been established. Eventually, this situation resulted in the exodus from the list of a number of members who found the sheer volume of inappropriate messages more trouble than they felt it worth to remain. This departure precipitated a crisis in SSREL-L similar to the forced removal of list members from Nurel-L.

As a result of this, Ploch began to more carefully monitor list content, and posted monthly reminders about the purpose of SSREL-L. He prompted participants that the "[primary] audience is researchers and teachers in this specialty" (i.e. the scientific study of religion; 'DP', 3 October 1994). Ploch continued:

> The list is intended for research scholars. Although others are not excluded, the assumption
> is that they will bring themselves up to speed with a minimum drain on the resources of the

list. SSREL-L provides a forum for the study of cultural phenomena called religion using the scientific method. SSREL-L is not intended as a place to proselytize for or defend any 'religion', or a place to hector or denigrate any 'religion' ('DP', 3 October 1994).

That is to say, however well or poorly the criteria were enforced, there was a clearly defined audience for whom SSREL-L was intended in the beginning. Any number of chat rooms and discussion lists are available to Internet users who wanted to debate the merits of Josh McDowell; SSREL-L was simply not the place. Once again, though, in similar manner to Nurel-L, once list content was monitored for suitability, message traffic declined, resuming its character of occasional requests for information and announcements about events of interest to its constituency.

Why was the experience of SSREL-L so similar to Nurel-L? A number of reasons suggest themselves. First and foremost is the subject matter. Despite colloquial wisdom that religion is one of the topics one ought not discuss in polite company, few topics evoke such intense interest and emotion. As many of the essays in this collection attest, religious discourse dominates the time many users spend on the Net. Discussion lists such as Nurel-L (with its added spice of sects, cults, and NRMs) and SSREL-L are natural venues for those with something to say. Second, when intended for academics and for their particular realm of discourse, unless lists such as Nurel-L and SSREL-L are actively restricted to this intended audience, the conflicting interests and agendas of many of those who do have something to say will almost certainly cloud the discussions.

Finally, specific communities evolve according to the pressures exerted and boundaries established by their participants. Despite intention, restriction, and protocol, both Nurel-L and SSREL-L provided e-spaces in which particular discourse structures emerged. In the early stages of its existence, SSREL-L's discussion architecture developed as one less bounded and more open – more 'free-wheeling' – than it became later, and participants came to expect that reality. When that changed, discussion volume declined. Similarly, for a good length of time, Scientology was *the* hot topic of discussion on Nurel-L. And, for various reasons, members came to see that as a recognizable part of the list architecture – for good or ill. Whatever other members may have felt, both apologists for and antagonists of Scientology came to expect that structure and reacted when the structure changed.

Put differently, however loosely defined, both Nurel-L and SSREL-L had particular e-communities in place when the structures of those communities were altered. Closer monitoring of SSREL-L content effected the same decline as the Nurel-L discussion ban on Scientology; the imposition of H-Net protocols and the Majordomo shift narrowed the list consituency in a manner similar to the monthly posting of the SSREL-L's purpose statement. These changes resulted in the fracturing of established communities and, in essense, required reinvention of those communities if the lists were to survive. Business as usual was impossible simply because the most popular items had been removed from the shelf, and a majority of regular customers had been banned – officially or unofficially – from the store.

PROBLEMS AND PROSPECTS FOR RELIGIOUS DISCOURSE IN E-SPACE

In terms of speed and storage, it seems that computer capability increases daily; as well, more and more individuals are finding their way onto the Net to advertise and shop, to investigate, intimidate, and retaliate. As such, religious discourse on the Net will continue to develop and evolve as the technology allows and the ability of users permits. Academics, members of particular religious communities, opponents of those same communities, as well as anyone interested enough to point their browser in that direction will continue to broaden the discussion. This is the goal, for example, of the H-Net consortium, and few would dispute that it is an admirable one. As noted, though, there are a number of problems inherent in the e-space environment; some have solutions already apparent on the horizon, others may resist resolution entirely.

In CMC environments such as Nurel-L and SSREL-L, these problems fall into three main categories: technical, ethical, and managerial/participant.

Despite its popularity, CMC of any type is in its *technological infancy* (Donath, Karahalios & Viégas, 1999; Herring, 1999; Turoff et al., 1999). Both synchronous and asynchronous text-based CMC is hampered by the inability to visualize quickly and graphically the flow and pattern of online discourse. Disrupted adjacency, overlapping replies, multilateral topic shifts within single posts – all contribute to this problem. In moderated asynchronous CMC, such as Nurel-L, some of these are exacerbated in the forwarding process.

The *ethical* nature of communication and research in CMC has been referred to here and elsewhere (see Paccagnella, 1997; Hadden & Cowan, in this volume). Copyrighted materials posted to the web without appropriate permissions, excerpts from public discussion forums taken and published without the author's knowledge or consent, and the various aspects of research protocols – all are issues which will require the diligence of scholarship as the Net and computer-mediated communication continue to expand.

Finally, the *managerial* and *participant* aspects of the text-based CMC environment will demand the attention of those who seek to refine and improve the medium.

Traffic on Nurel-L has never recovered to the levels enjoyed before the precipitation of the two crises discussed here. If the flow of message traffic can be analogized to liquid moving through a pipe, the discussion ban on Scientology reduced the volume in the pipe by a considerable margin, and the shift to Majordomo narrowed the diameter of the inlet to that pipe. What was a torrent at times has been reduced to a trickle.

Until the discussions of 1998–1999, moderation of posts on Nurel-L had only one goal in mind: the vetting of posts that could be construed as libelous. Several posts, for example, drew the analogy between treatment of the Church of Scientology by the current and immediate past German governments, and the treatment of the Jews by the Nazis. These posts were returned to the senders for modification before posting to the list. As noted, the decision finally to ban discussion of Scientology was greeted with relief by some and outrage by others. Some tried to evade the restriction by referring to "that group we are not allowed to mention," "a cult I can't name," or a "so-called church, but what's really a cult (no names)." After many attempts to explain to members why such posts would not be forwarded to the list, they were simply deleted when they came through the listserv.

Two issues presented themselves in response to the decision: academic freedom and censure, and the perceived monopolization of list space.

Academic freedom depends on the non-intervention of external authorities in discussions which scholars consider worthwhile. Whether these interventions come from government, university administration, or discussion list moderation, the appearance or perception of censorship can be as damaging as actual censorship. When this happens, list participants no longer react to what they do experience, but rather to what they fear they might experience if their posts violate the established protocols.

In all his administration and moderation of issues around list discussion of Scientology, nothing stands out more clearly than that Hexham sought to deal as openly and honestly with all participants as possible. He sought direction and input from list membership, and was willing to be guided by that feedback; 'inconclusive', however, accurately describes the response. And, whether members agreed with the particulars of his decision or not, he made the list fully aware of his reasons for terminating discussion of Scientology.

At various times, up to twenty individual members were involved in Scientology threads – less than ten percent of the total list membership at its high water mark in 1998. However, at that same high water mark (March 1998), 320 messages were posted to the list by 46 members under 45 separate subject headings. Many of the posts demanding that Scientological discussion be curtailed read as though the sender believed that there was limited bandwidth available, yet the message traffic indicates otherwise. It was simply not the case that only a certain number of messages could be put through per day, and Scientology was hogging the information pipeline. The sad reality of Nurel-L was that, while a number of members complained, few of those who did offered new threads to draw interest in other directions.

Thus, it seems to me that there are two caveats that present themselves out of the Nurel-L experience – one concerns management, the other participation. First, when establishing an e-space for the discussion of any topic, if traffic volume is of importance, then leave the parameters as open as possible to allow for the broadest possible discussion flow. If there are particular discussion parameters in place, however, then make sure these are clearly identified at the outset and readily identifiable in their breach. And, if there are such parameters in place, be ruthless in their application.

Second, as for list participation, the caveat is much simpler: Participate. Perhaps the best message of this nature was that sent by Hexham during the discussion over whether Scientology should remain a permissible thread: "Complaining about the posts is not too helpful if no one posts anything better."

CONCLUDING REMARKS

What can we learn from the Nurel-L and SSREL-L experiences?

Some members of Nurel-L in its Listserv incarnation were very angry that they were not allowed to participate in its Majordomo evolution. They viewed it as another moat dug around the ivory tower in which they believed far too many scholars had already taken up permanent residence. But is this a valid criticism, and how does one address it in the context of a discourse medium like the Internet? First, accessibility does not equal appropriateness. Simply because different individuals can post on Nurel-L, SSREL-L, or any other list does not mean that they ought to, or that their contributions are relevant to the purpose. In the case of Scientology, Nurel-L traffic regularly lingered in the polemic, and descended on occasion to simple name-calling. Little of the discussion was carried on at what might be called an academic level and according to scholarly conventions of evidence and argument. As Hexham pointed out, there are any number of e-spaces for that sort of discussion – not the least of which the venerable alt.religion.scientology.

Second, in both Nurel-L and SSREL-L, this dynamic points to the diversity of expectations of people who populate the Net. That is, different 'Netizens' want different things from their interaction on the Net. It is not too far a stretch to say that scholars access discussion groups for news, information, and a discourse carried out according to different conventions than many Usenet groups. In the context of Nurel-L, this exemplified a breach often seen in the interaction between academics and either the anticult or countercult participants. Put simply, academics often view anticultists as encroaching on discussions for which their agendas do not adequately qualify them; many anticultists, on the other hand, regard academics as naïve, stupid sometimes, often pawns and apologists for new religious movements.

In this tension, two very different and conflicting sets of expectations came together on the Nurel-L list. Whereas scholars viewed the list as an important source of information, the 'issue-oriented participants' saw it as another arena in which to carry on the battle. This is not to say that issues did not arise among academics, that sometimes strong disagreement did not make itself evident. However, these issues generally developed out of inquiries, news reports, or other information shared among list members; they were not brought to the list as the primary purpose for participation. Also, this is not to say that academics never argue, quarrel, backbite, or bicker; they do. It is to say, simply, that they approach the various discussions in which these occur from a different perspective and orientation – in the case of Nurel-L the broadly academic, in SSREL-L the social scientific.

Third, many of those who came to Nurel-L with particular agendas never granted Hexham the courtesy of acknowledging that this was *his* list. He established and hosted the forum, and while admission was not restricted, it was as though he had invited participants into his living room or office. Rather, they treated Nurel-L as though it were entirely *public space*, something less clearly defined in the Net environment than in the real world. In many discussions there was a sense of entitlement evident, a sense that 'issue-oriented participants' had the right to say whatever they pleased. And, when Hexham sought to exercise his authority in this regard, he was viewed as a tyrant.

Both Nurel-L and SSREL-L illustrate the natural adaptation of scholarly discourse to emerging technology. Their experiences, though, beg a couple of further questions. How might one consciously structure an electronic discussion list that is both effective and useful for the constituency it was created to serve? And, how does one maintain the level and credibility of discourse in a venue as accessible as CMC? One possibility is the example of New Religious Movements mailing list (NRMlist) now based out of Hartford Seminary. They formed as a result of a spontaneous discussion among religion scholars who received an electronic survey from the FBI about millennialism and violence. As new topics emerged, Nancy Ammerman volunteered to have the list hosted at Hartford Seminary. A number of issues have arisen for discussion, generated by the common scholarly interests of the constituency: millennial concerns (including the Megiddo report of the FBI),[7] pre-publicity to the Branch Davidian investigations and trial, the RTCG tragedy in Uganda, and anticult activity in Europe. An unmonitored list, principal gatekeeping of the group is through admission. In order to preserve the integrity of the discussion, the members have decided that it is a closed list. New members are added only occasionally, and only upon the recommendation of current list participants.

It should be noted that this work has addressed a very particular communications forum. That there is a place for vigorous theological debate, religious chat, and even polemic on the Web, is not in dispute. The number of different sites dedicated to these demonstrate that clearly. These, however, are not normally the needs of scholarship, and when venues intended for scholarship are taken over by them, experiences such as Nurel-L and SSREL-L can occur. Thus, the answer may not be so much "posting something better," as it is finding the correct balance of membership and purpose to promote vigorous *academic* discussion.

Both Hexham and Ploch deserve the thanks of scholars for having the foresight (not to mention courage) to help us communicate in e-space. They encouraged initial exploration of communication structures that offer us the opportunity to broaden considerably the circle of scholarly discourse. In doing so, Nurel-L and SSREL-L highlight the tremendous importance of cyberspace, and the new models of communication it engenders and demands. All indications are that the Web is here to stay. And, while many of us will continue to communicate face-to-face, happy now and then to hear a human voice, we will also continue to expand our communications through email, the ability to transfer files quickly and easily, the coming wave of conferencing via computer, and whatever lies just beyond the technological horizon.

NOTES

1. N.b., All notes are quoted exactly as they appeared on Nurel-L; no attempt has been made to correct spelling or grammar. With the exception of Irving Hexham ('IH') and Don Ploch ('DP'), the initials of participants have been changed to protect their anonymity. Diamond brackets (>) indicate quoted material within a list post.

2. For information about H-Net, an "international consortium of scholars and teachers ... committed to pioneering the use of new communication technology to facilitate the free exchange of academic ideas and scholarly resources," see http://www.h-net.msu.edu/about. In part, H-Net's charter reads: "The mission of H-Net is to assist humanities scholars worldwide to make use of new advances in electronic communication and information technology. At the core of H-Net are electronic discussion lists catering to specialized areas of scholarly interest" (http://www.h-net.msu.edu/about/charter.html; accessed 15 July 1999).

3. Consider, for example, http://www.carm.org, the Christian Apologetics and Research Ministry. Begun in November 1995, CARM is a densely packed, text-based site which includes pages on 'Apologetics', 'Major Cults' (including, interestingly, Christadelphianism), 'Minor Cults' (including 'Moonies', Theosophy, and Christian Identity), 'Evolution', 'New Age', and 'Religions'(e.g. Roman Catholicism). At first glance, all this seems quite impressive; the site owner claims 38,000 hits per week and over 20,000 e-mails received. However, when the document carminfo.htm is checked, one learns that "CARM is simply one guy, me, Matt Slick [B.A., M.Div.]. This site contains most of my notes from Bible studies, seminars, sermons, and Sunday School lessons" (Slick, 1998).

4. In North America, see, for example, *Premier* (September, 1993), *Quill* (November – December, 1993), *Time* (15 May 1998); for a series of articles entitled "Scientology Unmasked: Inside the Church of Scientology," published in the *Boston Herald* the week of 1 – 5 March 1998, see http://www.bostonherald.com/scientology. In the entertainment media, interviews and profiles of such film celebrities as John Travolta, Nicole Kidman, Tom Cruise, and Calista Flockhart, rarely pass without mention of their interest in (sometimes devotion to) Scientology. In Europe, see, for example, http://www.xs4all.nl/~kspaink for a collection of articles which have appeared in the Dutch press, including Karin Spaink's 'Party Coloured Laundry' and 'Religious Practices', both of which appeared in *Het Parool*.

5. One of those who joined the list to attack Scientology quite simply didn't believe Hexham in this, writing, "I have never been convinced by what Irving explained when I came onto the list: that he had been agressed by 'anti-cultists' but had not been aggressed by scienos" ('SH', 14 March 1999).

6. In response to a number of posts either questioning or complaining about the new list policy, Hexham posted the following explanation:

> Since a number of you very strongly object to the decisions I make while running this list, particularly regarding Scientology, allow me to impute motives to my actions, let me once more try to explain some simple guidelines.
>
> First, for any list to survive members must find it useful and informative.
>
> Second, when one particular theme dominates the list most members are not directly involved in the discussion begin to object. On this list it is not fear of Scientology [an allegation which had been made], but fear that the discussion of Scientology will kill the list through totally alienating the majority of members, which governed my decision to ban the topic.
>
> Third, there is a need to maintain civility. People may disagree all they want, but disagreements ought to be respectful. I am offended at the arrogant assumption on the part of some list members that any disagreement with their views is due to: (a) mercenary motives; (b) fear of a particular group; or (c) ignorance. The fact is intelligent people can and do disagree about many things and list members need to recognize the right of other people to disagree.
>
> Fourth, many decisions about accepting posts which are sure to provoke a strong response are very difficult to make. Therefore I try to include as many viewpoints as possible and allow discussions to continue until they seem to be irritating other list members.
>
> Fifth, there is no way that I am going to be able to satisfy everyone. So at some point I have to take a fairly arbitrary stance. When I do this the people concerned always think that I am discriminating against them. In fact, as Doug Cowan can affirm, we reject about

an equal number of posts from all sides for issues like those related to Scientology. ('IH',14 March 1999).

7. For the text of this report, see http://www.cesnur.org/testi/FBI_004.htm; accessed July 21, 2000.

REFERENCES

Aycock, A. (1996). 'Technologies of the Self': Foucault and Internet Discourse. *Journal of Computer-Mediated Communication, 1*(2). Retrieved July 21, 1999, from the World Wide Web: http://www.ascusc.org/jcmc/vol1/issue2/aycock.html.

Berger, P., & Luckmann, T. (1966). *The Social Construction of Reality: A Treatise on the Sociology of Knowledge.* New York: Penguin Books USA Inc., Penguin Social Sciences.

Donath, J. S. (1999). Identity and Deception in the Virtual Community. In: M. A. Smith & K. Kollock (Eds), *Communities in Cyberspace* (pp. 29–59). London: Routledge.

Donath, J., Karahalios, K., & Viégas, F. (1999). Visualizing Conversation. *Journal of Computer-Mediated Communication, 4*(4). Retrieved July 20, 1999, from the World Wide Web: http://jcmc.huji.ac.il/vol4/issue4/donath.html.

Gutstein, D. (1999). *E.Con: How the Internet Undermines Democracy.* Toronto: Stoddart Publishing Co. Limited.

Herring, S. (1999). Interactional Coherence in CMC. *Journal of Computer-Mediated Communication, 4*(4). Retrieved July 21, 1999, from the World Wide Web: http://jcmc.huji.ac.il/vol4/issue4/herring.html.

Hexham, I. (1999). NUREL-L. Retrieved July 2, 2000, from the World Wide Web: http://www.acs.ucalgary.ca/~hexham/links/nurel-i.html.

Kim, A. J. (1998). 9 Timeless Principles for Building Community: Erecting the Social Structure. *Web Techniques,* (January): 36–41.

Paccagnella, L. (1997). Getting the Seat of Your Pants Dirty: Strategies for Ethnographic Research on Virtual Communities. *Journal of Computer-Mediated Communication, 3*(1). Retrieved July 25, 1999, from the World Wide Web:http://www.jcmc.huji.ac.il/vol3/issue1/paccagnella.html.

Shirky, C. (1995). *Voices from the Net.* Emeryville, CA: Ziff-Davis Press.

Slick, M. (1998). About CARM. Retrieved March 12, 1998, and July 28, 1999, from the World Wide Web: http://www.carm.org/carminfo.htm.

Turoff, M., et al. (1999). Collaborative Discourse Structures in Computer Mediated Group Communications. *Journal of Computer-Mediated Communication, 4*(4). Retrieved July 25, 1999, from the World Wide Web: http://jcmc.huji.ac.il/vol4/issue4/turoff.html.

3. INTERNET FAITH: RELIGIONS IN CYBERSPACE

SURFING ISLAM:
AYATOLLAHS, SHAYKS AND HAJJIS
ON THE SUPERHIGHWAY

Gary R. Bunt

ABSTRACT

Surfing Islam discusses the phenomenon of Islam on the Internet, focusing on forms of Islamic expression and identity on-line, and the medium's application as a tool for religious propagation. The chapter analyses the impact of diverse cyber Islamic environments on those browsing the Internet, including the potential influence of various approaches towards the Quran. Religious experience and related symbols – in the forms of pilgrimage, mystical expression, and notions of Muslim authority – are evaluated in terms of their Internet manifestations.

INTRODUCTION

Say: "Were the sea to become ink for my Lord's words, the sea would be exhausted before the words of my Lord are exhausted, even if We were to bring its like to replenish it."[1]
The Quran

The Quran suggests God's words and knowledge are infinite, and cannot be written down. The analogy of an inexhaustible resource might be applied to the Internet, in relation to surfing the ocean of sites representing and discussing the 'Lord's words', Islam and Muslims.

Religion and the Social Order, Volume 8, pages 127–151.
Copyright © 2000 by Elsevier Science Inc.
All rights of reproduction in any form reserved.
ISBN: 0-7623-0535-5

The Internet is a significant part of many Muslims' lives, and numerous organisations and individuals are proactive in establishing a Web presence for Islam, utilising the networking and dissemination possibilities of the medium. The Internet already has ten million sites, covering a multitude of subjects, and it is estimated that this number will increase to two hundred million by 2005 (Nielsen, 2000, p. 347). This continued expansion means an inevitable proportional increase in Islam-related sites, and heightens the need to analyse, research, and record on-line developments concerning *cyber Islamic environments* (this writer's term).

It may be helpful to delineate some of the significant routes for research and study, based on examining forms of Muslim religious expression on-line. The choice of materials is associated with several years' experience in teaching Islamic Studies to undergraduates, including introductory and advanced courses. Teaching and research have increasingly required reference to Internet materials, as students introduce quotations from the Web within their work, and issues arise as to the Internet's legitimacy as an academic resource.

In 1996, the writer established a guide to Islamic Studies Resources, initially for students, although it acquired a wider readership, expanding from twenty sites to a hundred 'significant' resources.[2] Selectivity is the key: researchers 'surfing Islam' for the first time are faced with thousands of 'Islamic' sites fulfilling the propagandist virtue of *dawa* – the 'call' or 'invitation' to Islam. Listings of 'Islam' sites can be bewildering in their complexity, offering little insight into contents, whilst duplicating key themes and resources. Paring this down into a usable format of diverse and representative 'academic' materials has been an interesting objective. In terms of researching Islam on the Internet, developments have to be monitored closely – through observation of Islamic expression in political, theological and social contexts. Pages change frequently, and new sites and pages emerge daily. The concept of an ever-changing bookshelf is often presented as a metaphor to the notion of information on the Internet.

DEFINING WHAT IS 'ISLAMIC'

Defining what is 'Islamic' in this choice is itself revealing about cyber-Islamic environments, as the identities that manifest themselves under Muslim banners on-line represent broad interpretations and cultural approaches towards Islam, and many sites are not necessarily accepted throughout the Islamic spectrum. Indeed, there can be intra-Muslim antagonism on-line, as well as in the 'real' world. The notion of consensus or a global Muslim community may be contradicted by Internet representations of Islam (see Bunt, 1999).

This writer's interest in Islam and the Internet developed in the mid-1990s. During fieldwork, some Muslim religious scholars discussed how the electronic superhighway would impact upon the traditional networks of Islamic authority, altering the routes used to obtain a religious decision, and influencing the approach towards Islamic primary source materials. At this time, the Quran was already available for examination and reading in the 'non-conventional' form of a searchable hypertext (on this, see Bunt, 1997). Only a few pioneering Islam-related pages were available on-line. Text only interfaces were then being superseded by Mosaic and Netscape browsers, and it was an exciting experience (for some) just to download an Islamic image or graphic from a Web site – a lengthy process that often took several attempts, as computer systems buckled under pressure.

As technology has progressed and the Net expanded, there has been a subsequent battle for position, as various groups established their stalls (or cyber mosques) proclaiming versions of Muslim authority and religious beliefs to a global audience. 'Islamic' and Islam-related Internet sites now present diverse perspectives of what it means to be Muslim, and how Islam should be interpreted or approached (see Bunt, 2000).[3] These in themselves are a significant research resource.

Many Islamic Web site creators are not 'scholars' in the traditional sense, but present their *dawa* pages as part of an obligation or duty, based on Quranic injunction, and Muhammad's own example in propagating the message of Islam. The impact of this message in cyberspace is often associated with the effectiveness of Web design, and whether a sense of Muslim identity is conveyed. An 'Islamic site' has to look appropriate – judgement based on the graphics applied and how they are displayed (including images in the form of *jpegs* and *gifs*). To generate traffic, a site has to be connected to other 'influential sites', and score highly with search engines through integration of meta-data into site design. As will be seen below, key players frequently possess a memorable 'Islamic' domain name.

Cyberspace represents a new form of Islamic environment, drawing upon traditional notions of Muslim society and manners, integrated into an appropriate technical interface. Muslim cyber-communities have evolved rapidly, located outside of conventional space and time, but closely associated with contemporary and historical notions of Muslim identity and space. Many label themselves as 'Sunni' or 'orthodox' Muslims (representing the majority Islamic branch), although there are significant sites representing other interpretations and beliefs. There are many sites geared towards Shia Islam, and a substantial amount of esoteric material directed towards the 'mystically inclined' – under the banner of Sufi Islam. This is not to suggest that Sunni, Shia and Sufi are rigid and uniform categories, and indeed their complexity and fluidity are well represented on-line.

Substantial 'competition' exists between various Islamic Web sites – often sharing or reproducing similar content. There has been an increase in specialisation, focusing on particular Muslim communities. Sites serve as networking tools and meeting points for specific strands of Muslim belief. Some platforms apply wider use of technology than others. Scoring highly on several search engine queries for 'Islam' and 'Muslim' sites, the Nation of Islam – not necessarily accepted within all other areas of the Islamic spectrum – has utilised the Internet successfully for several years (notably the Final Call newspaper).[4] Overtly political Islamic messages from other global contexts generate a substantial on-line presence, such as sites associated with opposition to the Saudi Arabian government, the Taliban in Afghanistan or the Mujahideen in Chechnya.[5]

There are also 'Muslim' sites presenting concepts deemed radical and 'un-Islamic' in other Muslim contexts. A prominent example are those areas of cyberspace discussing 'gay Muslim' identities. These sites contravene 'mainstream' interpretations of the Quran, prohibiting homosexuality.[6] In such cases, the Internet facilitates Muslim individual or group expression, permitting the circulation of opinions about Islam, which do not find favour within home cultural-social contexts. Other examples include various Muslim women's groups, who find the Internet an appropriate and confidential medium through which to discuss religious and cultural issues, including gender related concerns.[7] Diverse religious perspectives and popular Muslim expression, including mystically inclined 'Sufi' orders, endeavour to present an interpretation of their own worldview on Islam, through video, sound files, and notions of religious understanding expressed in documentary format.

The net has become a tool of Muslim propagation, aiming at different audiences. Some sites reinforce ideologies as part of a networking process to an established 'membership' or readership. Others present a message to Muslims who hold different beliefs, perhaps attempting persuasion or sympathy towards a different worldview. There are also sites aimed at those who do not identify themselves as 'Muslim', endeavouring to gain converts to Islam, or to engage in theological dialogues with other religious groups. 'Answering Islam', 'Answering Christianity', and the 'Answer to Answering Islam' emerged in this highly charged area of 'dialogue', frequently accompanied by 'flaming emails' scorching through the ether between opposing factions.[8]

One of the interesting concepts associated with this 'dialogue' is that there is rarely face-to-face contact between individuals, and in many cases, pseudonyms are adopted. An Islamic Web site might be an individual production, or the development of a large organisation. 'Islamic Authority' as presented on-line can emanate with as much status from Swansea as from Mecca – and there may be few signals as to the status of those originating on-line material.

This subversion of traditional routes of knowledge and interpretation, together with the opening up of a new global on-line audiences, meant that authorities in mosques and religious schools began to pay greater attention to the new medium. Religious scholars can now be found learning hypertext mark-up language alongside classical Arabic in Islamic institutions such as Qom and Al-Azhar, working in English and other languages, endeavouring to present their worldviews on the Internet.[9] Some of this material is "preaching to the converted," whilst other sites seek to address a perceived imbalance in the nature of the Internet.

Muslim institutional awareness of the Internet heightened in the aftermath of SuraLikeIt's publication. This set of satirical, so-called 'suras' or Quranic verses was placed onto the Internet in 1998, hitting the headlines in parts of the 'Muslim world', SuraLikeIt's Internet Service Provider was America On-line, which – fearing a Rushdie-style 'fatwa' against it as much as a loss of business – shut the site down. It was too late: mirror copies emerged, which today can still be found on the Internet. Scholars who previously proclaimed the Internet as a hostile and dangerous environment decided that they had to enter cyberspace, to counter these and other opinions deemed detrimental to Islam (see also Bunt, 2000, pp. 123–130).[10]

THE QURAN IN CYBERSPACE

The Quran features strongly within cyber Islamic environments, and for the purposes of this discussion, emphasis is placed on approaches to the text in the English language. Translations from the Quran's Arabic text are problematic, as many authorities indicate that in order to fully comprehend this Revelation from God, it is necessary to understand the classical Arabic of seventh-century Mecca and Medina. This is the context in which God is said to have revealed the Quran to his Prophet Muhammad (570–632), during a period of 22 years.

The Arabic Revelation contained within contemporary versions of the Quran today is idealised as the exact duplicate of its original form, in every cadence, textual and linguistic detail. Translations introduce alternate shades of meaning and value-judgements – represented by the numerous and diverse translations available in the English language. These contain different nuances of understanding, and introduce theological issues requiring etymological analysis, and reference back to the original Arabic source. (It could be argued that there is a similar gulf between classical and forms of contemporary dialectical Arabic.) For the purposes of research on the Internet, issues relating to accessibility and 'usability' of Web sites join these considerations. How easy is it to approach the interface? What supplementary features are contained within the site, which enhances understanding of the text? What is the motivation behind a resource (commercial, ideological, cultural)?

The development of several Quran-centered sites indicates an assertion by Islamic site providers, as global opportunities for Web access increase, particularly within Muslim populations throughout the 'underdeveloped' world. The notion of Web access being simply for the élite is slowly diminishing, as computers become available in public places, libraries, universities, and homes.

The drive to place interpretations on-line has intensified, as this becomes a cost-efficient means of promoting specific variations within Islam thought and culture – often from 'modernising' sources at the cost of 'traditional' worldviews. New technologies, such as WAP telephone access, digital television, and inexpensive computers integrated into other 'desk-free' packages mean that these Quran sites will have an enormous audience (and influence) during the next decade.

With these considerations in mind, a selection of on-line Quran resources for research purposes is introduced here. The most technologically impressive is produced by Harf Information Technology, based in Nasr City in Cairo, Egypt. Harf produces a broad range of software, and constructs Web sites for other Islamic concerns. This on-line material is also available for purchase on CD-ROM. The Harf remit incorporates the presentation of substantial resources for free on-line usage, sponsored in part by the Saudi Arabian Ministry of Waqfs (religious endowments). This includes *al-Muezzin,* an adjustable program indicating the timing of five daily prayers, calculating the direction for prayer from any global location.[11] There is an extensive collection of photographs and video clips of the hajj (discussed below), showing all aspects of pilgrimage, accessible through a RealPlayer.[12]

The Quran 'translations' on the Harf site reach a global audience and market, being available in seven languages: Arabic, French, German, Malay, Indonesian, Turkish, and English. On clicking the English button, it may take several seconds before the Quran page fully downloads – due to current bandwidth limitations. The Quran Translation Main Page features the first chapter of the Revelation – *al-Fatiha* or the 'Opening' – with its Arabic text in a central box. In the left margin, the English translation is provided. Above the Arabic, a form (drawing on the page's JavaScript) allows the reader to select a chapter (*sura*) and verse (*aya*) number (the chapters are also listed separately on a single page, with names and number of verses). This works rapidly, bringing the reader to a new page from the text.

To the right of the Arabic, hyperlinks to two alternative recitations of the text are provided, from the highly respected and distinctive recitors of the Quran,

Shaykh Mahmoud Khalil Al-Husari and Shaykh Ali Abdul Rahman al-Hudhaifi. Their contrasting styles provide a useful introduction into the science of recitation, complemented through reading adjacent hyperlinked information explaining the basic rules of recitation. In Islam, recitation forms part of daily prayer, and its perfection and memorisation is an attribute (within this world and the Hereafter). Explanations about the context and language of the Quran, and the origins of specific chapters, would be a useful adjunct for researchers unfamiliar with these themes. The Harf site's other sections, for example on the sayings of Muhammad (*Hadith*) or the biography of the Prophet (*Sirah*), allude to specific sections within the Quran. Other elements within the site demonstrate the specifics of prayer, and extol the "virtues of the Quran" and its "miraculous nature." This may be of interest to those with prior knowledge of Islam, although as an objective 'research tool' it may be of less value.

In order to supplement and develop this initial research experience in the Quran, there are several other resources (from 'Islamic' and other institutions and organisations) which prove useful within an academic context, in addition to conventional source materials. For example, the Qur'an Browser Basic Home Page, produced at Brown University, is relevant for some research work. It contains a search box, through which passages, words, or word-parts can be retrieved from a choice of three Quran English language translations. These can be compared for nuances of meaning. Searchable indices of this kind offer rapid and efficient textual comparisons – although for Quran research purposes, some notion of a sura's context is still necessary.[13] This is located on the University of Southern California Muslim Students Association Islamic Server, one of the earliest searchable indices of the Quran, containing three translations (as on the Quran Browser discussed above) in which Boolean searches can be made.[14]

A commentary on the meaning of the Quran, based on an English translation of an Urdu text by the influential Muslim 'reformer' Sayyid Abul A'la Mawdudi (1903–79), presents one interpretation of specific verses and chapters, introducing context, historical detail, and theological dimensions of the Quran.[15] This is not a universally accepted commentary, although the site is linked on several academic institutions' religious studies' homepages as a reliable resource. Mawdudi's influence reaches far beyond its Indian subcontinent origins, and this Web site provides his supporters and their particular interpretation of Islam with a high profile and proactive presence on the Internet.

Cyberspace also contains a technical commentary on the Quran by Yasin al Jibouri, with a clickable, table-format interface, introducing the sayings of Muhammad and their contextual relevance within the exposition of the Quran.[16] This features as part of a site intended for researchers, Holy Qur'an Resources on the Internet, much of the material being unique to these specific pages, although often in the form of copied texts from other literature.[17] Specialist Islamic Studies' scholars may also find the *Tafseer Al-Mizan*: Exegesis of the Qur'an by Allamah Sayyed Muhammad Husayn Tabataba'i to be comprehensive. This draws on comprehensive scholarship from diverse authorities, but is revealing in its Shia origins in terms of interpretative issues and perspectives. Eight volumes are available online and theoretically searchable, although this writer's test run revealed only very general results. This hypertext equivalent of *Tafseer Al-Mizan* contains provides an illustration of Islamic scholarship in relation to the Quran, although its applications within a general context may be limited.[18]

The Quran can be experienced in many ways, and through the Internet it is possible to locate numerous indices of recorded recitations. Some are within commercial sites, including the Islamic Bookstore, which offers a "try before you buy" option on several forms of *tarteel* (recitation).[19] The commercial popularity of such recordings throughout Muslim communities means that many new recordings are produced annually on CD, demonstrating stylistic differences and emphases.

Not all recitation pages are *directly* linked to commercial concerns: Hamo's Audio Site features a comprehensive hyper linked listing of recitations in RealAudio format, although there is little in the way of explanation regarding context and style.[20] The comprehensive IslamiCity resource contains the entire Quran, in text, recitation, translation, and Arabic script – although without a direct commentary.[21] The Islaam.com site provides a useful range of high-quality recitations, from seven recitors, demonstrating diverse styles and choices of material; there are technical options, relating to file size, whether a recitation is downloaded or received in a streaming format. Islaam.com have made a great effort to produce a technologically proficient Web site, making good use of design features and ensuring an ease of browsing and accessibility.[22]

Radio Al-Islam – which claims to have been the first Islamic site on the Internet – contains recitations from the entire Quran. For a newcomer to the field, there is a comprehensive and varied listing of chapters and recitations, which might contribute to an understanding of diverse recitation techniques (even for non-Arabic speakers).[23] Simply click the number of the verse, and the recitation will commence using RealPlayer technology. The selection includes recordings made during pilgrimage and recitations by Bosnian Muslims.[24] Contents have been mirrored within the Mosque of the Internet's pages. There is also an exegesis on the opening verse, and a rendering of the text into an English-language translation audio file. The Mosque itself stresses that the recitation of the Quran in English is not endorsed as an appropriate practice within a prayer or mosque setting, Arabic being the appropriate medium.[25]

There are a substantial number of alternative Quran related resources available to surfers on the Web, but their utility as research resources is open to question. Often they are useful in conjunction with more 'traditional' sources. It is helpful to have an understanding of the motivation behind site creation, and an awareness of theological, ideological and religious approaches to specific perspectives and interpretations relating to the Quran. Having said that, these sites provide an inexpensive, searchable resource offering the potential for an extensive, information-rich research experience. This may be enhanced in the future, with the integration of video interactive features onto sites. There are many new Quran sites currently in development and with substantial investment, notably a site for the King Fahd Complex for the Printing of the Holy Qur'an in Saudi Arabia, which prints and distributes Qurans for global distribution. Harf Technology, drawing on its Quran interface discussed above, is constructing the site.[26]

A real time exploration of a Quranic text with a scholar thousands of miles away is already a technological possibility. Investment in print *dawa* is being transformed (in part) into investment in Web-based dissemination of interpretation and conceptual frameworks and resources. The role of specialist academics as guides to on-line resources, such as the Quran, may become enhanced.

Expansion of the Internet over the past decade—and the technological transformation of *dawa* – has led to English increasingly being applied as a medium for globalised discussion on interpretative issues. This is frequently (but not exclusively) centred on American-based resources, themselves often linked to various ideological organisations and institutions within the 'Muslim world'. Considerable energy and funding has already been placed into creating user-friendly Quran resources, and it can be seen from the above discussion that certain 'market leaders' are already well placed to project future influence within this critical area.

THE HAJJ: AN ON-LINE PILGRIMAGE?

The issue of 'objectivity' relating to cyber-Islamic environments is less of an issue when researching the opinions and resources associated with Muslim cultural and religious expression. The Web has proven to be an ideal medium for Muslim individuals and groups to put their worldview across, allowing researchers opportunities to understand (and discuss on-line) issues such as religious experience and diversity of expression.

Key Islamic symbols and concepts allowing researchers (from Muslim and other backgrounds) access to extensive and often unique multimedia resources. Search engines identify key terms, but can overwhelm a researcher, unless parameters are narrowed. A search for 'hajj' (the major Muslim pilgrimage), for example, produced over 35,000 references from one search engine.[27] Guidance may be required in terms of the quality and utility of resources. A first page of 'hits' relating to the hajj included a diverse selection of materials. Top of the list was a film by an American journalist, Michael Abdul Majeed Wolfe. This can be viewed on-line, and he discusses personal experiences, whilst taking a film crew around Mecca.

This is not the conventional pilgrim experience, although Wolfe is a well-informed guide – having previously written a book on pilgrimage (Wolfe, 1994). The basic quality of the streaming video, using average computer equipment, may encourage the purchase of a high-quality version of the documentary (available through this site).[28] As a research resource for those seeking knowledge about Islam, based on the personal experience of a Muslim, Wolfe's film is valuable when applied in conjunction with other materials.

Another highly rated page in this search was the Hajj and Umrah Foundation's listing of resources, based in South Africa. This efficient and well-linked site contains basic details of ritual practice, prayer, and advice for the major pilgrimage and minor pilgrimage (umrah). As well as introductory material, the site incorporates a complete book delineating hajj practices, illustrated with textual precedents from the Quran and other Muslim sources.[29] This is significant, in that it presents a specific 'theological' stance (that of the Al Quran was-Sunnah Society) on hajj practices. The site incorporates an interactive element, encouraging readers to provide contributions and information on their own experiences in Mecca and Medina:

> By the Grace of Allah (SWT) you are in our company for performing your Hajj. We would like to be of service to you during your journey ... We would also appreciate it if you would kindly read through the following 'gems' and titbits of information that may be useful to you. If there is anything that you would like to add to this list from your own research, please convey this information to us so that it can be distributed.[30]

Feedback includes several pages of personal observation, conveying a depth of experience beyond traditional frameworks. Ahmed Adam discusses his personal and primarily positive pilgrimage experiences, integrating it with appropriate religious contexts and explanations. The personal aspect is illuminating, and suggestive of cultural encounters: "The people of Medina are wonderful people, very polite, gentle and humble. I was hugged and kissed by the citizens of Medina on many occasions, much to the amusement of my wife Hanifa."[31]

Ahmed Adam provides specific travel information on hajj, suggestions on what to pack, and the prayers he found appropriate during different aspects of the pilgrimage. The overwhelming emotional impact of this pilgrimage is well expressed, when he views the focus of prayer within Islam – the Kaba in Mecca:

The view from the roof of the Kaba gives a stunning flow of human tide, a living river: each participant in the tawaaf [circling of the Kaba] melts away and becomes one: each person loses their identity. You cannot discern the individual pilgrims: all you see is a milky way, a vortex, a whirlpool, a sea of people all churning in an anticlockwise direction spinning slowly: this immediately brings to mind a typical spiral galaxy spinning majestically in an anticlockwise direction where each star loses its identity but the cluster of stars together give the galaxy its identity and all spin together into a black hole. Similarly, the beauty and the majesty of the tawaaf is not in the individual, but in the collectivity of the participants: the whole is better than the individual. Unity is better than division. This is the essence of Islam. This is its beauty. In this lies its strength and success.[32]

The account provides important local information as well, and criticism of those few individuals who 'transgressed' during the pilgrimage. This information provides color and insight into Ahmed Adam's experience:

For completeness sake however, I have to mention that I did encounter the occasional pilgrim who spat on the Holy ground (out of ignorance), the official who was unhelpful (out of ignorance or apathy or fatigue), the pushing and fighting at the Tawaaf (out of ignorance or over-enthusiasm), the fighting and shoving at the Jamarats (out of ignorance), the occasional toilets that are not very hygienic, the long delays and queues at every turn, and the heat that is sometimes unbearable and saps your energy to the bone.[33]

Similar dimensions of experiences – 'religious' and otherwise – are located in another account, also on the Hajj and Umrah site. If anything, it is more 'colorful', and certainly adds the human dimension to the religious. Mir Mohammed Assadullah's strongly held Muslim beliefs carried him through a demanding pilgrimage, where he was severely tested by some of the activities surrounding him:

With all praise for Allah, the Lord and Cherisher of worlds, the hajj rituals ended. I saw deception, corruption, selfishness, lewdness, ignorance, filth, robbery, broken promises, indulgence, name calling, back biting, yelling, pushing, arrogance, and more during these few days. I did get the answer to my question, if we were really that bad to deserve fire in the holy Mina. We deserved it. We deserved it well.[34]

For researchers using the net as a resource to discover more about Islam and Muslim cultural dimensions, these accounts are perhaps unexpected! In-between the 'religious material' (however that it defined), the Internet demonstrates effectively the personal angles relating to Muslim practices and experiences.

Technical information on the Kaba is contained on pages produced by the Islamic Gateway.[35] This includes highly detailed technical plans relating to key areas in Mecca, and a Glossary of Hajj Related Terms compiled by Abu Zahra, making good use of Web based resources. For example, key concepts and places are linked to various sound and image files, and the reference to the appropriate date for pilgrimage is linked into a scientific resource on the Islamic Calendar.

The future of Islamic cyberspace is hinted at on the 3D Kabah WebPage, created by Abid S. Hussain. This applies three-dimensional computer modelling, to produce animated video clips – notably a 'fly-through' the precincts of the Kaba. At the time of writing, four clips were available. Each is a substantial download (the largest being 14MB), although the download time is dependent on technical and local factors. The long wait is worthwhile, as the viewer is plunged from an aerial shot of the Meccan precincts, through two minarets, down to the front of the Kaba.

These unique animated images introduce a new dimension and understanding of the Kaba, devoid of pilgrims, and with a computer-enhanced aesthetic. Used in conjunction with film, such a virtual pilgrimage rather dates conventional text based materials on the Kaba, and hyperlinks to photographs alone start to become passé. A direct feed of 'live' pictures from a video camera – similar to that provided on Jerusalem's Western Wall – might be appropriate and complementary to the 3D Kabah within Mecca.[36]

The Google search engine brought up other sites relating to hajj, but not necessarily directly concerned with 'religious experience'. There is a substantial amount of cultural-religious data contained on the SoundVision site, connected to an American based commercial Islamic software company. This includes advice on practices during the *Eid ul-Adha* period (the celebratory Feast of Sacrifice, which occurs at the end of the hajj), 'excuse letters' for students to take to school in order to obtain time off, and electronic Eid cards. The site incorporates a comprehensive on-line Handbook of Umra and Hajj, which would answer many questions relating to ritualistic practices and objectives (these would have to be in advance of the hajj or umrah, as a pilgrim cannot take a personal computer/WAP phone on the hajj).[37] SoundVision links its discussion and advice into commercial products, such as CD-ROMS and books, which are promoted as a means of enhancing knowledge about Islam.

The search engine also listed travel companies offering pilgrimage packages: a resource such as Al Hajj Travel Agency Comparison is a Java comparative tool, through which prospective pilgrims can compare the various transportation and accommodation packages available, through a list of agents. Some of the agents have symbols besides their entry, indicating whether – in the view of the site's authors – they are an agency 'to use' or 'to avoid'. The site represents a consumer service, is produced as a guide based around 'Muslim values', and does not take commission from the agents listed.[38]

Within the Google search engine listing is a reference to what is described as "Hajj, the Correct Way." Arizona-based United Submitters International produces this Web site (part of a broader set of pages), claiming that many of the contemporary Muslim practices associated with the hajj are 'innovations' and 'corruptions'.

It is not the place here to discuss the validity (or otherwise) of these claims. However, it does raise some significant questions in terms of the type of opinions that can be found on the Internet in relation to different Islam religious expressions. Many Muslims would be offended by the United Submitters' claim that their practice is inappropriate, and some might question why this opinion was emerging from the United States! United Submitters assert that the 'orthodox' timing of Hajj, and practices relating to visiting the tomb of the Prophet Muhammad in Medina, consumption of 'blessed' Zamzam water from Mecca, and seeking blessing from the Kaba's black stone are all 'idolatrous rituals':

> Like many other rituals in Islam (Submission in English), Hajj was corrupted by traditions and innovations. Many of those who go to Hajj these days end by committing more sins than getting rewarded for the great deed of performing their Hajj.
>
> This Web site was designed to point to the true believers, the Quranic Hajj and expose the corruption in today's practice.
>
> We know that you did not come to this site by a mere accident, but by the will of God Almighty who sees to it that you either see the truth or refuse it. We all have to be tested. Welcome aboard.[39]

United Submitters International base their understanding on a literal reading of the Quran, negating the validity of the layers of 'interpretation' that have emerged since the Revelation appeared in the seventh century (Common Era). Other sources such as the sayings of Muhammad, certain esoteric interpretations, and texts associated with Islamic Jurisprudence are dismissed – whilst there is emphasis on the mathematical implications of the Quran:

> An intricate mathematical code, far beyond the ability of human intelligence, has been discovered imbedded in the fabric of the scripture. Like an ancient time capsule, it remained hidden until our knowledge grew sophisticated enough to decode its intricacies. This code was deciphered by computers.[40]

The site authors place significance on Jewish mathematical investigation into sacred scriptures, part of Revelation seen as the precursor to the Quran, which within Islam is considered the Final Revelation. The "prominence of the 19-based mathematical pattern" within the Quran and the universe is determined as being 'The Creator's Signature'.

This approach to Islam is not considered 'mainstream' in many other Muslim contexts, and the United Submitters have been the focus of some criticism. They are using the Web effectively to project their point of view, emerging prominently within Islam-related searches on various search engines. The extent to which this is having a direct influence on individual readers is open to question. It may expose Muslims to new concepts and ideas; they may enter the site seeking knowledge on the hajj, and find themselves exposed to the challenges of mathematical Quranic exegesis (!). The impact a site like this has on researchers – especially those approaching Islam for the first time – is one worthy of further consideration and research. The Internet is able to transform such 'minority' views on Islam, and provide them with an on-line prominence equal to that of the 'major players' within Islamic cyberspace.

SHIISM: SYMBOLISM AND WORLDVIEWS ON-LINE

Elsewhere in cyberspace, the domination of specific Iranian-centred approaches towards Shiism is represented on the Web as it is in the 'real world'. In terms of approaching Shia Islam as a researcher, there are a number of significant propagation related works. The Shia Encyclopedia is perhaps daunting as an introduction, providing theological and interpretative perspectives relating to the authenticity of Shiism as an Islamic worldview.[41] The Encyclopedia's home site – Al-Islam – is more accessible, detailing the historical and religious circum- stances that led to the evolution of this particular religious perspective. It may assume that the reader already has some prior knowledge about the religion, and might be useful in conjunction with other textual sources.[42]

Closer examination reveals information about culturally specific interpreta- tion: for example, there is a listing of pilgrimage sites of particular interest to Shia Muslims, itemizing tombs and shrines that might be meritorious for a visit. This listing incorporates shrines in Saudi Arabia, Iraq, Iran, Syria, Jerusalem, and Egypt. The significance of each shrine is detailed, alongside maps and photographs. In some cases, further detailed information about a shrine is avail- able through hyperlinks, such as the History of Mashad in Iran, which contains historical, architectural and religious information.[43] As well as enhancing any proposed pilgrimage, such information is relevant to researchers seeking quick and authoritative data. This might form the basis of a more extensive search, as there are many sites detailing Mashad and its significance. The Al-Islam site also has a link page to other information about shrines, including a listing of shrines destroyed in Saudi Arabia by King Ibn Saud in 1925 – and some inter- esting theories as to why this happened:

> According to some scholars what is happening in Hijaz is actually a conspiracy plotted by the Jews against Islam, under the guise of Tawheed ['unity' of the global Muslim commu- nity]. The idea is to eradicate the Islamic legacy and heritage and to systematically remove all its vestiges so that in the days to come, Muslims will have no affiliation with their reli- gious history.[44]

It is not proposed here to discuss these controversial remarks. However, it is important to highlight the fact that the Internet does produce an indication as to the polarity (on some issues) existing within the 'Muslim world', and that there is substantial diversity within on-line religious expression. It may be that the Internet will transform the way Islam is approached and analysed by 'outsiders' exposed to these views, which go beyond the Sunni-centric 'main-stream' opinions generated by certain Muslim platforms and organisations.

In terms of researchers being exposed to different conceptual frameworks associated with Islamic expression, attention should be drawn to the activities of different Shia perspectives within the Islamic Republic of Iran. The Internet was identified by Iranian agencies as a natural extension to other media, and a means to convey information about current affairs and Islamic issues to a main-stream global audience.

Any analysis of Shiism on the Web would have to incorporate discussion of the Sun's House, a site devoted to Ayatollah Khomeini. Its introductory page opens with religious music, an audio file quotation, and images of the Republic's founder – and provides a series of links which demonstrate that the concept of religious leadership within Iranian Shia society can differ extensively from that of other Muslim contexts. The site makes good use of multimedia, allowing the viewer access to archive materials, photographs and documentary clips analysing Khomeini's life and his religious role(s). The site is also available in Arabic and Persian, and there is some variation as to content and images – which might be worthy of future comparative research.[45] The overall site may present a different impression of Khomeini to that in many 'western' contexts. In fact, Khomeini is well represented in cyberspace, with various homages, together with other analyses.

A good example of a devotional page is that of Imam Khomeini's Homepage, which contains an extensive archive of material, produced by the Tehran company, Negaran. The video selections may surprise outside observers. Drawn from several sources, (including the Sun's House, whose video files were not functioning at the time of writing) they include film of Khomeini on his deathbed, edited together with symbolic images of flying doves and appropriate musical soundtrack. The film features mourning for Khomeini, and provides evidence of ritualistic practices associated specifically with Shia Islam.[46] Elsewhere on the site are clips of Khomeini in prayer, working from his hospital bed, and images from his funeral.[47] Video streaming technology currently does not provide 'T.V.' quality pictures on basic computers, and this combined with the occasionally blurred and poor-quality archive film often produces an ethe-real effect that – whilst not the intention of the site author(s) – lends itself to the subject-matter.

Also on the Khomeini site are photographs, twenty-eight tracks of Iranian devotional music (unfortunately lacking titles or performers' details), Khomeini's writings, and even stamps with his images on. This site presents an illuminating snapshot of Iranian Shia religious practices, symbolism and ideas associated with the notion of the Imamate (Shia religious leadership). Other perspectives associated with Shia Islam in Iran also have a substantial Web presence, and many religious institutions in the Republic are devoting time and energy to further developing Web sites as part of wider strategies associated with information technology.

Shiism is not exclusively Iranian – and there are many other sites from different global perspectives that seek to represent particular worldviews. Inevitably, there are a number of detractors – both from within Shia Islam towards other Shia branches, as well as from 'outside' Shiism. All of these may emerge in one search engine listing for 'Shiism', and to researchers – without the requisite experience or prior knowledge about Islam – this may provide difficulties. Analysis or guidance may be necessary to establish the biases of a particular site. For example, a search on Shiism produced a page produced by the Jamiatul Ulama (Council of Muslim Theologians) in Kwazulu-Natal, South Africa, on Abdullah ibn Saba. He is described on the site as the 'founder of Shiism', and the pages discuss the emergence within elements of contemporary Shiism of attempts to discredit him, on the basis that he was "a created and legendary figure." The Jamiatul Ulama are on neither side within these intra-Shia dialogues:

> In the face of the above evidence, the call of modern Shi'ahs to disclaim their roots has a sinister ring to it. They wish to discredit the claims of sound historiography in doing so, and came up with new explanations which might have some early political legitimism, but has no scientific basis and is not supported by corroborative texts. At most it can be said that though Shi'ism is not entirely based on the teachings of ibn Saba, it has borrowed many Saba'i characteristics which plays an integral part in modern Twelver (Ithna 'Ashari) Shi'ism.[48]

Such comments reflect the Jamiatul Ulama's own philosophy: "The organisation's philosophy, motivation and functioning reside in and derive from the teachings of the Holy Quran and the recorded lifestyle (Hadith) of the beloved Prophet of Islam, Muhammad (Sallallaahu Alayhi Wasallam) as exemplified by our pious predecessors."[49]

Jamiatul Ulama use the Web to disseminate this message (in English and Zulu). It is interesting to consider that, from within the minority Muslim context of South Africa, a site such as Jamiatul Ulama Kwazulu-Natal can emerge and present substantial critiques of other Muslim religious perspectives. Such criticism 'appears' prominently within search engine listings for 'Shiism' amidst sites such as the Sun's House and the Ayatollah Khomeini Homepage.

SUFISM: 'FACING GOD' IN CYBERSPACE

Evidence of diversity of expression can also be located from within the so-called mystical traditions of Islam, under the generic heading of 'Sufism'. Again, some researcher awareness is required when utilising the information on these sites, and the ways in which Islam is represented in such contexts. Web sites can range from detailed academic resources of Muslim philosophy, through to individual devotional pages. In terms of the former, one of the best sites to start exploration is the Sufi Home Page – part of Deb Platt's wider Mysticism in World Religions pages.[50] This would appear to be very much a labour of love, as Platt is not a religious studies academic, and has produced the site in her spare time since 1995. The Islam-related pages draw on the writings of mystics from the eighth to the twentieth century, including Ibn al-Arabi (1165–1240) and Jalaluddin Rumi (1207–1273), and provide useful introductions to their writings and lives. There is potential for comparison between and within different belief frameworks on this site.

More detailed listings and guidance on Sufism on the Web can be found on Transnational Sufism, from the Centre for the Study of Islam and Christian-Muslim Relations at the University of Birmingham in England. Research into the Web has formed a component of a project on transnational Islam in relation to a specific Sufi 'order'. This includes a list of Sufi-related resources, but the listing itself lacks the type of explanation useful for researchers and casual surfers.[51] More relevant and user-friendly for general researchers are the Sufism pages produced by Alan Godlas at the University of Georgia, including a hyper-linked essay on different aspects of mystical beliefs, featuring images, soundfiles, and references to external sites.[52] Similarly useful is a site by Fariduddien Rice containing links to over twenty-five different forms of Sufism, outlining basic principles, and recommending associated sites.[53]

Several Sufi sites have a 'home-made' design quality to them. Again, an interesting example emerges from South Africa, with the Al-Zawiyah Homepage based around the Alawiyah Tariqa (Sufi Order). The site opens with religious recitation audio file, and an image of the mosque on the Cape Town skyline. In its pages are photographs of the mosque's activities, including celebration of the Mawlid (Prophet's and/or saints' anniversary) in which children are seating in the mosque, all wearing 'traditional' white clothing. Elsewhere are photos of the rendering of devotional songs, pictures of a spiritual leader's visit, and a visit by the Shaykh to Nelson Mandela's prison cell on Robben Island. The site reproduces an article on the order, together with materials especially prepared for the site, such as translated prayers and papers on Sufism by two local scholars.[54]

Sufi sites may also be focused around an individual spiritual leader. One example comes from Jerusalem, centering on Shaykh Abd'ar-Rahman as-Shadhili. He is the spiritual mentor of the Tariqa Shadhiliyya. His significance (in the view of the site's authors) is emphasised on-line, through a Web site that incorporates an account of a meeting with the Shaykh, and discusses his role as one who can draw followers closer to God. This viewpoint is not necessarily one that would find favour elsewhere within the Islamic spectrum:

> This Way is the way to know God. I knew this after a meeting of only one hour when I met my Shaykh Abd'ar-Rahman as-Shadhili. No way is faster than this one and no way has more knowledge. The shaykh takes the hand of the murid [follower] and says to him, "Now you are facing God, face to Face." And the shaykh says, "This is who you are . . . " You see that your eye is really the Eye of God. There is only one eye.
>
> The Tariqa Shadhiliyya is the way of the person who forgets all things and returns back to the truth as in the beginning; a child in the Presence of God . . .
>
> . . . Pray for Muhammad and his family and the awliya (saints) and lovers of the truth. There is no difference amongst them, of who they are, where they have come from and what they are saying. They speak the language of God, because they are His children and lovers.[55]

This has echoes of philosophers and Sufis such as Ibn al-Arabi and Jalaladdin Rumi, and might be compared and contrasted through examination of their texts via the Web. It certainly introduces another dimension to understandings of Islamic cyberspace. The site contains detailed information about (this particular interpretation of) Muslim 'mystical' expression, and an archive of photographs centred on the Shaykh and Jerusalem. His role as a spiritual guide is emphasised throughout:

> God says, "Be My reflection in everything that you do. I have given you Myself and you can see Me in every human being. Give anyone love and mercy, if that is what he wants; and know you are giving it to Me." When you find the love, you find yourself. The secret of God is in the love. If you want to go beyond all that you have been to find the secret of God, then I am your brother to take your hand and guide you from the darkness to the light and to the garden.[56]

There are a number of such claims made elsewhere within Sufi circles, by guides seeking to take followers on a religious journey, in order to 'approach God'. Whether proximity is enhanced by access to such Internet sites is open to question, although this particular site comes with an option to purchase CD-ROMs of the Shaykh's prayers, and a variety of printed materials which might 'promote' this form of religious experience. Teachings are also available on-line, with titles such as 'Repentance', 'the Voice of God', 'the Reality of Human Essence', and 'the Divine Love'. These provide an overview of the mystical path, as defined by the Shaykh and his followers.

The global nature of Sufism is well represented on several sites by 'major orders' (Bunt, 2000, pp. 58–65). Other networks are also beginning to take advantage of the technology. The Senegal-based Muridiyya brotherhood, which was founded by Shaykh Ahmadu Bamba (1854–1927), and has links in West Africa, Europe, Reunion Island, Mauritius, Madagascar, Comoros, Seychelles, South Africa, and North America. The Web site contains materials in French and English. The lives of Bamba and his disciple Shaykh Sidi Ahmed Ibn Ismouhou Deymani (1870–1972) are rich in detailing Sufi practices, in an area underrepresented in other literature; Ahmed was from Mauritania, and the pages explain how Bamba's coming was foretold by Ahmed's grandfather:

> It is reported that Shaykh Sidy Ahmed [R.A] said that every time that a Qutb is about to come on earth all the Perfect saints are informed about it. For such an extraordinary event, all the saints went into a mystical retreat to ask their Lord [May His Name be Exalted] for the honour to welcome this Ghawthul Azam within their families. At the end of the retreat the Great Mauritanian Saint Muhammad Fadel [R.A.] had gathered all his family to inform them that the Saint will come from the Black African people.

> He shall come from a noble and virtuous family, where members will be engaging themselves in teaching the Qur'an and the sunna. The Imam Sabara was amongst the last to emerge from the spiritual retreat. When he was informed of the inspiration from Muhammad Fadel, he asked his Lord that the Pole of Poles visit Mauritania and may his descendance (sic) . . . be his disciples.[57]

GLOBALIZING ISLAM ON THE NET

Here we have a 'globalizing' Muslim order, whose founders travelled substantially to spread his message and increase the numbers of followers. Now similar activities are taking place on-line, and the Senegalese-based movement can represent its doctrine to a new international audience with ease. For researchers of Islam, such information offers fresh sources and angles on mystical expression, and an enhanced understanding of the networking possibilities provided by the Internet to Muslim platforms and perspectives. The current spiritual head of the Muridiyya, Shaykh Abdoulaye Dieye (1938–), networks strongly around the world – especially amongst university students – and has a substantial presence on this Web site. His writings (including a Sufi children's story) are available on-line. The French version of the site contains different materials, including biographical details of the 'Caliphs' that followed Bamba, placing some emphasis on Reunion Island.[58]

Sites such as this can take the researcher away from the Middle East centred focus of material about Islam, which dominates other forms of media. Researchers seeking information about Islam in contexts such as South East

Asia, the Indian subcontinent, and even Reunion Island can find contemporary data on the Web that is difficult to locate quickly elsewhere. For Muslims, such sites open up opportunities to discover alternate perspectives on beliefs, and even dialogue with practitioners. The notion of a globalised single 'community' or *umma* – articulated within the Revelation of the Quran – is for some now becoming a digital possibility.

This notion of individuality within Muslim expression on the Internet can be extended to the experiences that can be gained through 'visiting' different religious communities that have established themselves on-line. More mosques may consider a Web site an appropriate resource for their members, as well as informing outsiders about their activities. This could form a network of members, combing resources and exchanging information. A good example of such a model in action at a national level can be found in Singapore, a republic whose overall technical literacy has led it to be a force of innovation in the development of on-line resources for its Muslim minority. This is co-ordinated at central governmental agency level (which raises specific issues relating to religious identity and bureaucratic control).

There are seventy-one mosques in Singapore, and one third of these possess basic homepages. They include (in English and Bahasa Malay) 'what's on' sections, historical data, photographs and illustrations of buildings, membership and management information, and contact details.[59] Six of Singapore's historically significant mosques are highlighted in a separate listing, detailing their origins and current status. All mosque sites are centrally linked to a resource containing information on mosque building, management, and financial regulations.[60]

The pages contain the logo of the MUIS (Majlis Ugama Islam Singapura or Islamic Religious Council of Singapore), whose longstanding Web site has led the way in terms of governmental approaches towards the Internet – and is notably paralleled in adjacent Malaysia. This is perhaps *one* model on how communities can approach the application of the Internet. Content is in English and Malay, and demonstrates the MUIS agenda and activities. This includes the collection of the obligatory *zakat* tax (one of the five 'pillars' of Islam). MUIS promotes on-line a series of obligatory pre- and post-marriage preparation courses for couples, organised on 'Islamic lines' by the government's Family Development Department and MUIS.[61] The site features an On-line Matchmaking Service (including an application form), for Sunni Singaporean Muslims between twenty-one and forty-five years of age.[62] There is information on the MUIS' *Tahfiz Al-Quran* Centre, promoting the virtue of Quranic memorization.[63] MUIS provides guidance for local food producers on obtaining official Halal Food Certification, important for (some) local Muslim consumers as well as exporters to other Muslim markets.[64]

Governmental input into the religious lives of its citizens – including provision of information on-line – has been seen as a constructive model by some agencies in certain countries with Muslim populations. The Singaporean government has also attempted to censor the on-line lives of its inhabitants, and many of its censorship techniques have also been emulated in Muslim contexts.

The MUIS site is useful for researchers, seeking to obtain a flavour of Muslim life elsewhere, and an understanding of one government's approach towards its Muslim minority. It should be noted that those viewpoints from outside of what the government considers 'the mainstream' are not as accessible on-line, and Internet restrictions (in various forms) are in place in Singapore. The nature of the Web means that censorship can be circumnavigated, so one can find contemporary accounts of Shia activities in Singapore, 'published' outside of the republic. For example, the Shia observance of Ashura as a day of mourning is different to its ritualistic importance within Sunni Islam, and Shia practices for Ashura are not be openly endorsed by Sunni-centred MUIS. Through the Internet, an account appeared detailing Shia ritualistic observance in Singapore can be located, commentating on local practitioners:

> Apart from the men, women were also present. But one thing I noted with much embarrassment [was] that the outlook of the South Asian women (don't know whether they were Indians or Pakistanis) were not appropriate according to the occasion of the Moharram [month of the Ashura mourning period]. Though most of them were clad in black, but at the same time were not covering their head . . . then it was evident that they were wearing make-up also. On the other hand the Malay women were very much properly dressed.[65]

Shiism is not 'officially' approved in Singapore, although elsewhere in the above account it is noted that Singaporeans actively participated in the ritualistic practices. The site provides contact details for Shia activities, and reproduces a fatwa (juristic verdict) from Egypt's Al-Azhar University stating that Shia practices (from a particular strand of Shiism) form "a school of thought that is religiously correct to follow in worship."[66]

Singapore represents just one basic example of how diverse sources about Islam in a specific geopolitical context are available on the Web, and that 'official' agencies are now actively involved in promoting their interpretation of Islam on the Internet. Internal religious divergence may be actively suppressed, but this does not mean that its expression on the Internet can be similarly controlled (see Bunt, 2000, pp. 73–81, 83–88).

MUIS may have a substantial budget to produce pages about its perspective on Islam – but to researchers, it may be that individual efforts are just as significant. Home-produced pages may not be as slick as some of the 'major players' within Islamic cyberspace, but they do provide a sense of personal, Muslim values – and often reveal ethical agendas and spiritual motivations unique to specific understandings of Islam, perhaps with a regional and/or ethno-linguistic emphasis. The growth of Islamic materials in languages other than English on the Internet will inevitably increase the amount of this 'personal' material, and perhaps shift the current emphasis away from Muslim sites emerging from 'western' contexts, back to the traditional centers of Islamic learning. It may be that there will be an extension of the ideological and spiritual battle in cyberspace for the attention of those surfers interested in Islam-related Web sites. The increasing applications and utility of multimedia will contribute to this dialogue, facilitating an increase in on-line Islamic events and resources.

The quest to attain global readership (Muslim and non-Muslim) and influence inevitably will see substantial investment – from governments and benefactors – into research and development of cyber-Islamic environments. 'Official' Web sites promoting the 'right knowledge' connected with aspects of Islam are already a reality.[67] Academic and other researchers – from whatever background – should be made aware of the initiatives and ideologies behind various Islamic sites. Surfing Islam navigates an ocean of knowledge about Islam, Muslims, religious expression, and "the Lord's words."

ACKNOWLEDGEMENT

The writer gratefully acknowledges the invaluable assistance of his wife, Yvonne Howard-Bunt, at all stages during the preparation of this chapter.

NOTES

1. *Sura al-Kahf* (The Cave) 18:109. *The Qur'an: A Modern English Version*. Fakhry, M. (Trans.). Reading: Garnet Publishing Ltd, 1997, p. 185.

2. *Islamic Studies Pathways*, http://www.lamp.ac.uk/cis/pathways

3. A listing of the Web addressed (URLs) discussed in this article will be maintained and updated on the Virtually Islamic Web site. All URLs were correct at the time of publication: http://www.virtuallyislamic.com

4. *Nation of Islam On-line*, http://www.noi.org Final Call On-line, http://www.finalcall.com

5. *Movement for Islamic Reform in Arabia*, http://www.miraserve.com; *Taliban On-line*, http://www.ummah.net/dharb Islamic Emirate of Afghanistan, http://www.taleban.com *Jihad in Chechnya*, http://www.qoqaz.net

6. For example, see *Al-Fatiha Foundation*, http://www.al-fatiha.org *Queer Jihad*, http://www.geocities.com/WestHollywood/Heights/8977

7. See *Saudi Women Solidarity Page*, http://saudi.sexypage.net

8. *Answering Christianity*, http://www.angelfire.com/ak/BaltoMuslims/answers.html; *Answering Islam*, http://www.answering-islam.org; *Answer to Answering Islam*, http://www.submission.org/answering-Islam.htm

9. See *Ayatullah Khamenei, Qom,* http://www.wilayah.org/english/ahkam/index.htm; *Al-Azhar,* http://www.alazhar.org/index5.htm

10. See *SuraLikeIt UK,* http://ds.dial.pipex.com/suralikeit/original/index.shtml

11. *Harf Information Technology,* http://www.harf.com/software/emuezzin.htm

12. *Harf, Picture Album,* http://hajj.al-islam.com/eng/album/album.htm A RealPlayer can be obtained from http://www.realaudio.com/products/player/download.html

13. *Scholarly Technology Group, Brown University, Qur'an Browser,* http://www.stg.brown.edu/Webs/quran_browser/pqeasy.shtml

Also see: *Humanities Text Initiative, University of Michigan, The Koran,* http://www.hti.umich.edu/relig/koran

14. *USC Muslim Students Association Islamic Server,* http://www.usc.edu/dept/MSA/quran

15. *USC Muslim Students Association Islamic Server,* Syed Abu-Ala' Maududi's Chapter Introductions to the Qur'an, http://www.usc.edu/dept/MSA/quran/maududi

16. *Holy Qur'an Resources on the Internet,* Merits of the Recitation of the Holy Qur'an, http://www.quran.org.uk/ieb_quran_jibouri.htm

17. *Holy Qur'an Resources on the Internet,* http://www.quran.org.uk

18. *Tafseer Al-Mizan: Exegesis of the Qur'an* by Allamah Sayyed Muhammad Husayn Tabataba'i, http://www.almizan.org

19. *Islamic Bookstore,* http://islamicbookstore.com/islamic_audios/quranictarteel.shtml

20. *Hamo's Homepage,* http://www.mindspring.com/~hamoaa65.

21. *IslamiCity,* http://www.islamicity.com/Mosque/ArabicScript/sindex.htm

22. *Islaam.com,* http://www.islaam.com

23. *Radio Al-Islam,* http://www.islam.org/Radio/ch110.htm

24. *Radio Al-Islam,* http://www.islam.org/Radio

25. *The Mosque of the Internet,* http://www.mosque.com/ch1.html

26. See *Harf Technology,* http://www.harf.com/products/eng/SitesInf_6.htm

27. 35,099 hits for 'hajj'. *Google,* http://www.google.com

28. Michael Abdul Majeed Wolfe, The Hajj, ABC Nightline, *Astrolabe,* http://www.astrolabepictures.com/astrolabe/-vhajj.html

29. *Hajj and Umrah Foundation,* Shaikh Muhammad Naasir-ud-Deen Al-Albaani, Rites of Hajj and Umrah, http://www.mecjv.com/hajj15.htm

30. *Hajj and Umrah Foundation,* http://www.mecjv.com/hajj8.htm

31. *Hajj and Umrah Foundation,* My Hajj, Ahmed Adam, http://www.mecjv.com/myhajj.htm

32. *Hajj and Umrah Foundation,* My Hajj, Ahmed Adam, http://www.mecjv.com/myhajj.htm

33. *Hajj and Umrah Foundation,* My Hajj, Ahmed Adam, http://www.mecjv.com/myhajj.htm

34. *Hajj and Umrah Foundation,* Hajj - A Personal Experience, Mir Mohammed Assadullah, http://www.mecjv.com/hajj/hajj1417.htm

35. *Islamic Gateway,* Hajj and Eid al-Adha, http://www.ummah.net/hajjis

36. *AishHaTorah's Window on the Wall,* http://aish.com/wallcam

37. *SoundVision,* http://www.soundvision.com/hajj/index.shtml

38. *Al Hajj Travel Agency Comparison,* http://www.the-Webplaza.com/hajj/Comparison.shtml

39. *United Submitters International,* Hajj, the Correct Way,
http://www.submission.org/hajj

40. *United Submitters International,* Mathematic Miracle of Qur'an,
http://www.submission.org/miracle-history.html

41. *Shi'ite Encyclopedia,* http://www.al-islam.org/encyclopedia

42. *Al-Islam,* http://www.al-islam.org

43. *Al-Islam, History of Mashad,* http://www.al-islam.org/shrines/mashad.htm

44. *Al-Islam,* http://www.al-islam.org/shrines/baqi.htm

45. *The Sun's House,* http://www.irna.com/occasion/ertehal/index-e.htm

46. *Imam Khomeini's (R.A.) Homepage,*
http://www.honafa.com/khomeini/video/soog.rm

47. *Imam Khomeini's (R.A.) Homepage,*
http://www.honafa.com/khomeini/index-english.html

48. *Jamiatul Ulama Kwazulu-Natal,* Abdullah ibn Saba,
http://www.jamiat.org.za/isinfo/ibnsaba.html

49. *Jamiatul Ulama Kwazulu-Natal,* http://www.jamiat.org.za

50. *Mysticism in World Religions,* http://www.digiserve.com/mystic/index.html

51. *Transnational Sufism,* http://www.sellyoak.ac.uk/csic/csicressufilinks.html

52. *Alan Godlas, Sufism's Many Paths,*
http://www.arches.uga.edu/~godlas/Sufism.html

53. *Fariduddien Rice,* Islamic Sufi Orders on the World Wide Web,
http://homepages.haqq.com.au/salam/sufilinks

54. *Azzavia Homepage,* http://home.pix.za/mf/mfj1

55. *Sidi Muhammad Press,* Tariqa Shadhiliyya, http://www.sufimaster.org/tariqa.htm

56. *Sidi Muhammad Press,* About the Guide, http://www.sufimaster.org/about.htm

57. The term 'qutb' can be interpreted as a 'spiritual axis', and is used in connection with Sufi 'saints'. *Muridiyya International,*
http://freespace.virgin.net/ismael.essop/deymani.htm (R.A. represents Rasul Allah, or God's Prophet.)

58. *L'Ecole Soufie de Cheikh Abdoulaye Dieye,* Les Khalifes,
http://home.worldnet.fr/~acase/CAB.html

59. See, for example, *Masjid Al-Ansar,* http://www.mosque.org.sg/alansar/index.html

60. *Mosques in Singapore,* http://www.mosque.org.sg

61. *FDD,* http://www.muis.gov.sg/fdd/emain.asp

62. *MUIS On-line Matchmaking Service,*
http://www.muis.gov.sg/fdd/jodoh/menu-english.html

63. *Tahfiz Al-Quran Singapura,* http://www.muis.gov.sg/tahfiz/eindex2.html

64. *Halal Certification,* http://www.muis.gov.sg/services/halal.html

65. *Shia Muslims in Singapore and Kansas City,* Syed Kamran Raza, Moharram 2000 in Singapore, http://www.geocities.com/muslimbychoice/Moharram2000.html

66. *Shia Muslims in Singapore and Kansas City,* Sheikh Mahmud Shaltut, "On Permissibility of Following al-Shiah al-Imamiyah School of Thought,"
http://www.geocities.com/muslimbychoice/azhar-e.gif

67. See, for example, the *Official Ramadhan Web Site,* http://www.ramadhan.org

REFERENCES

Bunt, G. (1997). Islam in Cyberspace: Islamic Studies' Resources on the Internet, *Muslim World Book Review, 18*(1), 3-13.

Bunt, G. (1999). *islam@britain.net* 'British Muslim' Identities in Cyberspace. *Islam and Christian-Muslim Relations, 10*(3), 353-362.

Bunt, G. (2000). *Virtually Islamic: Computer-mediated Communication and Cyber Islamic Environments*. Cardiff: University of Wales Press.

Nielsen J. (2000). *Designing Web Usability*. Indianapolis, IN: New Riders.

Wolfe, M. (1994). *The Hadj: A Pilgrimage to Mecc*a. London: Secker and Warburg.

HOW RELIGIOUS ORGANIZATIONS
USE THE INTERNET:
A PRELIMINARY INQUIRY

Sara Horsfall

ABSTRACT

This chapter examines the ways in which five religious groups use the Internet. Each group has an active presence in the U.S. but an international membership. It was found that individual Web pages often predated official Web sites. Publicity and public relations is an important official use. The Internet also provides a means to counter negative rumors and critics. Another characteristic of Internet use is the publication of extensive religious texts. Directories of churches and centers as well of individual members is also important. Finally, international groups use the Internet to keep their members informed of the latest policies and activities worldwide. A typology is developed and ways in which the Internet will affect religious practice is discussed.

INTRODUCTION

Our modern age of computers is often called the Information Revolution, a time of social change comparable to that of the Industrial Revolution. This new revo-

Religion on the Internet, Volume 8, pages 153–182.
Copyright © 2000 by Elsevier Science Inc.
All rights of reproduction in any form reserved.
ISBN: 0-7623-0535-5

lution, it is said, will change our lives in countless ways – both in ways we can predict and in ways as yet unforeseen. It is realistic to think that religion will be as profoundly touched by these changes as other cultural institutions. In fact, religious concerns have a notable presence on the Internet.

There are hardly any U.S. based religious groups that do not have a presence on the Internet. Many well-established denominations have developed rather sophisticated Web sites. Other denominations are more appropriately characterized as being merely present; they have apparently not yet developed a strategy of what they seek to accomplish with their Internet presence. Some appear to focus on communicating with their own members, while others clearly seem to view the Internet as an instrument for communicating with persons and agencies outside of their regular constituencies. From a cursory examination of the pages of many established religious groups it is possible to discern several popular and recurrent uses.

A major use of the Internet for Christian groups is dissemination of information, such as directories – both on-line listings and comprehensive regional listings. Local church locators[1] appear to have heavy traffic. Information about the Bible is another popular use of the Internet. There are numerous on-line Bibles,[2] Bible searches and concordances.[3] There is evidence of an active religious community of Internet users in the several dozen Christian newsgroups. And there are a variety of resource sites for everything from search engines, voting indexes, art, clip art, evangelism, humor, jobs, music, prophecy, sermons, youth and children's ministry. There is also a group of eager Web hosts to help the less computer literate churches get started.[4]

The impact of the information revolution on religion is addressed here by examining the ways in which religious groups are using the Internet. A preliminary examination of religious Web pages made it clear that there is a seeming myriad of approaches that religious groups take in utilizing the Internet. I opted for a more in-depth examination of a small group of religious bodies (five) rather than attempting to reach some global generalizations about many religious groups. The five groups I selected differ widely in terms of the length of time they have been present in the U.S., membership size, beliefs, practices, and other important demographics. As it turns out, each of the five groups selected has an international membership, but that was not intentionally a criterion for selection. What the groups selected have in common is an aggressive commitment to make use of the Internet. By exploring groups that are actively committed to using the Internet, I hope to gain understanding about how religious groups are using the Internet as well as insights about what will be unfolding in the years ahead. The five religious groups selected are: the Roman Catholic Church, the Church of Jesus Christ of Latter-day

Saints (Mormons), the Church of Scientology, the Unification Church and Falun Gong.

An extensive Web search was conducted for each organization with subsequent examination of official pages as well as a number of unofficial sites. Even by limiting my investigation to this small number, it was not possible to examine all of the sites for each group, and it is likely that I have not achieved closure on all the uses of the Internet that these groups employ. Still, even this limited study reveals trends and common uses by these diverse groups.

To broaden what could be learned from an examination of the content of the Web pages, personal contact via email was made with six Webmasters whose pages identified them with their organization. Except for Falun Gong and Scientology, these contacts were not with Webmasters of official pages. A set of common questions was asked of each person contacted.

Responses varied from active back-and-forth email communication to a reply offering a phone number and invitation for a telephone interview. In each case, the contacted individual contributed considerable information and perspective both regarding their own Web sites as well as the official site of their faith tradition.

At the conclusion of my discussion of the five groups to be examined, I offer a typology that I hope will be valuable for further study of how religious groups utilize the Internet. The study concludes with a discussion of how the Internet has and will change the religious meaning system.

CATHOLIC USE OF THE WEB

A major Roman Catholic presence on the Internet is the Vatican site (www.vatican.va). Available in six languages (although some detailed pages are only in Italian), the Vatican site has an attractive, understated classical design. The content is extensive with church directories, directives, reports, and information on assemblies. One also finds commission proceedings and reports, publications and bulletins on Roman Catholic activities around the world, as well as the status and history of church policies. There are pages for the Institute of Sacred Music and the Pontifical Academies. There are news reports and extensive Library materials including 'Secret Archives' in Italian. The site has a multimedia page and a search engine.

The Vatican site seeks to disseminate information about and for Roman Catholics around the world. It also appears to be a reference resource for Vatican officials as well. There is little indication of evangelistic intent except for the well argued views on controversial social topics, such as abortion.

If the Vatican homepage may be characterized as official, authoritative and massive, it is but one of an extensive array of Catholic resources available on the Internet. There are sites with information on almost every aspect of Catholicism imaginable – the liturgy, its meaning, history, directives, the mass, sacraments, other ceremonies, prayer, music, hymns and chants. Internet pages offer information about catechisms, scripture, official church documents, church councils, papal writings, apologetics and explanations.

Catholic sites range from monthly magazines with topical discussions, to a site that contains the entire contents of St. Augustine's 'On Christian Doctrine'. There are sites on the history of the Catholic Church in various parts of the world. There is an on-line mass site offering audio homilies and the facility to make petitions and prayer requests. The Catholic Encyclopedia is also available on-line. Many Catholic schools and educational institutions have their own Web page, as do other of the various Catholic related organizations.

Several sites offer extensive directories (on-line AND non-on-line Churches) so that Catholics moving anywhere in the world can easily find a home parish. A group of sites dealing with Catholic news, history, art, and laws ranges from a virtual tour of the Sistine Chapel and the Vatican to discussions of the activities, spirituality and history of French working priests. Another group of sites deals with people – biographies of saints (e.g. Joan of Arc), all the Popes, a listing of current Bishops and church officials.

There are sites for Catholic Volunteer Services, for Religious Orders and Missions. There are pages devoted to helping people select Catholic related vocations. And pages devoted to helping Catholics solve some of the everyday family related problems: annulment, Catholic Singles, Catholic Sexuality, and marriage counseling (Retrovaille). Lastly there are numerous sites devoted to children and youth, including Youth Ministry, Teen Life, Young Adult Links, Dominican Young Adult Movement, Catholic Educator's Resource Center, Catholic Homeschoolers. There is a set of sites with no direct religious content – pages devoted to Catholic shopping, Catholic e-cards, movie reviews, and a site for inactive Catholics.

Another site with high Catholic visibility and usage is the Eternal World Television Network, or EWTN (www.ewtn.com). In addition to pages devoted to news events, and TV or radio programs associated with the network, it has an extensive series of pages devoted to Catholic teachings, and many speeches by the Pope. It also offers an interactive bulletin board and prayer request. Many of the pages are available in Spanish.

If much of the content of Roman Catholic pages can be characterized as information dissemination, there is clearly an evangelistic or proselytization component on the Internet. This can be seen in the evangelistic and/or devotional pages by individual priests and nuns – some sequestered in reclusive religious orders. The published sites are a means of disseminating their inspiration directly to the public.

Lay Catholics also have pages to promote their favorite aspect of Catholicism. According to John Ockerbloom, who for several years maintained a Catholic Resources site (www.cs.cmu.edu/People/spok/catholic.html), Web pages that promote an individual's take on Catholicism are not approved by the church, but neither are they opposed. Ockerbloom has never been officially rebuked, although lay persons have sometimes objected. And Ockerbloom notes, lay persons created Catholic pages on the Internet long before the appearance of the official Vatican site. He explains:

> Laypeople were active on the Net for years before the official bodies got involved, and still to a large extent dominate the on-line landscape. There has been a real explosion of lay activity on the Net (of late). Though the official Vatican site is probably the most visited official site (J. Ockerbloom, personal communication, April, 2000).

An example of the 'explosion' is the interest in mailing lists. There are more than 60 identifiable listservs on topics including Catholic Campus Ministry, Association for Rights of Catholics in Church, Catholic Spirituality List, CatholiCity, Home Schooling, Charismatic Catholics, Deacon Discussion List, Former Nuns mailing list, LesBiGay Catholic List, Order of St Benedict Discussion List, and Prayrosary. Some lists are moderated; some include people from other churches. Primarily lay people use the lists, but clerics and members of religious orders also participate in some lists. Lists are used for activism, for prayers and prayer requests, for discussion of issues, and for chatting. They are not primary means of disseminating information.

As for recruiting, according to Ockerbloom (personal communication, April, 2000):

> I didn't actually intend my site as a recruiting mechanism, and in fact never solicited questions, but I still got a steady stream of email messages from people who were inquiring about various aspects of the Catholic faith. I answered the ones that I could answer myself, referred people to other information sources when needed, and also told people to consult their local priests when appropriate. For those who were looking into converting, I recommended both on-line resources for more information, and also that they get involved in their local parishes, since this is an essential part of the process.

With close to one quarter of the U.S. population identified as Catholic, it is not surprising that the Catholic presence on the Internet is so large. A quarter of the Catholics on-line would represent 1/16th of the U.S. population. Most of the Catholic sites appear intended to be used first by other Catholics. But public availability of the information means that non-Catholics can and do access the Web sites, and the discussion lists. A secondary, if covert purpose, is proselytizing.

MORMONS AND THE INTERNET

The official position of the Church of Jesus Christ of Latter-day Saints, or Mormons, regarding the Internet is that it is a powerful technological tool that can be used for either good or bad. Members are encouraged to use it wisely. On the good side, it is thought to be divinely inspired in order to link Mormons around the world and to disseminate the Mormon doctrine more widely (P. H. Holmes, personal communication, March, 2000).

Compared with the Vatican site, the official Mormon site (www.lds.org) may be characterized as more functional, less international, and less extensive. There is a link to 'Media Information' leading to a basic press kit, including basic Mormon demographics, news updates, recent speeches by church leaders and other information that may be of interest not only to the press but to anyone who wants to learn more about the LDS. Visitors who click on 'What's New' will not only access new information about church activities, but have the opportunity to obtain a free copy of the Book of Mormon. Click on 'Family History Resources' and one will be offered a free videotape entitled 'Together Forever', that discusses the importance of family relationships both in life and after death.

One will also find a page countering common misconceptions about Mormons, mainly polygamy. More examples could be added, but it is clear that the leadership of the Mormon Church have conceptualized their official Web page as primarily an instrument for outreach – both public relations and proselytization, although there are facilities for members as well.

For members, resources include scripture studies, information on building strong families, and news – including information in 20 different languages about their semi-annual General Conference. In October of 1999 the Conference was broadcast live over the Internet for the first time, making it available in real time to members worldwide. The practical difficulties involved in receiving live broadcasts may limit the broadcast reception, however.

A major attraction of the site for non-Mormons is the FamilySearch™ Internet Genealogy Service. Mormons are acknowledged leaders in genealogical record keeping, much of which is available on-line. When FamilySearch was first made available, traffic to the site was so great that they had to access search time.

Unofficial Mormon sites number in the hundreds or even thousands (although noticeably less than unofficial Catholic sites). The entire Book of Mormon is available on-line, as are other official writings, historical and contemporary sermons, and essays. Several Mormon research foundations publish their findings on-line (e.g. Foundation for Ancient Research and Mormon Studies). There are on-line Mormon magazines, booksellers, lists of Mormon colleges, lists of Mormon grammar schools, sites on Mormon history, testimonies and tech support. There are sites for Mormons who are deaf, mentally ill or disabled; sites for singles and an LDS Matchmaker. There are at least four gay and lesbian Mormon sites, as well as some anti-homosexual sites that offer counseling.

One site offers a virtual tour of Temple Square and another offers help planning a wedding in the Temple. There are a handfull of women's sites including one with a list of names for Mormon babies. There are Mission Web pages – where missionary cohorts keep in touch. The most frequented Mormon sites offer Mormon clipart, genealogy searches (3 different ones), Temple schedule and photos, an LDS Chat and Teachers' Resources – most of which are accessed by other Mormons.

According to Canadian Webmaster, Nick Literski[5] (personal communication, April, 2000), most Webmasters are evangelistic.

> Very little has been done by the Church directly in terms of missionary efforts [on the Internet], but I would say that MOST individuals LDS-oriented pages have a missionary effort focus. My own is actually directed far more to established members of the Church. Even so, I have been told of various 'missionary successes' which have resulted from my page.

The Web is important to a large number of Mormons, but not, by any means, all. As Literski notes:

> The Internet is important to a rather select group. Most are American, and of course there is a level of technical savvy involved ... There are relatively few international LDS sites, but if my own site is any indication, many international users visit U.S.-based sites. I receive mail regularly from LDS members all over the world ... LDS use of the Internet is growing, however, with the expansion of the Church's official presence on the Web ... there is also a constituency of middle-aged to elderly LDS who seem to have purchased computers and Internet access SOLELY for email purposes. These individuals typically have a very, very limited understanding of the technology involved, and ask MANY questions of people like me (N. Literski, personal communication, April, 2000).

Mormons on-line are interactive. An LDS Resource site lists 24 Mailing lists, 14 chat rooms, and 10 message boards. There are several well-used newsgroups, as well, the most common being *alt.religion.mormon* and *alt.religion.mormon. fellowship.* A popular mailing list is called Words of Wisdom: a devotional quote is sent every day. According to Literski (personal communication, April, 2000):

> There are MANY LDS listservs, with a wide variety of specialized focuses and 'attitudes', for lack of a better description. Many have a high degree of traffic. The users, however, can only be considered a small group of LDS members ... The users of these listservs often 'know' one another as on-line presences, and will exchange private emails along with listserv postings. Certain individuals become well known, as do their attitudes and interests. This is largely a result of the small subset of users among LDS members ... On the other hand, these listservs also see a high degree of participation by critics of the Church, who post repeated and frequent messages in an effort to dissuade LDS from their beliefs.

In addition to the hundreds of pages created by LDS members, there are also literally hundreds more anti-Mormon pages – at least two dozen representing a significant presence. Many of these sites feature testimonies of those who left the Mormon Church. These testimonies are typically accompanied with arguments as to why leaving is the best choice along with information about the leaving process, including offers for counseling. These pages, in turn, have spooned pages by members that detail the history of hostility toward Mormons since the founding of the Church.

In sum, it seems that Mormon sites serve the membership, but have a missionary intent. Even those that do not have an overt outreach purpose are seen as contributing to missionary success. There seems to be a sizeable proportion of the Mormon population that use the Internet not only for outreach but for personal communication with other Mormons through discussion forums and email contact.

CHURCH OF SCIENTOLOGY ON THE INTERNET[6]

The official Scientology home page (www.scientology.org) bears evidence of considerable professional skill – a page designed to create an impact. Bells and whistles abound, beginning with a Real Player video that pops up when you click on "What is Scientology." The promo proclaims that Scientology is the "fastest growing religious movement on earth," and that the group has "The true secrets of existence." It concludes with an 800 number to purchase a copy of their book.

The site caters to people of different nationalities: a basic promo and book offer is available in 53 languages. There also is a series of pull down phrase boxes offering radio clips in multiple languages. The clips conclude with a book offer. Significant portions of the site can be accessed in up to fifteen languages, and virtually all pages are available in English, French, Spanish, Italian or German.

Complementing the extensive graphics and pictures on the Scientology site is a virtual tour of their churches and centers – a string of pages of photographs offering panoramic views of buildings, meetings and activities. And, one can listen to a brief excerpt of the 'Voice of the Founder', L. Ron Hubbard. As always, a bookstore offers yet another opportunity to purchase Hubbard's books about Scientology as well as his science fiction writings.

Although the initial impression is that all materials on-line come with a price tag, the Scientology site is substantial with vast amounts of on-line material. A second 'What is Scientology?' link on the front page reveals portions of the book offered for sale in the video promos. Another link offers contents of a second volume, *Scientology: Theology and Practice of a Contemporary Religion.*

On the 'Press Office' page there is information on current events involving Scientology. On my last visit to the site page, I found information about the group's status in Europe. The German government considers Scientology to be a threat and has prohibited its members from holding public jobs. The U.S. Department of State, charging that it violates religious freedom, has criticized Germany's position. The 'Press Office' page has position papers on a variety of causes championed by Scientology including drug prevention and rehabilitation, anti-crime programs and critiques of psychiatry.

In short, one can learn a lot about Scientology from their official Web site. For those willing to leave a name and address, there are some free commodities as well. An information packet about Scientology will be sent in three email installments. An invitation to a free showing of a Scientology-produced movie will be sent in exchange for information about the user. And there is a PDF file of the celebrated Scientology personality test for downloading. The user must send in a printed version of the test for diagnostic assessment. The test is then returned via surface mail, most likely with an invitation to a local center to learn more about the value of pursuing the Dianetics training program. Local churches are easy to find on the global map locator. A user clicks on the appropriate spot and it zooms in on a local Church of Scientology, giving a street map and times for the services.

Last, but not least, there is an invitation to 'Meet 15,000 Scientologists' worldwide. Again, one clicks on a Continent, then selects either a country or an individual name. Either one leads to individual pages that have highly similar content. Each member page begins with a heading: Welcome to my Web site. Some are accompanied with a photo. For all member pages there follows five categories: (1) About Myself, (2) My Success in Scientology, (3) My Favorite L. Ron Hubbard Quote, (4) Groups I Support, and (5) Favorite Links.

The first three categories have a brief paragraph about the member. The last two categories are identical for all 15,000 member pages. 'Groups I Support' leads to four Scientology organizations; 'Favorite Links' leads to 6 Scientology sites – *Dianetics*, Bridge Publications, L. Ron Hubbard page, Scientology, Association for Better Living, and *Freedom Magazine*. A final message offers contact with the member. However, rather than finding an email address, the visitor must leave their own name and address to be contacted by the Scientologist.

Scientology is clearly attempting to create the impression that many people are highly satisfied with their involvement in Scientology. While that undoubtedly is the case, one may have a different impression from reading the highly duplicative member Web pages. Critics of Scientology (easily located on the Web) have not missed the opportunity to charge the Church leadership with manipulating, or coercing individuals into mindless robotics.

In fact, one gets the impression that the design of many of the segments on the Scientology site was intended to counter negative propaganda. Performing arts stars are showcased. The message they communicate is that Scientology training successfully brings out the best characteristics of their members. Church projects and charitable activities are emphasized. Always, Scientology is portrayed as being involved in social reform and social betterment

This is seen in the several related Web sites. An impressive site showcases the founder L. Ron Hubbard. *The Freedom Magazine's* informative and interesting site helps to understand the group's commitment to the many dimensions of freedom. The World Institute of Scientology Enterprises (www.wise.org) site is intended for business and professional members who use Hubbard's management technique in their respective organizations. The Scientology Missions International (www.smi.org) site identifies the less formally organized centers run by non-trained members. The Association for Better Living and Education site (www.able.org.uk) showcases some of their social reform causes, such as World Literacy Crusade, Narconon – a drug rehabilitation and education program, and Criminon – a rehabilitation program for incarcerated individuals using correspondence courses.

Other Scientology pages are worth exploring if one is interested in learning more about this new religious movement. But the story of Scientology on the Internet is not complete without exploring Scientology's struggle with its adversaries who have effectively used the Internet to darken the group's public image.

Like all religions, the group has attrition, and disgruntled former members (apostates) eager to tell atrocity tales. The Church of Scientology has had more than its share of angry apostates, perhaps because of the large number of people they recruit, or because of the fee paid for training which makes the cost more tangible. In any case, the Internet has become an effective forum to disseminate their dissatisfaction to the world. It has also become a convenient way for former members to find and interact with each other.

The early anti-Scientology cyber-warriors used news groups and bulletin boards to spread messages of hate. With the advent of the World Wide Web in the early 1990s, the conflict began in earnest.[7] In 1993, the jealous lover of a member, Scott Goehring, started a newsgroup *alt.religion.scientology* using the name of Scientologist David Miscavige, who was head of the organization's powerful Religious Technology Center. Goehring's purpose was to provide a forum where Scientology, and particular members of the group, could be defamed. The ARS Usenet page generated thousands of postings daily, becoming one of the hottest sites on the Usenet system. Although a large proportion of the messages were posted by just a few individuals, the page also attracted thousands of visitors who knew nothing about Scientology except what they read on this site.

Also of concern to Scientology was the fact that anonymous contributors leaked confidential church material to ARS, and this material was then used on anti-Scientology pages along with official Scientology symbols and photographs.

Members of Scientology tried to fight back in a variety of ways. Their attempts at countering the accusations rationally by participating in the discussion were unsuccessful. They tried to cancel negative posts to the newsgroup, but critics set up a utility to identify illegitimate cancels. They tried to legally shut the ARS newsgroup down, on the grounds that it was created by fraudulent means (using a false name). Individuals posting to the newsgroup responded by accusing Scientology of stifling their freedom of speech. They tried spamming the message board and were denounced for dirty play.

The year after ARS was founded, a former Scientologist began posting segments of copyrighted materials on the newsgroup. Scientology lawyers sent cease and desist letters to the individual. Late in 1994, when the same individual commenced to publish more copyrighted material anonymously, Scientology filed suit for copyright infringement. In 1995 and 1996 Scientology filed no less than eight suits against persons who published segments of Scientology texts which they claimed were obtained illegally.

The courts ruled in favor of Scientology in each of the cases and Grady Ward has agreed to settle, paying the church $200 per month. Scientology's aggressive pursuit of their claim to the organization's intellectual property has been effective.

But this was not the end of Scientology's problems on the Web. The group was caught unprepared for the explosion of individual pages. Before they could set up their own page, there were a plethora of anti-Scientology sites. Anyone doing a search for 'Scientology' on any search engine would find an abundance of negative information. The church hastily constructed a personal Web page in the name of Leisa Goodman, the Church's head of Public Relations. This gave the group an official presence, but did not solve the search engine problem.

There is little question that the Internet, in the hands of a few former Scientologists, has been the Church's nemesis. By presenting a high quality Web site, Scientology seeks to portray itself in a positive light. Their achievement of this goal is accomplished with some drawbacks. Most seriously, a parishioners.org page, which identifies by name their internet adversaries: 30 individuals who "attempt to curtail the rights of others."

For our purposes, the whole controversy points to an interesting use of the Internet by both religious groups and by critics. Is it possible for a group that does not pay attention to critics on the Web to become a minor presence under their own name? Are efforts to 'flood' the Web with its 15,000 similar member pages to balance Scientology's presence a reasonable counter-measure? With Web materials so easily 'borrowed' and copied, how do groups deal with those who use their symbols and slogans in a negative way? These questions are of more concern to smaller, less well-established groups. Does the Internet, as one user queries, "bring more enlightenment and spiritual discrimination" or "increase intolerance and hatred?"

USE OF THE INTERNET BY THE UNIFICATION CHURCH

Another group that has encouraged use of the Web is the Holy Spirit Association for the Unification of World Christianity, or more commonly, the Unification Church. The large number of sites for "Unification Church" reflects the vast resources of church information available on-line, usage of the Net by members, and the large number of anti-cult sites. (The Unification Church has often been used by sociologists and by critics as an exemplary NRM – new religious movement, or in more derogatory terms, 'cult').

There are approximately 25 official sites for the Unification Church, each originating in different countries in the corresponding languages. In the U.S., the official Web site identifies the group as the Unification Church (www.unification.org). The official U.S. site has information for non-members including current events, information about Rev. and Mrs. Moon, a slide presentation of their teachings, current evangelism projects, a description of the global outreach, links to projects and education, and a bibliography of church publications available on-line. For members, there is a site for learning the Korean language and a page of Unification Community links. Under the latter, Damian Anderson's site (see below) is described as the 'most complete' unofficial news source; Gary Fleisher's site (see below) is described as a 'Library of Unification Resources'. There are a number of links to other member's pages as well.

The official Korean Web site (http://tongil.or.kr/ENG/CH/enindex.htm) identifies the group as the Family Federation. The site has information in both Korean and English. The English pages are more sophisticated than the official U.S. site, and have a more extensive selection of church materials, including a history of the church, a description of worldwide missionary work, and a biography of Rev. Moon and his achievements. Damian Anderson is identified as the source for some of the English language files. The Korean pages have a section devoted to missionaries that requires a login ID and password, so is off limits to non-members, and even to general Church members. They also include travel information for visitors to Korea. The site is also equipped to offer live broadcasts of church functions; times are announced on Anderson's

WorldTies mailing list. In theory, broadcasts extend access worldwide. In practice, receiving live broadcasts requires sophisticated equipment and computer savvy, limiting its audience.

European sites are available in English (UK), German, French, Italian, Spanish, Portuguese, Hungarian, Norwegian, Swedish, Japanese or Korean. Some of the national pages have separate Webmasters and different layouts. The main European page, and some of the national pages, are maintained by Paul Ettl, whose site is a mirror of Damain Anderson's in the U.S. In addition to the European site, there are at least 14 more international church Web sites that have no consistency or standard formatting except for the use of Church symbols and photos of Rev. Moon and his wife. Each reflects the personality and technical sophistication of the national Webmaster. Even the site title varies: Unification Movement, Family Federation for World Peace and Unification, Unification Church. Many local church pages in the U.S. are quite utilitarian with no apparent effort at attractive layout or graphics. Their primary function is to convey information to local members. Some local churches maintain mailing lists instead of Web pages, sending out pertinent information on a regular basis.

Three of the unofficial sites are so important to the church and to members that I called them quasi-official sites. They are not official, but have the backing of the church leadership. Members rely on these sites for the latest in church information. The three sites are those developed by Damian Anderson (www.unification.net), Gary Fleischer (www.tparents.org), and Paul Ettl (www.ettl.co.at/unification).

Anderson's site is the most extensive. He caters to both members and non-members. Church information includes an extensive collection of Rev. Moon's speeches and complete texts of church publications – including some meant for 'inside' consumption. (For example, 'The Tradition' contains details of private church rituals.) A link to the church bookstore is an alternative to on-line texts. A page of news covers events within the church as well as non-church developments worldwide that are deemed significant. Member testimonies and sermons are featured prominently. A link to another member's site gives email addresses (approximately 1500) of church members. There are links to national sites in different languages – Chinese, Dutch, Farsi, French, German, Estonian, Hungarian, Japanese, Italian, Kiswahili, Lithuanian, Macedonean, Norwegian, Portuguese, Polish, Russian, Swedish and Thai. And finally there is a page of links to church related organizations and activities. According to the cumulative statistics on Anderson's site (which he keeps for 'historical purposes'), daily access during the first three months of 2000 averaged 6,330.

Paul Ettl's mirror site contains a page of .midi files of Holy Songs, an address list of churches worldwide, and makes all of Anderson's voluminous material available to members in Europe. Gary Fleischer's page has a collection of church materials – speeches and texts – that complement Anderson's extensive files. His stated purpose is the "free exchange of information." Visitors can submit a favorite link or information they want published on his page. Fleicher's page includes resources for members who want to set up their own Web page: photos of Moon and his family and various church events, church logos, directions for putting logos on a Web page, and links to computer information. Finally there is an invitation for the visitor to send a message to Reverend Moon through the Webmaster, who promises to forward or hand deliver the message.

Anderson also moderates a popular and rapidly growing church listserv and several mailing lists.[8] Unification Evangelism listserv, with nearly 700 subscribers, is for members. It is monitored and most postings are supportive of the church. The Internet evangelism focus leads to lively discussions, criticisms, testimonies and international activity reports. The WorldTies mailing list (church news, announcements, reports, testimonies and sermons) has more than 1900 subscribers. It serves as a quasi-formal means of communication; church leaders make it a point to keep Anderson informed. It also connects members who are otherwise isolated. The True Family Values News (TFVN) mailing list (national and international news items that relate to church morals and values) has approximately 1560 subscribers. The Unification Texts mailing list (daily speeches of Rev. and Mrs. Moon) has more than 900 subscribers. More than 500 World Scripture subscribers receive one section of world scripture daily.

Anderson's purpose for all his Internet activity is evangelistic. He wrote his own software to be able to accommodate his various activities. He explained to me in a lengthy phone conversation that he often gets responses from people who access his pages – members and non-members. Frequently they thank him for the material. For example, one American church member with a Japanese wife, living in Japan for several years, wrote the following:

> Needless to say, I don't know much about anything that's happened in our movement in the last 8½ years. I feel a bit like Rip Van Winkle waking up from a 100 year sleep without a clue as to what has happened during my sleep. Your work, with the various lists and the Unification Church Home Page, is my lifeline to our Movement. I'm incredibly grateful (WorldTies listserv).

There are at least two other popular listservs for Unification Church members, or ex-members. Global Village International (GVI) was one of the first list to be established. According to one active church member it "is now pretty much dominated by old, tired and cynical members and a lot of ex-members."

The church is frequently the topic of conversation and comments are often critical.

Home Harbor Inn (HHI) is described by members as a middle-of-the-road list administered by two church members. It has a threshold of 65 posts per day, and interested persons can sign up on the Web. The list is monitored and anti-church postings are not allowed, although constructive criticism is.

Anderson's Unification Evangelism is the most conservative of the three list-servs. Other listservs exist, such as one for a select group identified as National Messiahs – people with missionary responsibilities in a foreign country. A popular theme for the NM listserv of primarily western members is the problems working with their Korean and Japanese counterparts. There have been some newsgroups, but currently most discussion is carried on through personal email or listservs. One reason for this is the hesitancy to have their views published for public consumption.

Other member Web pages (mostly from the U.S.) tend to be family oriented with pictures of the Webmasters' family. Teachings of the church are usually included in some form, but the pages vary considerably in additional content. Links to spiritual, religious or moral sites not directly connected with the Unification Church: Dr. Laura, Rush on-line, a speech by Charlton Heston, Shiatsu, Reiki and QiGong books with a link to Amazon.com; enneagrams and a Bible search are examples of the broad array of materials one can find. One member advertises his telecommunications business; another included writings of his children; another has personal commentaries on subjects such as Heaven's Gate, Allen Ginsberg and Tiger Woods. A known church musician/songwriter sells his recordings. Another enterprising member set up his own BFam server and sells space on it to church members.

In addition to the official church sites and unofficial member pages, there are numerous sites for the many church-related organizations. Those organizations that are directly affiliated with the church are identified as such on their Web page and have links to church sites. Organizations that are separate businesses or entities don't have links to church sites. Examples of the latter include *The Washington Times*. Like other newspapers it has news stories, stock quotes, and other related news information. Similarly, *The Middle East Times* has news relating to the Middle East. Paragon House Publishers has a sophisticated search function on its site. On the other hand, a site directly affiliated with the church is the Unification Theological Seminary. In the last two years it has expanded its Web presence to include long distance education for students throughout the country and around the world.

An important use of the Web by Unification Church members not yet mentioned is education – resources and activities for children. Those who home school their children have set up extensive home school resources. Others make Sunday School materials available on-line. Children are encouraged to use the Internet – send each other emails, visit the several sites set up for children, and make use of the Internet resources of information. At least one Second Generation (children of members) has established her own site – a youthful collection of talk and advice, testimonies and email addresses of other Second Generation.

In concluding this segment of the work, there are three things that are important to note about the development of the Unification Church presence on the Internet.

- First, those who used the Internet and initially set up pages with information about the church were not church officials but members who worked with computers and were technologically knowledgeable. The official Web sites came later and made use of the materials already available.
- Second, unlike Scientology, which seeks to control the use of symbols and pictures, there seems to be no attempt to regulate the use of materials on-line. In fact, access to files of the symbols, and photo files is quite free, including directions for importing them into a Web page.
- Third, there is no apparent effort to present a unified image to the world. Use of the Web by Unification members seems to reflect the decentralized development of the Web in general, perhaps leading to a variety of forums for people of different 'political' leanings (conservative versus liberal listservs).

FALUN GONG WEB USE

A very different use of the Internet is that of the Chinese group Falun Gong. Under the leadership of Hongshi Li, this group originating in Mainland China in 1992 as one of many Qigong groups of traditional meditation and exercise.

In 1996 Li disassociated his group from the government recognized Qigong Association because of the superficiality of the latter's emphasis on healing and "displays of supernormal powers." Li's goal is nothing less than 'spiritual enlightenment'. But outside the approved society, Li's group lacks legal protection and status.

The Chinese government subsequently cracked down on all Qigong practitioners, but especially Falun Gong. In April 1999, 10,000 Falun Gong adherents silently meditated in public to protest government treatment. According to Amnesty International, prior to banning the Falun Gong last July, approximately 21,000 Qigong practitioners were arrested. By late April 2000, news reports from China are that "defiant protests are a daily sight in Beijing's Tinananmen

Square." The group became international in 1994 when Li traveled outside China. He currently lives in New York State and the group claims 100 million practitioners in 30 countries around the world.

According to Jillian Ye, a volunteer in Toronto, all Web sites around the world are created and maintained by volunteers. Practitioners discover which sites are the best and refer others to them. At the moment the New York (http://falundafa.org) and Toronto (http://falundafa.net) sites are the most extensive and sophisticated, hence most often listed in the literature around the world as the main sites.

(Since the first writing, the following sites have changed, but the general content is the same). The New York site is professional, simple and easy to get around. A prominent link features a photo of the founder. 'Introduction' leads to a general explanation of the group. 'Start to Learn' includes an explanation of the practice with four steps of involvement: join a group practice, study Buddhism, study lectures of Master Li, and attend a 9-day workshop. The multimedia link leads to numerous real time audio clips of the founder's speeches. 'Books On-line' leads to a voluminous amount of material (several complete books) available for on-line viewing or zip file downloading in a variety of languages. Bookstores that have their materials around the world are also mentioned. There are repeated reminders to the reader that all activities and information is free.

The site also features 'Current News Regarding Falun Gong Around the World' and 'Falun Dafa Bulletin Board'. A notice dated June 1999 explains their legal situation in China.

> According to the media reports, the Central Committee of the chinese [sic] Communist Party recently held an emergency meeting regarding Falun Gong. They decided internally to categorize Falun Gong as an evil cult and developed a series of extreme procedures to sternly repress Falun Gong ... As a matter of fact, anyone who takes an objective look at the situation can see very clearly that the authorities have a big misunderstanding of Falun Gong.

The New York site is available in Chinese or English although the English sometimes gives the impression that it was first written (or spoken) by a non-English speaker. There are links to pages in 22 different countries in a variety of different languages. The Web addresses in the different countries are often the same except for the country code (e.g. .ca for Canada). Each country site generally also has the same four or five links – with the exception of the Multimedia link which most don't have. Still, the connection between the sites, languages and materials is seamless. Contact names, phone and fax numbers and email addresses are given for cities around the world.

Some national sites also have maps of the parks where followers meet to do their exercises in the early morning. For parks in Mainland China the message reads: "Too many to be listed. Falun Dafa practitioners can be found in public parks in all the cities every morning." For Iran, another government that is sensitive to religious practices, the contact is located in Sweden. The whole site appears to be updated frequently; the information available is recent. There are requests to send the Webmaster updates if they have missed an address or contact person. It is a truly international site.

The Web pages are important to new contacts, according to Ye. "A lot of people find out about us through the Web," she explained. Then they either contact someone, or go to the park for the practice. Half or more of the Falun Gong practitioners outside of China use the Internet. "I say half, because we have a lot of elderly people, and they may not use the Internet."

Email is a major means of communication between members. It was even more important in the beginning stages, when there were not a lot of practitioners nearby. "We were all eager to hear from others," Ye explained, so they emailed the Webmasters, and exchanged experiences. Now practitioners go to the annual conferences where they meet others, and subsequently keep in touch through email. Someone in Texas started a listserv about a year and a half ago – to enhance individual understanding and get inspiration from other practitioners. But some discussants became argumentative, insisting their views were right. According to Ye, each practitioner is required by Falun Gong to acknowledge that what they say is only their opinion, and may be wrong. The arguments went against the teaching. Many discussants recommended the list be shut down. After about six months, it was.

A major use of the Internet for Falun Gong is to publicize events in China and counter the Chinese government charges. The following appeared under 'Current News' on the New York site. March 2000

- Three fabricated Dafa articles are spreading in Guangdong Province and some other regions of southern China. The fabricator usurped the name of Minghui Web site to create confusion. This is because many practitioners can not log on to Minghui, while others did not pay attention to the warning message on Minghui against rumors before encountering fabricated Dafa articles.
- Yu Hui, a practitioner in Shenzhen, was sentenced to one-year labor camp for insisting on practicing Falun Gong.
- A Dafa disciple in Shenzhen, was detained in Futian Detention Center on suspicion of sending the above mentioned two articles to Minghui Web site for publishing.
- In late February, one practitioner was beaten for going on hunger strike. Another practitioner was beaten also because he tried to offer some explanation in the other's behalf. [Their] screams could be heard all across the cells.

- Xia Hai, a graduate student of, 26 years old was sent to the Xinhua Labor-reform Farm for labor-education due to appealing to the Central Government in Beijing on behalf of Falun Gong. [The] prison administrators only allow him ... an extremely thin quilt at night
- Ms. Guozhen Su was sent to a labor camp ... for two and a half years because she ... appealed to the Central Government on behalf of Falun Gong. No one is taking care of her [blind, old] mother.
- More than 3000 Falun Gong practitioners who were sentenced to one-year labor education ... in the Heizuizi Female Jail in Changchun City. [They] were physically abused and forced to work.

The New York and Toronto sites include reports from western news agencies. A Reuters report describes their protest outside the U.N. buildings in Geneva. An Agence France Press report describes the situation of foreign journalists in China: "Foreign journalists have been routinely followed around the city throughout the NPC [National People's Congress] meeting to prevent them meeting with Falun Gong members, triggering a complaint from the Beijing Foreign Correspondents Club." The New York site also has an appeal to journalists. "Please do not use the pejorative vocabulary of the Chinese Government in describing Falun Gong as a cult or sect. It is neither. It is not an organization, not a political group and has no structure. All activities are conducted by volunteers."

The Webmaster of the New York site defends Falun Gong.

Falun Gong practitioners cultivate their Xinxing, and behave as good people. They absolutely do not participate in politics nor oppose against the government. Over one hundred million good people have contributed to the social stability of china [sic], enabled the morality level of chinese [sic] society to re-ascend, and greatly improved peoples' health which has saved a tremendous amount of medical expenses for the government ... Why is it dictatorially attacked as an 'evil cult' and categorized as a target to be outlawed? Why was the rumor of so called 'Xiangshan Mass Suicide' started deliberately?

There are also defensive statements by Hongzhi Li, and an appeal for assistance.

'Some people have spread rumors that I deceived people by changing my date of birth. During the Cultural Revolution, the government misprinted my date of birth. All I did was simply to replace the misprinted date of birth with the correct one. As for the fact that Buddha Sakyamuni was also born on this day, what does that have to do with me? Many other people were also born on this day. In addition, I have never claimed that I am Sakyamuni ... We are calling for all governments, international organizations, and people of goodwill worldwide to extend their support and assistance to us in order to resolve the current crisis in China'.

Another Falun Gong site, identified as a Witness Page, has testimonies from practitioners. A Chinese man educated and employed in the U.S. returned for a visit to China after learning Falun Gong. His story gives further insight about the situation in China, and demonstrates an important use of the Internet.

> I first met a few Beijing practitioners ... [They now] stayed home alone and seldom discussed and shared experiences with others. Later ... practitioners came to Beijing from other provinces ... Dozens of practitioners lived together in a big room, studying and discussing Fa together everyday ... Some of them went to study and practice at Tiananmen Square ... A dozen practitioners were detained everyday. [A]nother dozen practitioners came to Beijing from other provinces [to replace them] ... Some went to the Tiananmen Square directly ... Some studied Fa ... first, because they felt that they still had some attachments to let go of. They would go out once they felt there was nothing to be feared.

The man went to a conference in the Province of Guangyuan where practitioners shared their experiences of going to Beijing. Their stories were described as 'moving'. Attendees then each wrote their experiences to be read aloud. "Each draft was read several times. We were all moved to tears by the authors' realm of cultivation while listening to it." After the conference the man went back to Beijing, and Tiananmen Square where he was arrested and tortured for several days.

> Later on I returned to America after I got my passport back. Before I came back to America, the government officials and my family members persuaded me repeatedly not to speak about the fact that I had been beaten and tortured by the police. I thought then that it was impossible. Tens of millions of Falun Gong practitioners have been persecuted, tens of thousands of them have been beaten and tortured by the police. Few of them had any chance to speak out the fact to the rest of the world, how could I withhold the fact for the protection of my family and myself?

Even though the number of people who use the Internet in China has decreased since the ban on their group last year, it is still a very important means of communication. The Chinese government has tried to block Internet communication. They have blocked access to major Falun Gong sites (Chinese practitioners cannot access them). They have shut down Web sites created and maintained by Mainland Chinese, and arrested the Webmasters. And they block email to and from China if it has anything relating to Falun Gong in the address or subject lines. Just after the ban, the two free email servers in China were both shut down. Despite all of this, messages still get through, and Falun Gong practitioners continue to defy the government. (Since the first writing, editors of the http://clearwisdom.net have encouraged the practitioners to set up web sites, mirror sites, and to repost articles so that material is not lost. "everytime we reach a historically critical period, the site is viciously attacked. This was the case on July 20th ... it has undeniably created many inconveniences in terms of the flow of information ...").

GENERAL CHARACTERISTICS OF INTERNET USE BY RELIGIOUS GROUPS

Information and communication are the specialty of the Internet. And these two factors describe the key usage of the Internet by religious groups. Communication can be divided into communication with those outside the group, and communication within the group. Information is more or less covered by communication – but there are some aspects that warrant a separate category as well. The following is a typology of communication and information usage of the Internet by the religious groups examined.

EXTERNAL COMMUNICATION

1. Evangelical Outreach

Almost all of the sites and pages have an evangelistic element, more or less prominently displayed according to the nature of the group. Each group, however subtly, is advertising a way of life and a religious practice to which they are inviting others to join. This is especially true of the official pages. Evangelism is part of the Mormon encouragement to use the Internet. It is overtly stated as the purpose of the Unification Evangelism listserv. It is obvious in the 15,000 Scientology member pages each with the same links to related organizations. It is seen in the use of the most sophisticated and extensive sites as official pages in Falun Gong. Even the Vatican page, while not directly evangelical, is certainly not contrary. In conclusion, evangelism is a major motivation for the investment of time and money on Web pages for all the groups.

Some groups are having success in their Internet outreach. Nick Literski, whose site is not intended to be evangelistic, frequently gets evangelistic requests. Non-members contact Damian Anderson through his Web site and through his mailing lists. Web sites are a recognized way for people to find out about Falun Gong. Success at Internet outreach is less obvious in the case of Catholics and Scientology, but it is safe to assume that they too get requests from persons interested to know more about their beliefs. The mere presence on the Internet is enough to reach at least some people.

Whether people are actually converted through their Internet experience is another matter. It is more likely that published materials, including testimonies and other accounts, provide the impetus for an uninitiated individual to seek personal contact with someone. Nick Literski refers individuals to others. Those who contact Falun Gong are encouraged to meet with others to practice meditation or to attend a workshop. Scientology has photos of their church centers, a sort of invitation to come and visit. No one indicated that the Internet information is sufficient in itself for a religious experience.

2. Publicity/ Public Relations

(1) Closely related to evangelism is *public relations strategy.* Some sites have Press Office links prominently featured on the first page (Mormon and Vatican). Those without such a link have similar material easily accessible – basic facts about the group, summary of beliefs, summary of history, news about current projects and events.

(2) A very important aspect of publicity is *countering negative publicity.* Like evangelism, and even publicity, this is more obvious on some pages than in others. It is impossible to spend any time on the Scientology site without encountering "their side of the story" about events in Germany or their explanation as to why they receive negative publicity. The Mormon site has a link specifically addressing misconceptions. The Unification Church has news about anti-cult activity, and Damian Anderson has his multi-volume "Responses to questions about Unificationism on the Internet" where he counters a variety of charges. The Falun Gong sites publish material about their activities in China and state their side of the issues in a variety of pages on the New York site.

(3) Another equally important aspect of publicity is *activism – campaigns and promotion of values* important to the group. Mormons have a Family Resources Link. The Vatican page features links related to Lent and Jubilee Events. Scientologists promote their causes in a variety of places and ways on their site. The Unification site promotes family values as much or more than its own ideology. To that extent, member pages freely promote a variety of related sites including those having to do with abstinence, and family values. Unification member pages link up to a variety of non-church related sites that promote corresponding values.

3. Directories, addresses and contact information

Every group maintains some sort of address/contact list, indicating an important use of the Internet. In some ways, these lists are less important for external communication than they are for internal communication (see below). Locations of meeting places, email addresses and phone numbers of contact persons are regularly included on sites of all groups – some more openly than others. Anyone wanting to contact someone from the group can, in most cases, select the type of person they want to contact by viewing page contents where their address appears. For Falun Gong, individual contact through the Internet is less important than the location of the parks where practitioners meet. It is likely that media personnel and academic researchers would also make use of the address lists to note demographic characteristics about the group. Frequently the Internet-published directories are more up to date and comprehensive, as well as being more available, than published hardcopies.

4. Legitimization

An important function of publishing material on the Web is legitimization. Small groups can easily be dismissed by others as inconsequential because of the few number of people in any one place. A group that is 0.01% of the total U.S. population would have a presence of approximately 10 people in a community of 100,000. But their presence on the Internet is unrelated to the number of people associated with them. The Religious Tolerance site, for instance (www.religioustolerance.org; see B. Robinson in this volume), is maintained by a handful of people. Yet the extensiveness of the site (and reliability of the information) gives it a considerable presence. Similarly, small groups that represent only a handful of people in any one locale, can 'gather' on Internet sites and just in terms of numbers, make an impressive showing. If the Web site is sophisticated, extensive, and interesting – the group's existence can be legitimated in virtual space in a way that it never would be otherwise.

Similarly, groups that receive negative publicity – for whatever reason, can tell their side of the issue in a format that reaches far more people than any other communication medium. That is, groups have a chance to 'set the record straight' through the use of the Internet in a way that they cannot do elsewhere.

INFORMATION SHARING

1. Publication of religious texts/material

Although related to external communication, this use of the Web is more impersonal. The extensiveness of materials available goes far beyond simply communicating with others outside the group. All the groups examined here, except Scientology, offered *completed volumes of texts* on-line, many in a variety of languages. In the case of the Bible, numerous translations and versions are available on-line, including those in several dozen different languages, as well as Greek and Hebrew texts, and ancient texts. All material is offered as a public service, free of charge. Some material is formatted in .zip files for easy downloading. This availability of texts is in keeping with information on the Web in general.

Related texts are also available on-line. The Apocrypha, at least some of the Dead Sea Scrolls, and a variety of early Christian texts can be found on various sites. Other groups have a wealth of related materials available, as well. Among the groups studied here, Catholics, Mormons, Unification Church and Falun Gong all have extensive pages of material.

In addition to published volumes, there are *commentaries* on almost every topic of concern. Similar to official explanations, commentaries represent individual interpretations of the belief system. They are different from informal communication in that they are a more organized and systematic delineation of thought. There are entire sites devoted to commentary – theology and apologetics. Commentary is available through links on a number of sites, including the official sites.

2. Study Aids: Bible Searches/Text Searches/Concordances

Most sites with published texts have search functions available (Mormons, Unification Church, Falun Gong, Catholics). Like the traditional Christian groups that access Bible searches and concordances, the five groups studied here also make use of this computer function. Study of the Biblical and religious texts, whether for individual meditation, sermons, or academic purposes is an important use of the Internet. Access to these searches is convenient, cheap, and likely to be more extensive than a search using published materials. Some searches are for phrases as well as individual words. Concordances and other Bible study aids are also available.

3. Mormon Genealogy

Publication of other material, such as the genealogy records of the Church of Jesus Christ of Latter-day Saints (Mormons) is also important. Belief in spirit baptism has led to some of the most extensive genealogical records in the world made available to the public. This information is used by the general public. In addition to genealogical records, there are links to other records, search engines and programs available to the user, some free, some for a fee.

4. Sale of Material

Most of the religious sites have material available for sale – ranging from publications to momentos and gifts. In the case of Falun Gong, the seller for the material is Amazon.com or another bookseller. In the case of the Vatican, the user is referred to local sales sites. Neither of these two sites intend to make a profit on sales. Scientology, on the other hand, has material available in many places. Most other official sites have a book store with on-line material for sale from their offices.

INTERNAL COMMUNICATION

1. Directories, addresses and contact information

Internal communication is similar to external communication, although the purpose is different. For instance, directories. These lists have more importance to group members than to those outside the group. They are a means of contacting each other, a means of locating someone, etc. This is an especially useful aspect of Internet use for religious groups that have an international or widely dispersed membership.

2. Official dissemination of material: Policy/Directives/Doctrine

The Vatican site is the clearest example of using the Web for disseminating information. All the recent news, directives and announcements are available in a variety of languages for the congregants who are dispersed worldwide.

Another international organization, the Mormon site publishes the news from their major conferences in a variety of different languages. It also uses live video broadcasts for members who cannot attend the conferences in person.

International dissemination of information is found in the Korean site of the Unification Church, where there is a log-in page for missionaries. The Unification site also reports church news and offers live video broadcasts of events in Korea. The WorldTies mailing list provides another way for Unification Church members to learn the major church directives and announcements.

For the Falun Gong, news from around the world is probably one of the most important aspects for members who would like to keep abreast of events in China.

It is likely that dissemination of official directives or announcements through the Internet is likely to be more important to groups that have a dispersed membership. But official contact with members is important even to those located within a specific area. This is especially true of published texts and materials. It is likely that members more than non-members use them. Text searches, whether for inspiration or academic, are likewise probably more used by members than non-members. Even the bookstore offerings are likely to appeal more to members than non-members.

3. Discussion Among Members

Discussion among members is a very important function of the Internet for religious groups. Some of the discussion is public, published on the newsgroup pages. Other discussion is through private, perhaps monitored, listservs. And a third means of discussion among members is through email – as described by Jillian Ye of Falun Gong.

4. Published Testimonies

Related to discussion among members, is the publication of testimonies of members. These non-interactive accounts are generated by the membership, intended for anyone who will 'listen', but primarily for internal consumption and for conversion. They appear on individual pages, on listservs, and on mailing lists. They have an experiential quality even though they do not appear in 'real time'. As a standard part of religion, testimonies are intended to inspire others to a deeper faith and commitment.

5. Sharing Resources/Web resources

A major use of the Internet by group members is to share resources. This use ranges from individuals who sell various products on-line to helping others set up Web pages and information on using the Internet. There is also a lively dissemination of economic enterprise information among members of some groups, particularly the Unification Church, through email, listservs, or published on individuals' homepages. Announcements, and bulletin board sharing is also prominent. Members with frequent computer access keep others informed about sites promoting their causes. One notable sharing of resources is Web programs and filters. Several Christian organizations sell Internet filters for concerned parents. Related are Internet locations for members to put up Web pages, or receive email.

6. Education

Members of religious groups who home school their children use the Internet for education in many different ways – as a source of general information as well as to contact other homeschoolers (both adult-teachers and students). Parents and teachers who are not involved in home school make use of the

Internet for dissemination of Sunday school material, and other educational opportunities with the particular moral bent that is important to them.

7. Daily Inspirations/Prayer Requests

A unique use of the Internet by religious group is the growth of inspirational mailing lists. These are lists run by a member who selects inspirational readings to send at regular intervals to all those on the mailing list. Like the testimonies, although not in 'real time', these have an experiential effect, in that they are intended to inspire the reader to a deeper faith or increased commitment.

HOW THE INTERNET HAS CHANGED RELIGION

We started out asking how the Information Revolution has impacted religion. After examining use of the Internet by several groups, and developing a typology of use, we are in a better position to comment. Using the common components of religion – beliefs, ritual, experience or subjective involvement, and religious community (McGuire, 1997) – it is not hard to see all of them are or will be changed.

1. *Beliefs are impacted by the vast published resources on the We*b, including published texts as well as commentaries.

In some ways, the amount of material commonly available because of the Internet parallels the immediacy of Christian teachings to the common person when the Bible was translated into the vernacular. Knowledge is no longer the privilege of the elite but is available to anyone who has the time and interest to search for it.

The impact of this may well lead to a Personal Reformation similar to the Protestant Reformation. Individual congregants can now develop their own theology supported by a variety of information, official and otherwise. Those in remote locales and countries are less dependent upon others for access to published texts, searches and commentaries. They no longer have to wait for hand-carried materials, or mail service, but can access information directly. Remote members may end up being more informed since they are more reliant upon the medium.

Just as published materials are more available, however, so are the contrary arguments and anti-material. Anyone using the Internet is likely to encounter material that is hostile to his or her beliefs. Isolation from these negative opinions is not possible. The ramifications of these encounters could go either way – influence believers to lose their faith, or make their faith stronger.

2. *Religious community is perhaps more affected by the Internet than other components of religion.*

For those on the net, one's community is no longer the immediate physical locale. Computer communication makes daily contact with people anywhere in the world a possibility. Those that one 'meets' through listservs, discussion pages, bulletin boards, homepages, announcements, etc., can be part of an immediate personal community (Wellman, 1999).

A larger community means larger groups of like-minded members. An individual who is a minority within their own locale may be part of a substantial subgroup in the larger community. The Internet provides a way to meet and interact with this subgroup. Members who 'meet' over the Internet, however, are likely to establish themselves through common real life experiences – acquaintances, events, group activities – as a means of verifying membership and trustworthiness.

For international groups that are small and mobile, the Internet provides an important and convenient forum for interaction. It is less a case of 'meeting' people in a distant country than maintaining contact with those one already knows. This is particularly true for some countries, such as the former USSR. In the predominantly Muslim countries near China, the Internet and phone are the main means of communication, since mail is unreliable or non-existent.

The expansion of the community does not seem to spell the end of the importance of contact with others. To the contrary, it appears to be more important than ever. Neither does it seem to replace face to face experiences with others. So Durkheim's cult of the individual notwithstanding, it seems that Internet communities will not replace real time community experiences. Rather the two augment each other.

3. *Experience or subjective involvement is impacted through the information available.*

Whereas the Web material is unlikely to convince anyone who does not want to be convinced, it is a powerful resource for the novice. Potential believers can read and study religious material on-line, using it to help them make important decisions, which are likely to then be shared with others. The exception is the category of testimonies.

With a larger religious community from which to draw, more dramatic testimonies are available to a larger group of members. Since the purpose of a testimony is to 'move' the listener to new levels of faith, each reader may be led to an 'experience' while reading, with no one else around. Another exception could be the inspirational mailings. Whether they actually lead to an experience, the intention is a form of cyber-devotional.

4. *Even ritual is impacted by the information revolution, although less than the other components of religion.*

Those who replace attendance at church or religious meetings with Internet participation may be few. Take, for instance, Falun Gong. Although the Internet is a vital part of conveying information about their organization, adherents still meet daily to practice their faith. And though some may first contact the group through the Internet, indicators point to a personal follow up. Conversion and group loyalties are likely to develop in person.

There are other groups that we have not examined in depth who are known to have a high percentage that use the computer. Wicca, for instance, is said to be exceptionally computer literate. But even they meet periodically and in person, although they maintain active Internet communication. There are some so-called cyber churches, offering a place for the user to worship in solitude. But as is the case with the groups examined, it is likely that few participate to any great extent. Internet participation in religious matters doesn't seem to eliminate real time worship and meetings.

But there are two ways the Internet is likely to impact religious ritual. First, the availability of detailed knowledge of so many different forms of worship is likely to lead to a greater blending of traditions. Examples might include the use of meditation by charismatics, or the use of testimonies by the more reclusive groups, or evangelism by groups that normally view faith as an internal phenomenon that is kept to oneself. A second probable impact on ritual is likely to be seen in cyber devotionals – such as the Mormon listserv of daily quotes, Damian Anderson's Unification Texts, or even the inspirational messages on the pages of priests and nuns. The extent to which they replace traditional devotional practices is, of course, yet to be seen.

CONCLUSION

Those most affected by the Internet are obviously those who use it. However even those who do not use it are affected by it indirectly through availability of information and contact with others in remote locations. Use of the Internet for communication and information has broadened the religious community. The immediacy and ease of transmission offers a wide audience means of not only learning about each other, but actually 'speaking' with each other and sharing resources a variety of resources, from inspirational texts, historical information, genealogical information, music, artwork.

NOTES

1. CHURCH LOCATORS http://www.church-profiles.com; http://www.christianity.net/ churchlocator http://www.netchurch.com; http://www.churches.net/churches; http:// www.netministries.org/churches.htm

2. ON-LINE BIBLES: On-line Bible: http://www.on-linebible.simplenet.com Jesus Saves: http://JESUSaves.com/bible World Wide Study Bible: http://ccel.wheaton.edu/ wwsb Bible Gateway: http://bible.gospelcom.net etexts at University of Virginia: http://etext.virginia.edu/rsv.browse.html On-line Chinese and English Bible: http://www. ccim.org/~bible Virtual Church Web Bible: http://www.Internetdynamics.com/pub/vc/ bibles.html

3. BIBLE SEARCHES/CONCORDANCES: Bible Gateway: http://bible.gospelcom.net Bible Browser Basic Home Page: http://www.biblesearch.com University of Virginia etexts: http://etext.virginia.edu The Unbound Bible: http://unbound.biola.edu Search the Bible: http://supernet.net/~chrisd/home/bible.html

4. WEB HOSTS: http://www.netchurch.com http://church-on-line.com http://www. churchlink.com http://www.churchesontheWeb.com

5. http://www.ldstemplepage.org/index.html

6. Information for this section came from discussions with Scientologists and Webmasters as well as surveys of Internet pages.

7. Details of this controversy are complex. Even those involved admit to hazy points. For Scientology's explanation, see: http://cti.itc.virginia.edu/~jkh8k/soc257/nrms/ scientology_briefing.html For further information, see:http://bernie.cncfamily.com/ legal.htm

8. On November 12, 1999, Anderson gave the following subscriber numbers: WorldTies 1315, TFV News 1288, Unification Texts 678, World Scripture 406, Unification Evangelism 556.

REFERENCES

McGuire, M. (1997). *Religion: The Social Context.* Belmont, CA: International Thompson Publishing Co.

Wellman, B. (1999). *Networks in the Global Village.* Boulder, Colorado: Westview Press.

DISPATCHES FROM THE ELECTRONIC FRONTIER: EXPLORATIONS OF MAINLINE PROTESTANT USES OF THE INTERNET

Ken Bedell

ABSTRACT

This chapter presents the results of nearly a year searching Web sites for evidence that people are actively using the Internet to create new ways of supporting or enhancing their spiritual life or their participation in spiritual communities. The thesis guiding this inquiry was that emerging activities outside of traditional institutions would provide pointers to trends in religious expression and spiritual community formation. My conclusions are: (1) people are eagerly adopting Internet solutions to communication problems of existing religious interest or commitments, (2) they think of religion as one of the countless topics that can be researched on the Internet and, (3) they expect the Internet will play an important role in religious life in the future. Contrary to what I anticipated, there was little evidence of widespread use of the Internet to form new religious communities or to support new spiritual practices.

Religion on the Internet, Volume 8, pages 183–203.
Copyright © 2000 by Elsevier Science Inc.
All rights of reproduction in any form reserved.
ISBN: 0-7623-0535-5

INTRODUCTION

This is a report on almost ten months of looking at the Internet, asking people to engage in conversation about their experiences and observations, and trying to figure out the extent and nature of religion on the Internet. Even though there is the appearance of using traditional social science methodologies such as questionnaires, focus groups, and interviews, data was not gathered from representative samples, so statistical tools of analysis cannot be used to make generalizations about larger populations. The methodology of this applied research project included using tools developed by futures researchers and qualitative researchers.

This is a report on an ethnographic study. It is really anthropology rather than sociology. I saw myself as a visitor to the electronic world of the Internet where I wanted to try to understand not only what people are currently experimenting with, but what the potential is and where the promise lies. So this is a report on a visit. As I wandered around in the environment of the Internet, I counted things, I took extensive notes, I coded and analyzed, I made a tentative conclusion and asked for feedback.

The report is organized around four general observations that reflect my findings and conclusions. For each, I offer the reasons that shaped my observations and, when available, data to support my belief that the generalization were worthy of consideration. Each observation is followed with a discussion of what I see as the implications of the issue for people who are engaged in planning or designing Internet applications for religious organizations. The project, thus, is firmly grounded in applied social science research for established religious traditions.

DESCRIPTION OF THE PROJECT

The project was grounded in a number of assumptions and a hunch about both the Internet and the nature of religious activity. These included the following five assumptions:

(1) Individuals and organizations are increasingly integrating the Internet into their daily lives and organizational processes.
(2) The flexibility and accessibility of the Internet allow initiatives to come from a variety of sources and the Internet allows people to respond to those initiatives outside traditional channels.
(3) Because the Internet is accessible and many aspects are public, it is possible to look at public activities to observe ways that individuals and organizations are using the Internet for activities related to religion.

(4) Internet activity involves millions of people so a Web site where individuals could complete a questionnaire to tell us about how they use the Internet for religious related activity could be used to identify the types of activity people are engaged in on the Internet related to religion.

(5) Since using the Internet to ask people about their use of the Internet and expectations from the Internet may bias results, talking to people on the telephone may allow them to provide a more objective report on their own experiences or expectations.

The hunch was that people are actively using the Internet to create new ways of supporting or enhancing their spiritual life or their participation in spiritual communities. I thought that while institutional religion searches for ways to fit the Internet into current patterns of religious institutional culture, new forms of religious activity would emerge outside these institutions. My hunch, also, was that these emerging activities would provide pointers to trends in religious expression and spiritual community formation.

THE RESEARCH STRATEGY

(1) I set up a Web site where the project was described and two questionnaires were posted to collect data from anyone who found the site and was willing to fill out the forms. The site also included a guest book for people to register with the project. The questionnaires and most of the descriptive information about the project were translated into Spanish so the site was bilingual. More than 600 people filled out questionnaires and more than 350 people registered with the project.

(2) A search of the Internet was conducted using several search engines to find Web sites that related to religion. A database was developed that consisted of more than 350 sites that were not sponsored by local congregations or denominations. Email messages were sent to individuals responsible for the sites asking them to respond to our provider questionnaire and to help us recruit people to respond to the questionnaire.

(3) The Web address for the questionnaire was posted on several denominational Web sites including the United Methodist and the Christian Church (Disciples of Christ) sites. The United Methodist News Service distributed a news release about the research. National Public Radio aired a description of the project including the Web site address. The Web site address was included in articles in the *Pittsburgh Post-Gazette* newspaper and the *United Methodist Reporter*. On the Internet, the address for the Web questionnaire was posted on several mailing lists.

(4) United Methodist Communications provided data on activity at their site, The Upper Room; and Stephen Rose also provided activity information. The 350 sites on the database were searched for information about activity on those sites.

(5) Software to download related sites was used to develop an off-line set of data from theological schools, students and faculty at the University of Chicago and St. Louis University. These databases are the text of Web pages and were used for text analysis.

(6) A mailing list was set up to serve as a focus group to discuss issues raised by the research and to obtain feedback from Internet users. People who visited the Web site for the project were recruited to participate in the discussion.

(7) An on-line international discussion organized by Peter Horshfield in Australia was monitored. This discussion called xt-mediaculture focused on theoretical issues related to the subject of this research and provided a window into the thinking of several academics.

(8) Interviews were conducted with 50 people over the telephone. Most of these interviews were with people who provided telephone numbers when they registered with the project.

Generalization No. 1: Internet is being used by religious people

People are eagerly adopting Internet solutions to communication problems of existing religious interest or commitments. Increasingly email is replacing or enhancing communication by telephone, mail and fax. The computer is seen in an instrumental sense of making it possible to communicate more easily, more clearly, and less expensively.

In telephone interview after telephone interview people told me about their individual use of the Internet to facilitate communication. A pastor told me that he received an invitation to preach at a neighboring congregation by email. The negotiations were made by email and all arrangements for the service were conducted by email. Another person looked in his email directory and reported that he has about ninety addresses of people that he occasionally corresponds with, but there are ten or twelve with whom he regularly communicates. A person who works with religious educators told me that at first she was reluctant to start using email, but now finds it to be invaluable as a way to connect with people across the country. I heard stories about email that was received by a retired seminary professor after major surgery.

Responses to the questions about personal email and public email that related to prayer requests were almost identical. It did not seem to matter to people whether they learned about a prayer request from a public source like a web page or from a personal email message.

It appears that the Internet is being adopted as a place where the distinction between public and private sources of information is somewhat blurred. If not blurred, then both are being taken with equal seriousness. One person I interviewed told about sending email to the author of a book that she read. In reading the book she learned the public presentation of the author, but in exchanging email she entered into a more direct relationship with the author. As she pointed out, this use of the Internet was beyond what she would usually do. She would not likely telephone the author of a book that she read. If she did write a letter, she would not expect a personal response. In this case the Internet enhanced her communication about a religious topic.

A survey of ECUNET (a denominational sponsored private email system) users that was conducted by the ECUNET board provides additional evidence that people in the religious community find email to be extremely useful. One ECUNET user sent me an email message when she learned about the research explaining that she had not used the Internet because ECUNET meets all her needs.

At the moment the use of computer communication may be limited to a small percent of all the participants in religious organizations. However, their enthusiasm suggests the use of this technology will continue to increase. I heard only two cautions:

- the volume of communication can become so great that strategies need to be developed to determine which messages to respond to or even read, and
- electronic communication is not a complete replacement for face-to-face meeting or other forms of communication.

It seems reasonable to assume that computer aided communication through email is not just a fad or a phenomenon supported by a small number of enthusiasts or hobbyists. An article in The Futurist magazine (Hallal, Kull & Leffman, 1997, p. 27) reports that a panel of the George Washington University forecast group predicts that by 2008 about 80% of all people in industrialized nations will have access to the Internet.

Implications

It may seem obvious that religious people are using email extensively. I offer this observation first because it has immediate, if short term, implications for denominational and other planners.

While this report is being written, ECUNET is in the midst of trying to determine its own future. ECUNET has pioneered efforts to make a computer communication system useful for church workers and others. It provided two important functions. First, ECUNET offered a reasonably priced system for people to have access to email that included a user-friendly interface. Secondly, it provided an on-line community where church people could discover ways to use email for individual communication and group discussion.

Today obtaining access to email is not a problem. JUNO is one example of many services where anyone with a computer, modem and a telephone line can receive a free email account. In many places a free telephone number is available to use to send and receive email. Some places require a long distance telephone call to access the otherwise free service. Increasingly, public access to the Internet is available free of charge at public libraries. Anyone who can go to one of these computers can obtain a free email address. With a personal (and completely free to the user) HOTMAIL account anyone can send and receive email. These are just two of the many ways that individuals can obtain access to their own email account. All this is to say that church leaders do not need to worry about the issue of how to make email available. The only thing they might do is to inform people, especially economically disadvantaged people, about the possibilities that are available to them.

There are two areas where denominational leadership is needed. The first is in intentionally training and supporting the use of email on the part of church leaders and pastors. It appears to make a big difference if denominational leadership and resources are used to encourage the development of electronic communication skills.

A comparison of the United Methodist Church and the Presbyterian Church illustrates this. The Presbyterian Church for more than a decade has encouraged national, regional and local staff to learn how to use electronic communication. They provided economic support to greatly reduce the cost of using email for all Presbyterians. The result is extensive use of PRESBYNET across the church and the integration of email as central to communication across the denomination. In contrast the United Methodist Church 'officially' participated in ECUNET, but did not develop a church wide program to encourage denominational leaders to use email nor provide economic incentives to United Methodists. The result is that United Methodist denominational staff have been slower to pick up the use of email and United Methodist pastors and lay leadership is not as well connected as Presbyterians are.

The second place where denominational leadership is needed is to ensure that easy-to-use chat room and mailing list software is available to the denomination and to local congregations. Supporting this activity at the denomination is quite easy. However, local congregations need a great deal of help at this point to understand how to use this technology to support their work. Thousands of congregations are setting up homepages to support or describe their ministries. It is very easy for them to obtain space on the Internet to post these sites. However, obtaining access to easy to use mailing list software is much more difficult at this point.

What is needed is a system for local congregations that would provide many of the functions at a local church level that ECUNET provided at a denominational level. The system needs to be designed with an awareness of the advances in technology that have occurred since ECUNET was conceived. But local churches have similar needs to those that originally drove the creation of ECUNET. There are groups of people who can benefit from increased communication and contact. For example, a church school class or a youth group can exchange messages and keep in touch between regular weekly meetings. There are people who live at a distance but want to keep connected, like young people in college or the military. There are some cases where connections across boundaries are enriching such as community interfaith discussions just like ECUNET fosters ecumenical discussions.

Beyond the local congregational uses that are similar to ECUNET's purposes, recent technology makes it possible to design local congregational systems that foster the development of community and intimacy within the congregation. Recently, some congregations have found that a pictorial directory is helpful in keeping people connected. With the Internet this concept could be greatly expanded so that information is available about members, for members.

Generalization No. 2: People expect religious information to be on the web

> People think of religion as one of the topics that can be researched on the Internet. Internet research has two senses. First, there is the search for the answer to a question of fact. Second, is the exploring of an unknown area of knowledge. Just like people expect to find religious topics as part of an encyclopedia, they expect to find them on the Internet.

When people were asked in the questionnaire to rank the importance of possible uses of the Internet by a local congregation, the items related to distribution of information floated to the top. Eighty-three percent of the respondents said that they value having the local congregation provide information about services and programs. This was the most popular item on the list. Less than 20% thought this information is not a priority.

More than 99% of the respondents who have access to the World Wide Web said that they look for information about religion on the Internet. Almost one fourth report that they look for information on a daily basis.

Most of this desire for religious information appears to be from the same tradition that people belong to. Forty-seven percent of the same group of people say that they hardly ever or never look for information about religious traditions

Table 1. Possible Use of the Internet by Congregations

Possible congregational use of the Internet	Total % indicating importance	Top priority	In top 3 priorities	Not in priority list
Display information about services and programs	89	40	64	20
Distribute announcements to members	80	21	48	33
Request prayer and other support for those in need	71	10	26	47
Keep in contact with members who are unable to leave their residences	63	4	21	59
Distribute information about the history or traditions of the congregation	61	6	25	58
Sign-up for events or register for meetings	60	2	11	61
Keep in contact with people who have moved away	58	2	10	69
Display information about staff or members	56	1	14	68
Distribute information about people who are hospitalized or have special needs	55	4	22	61
Publish the church directory with members email addresses	53	5	18	64
Distribute sacred writings, scriptures or other religious literature	53	7	19	67
Tell faith stories or testimonies of members	50	3	14	69
Conduct educational classes	42	2	14	74
Evaluations of worship or programs	37	1	4	85
Conduct business meetings	24	1	4	91
Conduct worship or spiritual meetings	22	4	7	87

(Note: First column is percent of respondents who indicated the item is important. Other columns are also in percent of respondents.)

that are not their own. This suggests that many people are only interested in being able to find information about their own tradition.

The questionnaire asked people to rank the importance of national or denominational Internet services. Here providing information was extremely important. Respondents wanted to be able to get news about religious organizations from the Internet. They also wanted to be able to get information about social action and relief opportunities. Somewhat lower on the list was information to help them fulfill responsibilities in local congregations.

Table 2. Percent of Respondents who Look for
Information about Other Traditions

Do you ever look for information on the World Wide Web about religious traditions that are not your own?	
8	Never
39	Hardly ever
34	More than 12 times a year
11	More than 4 times a month
5	More than 3 times a week
3	Most every day

This hunger for information was almost universal. At all levels of church organization people expect that they can find answers to questions on the Internet and they expect religious organizations to provide it. Only 11% of the survey respondents thought that they would not use a large religious library on the Internet.

There was much less unanimity regarding paying for publications on the Internet. Almost 20% did not have an opinion about paying for publications on the Internet. Two-thirds of respondents did not want to pay for on-line publications or wanted to pay less for on-line publications than for printed publications. Even though only 13% were willing to pay the same or more for the publications, there was a great deal of interest in using the Internet for research.

It was surprising to see how often the word research came up in interviews. When I asked people exactly what they meant by research they often seemed surprised that I would ask. They were talking about finding the answers to questions and learning about specific topics. This appears to be a different vision of the Internet than Bill Gates has in mind in his book *The Road Ahead*. There he talks about the similarity between the Internet and television. After explaining that television is just enhanced radio he writes, "But no broadcast medium we have right now is comparable to the communications media we'll have once the Internet evolves to the point at which it has the broadband capacity necessary to carry high-quality video" (Gates, 1996, p. 72). He thinks the power of interaction on the Internet is the ability to choose what entertainment to purchase that is then delivered over the Internet. This seems very different from research.

Implications

As Jon Katz concluded in his *Wired* Magazine report on a survey of Americans related to technology:

Table 3. National Religious Organizational Use of the Internet

National Religious Use	Total % indicating importance	Top priority	In top 3 priorities	Not in priority list
News about the activities of religious organizations or religious leaders	81	16	35	50
Information about social action or relief opportunities offered by religious organizations	79	6	32	43
Resources for personal study	76	7	23	54
The official pronouncements or press releases from religious organizations	71	7	18	57
Information about the organizational structure of religious organizations with addresses, phone numbers and email addresses	70	9	25	54
Calendars with information about future meetings	69	3	16	65
Resources for leadership in a religious organization	67	5	18	60
Resources for teaching in a religious or church Sabbath school	65	5	17	65
Resources for daily personal devotionals	65	7	24	61
Religious teachings from the perspective of a particular tradition	58	9	21	65
The address and times of meetings or worship services of local congregations	57	10	17	69
Daily text inspirational message or stories	56	15	24	67
Calendars with public appearances of religious leaders	45	0	4	88
Statistics about membership, attendance or finances	38	2	7	85
Daily audio inspirational messages or stories	26	2	5	92
Daily video inspirational messages or stories	20	2	4	94

(Note: First column is percent of respondents who indicated the item is important. Other columns are also in percent of respondents.)

While there are thousands of Web sites devoted to spirituality and religion, I've seen little in the on-line world to make me believe that Digital Citizens readily embrace institutions like organized religion and incorporate prayer into their daily lives ... I suspect the poll was picking up a trend that other surveys have also found about younger Americans: they have a deep spiritual – as opposed to religious – bent. With that possible distinction in mind, I remain convinced that this group is allergic to preaching and piety, whether it comes from the White House or the Vatican (Katz, 1997, p. 274).

Table 4. Percent of Respondents who Would Use a Large Internet Library

If Religious literature that is of similar quality and quantity to what you would find in a public library or a large book store were available for you to search and browse on the World Wide Web, do you think that you would look at that literature?

1	Never
10	Hardly ever
44	More than 12 times a year
22	More than 4 times a month
12	More than 3 times a week
12	Most every day

The *Wired* survey is consistent with the theory that organizational loyalty and connections are not the driving force behind people's interest in getting information about religion from the Internet. Rather they want information that will assist them in determining not only how they will respond to institutions but how they will take individual actions.

This means they want information that will primarily help them determine their own actions. Therefore, it is not surprising that news and information about social action opportunities are the most popular items on a list of possible denominational uses of the Internet. If this analysis is correct then it calls for a radical rethinking of the function of denominational staff persons. The traditional role of a denominational staff person is to work for the lower levels of the denomination in one of two ways:

- Working on projects that are beyond the scope or ability of lower levels of the denomination to accomplish; and
- Providing guidance to lower levels of the denomination on how to do things.

Most mission work falls into the first category. The denomination organizes the recruitment and training of missionaries and determines what they work on. The development of curriculum materials is an example of the second. Here 'experts' write and publish curriculum material for use in local congregations. Although seldom expressed in this way, the idea is that people in local churches don't know how or what to teach so they must be told by denominational staff people.

The Internet makes it possible for people to have sufficient information so that they determine what mission projects are important and how they will support them. Research and learning are viewed from the perspective of *discovering* rather than *receiving* material from experts.

Obviously there are already some denominational programs that are not what most would considered *traditional*. The point is that as Internet users grow in number, they will increasingly be looking for more and more information on the Internet that helps them decide on actions to take and they will be doing their own research.

This will require increased attention to providing current and in depth data. This has implications for most areas where denominations provide information. For example, Internet users will not look for news that is public relations. They will want news that includes references to background material and offers links to a variety of sources with alternative perspectives.

Observation No. 3: Religious users have high expectations

Current users of the Internet who are also interested in religion have an expectation that the Internet will play an important role in religious life in the future. While there is no clear consensus about exactly what applications religious organizations or religious people will use, many of the people we talked to have very specific ideas about ways that the Internet can and should be used by religion. Even people who are critical of particular current applications of the technology usually have ideas about how the technology 'should' or will be used in the future.

It would be nice for denominational planners if the current users of the Internet had a clear consensus about the future use of the Internet. However, I found that people have very different views of what is essential. One illustration of this is the attitude people have toward the distribution of devotional material on the Internet. In several interviews people described how important receiving devotionals over the Internet is to them. There were other people who said that this is not something that would interest them. The questionnaire asked about devotionals. Although only 56% said this is something that is important for a denomination to sponsor, 15% listed it as the highest priority for denominations.

Most people had very specific ideas about ways that the Internet should be used. These were often, but not always, related to people's current situation. For example, local pastors had ideas about ways that the Internet could benefit local congregations. The staff person in a regional office had ideas about ways that her work could be made easier because of the Internet. A pastor who works with homeless people suggested the development of an Internet resource to help people working in this specialized ministry.

Most often the ideas suggested were related to specific agenda. One person in the focus group presented an argument that historically high expectations for new communication technology are replaced by a reality of people figuring out how to use the technology without replacing other forms of communication.

Implications

The Internet is not something that can be ignored or dismissed by religious leaders. However, it would be equally impossible to respond to every suggestion and to fund all possible uses of the Internet. Many of the people I interviewed spoke very appreciatively of the services that they find on the Internet related to religion. News services and mission information were mentioned repeatedly. However, most people expect and want the number and quality of services to continue to increase.

One possible strategy is for denominational offices to view the Internet as a way to facilitate coordination and support of ministry. The General Council of Ministries of the United Methodist Church is considering such a proposal. The research office of the agency is looking into developing an on-line support system for research in the United Methodist Church. With this model the research office would do very little research itself. Rather the office would identify places where people are doing research or are interested in doing research. Using the Internet these projects would be supported and the results distributed across the church.

In the example of the minister who wants resources for ministries to homeless people, this model suggests that the denomination not hire a Web master to design Web pages and coordinate collecting and editing information. Rather, the denomination would provide technical support, training, and access to Web page space and mailing list technology, legitimacy and a community of support so that a person involved in the ministry could collect and edit material.

In this way a single national staff person might be able to support and encourage one hundred or more editors in specific areas of expertise. The actual determination of what Internet content is developed would largely depend on the existence of individuals who value making sure the data is widely distributed.

Generalization No. 4: Inspiration from friends

Some individuals report that their prayer life has been improved because of access to information on the Internet, some report obtaining help over the Internet for preaching or teaching, and others say they use the Internet to enhance their spiritual life. However, I was not able to find evidence of widespread use of the Internet to form new religious communities or to support new spiritual practices. One possible exception to this is the emerging practice of college students and others of sending email messages containing inspirational stories and messages to a long list of friends.

It certainly is possible that there is a large underground of Christians using the Internet to meet their spiritual needs and developing new forms of community.

It is difficult to provide evidence for this, however, since it is something that my research efforts did not find.

One reason that I believe this is not present is that I systematically searched the homepages of students at the University of Chicago and Saint Louis University, and they did not reveal pointers to spiritual resources or religious Internet sites. Both of these universities, like most colleges and universities, provide free space on their computers for any student or faculty member to post a personal Web page. Most of these Web pages are very personal with pictures of friends and families and information about the interests of the person. Sometimes the page is used to promote a specific agenda. For example, at the University of Chicago a student leader of a Christian group used his Web page to promote the Christian group. However, the vast majority of the pages are just about the person.

The amount of material in the Web pages at these two institutions is tremendous. There is over 500 megabytes of data. I used word search software to try to find references to religious sites or descriptions of spiritual or religious issues. I could find no pattern of either religious reflection or references to religious Internet sites. I did find references to environmental issues and political issues, but these were not explicitly connected to spiritual foundations.

In one of the telephone interviews it was suggested that college students do not think of the Internet as a place where they share about their spirituality. That may be the case, but if so then it seems that the Internet is also not a place where they are developing new forms of spiritual community. The students' Web pages were filled with information about their families, their hobbies, their relationships and their opinions on popular culture.

There are a number of attempts by clergy to develop Internet ministries. While these sometimes have very loyal followings, I have not been able to identify any with large followings. This may be partly because the Internet is an environment where small groups can experiment without the necessity of growing large.

It seems important to note, however, that at various times in history there have been new forms of religious practice that emerge and are very quickly embraced by large numbers of people. A good example of this is the adoption of camp meetings by frontier Americans. In this case frontier life made it difficult to participate in weekly religious group activities. When religious leaders offered camp meetings as an alternative, large numbers of people responded.

There are areas where large numbers of people are responding to an Internet initiative. One area is support for computer software. Microsoft has a large Internet system of providing support for its products with thousands of customers using this resource daily. It is difficult to find a hardware or software vendor that does not use the Internet extensively for support services. This activity seems to just make sense to Internet users.

Another example is on-line bookstores. Although Amazon.com, a large Internet book vendor lost $33.6 million in 1997, people purchased a daily average (including weekends and holidays) of more than $400,000 worth of book from Amazon.com in that year. Again it seems to make sense to Internet users that they can purchase any book they want at a discount and have it shipped to them in a day or two. I could find no product or service on the Internet related to religion where people are responding in such large numbers or where the activity just seems to make sense to Internet users.

In the previous section I noted the enthusiasm and variety of interests that can be found in religious users of the Internet. Here I want to emphasize that I could not find a focused public use of the Internet for religious purposes. In the frontier of the Internet, I could not find the equivalent of the camp meeting.

There are two possible structures that might yet surface. The first is built on a variation of the E-commerce model. In 1999, the Family Christian Stores launched (iBelieve.com). This was followed by (Beliefnet.com), which went on-line the first week of the new millennium. Both sites aim to combine commerce with Web sites that encourage interactive participation on issues relating to religion and morality. Both have considerable equity backing (Broadway, 2000).

A second possible candidate for an emerging use as a structure for the creation of community is not public and, therefore, much more difficult to observe and to document. This is the grassroots sharing of stories, inspiration and spiritual reflection among people who know each other and between people who meet on the Internet.

People that I interviewed in a variety of ways reported this sharing of inspiration to me. Several people talked about being able to discuss religion with people with very different perspectives. One person told about intentionally developing relationships with people on different continents to learn how they view religious issues. A college chaplain reported on an initiative of a small group of women at a Catholic college who organized a discussion with a group of young men on a Baptist campus to discuss religion. People told me about engaging their own children in discussion about religion.

One of the questions asked on the survey questionnaire was: "Do you pray for other people because they send you personal email prayer requests?" Only 4% responded that they have not and do not think that they ever would. Seventy percent of the respondents said that this is something they have done and 26% said they have never done it but think they might do it someday. Responses were almost exactly the same to the question: Do you pray for other people or

Table 5. Percent of Respondents Who Pray Because of Email Messages

Do you pray for other people because they send you personal email prayer requests?	
4	No, I have never done that, and I don't think I ever will
26	No, I have not done it, but I might do it someday
22	Yes, very rarely
27	Yes, More than 12 times a year
8	Yes, More than 4 times a month
6	Yes, More than 3 times a week
7	Yes, Most every day

about situations because of public information that you receive over the Internet? When people were asked: Do you ask other people to pray for you by sending them an email message? they were a little less likely to say that they expect to do this in the future. Ten percent of the respondents say that is something they would never do. The remaining 90% have either done it or think they might.

Sharing about religion is sometimes more formalized. A pastor in Ohio sets up mailing lists specifically for people to discuss spiritual issues. ECUNET has many formalized groups with sharing about spiritual experiences or ideas. The observation above that Internet sites with religious content do not have large audiences that compare with Microsoft or Amazon.com may be because the sharing of spirituality on the Internet is much more intimate. It is between individuals and within smaller groups. People are likely to actually know each other or to become known to each other. The pastor who posts her sermons on the Internet may not have thousands of people rushing to read them each week, but there are a small number of people who find them helpful and these people can and do communicate with each other.

A closely related activity was reported to me in two different interviews. In one case I talked to an editor of an on-line religious publication that is designed to appeal to Internet users. She told me that she sometimes visits public chat groups and looks for people who are raising fundamental questions or appear to have spiritual needs. She then engages in on-line conversation and invites them to use the resources of her magazine. A minister of a local congregation told me about his night time ministry of monitoring on-line discussion groups and chat rooms to identify people with spiritual and religious questions. In both of these cases the Internet is a place to engage people in spiritual discussion.

Implications

If I have correctly identified at least one aspect of spiritual activity on the Internet then a new perspective on pastoring is called for. The minister of people who are using the Internet to share inspiration and to discuss spiritual matters needs to be primarily a listener and not a proclaimer. Skills of hearing spiritual issues and connecting them to faith stories are more important then being able to present doctrine clearly. Telling stories is more important than preaching. Empathy is more important than analysis. Dialog is more important than dogma.

There are several characteristics of the Internet that have important implications for religious communities and faith development. These include the potential for interaction between people separated by great distance or culture, the sense of intimacy, the sense of immediacy, and the potential of anonymity. These characteristics need to be understood by pastors so that they can engage people in the electronic environment with integrity. I believe that the grassroots spiritual development that I have described can be enhanced by a supportive professional clergy who celebrate, encourage, and participate in dialog and exchanges over the Internet.

OTHER ISSUES

There are four additional issues that were not considered to be part of the inquiry, but which came up with sufficient frequency in the interviews and questionnaires. They deserve at least brief mention because they call attention to common concerns for all that used the Internet:

- The authority of information;
- Misrepresentation of organizations or ideas;
- Protecting unsophisticated readers from what are perceived to be dangerous ideas; and
- The problem of uncivil behavior on the Internet.

In one sense, all of these issues can be understood as rooted in a need for people to develop Internet literacy. Literacy is, on the one hand, learning the fundamental skills of communication – reading, writing and speaking. Discerning the authority of information is something we all do all the time. Internet communication is different only in the sense that editors, publishers, broadcasters, teachers, preachers, etc. do not screen the content prior to its entering the public domain.

Some persons learn to demand very high standards to consider information authoritative; others believe that supermarket tabloids are a more reliable source of information than most newspapers that are generally considered to be authoritative.

Concern that the Internet contains considerable misinformation, and that people manipulate information for their own purposes, mirrors uneasiness that people often express about other media as well. Much of the concern people are expressing is almost certainly the uncertainty about the Internet as a source. This is understandable in light of the fact that this medium is still very new.

When it comes to Internet information about religious beliefs and practices, many feel certain angst that others might be using the Internet for deception. This may involve telling untruths about a faith tradition to a believer of that tradition. Or, on the other hand, faith traditions that are 'heretical' may be misrepresented as orthodox beliefs. The former may be intended to undermine, even shatter belief, while the latter involved deceptive practices to lure people to 'errant' beliefs.

These are certainly legitimate concerns, but beneath the surface of deception, or perceived deception, is the question of how the Internet impacts are awareness of the beliefs of others. Our survey results indicate that many people do not explore information about faith traditions other than their own. Still, many others do.

American society is becoming increasingly pluralistic. We face not merely the proliferation of Christian denominations, but a growing presence of non-Christian faith traditions. Most faith traditions would wish to argue that they have a legitimate concern with protecting their own from aggressive proselytization by other faith traditions – especially their youth who may be perceived as being more impressionable and, hence, vulnerable.

I would wish to argue that this is a perfectly legitimate concern. Let us acknowledge that the Internet does present a potentially threatening environment in which a few may practice deception and fraud to mislead others in matters of faith. Understanding when and how this occurs is part of cyber-literacy. Let us also acknowledge that the Internet has also brought forth voluminous information about hundreds of faith traditions – accessible in ways and in details that have not heretofore been available. Furthermore, this flood of information is substantially accurate.

Let us not only welcome the opportunity to learn about other faith traditions, but also let us work to place this goal on our own denominational agendas. As a culture and as peoples of faith, we should be concerned that we do not create a society that becomes increasing divided along the lines of faith traditions.

This goal of cultural inclusiveness of all faith traditions can perhaps best be achieved by promoting tolerance and respect for traditions that believe differently than we believe. Learning about other faith traditions is an important step toward understanding and respect. And this, perhaps, is an agenda item that established faith traditions should place high on their list as they consider how to put the Internet to work to achieve their interests and goals.

Table 6. Demographic Characteristics of Respondents to On-line
Questionnaire

Age	Number	Percent of Respondents
Less than 18	1	0
Between 18–30	34	9
Between 31–50	215	57
Between 51–70	118	31
Over 70	10	3

Gender	Number	Percent of Respondents
Female	124	32
Male	259	68

Country	Number	Percent of Respondents
USA	356	92
Canada	11	3
South & Central America	2	1
Australia	2	1
Europe	4	1
Other Places	10	3

SUMMARY OF GENERALIZATIONS

(1) People are eagerly adopting Internet solutions to communication problems of existing religious interest or commitments. Increasingly email is replacing or enhancing communication by telephone, mail and fax. The computer is seen in an instrumental sense of making it possible to communicate more easily, more clearly, and less expensively.

(2) People think of religion as one of the topics that can be researched on the Internet. Just like people expect to find religious topics as part of an encyclopedia, they expect to find them on the Internet. But, more importantly, people are looking for information that they can use to determine their own actions.

(3) Current users of the Internet who are also interested in religion have an expectation that the Internet will play an important role in religious life in the future. While there is no clear consensus about exactly what applications religious organizations or religious people will use, many of the people I talked to have very specific ideas about ways that the Internet can and should be used by religion. Even people who are critical of particular current

applications of the technology usually have ideas about how the technology 'should' or will be used in the future.

(4) Some individuals report that their prayer life has been improved because of access to information on the Internet, some report obtaining help over the Internet for preaching or teaching, and others say they use the Internet to enhance their spiritual life. However, I was not able to find evidence of widespread use of the Internet to form new religious communities or to support new spiritual practices. One possible exception to this is the emerging practice of college students and others sending email messages containing inspirational stories and messages to a long list of friends.

ACKNOWLEDGMENTS

The Centre for the Study of Communication and Culture at St. Louis University provided office and library facilities for this study. It was paid for by a grant from the Louisville Institute to United Methodist Communication.

REFERENCES

Broadway, B. (2000). Prophets of Profit. *Washington Post,* February 5, B9.
Gates, B. (1996). *The Road Ahead.* New York: Penguin Books.
Hallal, W., Kull, M. D., & Leffman, A. (1997). Emerging Technologies: What's Ahead for 2001–2030. *The Futurist,* November–December.
Katz, J. (1997). The Digital Citizen. *Wired,* December, 66–82; 274–275.
Mitchell, K. (1998). Print and on-line readers cast their votes. *InfoWorld,* March 23, 15.
Rogers-Melnick, A. (1998). Churches finding a home on Web. *Pittsburgh Post-Gazette,* March 11, C1.

METHODOLOGICAL APPENDIX

Internet users and providers of information and services on the Internet are a diverse and complex group of people and organizations. This project was not designed to discover or document the characteristics of Internet users. However, interpreting the data collected required giving careful attention to the nature of the population providing information. A variety of sources of data were used.

A great deal of data was generated from contacts that were first made through the project's own Web page. People were invited to register with the project. With their registration they volunteered information about themselves. A total of 386 people registered with the project. They provided the information listed on Table 6.

Caution must be exercised in interpreting the results of the on-line questionnaires beyond the context of this research project. This project does not include a comparison of the results of the questionnaire with a random sample of a larger defined population. However, there are other studies that illustrate the potential problems that can result from making assumptions about generalities from on-line surveys. On March 23, 1998, *InfoWorld* reported on the comparison between results of an on-line volunteer survey and a random telephone survey of readers. The random survey of readers indicated that 33% chose Microsoft Office as the product of the year with no other product receiving more than 5% of the votes. In an on-line survey that asked exactly the same questions, 37% chose Red Hat Linux with no other product receiving more than 10% of the votes including Microsoft Office. Obviously the volunteer on-line survey results did not reflect the results from a random telephone survey of the magazine's readers.

ONLINE-RELIGION/RELIGION-ONLINE AND VIRTUAL COMMUNITAS

Christopher Helland

ABSTRACT

This chapter develops a heuristic device for a general classification of religious and spiritually focused Web sites. It is argued that religion on the Internet manifests itself in two forms. The first is characteristic of institutionalized religious structures, representing the harnessing of the medium as a traditional form of one-to-many communication. The second form represents a direct reaction to religion in the secular world, allowing for a new manifestation of religious interaction, participation, and community.

INTRODUCTION

"Are you ready?" Cisco Systems asks viewers in their latest television ad for the Internet. With the rapid developments in computer-mediated communications, I don't think anyone is. The industrialized world is travelling at such speed down the information and technological superhighway that most people

Religion on the Internet, Volume 8, pages 205–223.
Copyright © 2000 by Elsevier Science Inc.
All rights of reproduction in any form reserved.
ISBN: 0-7623-0535-5

have become numb to developments that blur past our windshield before we even recognize their impact on our changing cultural scenery. In true McLuhan form, the only view we really have of this forward motion is through the rearview mirror of our progress (McLuhan, 1999 [1964]). In the midst of this change, I can't seem to remember what it was like not to have email or the World Wide Web at my fingertips. And I'm not alone.

There are now an estimated 304 million Internet users worldwide. Use in Japan has increased 128.8% over last year; in Canada, households with at least one regular Internet user are up from 35.9% in 1998 to 41.8% in 1999. The most popular place for Internet use is now the home and not the workplace.[1] To continue the *on-lining* of the globe, Internet support companies count their subscribers in the tens of millions and give away their Web browser software free in magazines and on street corners. The Internet and World Wide Web (WWW) now provide not only commercial ventures like banking and stock market participation, but also online psychotherapy and counseling, interactive music lessons, unlimited sexual exploitation, and the topic of this volume, religion.

Despite the assumption that computer-mediated communications would be a secular undertaking based upon its technological encapsulation of modernity, religion and religious beliefs have permeated the Internet from the beginning. Religion has now become so prevalent on the Web that statistics gathered by the Time Warner Company estimate that there are almost three times as many WWW sites concerning God than there are sex.[2] Both traditional and new religious groups are actively establishing themselves at such a rate in cyberspace that is impossible to keep track of all the activity.

Religion on the Internet raises several issues concerning the social phenomena of religious participation. The Internet is not a device that functions outside of the parameters of the social world built by humanity; it is a mirror that reflects the enterprise of world building. "As above so below" (or vice versa) appears to hold when considering the manifestations of Internet participation with the 'non-virtual' lives of those who go on-line. The alterations that have occurred in religious belief systems, religious participation, and religious communities in the Western world over the last half of the twentieth century are reflected through this medium. These transformations have been coupled, or intertwined, with the development of the technology and structure of the Internet itself (Noble, 1999).

The purpose of this work is to establish a theoretical framework and heuristic device for examining religion on-line, and contribute to the discussion of virtual community, religious praxis, and belief system structures. To demonstrate this theory I will present the study in three sections. The initial focus will be secularization theory, examining the alterations that have occurred in religious participation with the rise of the secular society. The investigation will then shift to explore religious beliefs and practices that are flourishing outside of traditional religious structures.

The final section will examine religion on the Internet, demonstrating that there are two forms of religious participation on-line. One of these is based upon traditional religious hierarchical structure, attempting to harness the Internet as a tool of top-down, organized communication. This use of the Internet represents what I would classify as *religion-online,* an organized attempt to utilize traditional forms of communication to present religion based upon a vertical conception of control, status and authority. The second represents a new development in religious praxis, reflecting the configuration of the Internet medium itself. This form of religious participation can be designated as *online-religion,* and has several distinct characteristics that stem from new forms of communication protocols based and the ideal of unstructured, open, and non-hierarchical interaction.

Online-religion offers participants a form of religious liminality outside of traditional religious structures. Within this liminal state there are alterations in the control, status and rank of the participants, coupled with selective anonymity and equality. The community developed by these participants represents *virtual communitas,* a virtual space where interaction and sacredness ebbs and flows in a continual state of transition.

THE GREAT DEBATE:
RELIGION IN THE SECULAR WORLD

The great debate occurring over the process of secularization is ongoing and heated. Due to the focus and length of this study I will only be addressing certain issues of the secularization process in the Western world that I believe are relevant to the study of religion in the new public space of the Internet. The manifestation of religion on the Internet is directly opposed to the assumptions made by some secularization theorists that religion in the Western world is declining.[3] This is particularly so because the significant number of people experimenting and participating in religion through the Internet would generally be considered educated, scientific, and certainly modern by technological standards. However, it is important to recognize several alterations in religious participation that have occurred with the advent of modernity. For examining this issue, Berger's original work on the secularization theory is insightful and I believe still helpful in exploring these religious changes.

Berger addressed the issue of secularization with a form of reverse sociological engineering.[4] He recognized that (in what he considered Western or industrial society) there was a decline in traditional religious participation, a separation between church and state, and a number of transformations that had occurred in religious practices which removed them (or forced their removal) from society (Berger, 1967). He defined secularization as "the process by which sectors of society and culture are removed from the domination of religious institutions and symbols," (Berger, 1967, p. 107). This was evident not just in the political sphere but also by the decline of religious symbols "in the arts, in philosophy, in literature and, most importantly of all, in the rise of science as an autonomous, thoroughly secular perspective on the world" (Berger, 1967, p. 107).

Examining the public or social dimension of Western culture, Berger noted that within this sphere, religious participation had been declining and the traditional monopolistic religious structures were losing their ability to influence politics and, in similar vein, the entire Western social world. Religious authority had been challenged by alternative plausibility structures, or belief systems, that counteracted its religious claims and contested its basic assumptions concerning divine intervention in worldly matters.

Berger developed a correlation between the secular work place and the secularization of the individual. "The original carrier of secularization is the modern economic process, that is, the dynamic of industrial rationalism ... Today, it would seem, it is industrial society in itself that is secularizing, with its divergent ideological limitations serving merely as modifications of the global secularization process" (Berger, 1967, p. 109). In this case he extrapolates from an observable social trend (the secular workplace) to draw conclusions about the religious states of the individuals participating in that workplace.[5]

With these secular developments, religion became a matter of private choice. The secular environment encouraged a form of private, family-centered religious participation, rather than outward social expressions. Governments, for the most part, no longer enforced one belief system over another, and individuals were left to choose their own affiliations. This allowed for an environment of religious pluralism, voluntary allegiance, and a competitive religious market place. As a result, religious organizations also had to develop the bureaucratic machinery to compete for participants.

Shortly after Berger presented his theory concerning the secularization process, several individuals attempted to acquire statistical data to support or discredit the theoretical paradigm. Wilson (1970) reviewed such a survey and found that 96% of Americans and 76% of the population in the United Kingdom believed in God. What these numbers demonstrated was that secularization was affecting religion, but significant forms of belief remained at the individual level. Religion may have left the workplace, governments, and schools of America, but it certainly had not left the lives of the American or British populations.

Commenting on these statistics, Bellah noted a changing trend in religious beliefs systems:

> The central features of the change is the collapse of dualism that was so critical to all the historic religions . . . There is simply no room for the hierarchic dualistic religious symbol system of the classical historical type . . . Behind the 96% of Americans who claim to believe in God there are many instances of massive reinterpretation . . . The dualistic world-view certainly persists in the minds of many of the devoted, but just as surely many others have developed elaborate and often pseudo-scientific rationalizations to bring their faith in its experienced validity into some kind of cognitive harmony with the twentieth-century world (Bellah, 1976, pp. 39–44).

Despite statistics that assert that belief in God is still an interdependent component of the lives of a great percentage of the population (e.g. Bibby, 1993), there has been a decline in traditional forms of religious participation. In the most recent analysis from Statistics Canada this decline in Church attendance has been noted and recorded as a social trend. Statistics from 1985 to 1996 compiled by both Statistics Canada and the United States General Social Survey demonstrate that weekly attendance and participation in traditional church institutions is declining. Those reporting that they did not attend any church service during the year have risen sharply (Clark, 1998), and statistics compiled from 1957 to 1988 demonstrate that this trend has been underway for some time. Despite occasional fluctuations in attendance, the overall percentage attending a church or a synagogue on a weekly basis has been reduced in Canada by almost 30% since 1945 (Baril & Mori, 1991).

These figures both support and contradict Berger's theory. Traditional religious participation in the institutionalized social setting of the church has declined and would appear to coincide with the secularization theory that religion is diminishing. On the other hand, religious beliefs remain strong and are maintained within a large percentage of the population. This contradiction has been studied in a number of ways. In a more recent examination of this phenomenon, Berger has concluded that his original theory – that religion would: (1) become more this-worldly, as a form of hybridized Protestantism, and (2) slowly disappear from the social setting (Berger, 1967) – was not consistent with the actual transformation of religion within contemporary culture. Berger has reversed his belief in the secularization thesis and written against it on several occasions (Berger, 1982, 1997, 1999):

> I think what I and most other sociologists of religion wrote in the 1960s about secularization was a mistake. Our underlying argument was that secularization and modernity go hand in hand. With more modernization comes more secularization. It wasn't a crazy theory. There was some evidence for it. But I think it's basically wrong. Most of the world today is certainly not secular. It's very religious (Berger, 1997, p. 974).

Berger's recent study of *desecularization* specifically focuses upon religious organizations and institutions that are thriving in the political social sphere (Berger, 1999). It is an important study of the transformation of religion in modernity/post-modernity but in a similar manner as his original work on this subject, he has not addressed issues concerning the vast numbers of people that do not belong to these groups yet maintain religious and spiritual beliefs outside of the traditional religious organizations. His original theory, that there is a form of religious *individuation*, is certainly valid, in that there has been a polarization between the public sphere and the private sphere concerning religious matters (Berger, 1967, pp. 133–135). Yet the hypothesis that religion in the private sphere would eventually taper off has not played out.

The secularization process has led to a separation between church and state, the rise of religious pluralism, the development of the religious market place, and a separation between personal religious beliefs and the secular world. Vast numbers of individuals are maintaining religious and spiritual beliefs without participating in any form of organized religion. Their beliefs are for the most part private, yet they are maintained in the modern world despite a secular worldview that fosters atheism or agnosticism. It is this form of private and personal belief that I will examine in the next section of the chapter.

'WE STILL BELIEVE':
RELIGION IN THE PRIVATE SPHERE

In a prolonged study of religious and spiritual belief systems in Canada, Bibby has concluded that:

> Intrigue with mystery is almost everywhere; people are fascinated with the supernatural; they want to find out how to make life more meaningful; they seek out the churches for rites of passage; almost all continue to identify with religious tradition; and, their biographies typically are characterized by religious memories (Bibby, 1993, pp. 178–179).

These beliefs in the supernatural (e.g. ESP, near death experiences, divination) appear as an almost separate form of religious observance outside of traditional institutional belief systems. Several new religious movements have been organized around these alternative beliefs and many systems of classification have been developed to examine them (see, for example, Wilson, 1970; Wallis, 1984). A general encomium could include: "(a) this-worldliness, (b) self-spirituality, (c) dehierarchization and dedualization, (d) parascientificity, (e) pluralistic, relativistic, fluctuating, seeking faiths, and (f) loose network-type organizations (indeed, religion without religion)" (Lambert, 1999).

Despite the rise of new religious movements with the demonopolizing of religion (Berger, 1967, p. 135), participation rates in these groups still remains relatively low and highly transitory (Dawson, 1996). Statistics Canada estimates that although participation in groups recognized as sects, cults, and para-religious movements has increased 109% from 1981 to 1991, the total numbers are only 0.1% of the population. These figures in no way account for the large number of people in Canada who can be considered religious, yet do not participate in any traditional religious organization.

Complicating matters even further, many participants in mainline traditional belief systems may hold alternative personal views, heterodox to the tradition in which they belong (Lewis & Melton, 1992). In the World Value Survey (WVS) conducted in Europe in 1990, 40% of those who said they believed in the resurrection of Jesus Christ also said they believed in reincarnation; the rate increases to 50% for young adults (Swatos & Christiano, 1999).

In our contemporary religious culture it appears as if there are two manifestations of religious systems. One is structured and appears in the public sphere based upon traditional forms of highly bureaucratic and institutionalized beliefs, controlled by the elite of the organization. The other has its locus within the individual, fluctuating and altering as the beliefs change with the individual's perception and interpretation of what it means to be religious or spiritual in the modern world.

Statistics from the European Value Survey (EVS) demonstrate that only 25% supported the belief that there was one true religion, 53% believed that there were interesting, or valuable insights in all the great religions, while 48% of the baby-boomer population believed that "All the religions of the world are equally true and good" (Lambert, 1999, p. 320).

Although surveys such as the EVS or PROJECT CAN 90 demonstrate that there are religious beliefs outside of the institutionalized public religious sphere, it is very difficult to see where these beliefs become manifest. Even if large numbers of people maintain them, the secular environment does not encourage promotion of these beliefs. (An example could be the belief in near-death experiences or UFOs. Many people may believe in these phenomena, yet for the most part it isn't discussed at work or with associates; it remains private to the believer.) While one avenue for locating these beliefs is to examine sales in 'Religious' or 'Spiritual' books, this is a static examination of the phenomenon and does not demonstrate the depth and complexity of the social manifestation of these individual beliefs (Wuthnow, 1998). Surveys may be effective in the study, but they also contain methodological difficulties and limitations.

With the development of Internet technology, people have begun expressing their personal religious beliefs through the medium of cyberspace. Religion has been projected into the public world without the constraints of traditional church organization, authority, or even architecture. The Internet and World Wide Web have allowed for the creation of a unique public space in which individuals can participate from the privacy of their own homes. The Internet has eroded the boundary between traditional public space and, although the WWW is replete with the social manifestations of the secular world, it is also abounding in private expressions of religious belief.

HIGH TECH BELIEF: RELIGION AND THE INTERNET

Before beginning an examination of religion on the Internet it is important to recognize that this form of communication has its limitations, despite the positive spin given it by the media and companies that have a vested interest in its promotion. There is a 'digital divide' created by social and economic constraints. Only 2% of Latin America, for example, has Internet access.[6]

When the individual is on-line, there are also restrictions concerning the nature of the communication. Most interaction is text based; people must watch the screen and type messages to engage other participants. Emotions and feelings are expressed through symbols, abbreviations, and fonts. While microphone interfaces, sound cards, live video feed, and Voice Portal Technology are now allowing for some individuals to speak, hear, and see each other on-line, this technology is still evolving.

'Internet' is a term used to describe interconnected Webs of computer networks. Called ARPANET, it was designed originally by the U.S. Army to connect computer systems in several parts of the country. Similar systems of interconnected computers were also developed in France to allow different computer systems at different universities and military centers to communicate without humans having to translate and input data from one system to the other (Kitchin, 1998).

With the development of a program called MODEM, public access to these systems began in 1977. Through this system, microcomputers (home based computer systems that were not connected to a larger system) were able to communicate with each other through telephone lines (Kitchin, 1998). This can be seen as the first public manifestation of the Internet. Systems were established in Chicago and Santa Cruz, and individuals could communicate with others who were using the same MODEM program. The system in Chicago was used as a forum for communicating about computer uses. The Santa Cruz system was more structured and allowed for thematic discussions among users. Known as BBSs or Bulletin Board Systems, discussion topics were generated and regulated by the users of the system. The Santa Cruz BBS (called Communitree) included a section devoted to religion and spirituality (Rheingold, 1993; Zaleski, 1997).

As Rheingold notes, in the early years of the BBS, use of MODEM was restricted to computer hobbyists. This was an elite group of individuals with the technical knowledge, money, and education that allowed them to go on-line before Web browsers like Netscape Navigator or Microsoft Explorer opened the way for mass public use (Rheingold, 1993, p. 134). It seems somewhat surprising that one of the original BBSs designated part of its forum for religious and spiritual discussion. A BBS called ORIGINS started a 'create your own religion' discussion area (Rheingold, 1993, p. 134). The original declaration of the BBS was: "ORIGINS has no leaders, no official existence, nothing for sale. Because it started as an open computer conference, no one knows who all the creators are" (Rheingold, 1993, pp. 134–135).

This form of non-structured religious participation now permeates the World Wide Web. It ranges from homemade to professionally designed Web sites; they contain doctrinal information to message boards and chat rooms; they range in belief from Christianity to Neopaganism. Homemade Web sites exist, for the most part, without any church or institutional support. They have been created and maintained by individuals who wish to participate with religious and spiritual matters on their own terms.

Religion and spirituality account for the largest number of homemade pages supported by the Lycos search engine, outnumbering any other category by several thousand. Other accommodations to religion and to spiritual beliefs have also been established on the WWW. One example is Yahoo (www.yahoo.com), which has an active 'Religion and Beliefs' section supported by their chat room software and allows for discussion rooms on Astrology, Christian Chat, Christian Teens, Islam Chat, Jewish Chat, Jewish Teens, Paganism, and Religion.

Chat rooms may appear chaotic at first; often several discussions are going on at once and the topics fluctuate rapidly. In these spaces everyone not only has their own virtual soapbox, they also have a VR bullhorn. However, there is order in this apparent chaos. Often individuals know each other through previous interactions. And, although the content varies, people are often very well educated and lucid in their discussions (during one interaction in the Yahoo religion chat room I misspelled Feuerbach and was quickly corrected).

This type of religious participation fits the classification outlined earlier regarding non-institutionalized or private religious belief systems. People using the BBSs or chat rooms ask questions ranging from magic to charisma, and anyone using the system can post responses or information about religious and spiritual practices (Rheingold, 1993, p. 135). A more current (and commercial) example of ORIGINS can be seen at www.espirituality.com. Recently developed and on-line as of June 2000, it offers a variety of 'boards' for discussions ranging from dream analysis to divination, along with up to date information on 'new age' topics. Through correspondence with the site's founder, Tidiani Tall, I learned that they average 30,000 hits per day, an impressive number for such a new venture.

FROM THE BOTTOM UP: ONLINE-RELIGION

The medium of Internet communication has provided the opportunity for individuals to interact with "unrestricted freedom of expression that is far less hierarchical and formal than real world interaction" (Kitchin, 1998, p. 80). This form of communication mirrors the ideal structure of the Internet itself: an unregulated, open-ended, non-hierarchical communications network.[7] As Zaleski notes, the World Wide Web is:

> organized laterally rather than vertically or radially, with no central authority and no chain of command. (Individual Webmasters have power over Web sites, as do sysops, or systems operators, over bulletin board systems, and moderators over Usenet groups, but their influence is local and extremely responsive to the populations they serve.) Moreover, on the Net, at least as of this writing, freedom rules. The Internet is anarchy in action, a libertarian cyberland, and it nurtures direct (albeit virtual) contact between individuals, without hierarchical intermediaries (Zaleski, 1997, p. 111).

It is within these parameters that a new form of religious participation is occurring. This form of religious participation I choose to recognize as *online-religion*. Individuals are interacting with the religious beliefs systems presented on the Internet; they are contributing personal beliefs and receiving personal feedback. It is a dialectic process; the beliefs are developing and altering, adapting and fluctuating in the direction the participants wish to take them. On the Web, particular manifestations of community are developing around this form of religious interaction, virtual religious communities that are best classified as expressions of virtual communitas. A theoretical framework developed by the anthropologist Victor Turner is a useful tool for understanding these interactions.

In Turner's anthropological study of tribal religion (1969), he recognized a pattern of religious participation based upon a form of anti-structure. This manifestation of religious interaction has a surprising number of similarities with the current phenomenon of religion on the Internet. His study recognized that particular forms of religious interaction provided a liminal and unstructured environment for the participants, which was in direct opposition to the socially structured world the people normally inhabited:

> It is as though there are two major 'models' for human interrelatedness, juxtaposed and alternating. The first is society as structured, differentiated, and often hierarchical system of political-legal-economic positions with many types of evaluation, separating men [humanity] in terms of more or less. The second, which emerges recognizably in the liminal period, is of society as an unstructured or rudimentarily structured and relatively undifferentiated comitatus, community, or even communion of equal individuals (Turner, 1969, p. 96).

Within this space the 'liminal personae' (threshold people) are ambiguous, "as liminal beings they have no status, property, insignia, secular clothing indicating rank of role, position in a kinship system – in short, nothing that may distinguish them from their fellow neophytes or initiands" (Turner, 1969, p. 95).

Because it acts as a great leveler once people have gone on-line, Internet participation forces this same form of liminality upon its users. Status disappears, no social class has dominion over any other, and everyone is forced into an accommodation of equality in which a particular form of non-structured interaction can take place. There are no racial, gender, or class signifiers presented, "unless you choose to disclose it, no one knows whether you are male, female, tall, short, a redhead or blond, black, white, Asian, Latino, in a wheelchair or not" (Kane, 1994, p. 204). People establish their presence within the medium through the use of the written word. Although it requires knowledge of specific guidelines and protocols to allow for this form of unbridled interaction, once the participant is cognizant of the rules employed by chat rooms or BBSs they obtain their liminal status.

There are exceptions; some individuals, such as programmers and monitors, do exercise a great amount of authority over certain environments on the Internet (Stone, 1991). However, this control is used only in extreme circumstances and is often regulated by the users themselves. In MUDs ('Multiple User Dungeons') and MOOs ('Multiple User Object Oriented' environments), the 'God' of the cyberspace (i.e. the creator of the environment) can regulate the space which the 'Avatars' (i.e. the virtual presence of the participant) inhabit, much like the ritual elder recognized by Turner (Turner, 1969, p. 96).

Within the liminal state, people are immersed in a condition of "sacredness, of homogeneity and comradeship. We are presented, in such rites, with a 'moment in and out of time', and in and out of secular social structure, which reveals, however fleetingly, some recognition (in symbol if not always in language) of a generalized social bond that has ceased to be and has simultaneously yet to be fragmented into a multiplicity of social ties" (Turner, 1969, p. 96). Rather than community, Turner classifies the social bond that occurs in this liminal stage as *communitas*, "to distinguish this modality of social relationship from an 'area of common living' " (Turner, 1969, p. 96).

Distinguishing *communitas* from community is particularly relevant when addressing issues concerning the concept of virtual community. This discrimination recognizes that "communities do not have to be solidary groups of densely knit neighbors but could also exist as social networks of kin, friends, and workmates who do not necessarily live in the same neighborhoods" (Wellman & Gulia, 1999, p. 169).

Rheingold did extensive research on virtual communities and published his findings in 1993. After *The Virtual Community: Homesteading on the Electronic Frontier* had became widely circulated, cultural studies scholars as well as the general public began both to support and develop the concept of virtual community and to challenge the notion that a community can develop through the Internet medium.

However, despite its detractors, I believe three reasons argue in favor of some type of on-line religious community formation. First, because *communitas* is centered upon the liminal individuals and their experience, it is a community of free choice and free association that has at its core a religious dimension drawing the participants together. It is a community based upon social networks rather than geographical space (Wellman, 1988). Second, situating the requirements for a community based upon "tradition and history of location" excludes the marginal members of a community who do not belong to the dominant group (Simpson, 1999). It does not give room for, or recognize, those groups situated around alternative belief systems or histories.[8] Religion in contemporary Western culture is also a matter of choice more than locale or tradition. For the most part people are choosing when to involve themselves in religion and when not. And, often, individuals are choosing to participate in religious organizations to which their parents may or may not belong (Stark & Bainbridge, 1985). Finally, although the question of virtual community is complicated and multi-dimensional, if participants explicitly state that they are experiencing a sense of community on-line, it is distinctly questionable to tell them they are not.

As Turner developed his *communitas* theory, he expanded it cross-culturally to examine the phenomenon in a number of religious and para-religious settings. He categorized three forms of *communitas*, all of which can be found in online-religious groups. These are: (1) existential or spontaneous communitas, (2) normative communitas and, (3) ideological communitas.

Existential Communitas

Existential or spontaneous communitas "William Blake might have called 'the winged moment as it flies' " (Turner, 1969, p. 132). It is an open ended, unrestricted, environment with no constraints or limitations placed upon the participants, "what the hippies today [1969] would call a happening." For example, this is the form of *communitas* which occurs in unregulated religious chat rooms (and many of the religious Usenet groups) where topics, content, and expression are generated spontaneously by and flow freely among the participants. Sites such as http://chat.yahoo.com have chat rooms devoted to open religious and beliefs discussions under various sub-headings (see above). Http://dir.lycos.com/Society/Religion_and_Spirituality, on the other hand, offers thousands of different religious sites, many of which offer this form of religious interaction. Http://www.espirituality.com (see above) provides similar venues for a wide variety of New Age interests and concerns.

Because there is no authority to set limits on the discussion, people will argue with each other, support one another, and even make 'virtual' sexual passes at some participants while others join and leave the room as their whims dictate. This atmosphere can be pleasant or uncomfortable, sometime hilariously entertaining or extremely offensive; it is a 'happening' to be sure.

Normative Communitas

Normative communitas may be the most common arena for the development of online-religion. This *communitas* does have a type of structure in that the membership of the group is mobilized in pursuit of certain religious goals. The structure, however, is based around speculative, philosophical, and mythic ideas. "Here there is usually a great simplification of social structure in the British anthropological sense, accompanied by a rich proliferation of ideological structure, in the form of myths and sacra . . . Rules that abolish minutiae of structural differentiation . . . liberate the human structural propensity and give it free reign in the cultural realm of myth, ritual, and symbol" (Turner, 1969, p. 133). This form of religious participation can be found in a number of 'official' religious Web sites, as well as individual sites posted and supported free of charge by Web server companies.

Belief systems vary and range from new religious movement such as Ashtar Command (http://ashtar-lightwork.tripod.com) to eclectic 'new age' pages (www.spiritWeb.org; www.espirituality.com), Christian (www.biblenet.net), Muslim (www.islamworld.net), and Jewish (www.havienu.org) sites. The important point is that those who log-on are afforded the ability to interact with the belief system, contributing their own experiences and views to the religious group while receiving feedback from other participants.[9] Interaction is regulated, but not in an extreme manner. Unlike existential communitas, though, where anything is tolerated, in this setting participants must focus their discussion around the general precepts, goals, or beliefs of the organization.

Myths and alternative belief systems are often supported through hyperlinks to other Web sites, creating a much stronger plausibility structure for the belief system and larger community of believers. In Berger's study of the secularization process he recognized that religion was losing its ability to provide plausible conceptual systems for religious groups and activities, thus affecting the felt validity of their truth claims. While science is recognized as one of the strongest factors in contributing to the loss of religious plausibility, some religions on the Internet have developed the ability to draw from the appearance of science or unrelated scientific Web sites to support their claims. UFO religious groups, for example, will often hyperlink to official and scientific-looking Web sites which support, and appear to validate, the group's belief in UFOs; this provides support for the plausibility structure of the religious myth around which the organization is built.[10]

Ideological Communitas

Ideological communitas, the final classification, "can apply to a variety of utopian models of societies based on existential communitas" (Turner, 1967, p. 132). In this state, "a fairly regular connection is maintained between liminality, structural inferiority, lowermost status, and structural outsider on the one hand, and, on the other, such universal values as peace and harmony between all men [people]" (Turner, 1967, p. 134). This form of communitas attempts to maintain the liminal status of its participants in the development of a community outside of the normal structure of the society.

In the context of religion and the Internet, *ideological communitas* is best represented by those technopagan groups that recognize a spiritual force within cyberspace itself – a force they feel they connect with and experience in their collective worship through the Internet medium.[11] Technopagan groups often hold 'live' interactive online rituals during the solstice or equinox, however it is often difficult to find the technopagan sites hosting these events without significant contact through the Usenet newsgroups. Mark Pesce, for example, (www.hyperreal.org/~mpesce/), the designer of VRML (a revolutionary computer language that turns the Web into a three-dimensional environment) and a practising witch, developed both an on-line 'Yule ritual', following the death of a close friend, and 'Cybersamhain', an on-line ritual "publically performed on 27 October 1994" (Pesce, N.d.).

Examining one such technopagan on-line religious ritual, O'Leary noted that both the ritual and the participants "constituted something close to an actual neopagan congregation, a community of people gathered regularly to worship even though they had never seen each other face to face" (O'Leary, 1996, p. 794). Individuals like Pesce promote this form of *communitas*, which recognizes the development of computer-mediated communications as an evolutionary step in the spiritual development of humanity (Zaleski, 1997, pp. 254–278).

The technopagan belief system is a syncretism drawn from, among other things, the theoretical writings of Teilhard de Chardin (concerning his concept of the noosphere), science fiction such as William Gibson's *Neuromancer* and Neal Stephenson's *Snow Crash*, New Age beliefs, traditional paganism, and shamanism. Technopagans believe that there is more to the magical realm than the gods and goddesses (or spirits) of earth, air, water, and fire, there is also a "ghost/god in the machine," a spiritual presence in the cyberspace created by modern technology. The goal of this form of *ideological communitas* is to create or maintain a permanent liminal community based upon the anti-structure of the Web itself (Davis, 1998).

With *online-religion*, the *existential* and *normative communitas* experienced by the participants is not a permanent state of being. Turner viewed these states as liminal transition periods on a spiritual path, aiding in the transformation of the individual from one state to the next. In the on-line world and not the tribal, it is a liminal space that may be engaged at will and left when desired. In this way the participants may experience a form of anti-structure within their daily structured lives, and they may or may not choose to develop their participation into face-to-face meetings. Through this form of religious interaction they may be obtaining the spiritual and religious input in their lives that they feel is necessary in a modern world. *Virtual communitas* may even strengthen religion and spiritual beliefs by allowing for a unique public space for individual and personal spiritual exploration without the restraints of traditional organization and community. In this way *virtual communitas* may be a *fait accompli* in and of itself rather than a means toward some religious end.

Online-religion may also be a low commitment form of religious participation. Because of its essential anti-structure, its unregulated, unsupervised commitment requirements, online-religious participation does little to foster a more developed personal investment. Members can come and go as they choose, participate as they wish, belong to several 'movements' at once, and 'sample' different religions without feeling like they are actually members in any way.

FROM THE TOP DOWN: RELIGION-ONLINE

On the other hand, rather than use the Internet as a medium to more freely explore their faith, many established religions continue their institutional structures on-line. Zaleski noted this form of control over the participants of some Internet religious sites, commenting in particular on the official Vatican Web page. "The Holy See Web site is wonderful," he writes, "but it also commits what, in cyberspace, must be considered two cardinal sins. It offers no links to other sites, and so gives lie to the terms Internet and Web ... The Vatican's site also uses the Net strictly as a broadcast medium ... This is cyber religion as if from a mountain-top enclave, and it does not bode well for the future of the Roman Catholic Church online" (Zaleski, 1997, p. 128).

I disagree with Zaleski that the presence of the Catholic Church on-line is threatened in any way. Their development of the site fulfilled Pope John Paul II's wish that, "with the advent of computer telecommunications and what are known as computer participation systems, the Church is offered further means for fulfilling her mission." The original Vatican site that opened in 1995 had more than 1 million people log on in the first two weeks, 200,000 on the first day. What has to be recognized in the study of religion and the Internet is that there are two distinct forms of religious participation occurring.

Controlled religious interaction at sites such as the Vatican (www.vatican.va), the Church of Jesus Christ of Latter-day Saints (www.lds.org), and even new religious movements (e.g. www.paoWeb.org) represent *religion-online*. Here the religious organization has adapted the medium to a traditional form of one-to-many communication. They have retained complete control over the belief system and presented it to their practitioners without allowing for any reciprocal input from those receiving the message. Although this may allow for a widespread audience, the effects on the practitioners may be similar to that of television worship (Wolff, 1999).

If the Internet can be considered an electronic frontier (Healy, 1997), then organized and institutionalized religion are trying to establish not only a presence there, but the same level of control they exercise in the 'real' world. (The Vatican has recently decreed that 'virtual infidelity' is a real sin.) However, I do not believe that the Internet will allow for one form of religion to dominate or monopolize the medium. As technology such as WebTV and live-stream video develop, *religion-online* will continue to establish hierarchical religious organizations on the Web, catering to their practitioners in a one-to-many form of communication. With millions of Web sites devoted to religion and spirituality, a large number of which are supported privately, *religion-online* will most likely have appeal to those already associated with particular movements or traditions. In the long term, it is unlikely that the Internet, in and of itself, will provide adequate means for religious recruitment (Dawson & Hennebry, 1999).

CONCLUSION

Both *religion-online* and *online-religion* represent the presence of religion in contemporary Western culture. On the Internet there are organized traditional religious structures functioning as they do in society today, alongside personal and individual non-hierarchical religious systems. Each has found their place in the virtual space created by computer-mediated communications. Religion on the Internet demonstrates an important development in the accommodation of religion with modernity. I do not believe that religion on the Internet will replace religious structures or decrease the level of organized religious participation occurring in the West. Rather, religion on the Internet functions as a supplement, a venue that allows for participation without traditional structures placed upon the practitioner.

In a modern and secular world the Internet has provided a unique public space that allows for unbridled religious participation. Individuals can act in the privacy of their own homes, participating in religious belief systems without fear of reprisal, ridicule, or repercussion from the secular world. This unique new space blurs the boundary between the private and the public sphere, allowing for a new form of religious participation in the modern world. Private religious belief systems are difficult to express in the secular environment; individuals are not encouraged to talk about their religious beliefs at work, school, or in many social settings. Even within the private sphere of the family, religious beliefs may vary among the family members. In this sense, the Internet has reflected a significant and complicated phenomenon into a space where restrictions have been removed and the individual can express what they want, when they want, and to whomever will listen, becoming participants in the new religious expression of *virtual communitas.*

NOTES

1. Statistics concerning Japan can be found at www.nua.ie/surveys/. Canadian statistics are based on a cross-country average (www.statcan.ca/Daily/English/000519/d000519b.html).

2. While the statistics gathered by Time and posted on their WWW site state that there are 1.7 million sites concerning God and only 0.7 million concerning sex, this demonstrates one of the great difficulties in studying Internet communication – accountability. Although *Time* is a distinguished organization, they have not posted the date for which their information was tabulated. It may be several months or years old, and with the highly fluid nature of the Internet completely outdated. Despite this possibility, the information amply demonstrates that religion on the WWW is a significant phenomenon (see www.time.com/time/godcom/home.html).

3. A recent special issue of Sociology of Religion (1999, no. 60) on the secularization debate has presented a fairly unified front concerning the secularization theory. Although some sociologists still support the original assumption that religion is on the decline and will continue to do so until it is an insignificant component of the social world, most now agree that this is not the case.

4. By reverse engineering I am referring to the process often used to establish how certain technologies were developed or created. For example, Company A is attempting to comprehend a finished product that was developed and produced by Company B.

Using the finished product as the starting point, A's engineers work backwards to determine how the product was developed.

5. Sociologists have never been able to support statistically the theory that the secular work place leads to a decline in personal religious beliefs. This is highlighted by more recent studies of Asian countries that are modernizing their secular economies while maintaining their religious belief systems (Nakamura, 1986).

6. For world Internet demographics, see http://www.nua.ie/surveys/how_many_online/index.html

7. Questions concerning the ideal structure of Internet interaction and the reality of this form of communication are still heavily debated. In truth, arguments can be supported for each perspective. While the passage quoted from Zaleski is valid, it is also a valid argument that the Internet has presented new forms of authority and structure.

8. A well researched example of this form of marginal community on-line can be seen in the study Correll undertook of an virtual lesbian café (Correll, 1995).

9. For examples of Muslim, Jewish, Christian, Hindu, Buddhist, and Neopagan Usenet conversations, see www.time.com/godcom/communion.html

10. See Ashtar Command (http://ashtar-lightwork.tripod.com) which links to other new age sites, to sites concerned with UFO implant removal, and to www.ufoseek.com a site containing hundreds more religious and non-religious links.

11. For a detailed listing of technopagan resources see www.technopagan.dhs.org for Usenet newsgroups concerning technopagan events and beliefs see alt.pagan and alt.magick

REFERENCES

Baril, A., & Mori, G. A. (1991). Leaving the Fold: Declining Church Attendance. *Canadian Social Trends, 22*, 21–24.

Bellah, R. (1976). *Essays on Religion in a Post-Traditional World.* New York: Harper and Row.

Berger, P. (1967). *The Sacred Canopy: Elements of a Sociological Theory of Religion.* New York: Doubleday.

Berger, P. (1982). From a Crisis in Religion to a Crisis in Secularity. In: M. Douglas, & S. Tipton (Eds), *Religion and America: Spiritual Life in a Secular Age* (pp. 1–18). Boston: Beacon Press.

Berger, P. (1997). Epistemological Modesty: An Interview with Peter Berger. *Christian Century, 114*, 972–75, 978.

Berger, P. (1999). The Desecularization of the World: A Global Overview. In: P. Berger (Ed.), *The Desecularization of the World: Resurgent Religion and World Politics* (pp. 1–18). Grand Rapids, MI: William B. Eerdmans Publishing Company.

Bibby, R. (1993). *Unknown Gods: The Ongoing Story of Religion in Canada.* Toronto: Stoddart.

Castells, M. (1996). *The Rise of the Network Society.* Oxford: Blackwell.

Clark, W. (1998). Religious Observances, Marriage and Family. *Canadian Social Trends, 50*, 2–7.

Correll, S. (1995). The Ethnography of an Electronic Bar: The Lesbian Café. *Journal of Contemporary Ethnography, 24*, 270–298.

Davis, E. (1998). *Techgnosis: Myth, Magic, and Mysticism in the Age of Information.* New York: Three Rivers Press.

Dawson, L. L. (1996). Who Joins New Religious Movements and Why: Twenty Years of Research and What Have We Learned. *Studies in Religion/Sciences Religieuses, 25*(2), 193–213.

Dawson, L. L. & Hennebry, J. (1999). New Religion and the Internet: Recruiting in a New Public Space. *Journal of Contemporary Religion, 14*(1), 17–39.

Healy, D. (1996). Cyberspace as Place: The Internet as Middle Landscape on the Electronic Frontier. In: D. Porter (Ed.), *Internet Culture* (pp. 55–68). New York: Routledge.

Kane, P. (1994). *Hitchhiker's Guide to the Electronic Highway*. New York: MIS Press.

Kitchin, R. (1998). *Cyberspace: The World in the Wires*. New York: John Wiley and Sons.

Lambert, Y. (1999). Secularization of New Religious Paradigms. *Sociology of Religion, 60*(3), 303–333.

Lewis, J. R., & Melton, G. J. (1992). *Perspectives on the New Age*. New York: State University of New York Press.

McLuhan, M. (1999 [1964]). *Understanding Media: The Extensions of Man*. Boston: MIT Press.

Nakamura, H. (1986). *A Comparative History of Ideas*. London: Routledge.

Noble, D. F. (1999). *The Religion of Technology: The Divinity of Man and the Spirit of Invention*. New York: Penguin Books.

O'Leary, S. D. (1996). Cyberspace as Sacred Space: Communicating Religion on Computer Networks. *Journal of the American Academy of Religion, 64*(4), 781–807.

Pesce, M. (N.d.). *Rituals for Samhain and Yule*. Retrieved July 10, 2000, from the World Wide Web: http://www.hyperreal.org/~mpesce/rituals.html

Rheingold, H. (1993). *Homesteading on the Electronic Frontier*. Reading, MA: Addison-Wesley.

Simpson, J. (1999). The Search for Community in America: Comments on 'Visions of the Good Society and the Religious Roots of American Political Culture'. *Sociology of Religion, 60*(1), 41–45.

Stark, R. & Bainbridge, W. S. (1985). *The Future of Religion: Secularization, Revival, and Cult Formation*. Berkeley and Los Angeles: University of California Press.

Stone, A. R. (1991). Will the Real Body Please Stand Up? Boundary Stories about Virtual Communities. In: M. Benedikt (Ed.), *Cyberspace: First Steps* (pp. 81–118). Boston: MIT Press.

Swatos, W. H. Jr., & Christiano, K. J. (1999). Secularization Theory: The Course of a Concept. *Sociology of Religion, 60*(3), 209–227.

Turner, V. (1969). *The Ritual Process: Structure and Anti-Structure*. New York: Aldine De Gruyter.

Wallis, R. (1984). *The Elementary Forms of the New Religious Life*. London: Routledge.

Wellman, B. (1988). The Community Question Re-Evaluated. In: M. P. Smith (Ed.), *Power, Community and the City* (pp. 81–107). New Brunswick, NJ: Transaction Books.

Wellman, B. & Gulia, M. (1999). Virtual Communities as Communities: Net Surfers Don't Ride Alone. In: M. A. Smith, & P. Kollock, (Eds), *Communities in Cyberspace* (pp. 167–194). New York: Routledge.

Wilson, B. (1970). *Religious Sects: A Sociological Study*. Toronto: World University Press.

Wolff, R. F. (1999). A Phenomenological Study of In-Church and Televised Worship. *Journal for the Scientific Study of Religion, 38*(2), 219–235.

Wuthnow, R. (1998). *After Heaven: Spirituality in America Since the 1950's*. Berkeley and Los Angeles: University of California Press.

Zaleski, J. (1997). *The Soul of Cyberspace: How New Technology is Changing Our Spiritual Lives*. New York: HarperCollins Publishers.

ON-LINE ETHNOGRAPHY OF
DISPENSATIONALIST DISCOURSE:
REVEALED VERSUS NEGOTIATED
TRUTH

Robert Glenn Howard

ABSTRACT

This chapter discusses and applies a mix of rhetorical and ethnographic analytical methods to document and analyze a small Internet community. Providing an easily identifiable and wide-spread discourse, engaging in both on-line and face-to-face discourse with American Evangelical dispensationalists creates a window on the evolving modes of Internet expression. Developing out of informal electronic expression, dispensationalist debaters utilize complex vernacular rhetorical techniques. In 1999, this community's debates were a feverish rush. In this rush, a rhetorical tension emerges between the desire to negotiate about truth and the desire to express an experienced or revelatory Truth. This article explores the possibilities and limits of the hypothesis that the medium of the Internet encourages and privileges more negotiative rhetorical techniques based on the methods it has developed for this purpose.

Religion on the Internet, Volume 8, pages 225–246.
Copyright © 2000 by Elsevier Science Inc.
All rights of reproduction in any form reserved.
ISBN: 0-7623-0535-5

INTRODUCTION

As a new millennium begins to dawn across the Western world, radical changes in the everyday lives of many North Americans are being driven by new technologies. Primary among these is the expansion of local area computer networks into a massive wide area network loosely called 'the Internet'.

If a moment must be chosen to mark the first conception of the Internet, one might consider the 1962 vision of an 'Intergalactic Network' of MIT's J.C.R. Licklider (Hauben, 1995). He conceived of a globally interconnected set of computers through which individuals could quickly access data and programs from any location. Unlike many of the life-changing inventions of the millennium, though, the Internet is not the product of any single human genius or moment of revelation. Instead, it is the slow evolution of applied computer technologies. From this development two key characteristics emerge that define and shape the modes and norms which on-line communication has taken, and of which any socio-cultural research conducted on Internet communication must be aware. These two key characteristics are:

- a driving desire to develop the ability to share documents openly and freely across great distances; and
- a level of computer coding that could be shared universally by all computers attempting to access the networked information.

Since the Internet was developed out of and through existing computer systems, a common reference point was needed. At the beginning, and in large part still, this reference point is the ASCII text code and the Hyper Text Markup Language (HTML).

It is precisely this characteristic of striving to share information that formed the Internet technologies as we know them today. Further, the necessity to share common base-line information encourages the adoption of similar communicative technologies. From a cultural or sociological perspective, however, this same desire and its resulting technologies create a feedback loop in which individuals using the Internet are engaging technologies whose very design encourages the open sharing of information based on common shared communicative modes.

Unlike the unilateral transfer of information characteristic of mass media broadcasting, the Internet is multilateral. Because of its design as a multilateral medium, individuals using the Internet tend to engage in complicated discourse with multiple other individuals. Thus, to try to analyze the cultural impact of this new technology using mass media models of communication, quantitative analysis, audience sampling, and so on are not enough to draw a full picture of the developing Internet behaviors. Instead, we must accept that the multilateral communication on the Internet creates a sort of dynamic electronic community.

Relying on community-focused models of communication, my approach is rooted in the nexus of ethnography and rhetoric. Because the Internet is multilateral, it develops its own dynamic communities. Because these communities are based primarily in the exchange of language, they are identified with the help of the post-modern rhetorical idea of 'discourse'. Hence, my analysis of Internet communities is a result of my own long term participation in a specifically bounded discourse community: Evangelical dispensationalism.

A brand of fundamentalist Christianity, dispensationalism presents a rich field for analysis precisely because it is a discourse that is not typically associated with the free exchange of diverse and new ideas. I contend that all discourse on the Internet will foster a desire to exchange information precisely because the very structure of the Internet is one which was designed to make the free exchange of information and ideas possible across space and time: Licklider's vision of an 'intergalactic network'. That is to say, Internet mediated discourse will exhibit strongly negotiative rhetorical strategies.

In order to gather data to test against this hypothesis, I have had to develop new research methods. This study attempts both to describe those methods and to present the preliminary results that they have yielded. Instead of fully validating my hypothesis, however, my research has proven Geertz's famous statement about ethnography: "Cultural analysis is intrinsically incomplete. And, worse than that, the more deeply it goes the less complete it is" (Geertz, 1973, p. 28). My research has complicated my understanding of Internet behavior as much as it has clarified it. I hope this article shows by this very fact that the methods I have developed for the documentation and analysis of on-line communication have proven a rigorous basis for further development and application.

BACKGROUND

I have been involved in on-line dispensational discourse since 1994. Developing quite accidentally out of my desire to locate individuals who watched the dispensational televangelist Jack Van Impe's weekly television broadcast, I emailed each of the few Christian newsgroups looking for research respondents. Having really only used the Internet for email correspondence to that point, I was shocked by the range and diversity of response. Within hours, I received responses to my query that quickly escalated into the hundreds. Soon, I was a member of various private email lists where everyday dispensationalist Christians hotly debated theological issues not unlike scholars and theologians at an academic conference (see Howard, 1997).

Since that initial research, my project has evolved to explore the socially instilled rhetorical strategies that individuals choose to employ in the everyday contexts of their lives. I have sought to do this through the examination of beliefs associated with an impending apocalypse. Apocalyptic communication is excellent for this research because it presents, based on the influence of Hal Lindsey and other popular writers and evangelists, a well defined American discourse known loosely as 'dispensationalism' (Lindsey, 1970, 1994; Wojcik, 1997).

The basic teaching of dispensationalism is that human history exists as a series of divinely mandated epochs or 'dispensations'. The current state of affairs, the current 'dispensation' is 'The Church Age'. Beginning with the crucifixion of Christ, this dispensation will end with the Rapture – the moment when all true believers will be lifted bodily from the earth to escape the onset of an age of human strife and turbulence that will finally result in the millennial reign of Christ (Boyer, 1992, pp. 86ff). Mixed with a general rise in evangelical activity in America, there is a new fixation on events surrounding 'The Tribulation' and the Endtimes.

Although the influence of dispensationalism is well documented in contemporary religious sects as diverse as the Seventh-Day Adventists (including the Branch Davidians), The Church of Jesus Christ of Latter-day Saints, the Christian Identity Movement, as well as Aum Shinrikyo, and the Solar Temple, by the 1990s dispensational thinking had become diffused across general Evangelical discourse (Palmer & Robbins, 1997; Strozier & Flynn, 1997). Grounded in a common tradition of evangelical ministry, writers and preachers like Hal Lindsey, Pat Robertson, Jack Van Impe, and others have established a well defined and clear American dispensationalist discourse. The popular writer Hal Lindsey is particularly well known for works that tapped, defined, and helped normalize this premillennial discourse. In 1970, his first major book, *The Late Great Planet Earth*, sold 7.5 million copies making it the largest selling non-fiction book of the decade (Wojcik, 1997, p. 8).

Discussed by televangelists and by Christians at church socials or between friends, one characteristic of this pan-Evangelical discourse has adapted particularly well to new electronic media – and, in particular, to Internet communication. Even in its obsessive focus on the conclusion of time itself, that characteristic is one of reverential debate in which the exchange of potentially important but unknowable facts takes on aspects of spiritual devotion. In his introduction to *The Late Great Planet Earth*, Lindsey stated, "I am attempting to step aside and let the prophets speak. The readers are given the freedom to accept or reject my conclusions" (Lindsey, 1970, p. 6). Much as Lindsey himself implies, many Evangelical Endtimes debaters find sanctity in debate, not in final conclusions.

In 1991, Christian vernacular expression on the Internet was small. But by 1994, a number of large and broadly inclusive Christian newsgroups were in full bloom. On those groups, however, millennial discourse came only in short bursts. In the late 1990s, the Christian Internet communities had diversified and expanded. In so doing, Christians offered themselves more niches for millennial expression. This development seems a typical pattern for contemporary electronic communication. The effect of this pattern on communicative behavior is, however, debatable.

On the one hand, more diversity in smaller discursive niches might allow individuals to limit their media and/or vernacular influences to only those with which they already more or less agreed. Some argue that such individuals would then become more easily influenced by dogmatic leaders. However, the behavior I have documented indicates that individuals involved in electronic media do not immerse themselves in a single newsgroup, email list, Web site or discourse community. Thus, they are not, for the most part, easily influenced by single-minded or dogmatic argumentative techniques.

For instance, many individuals watching Jack Van Impe's weekly Christian dispensationalist television broadcasts also talk to their friends about his show. They engage both popular media and face-to-face human interaction in a dynamic interchange of influence and expression. In 1994, many of these people were also beginning to explore the Internet and participate in email discussions about Van Impe's show, comparing its information with previously held beliefs or other discursive influences. Then, many of these same individuals also communicated with an untold number of others through chat rooms, newsgroups, and Web sites.

As these individuals widen and diversify the multiple discourse communities they participate in, they must also, by the very act of widening and diversifying, accept more and different ideas into their discourse. Internet communities who engage in dispensationalist discourse actually debate, in a continuous cycle, the same core issues which form easily identifiable narrative sets based on the popular ideas of dispensationalism and normalized into a fairly standard narrative set by such writers as Lindsey (Howard, 1997, 1998b).

In Christian discourses such as these, there are repeating patterns that can be usefully considered 'vernacular rhetoric': rhetorical techniques that are employed by individuals without formal training in rhetoric.[1] In the case of many Evangelical dispensationalists in 1994, I found a rhetoric of open debate which included the desire to entertain different millennial possibilities (Howard, 1997). While for other individuals, such as the Heaven's Gate group, I have found a flat rejection of debate based on a deep conviction that Truth had already been 'revealed' to that group or its leaders (Howard, 1998a).

Revelatory Truth is a truth known wholly and immediately. *Negotiated truth*, on the other hand, is pursued through open dialogue among different individuals. It is the formulation and reformulation of beliefs based on new influence sources. While experience can act as a final authority, negotiation can only support truth if the negotiating parties are willing to continue communication. Developing out of informal electronic expression, apocalyptic debaters utilize both of these complex vernacular rhetorical techniques – often simultaneously.

RESEARCH METHODS

With my initial posts to and responses from dispensational email lists in 1994, I had rather unwittingly become involved in the on-line dispensationalist community at its very beginnings. To better take advantage of this involvement, I decided to more directly participate in this on-line discourse. To this end, I built *The Millennial Information Exchange* World Wide Web site in 1996 (http://www.endnear.com). This site provides a publicly accessible forum in which anyone can read and post their ideas.

The M.I.E. Web site functions as a way for me to participate in the on-line dispensationalist community. My actual research data, however, is encoded onto CD-ROMs and is not publicly accessible. Since the summer of 1999, I have been systematically downloading and saving Web sites, emailing questionnaires, and engaging in email discourse with millennial Web site builders. After I established relationships with individuals on-line, I have traveled to interview many of those whose Web sites I have archived. Including transcribed interviews, these electronic archives are already substantial: over 250 complete Web sites, some 50,000 emails, survey responses, and interview transcripts totaling nearly three gigabytes of data in more than 60,000 individual files.

The collection of this data is not random. Instead, it is the result of both experience within the on-line dispensationalist community and an organized effort based on methods developed out of that experience.

In the past, the study of individuals within locally defined communities in the non-electronic world could be adequately addressed by assuming that those individuals comprise a single discourse community or folk group with little or no outside influence (Redfield, 1930). However, groups such as these are an increasingly rare phenomenon. Where it has emerged, electronic communication has so radically changed the way human discourse is conducted that new approaches must be developed to address contemporary communicative events of all sorts.

On the Internet, individuals involved in multiple discourse communities simultaneously engage one another on multiple topics informed by potentially unlimited sources of influence. By implication, no two individuals necessarily share all of the same influences. However, by defining a single discursive matrix, we can establish if and to what degree a given individual is engaged in a particular discourse. To develop this model, I have turned to terms common in the study of rhetoric, 'discourse community' primary among them.[2]

Discourse refers to any communicative activity that surrounds specific and observable communicated elements. Individuals who engage in a discourse comprise a discourse community. My term, 'influence community', expands this communicative domain by referring to individuals who are influenced by a single mass media source without necessarily engaging the creators and/or disseminators of that source in other discourse.

Discursive communication can be seen as necessitating at least bilateral, if not multilateral, communicative behavior in which all members of the community are both audience and expressers. Influence communities can be discursive, but do not have to be. Instead, they can encompass both discourse communities' multilateral ('two-way or more') communicative characteristic as well as mass media's unilateral ('one-way') characteristic. For example, individuals who watch a particular soap opera every day comprise an influence community, but not necessarily a discursive one. At the same time, individuals who watch that same soap opera and also communicate about it in an email discussion group participate in a discourse community based on the single influence of the soap opera.

While the examination of influence communities is highly developed in journalism and mass communication studies (see McQuail, 1994, pp. 33ff), the study of discourse has long been the purview of rhetoric. Many studying the new forms of electronic communication find them to be far more discourse-oriented than the quantitative analysis models of television or newspaper communication were designed to examine.

For this reason, my descriptive rhetorical concept of a 'discursive matrix' becomes useful. A discursive matrix refers to a theoretical model of the shared ideas or issues that are necessary to define a given communicative behavior as related to or participating in a given discourse. By using such rhetorical terms, we can consider each individual involved in more than one of these communities as a unique nexus of the various discourses and influences he or she engages in or has been exposed to.

In order to establish if a particular communication is engaging in a particular discourse, I sought to locate definitive traits of dispensationalism. Because the on-line behavior I am documenting is heavily focused on the debate of certain common issues, I have named these definitive marks 'exchange issues'.

Exchange issues are the basis for much dispensationalist discourse on-line. In order for an individual to engage in 'exchange issue'-driven discourse, both sides of the communication must have a certain competence in the discourse. In the case of on-line dispensationalists, one of the most common exchange issues serves as an example. This issue is the 'pre-trib vs. post-trib' debate, which centers around the order of specific events that dispensationalists expect to see occur in the near future. In this case, the 'pre' and 'post' refer to whether Christians will be Raptured before or after the Tribulation.

Regardless of a particular debater's position on this exchange issue, he or she must be familiar with one of the basics of dispensationalism: that true Christians will be saved in the Rapture at some point. This, of course, implies a knowledge of the broader discourse of Evangelical belief. This, as well as some familiarity with the Bible, are necessary for competence in the on-line dispensationalist discourse.

Setting out both to familiarize myself with the basics of dispensationalist discourse and to establish a method for assessing competence in that discourse, I began to read the major modern writers of Dispensationalism. Having already analyzed Jack Van Impe's dispensationalist broadcasts for over a year, I found in Hal Lindsey's writings an almost exact replication of a basic narrative set. From this set, the typical exchange issues arise and are discussed by on-line millennial debaters.

For example, from watching *Jack Van Impe Presents* regularly over a two month period in 1994, I constructed a schematic of his Endtimes narrative. Immediately following the United States' ground assault on the Iraqi forces occupying Kuwait:

1. Iraq surrenders and negotiates peace;
2. Palestine peace "becomes international in scope";
3. A world leader rises out of revived Roman Empire (the European Union);
4. EU originates and consummates international peace treaty;
5. A World coalition of nations is the 'New World Order' President Bush spoke of during the Gulf War;
6. Russia breaks away from world organization and attacks Israel at the three-and-a-half year point of a seven-year peace treaty;
7. The majority of the Arab world aligns itself with Russia against Israel;
8. England and America ("the English speaking world") and Saudi Arabia "will raise a voice of opposition" against Russia;
9. "Three-and-a-half years of skirmishes" climax in Jerusalem;
10. "Messiah will come to end the war, but not wipe out the world."

At the time Van Impe set out this schema, number 1 and, arguably, number 2 had already occurred. The following eight events were, by implication, on the immediate horizon. From Van Impe's perspective, all these predictions are well grounded in Biblical teaching. While there are some interesting differences between this model and that which pervades Lindsey's work, the same basic belief structure informs both (see Howard, 1997; Wojcik, 1997).

This belief structure serves as a baseline series of narrative events that defines on-line dispensationalist discourse. It must be kept in mind, however, that an individual engaging parts of this narrative set is not exclusively or even necessarily a believer in contemporary dispensationalism. However, even though individuals engaging in debates may or may not be believers, from this discourse-centered approach when an individual debates a dispensationalist issue, even if only for a moment, he or she is involved in dispensationalist discourse.

This leads us to new and complicated questions about who the primary participants in this discourse are. Having established what sort of discourse constitutes dispensationalism, individuals heavily involved in this discourse must be located. When downloading dispensationalist Web sites, I also followed each link from those sites and downloaded the linked site. In this manner, while I have not exhaustively cataloged all dispensationalist Web sites, I have documented a core group of sites that are all linked to one another.

Because there are many hundreds of sites involved in dispensationalism even though it is a relatively small discourse, this catalog had to be limited in order to archive them in any detail. To this end, I began eliminating sites from the research which were: (a) not based in the United States, (b) run by trained ministers, or (c) part of a for-profit evangelical career of some sort. Although I have archived some sites belonging to major figures in dispensationalism, the focus of my research, in keeping with its examination of 'vernacular' rhetorics, is on amateur site builders whose use of the WWW is not their primary occupation.

Having established a catalog of over 250 Web sites, I began contacting Web site builders via email. I asked both permission to archive the site and a couple of basic questions to establish if the Web site would fit the criteria of the research. When that email was answered, I sent a second asking if I could forward a questionnaire for the Web site builder or builders to fill out and return. That questionnaire included basic demographic questions, as well as some questions to establish how conversant the individual was with dispensationalist discourse.

As these responses were returned, they were cataloged; some raised further questions in my own mind, others had questions of their own. Each of these was responded to. In some cases, I asked or was invited to join and archive the correspondence on email lists associated with some of the Web sites. Thanks were sent and so forth, and all of this correspondence was organized as it was collected. While this went on, I began a second catalog of those individuals I might be able to interview at a later date. In the coming months, I would re-email, as many as three times, individuals who did not respond to my initial contact.

For those who had agreed to have their site archived, I downloaded and saved their entire Web sites using commercial software designed for that purpose. Placing exact duplicates of each Web site into separate folders together with their Web address, this first run of downloading went on in an intensive session during the Fall of 1999.

Interested in documenting any apprehension surrounding the turn of the year from 1999 to 2000, the second downloading run of these same sites took place in the Spring of 2000; a third run is planned for Fall of 2000. Further 'snap shots' of my primary Web sites are planned for the Spring and Fall of 2001. The current number of sample sites stabilized at 120 – some have already disappeared and a few others were added as it seemed appropriate.

While this downloading was going on, I also organized and conducted interviews with as many Web site builders as I could travel to visit. Individuals who agreed to fill out the electronic questionnaire, and were in an area I could to travel to, were asked if they would be available for a face-to-face interview. When an interview was agreed to, I sought to organize interview schedules. These resulted in long road trips from Montana to Seattle, and to San Diego. Further, some air travel afforded me the opportunity to do interviews as far east as Florida and North Carolina.

As with many ethnographic interview projects, these interviews followed a basic formula which established similar data for each. At the same time, individuals were encouraged to draw the conversations in ways they thought fruitful. As time and funding have permitted, these interviews are being transcribed and added to my data archives as text files.

At this point, these archives had become rather unwieldy in size. I moved them from my computer harddrive onto CD-ROMs and made basic HTML pages to facilitate navigation in the raw data. As the addition of these HTML pages suggests, I envision these archives being useful to future researchers in both religion and Internet communication. In the future, I hope to make it available for that purpose.

While the Modern Language Association and other publication-oriented organizations try to treat WWW documents in the traditional ways which published texts have been treated, Internet documents do not share the fundamental characteristic of published works in libraries. Simply stated: published texts do not change and hence can be cited. Once cited, those texts can be located via various library and publishing systems to verify that what is cited actually exists in the published text.

WWW documents – amateur or personal ones in particular – are constantly appearing, changing, and disappearing from individual harddrives all over the world everyday. As new technologies are developed, these sites are already fundamentally changing in character and appearance.

While some sites might survive into the future as the result of random business or institutional practices and some could be resurrected via the dawning field of electronic archeology, these archives represent an organized sample of a large cross-section of individuals who share a common discourse based on the discursive set popularly established by Hal Lindsey long before Internet technologies were readily available. Why settle for archeology when we have the ability to augment such future efforts through the application of systematized ethnography and archiving? Such archives offer a series of snapshots of a discreetly bounded discourse at specific intervals during these early years of Internet communication.

In the following cases, I apply my basic hypothesis that discourse on the Internet will foster a desire to exchange information and thus encourage negotiative over revelatory rhetorical strategies to four very different Web sites that are included in the archives. I hope the utility and rigor of my ethnographic methods will become clear through these examples.

CASES:

www.alphathroughomega.com

A stark default gray background with no graphic images at all, 'Gene' and 'Susan's' Web site is the result of Gene's direct communication with God.[3] Gene is an employee of Intel and his wife, Susan, is a homemaker. I interviewed them together over breakfast near the Intel headquarters in Hillsboro, Oregon, on October 5, 1999. Although Gene is a skilled computer technician, he is also skilled at casting out demons.

God has led Gene to present a fairly typical Evangelical Endtimes scenario. On the front page of his Web site, he has listed representative topics for Endtimes debaters under the names: 'End Times Studies', 'Doctrinal Errors In The Churches', 'Open Letter to Satanists and Occultists', and so on. Through the link, 'End Times Studies', he has created a series of pages that outline a standard dispensationalist chronology of events associated with the Endtimes. These pages include descriptions of the 'Tribulation Period', a time when anti-Christ will take control of the European Union and persecute Christians during a massive Third World War. In addition to these standard topics, Gene and Susan also use a common argumentative style in which a Biblical quote is presented, then followed by the correct interpretation that has come to Gene through God's direct guidance.

On one such page, 'REVELATION 3:10' is the passage quoted. Here, Gene discusses the 'Rapture' (Alpha thru Omega, End Times Bible Study). The most commonly debated topic in this discourse, it is clear that Gene is on the 'Post-Tribulation' side of the issue. Unlike Hal Lindsey or many other popular dispensationalists, Gene does not believe that the Rapture will lift the true believers from the chaos of impending apocalypse. Instead, side-by-side with the sinners, these believers will have to weather the plagues of war, disease, and natural catastrophe. While acknowledging that his view is different from other dispensationalists, Gene is not interested in exploring the possibility that he might be wrong because his knowledge is the result of direct experience with God.

On another page, it is clear that Gene and Susan are also involved in the 'spiritual warfare' movement (Alpha thru Omega, Spiritual Warfare Training). They both have a long relationship with demons. Gene showed me his 'Warlock' tattoo as proof he was "into the occult." In fact, he was so deeply involved that he became possessed by a demonic spirit. This occurred while Gene was in the Navy, before he met Susan. His personality changed. He became distant and emotionless, and he gained minor supernatural powers: mind-reading, seeing the future, and partial control of the weather. Because of these powers, he got quite a reputation aboard ship ('Gene', personal communication, October 5, 1999).

Dramatic spiritual beliefs animate Gene and Susan's daily lives: from wrong turns into demonically controlled parking lots to apartment neighbors attracting demonic attacks through their occult rituals. Both Gene and Susan believe they have been subject to earthly manifestations of demon attacks in the well known forms of fog, sense of presence, temperature drops, and other sensory phenomena.[4] Their belief in demons is based on these personal experiences, and are a result of Gene's turning away from the powers of Satan. From this wealth of direct personal experience, they offer advice and help for others on their Web pages. For example, another page on their Web site contains a short how-to section on 'hedges', the practice of spiritually cordoning off demonic forces (Alpha thru Omega, Hedges).

Gene and Susan present a typical scenario for the Endtimes. Their arguments against a pre-Tribulation Rapture further indicate they are aware of and participate in the Evangelical discursive community of Endtimes debate. Like many Endtimes debaters, Gene feels his very words, as he writes them for the Web, are directed by a special personal relationship with God. He knows that relationship exists because of his personal experiences of God, angels, and demonic forces.

Gene presents an excellent, if extreme, example of an individual operating in a world of revelatory rhetoric relying heavily on personal experience narratives in his appeals to authority both in person and on-line. However, his site is relatively unknown because, in part, it fails to conform to the expectations of Internet communication which demand, at least, the appearance of an openness to response, debate, and change of one's expressed opinions and beliefs.

CASES:

http://ldolphin.org

At the other end of the spectrum, Lambert Dolphin's site presents an example of highly negotiative rhetoric. Based on its links from other dispensationally oriented Web sites, as well as personal testimony of interviewees, his site is extraordinarily well known. While I have been in email contact with Lambert since 1994, his site is a little bit older than that. I finally managed to interview him face-to-face in August 1999. Though not totally devoted to millennialism, his site is one of largest independent Christian sites on the Web: 69.9 megs for some 1449 files. The bulk of this material is a section entitled 'Lambert's Library' (Dolphin, 2000).

Because his site is so large and has been around for so long, Lambert is probably the best known amateur evangelist in the online Endtimes community. His resumé, which is also available on his Web site, contributes a long list of credits accumulated from a career in sound and light wave research at Stanford University in Palo Alto, California. Lambert is a retired physicist, and this fact bolsters his on-line authority (Dolphin, 1996).

He told me the reason he first put up the site:

> I started just filing things on my Web site . . . and it became handy to find things there and that motivated me to write a little bit more deliberately for the Web site specifically. So the email comes in and finds what I have to say interesting and worthwhile or it generates comments; so I think it is worthwhile (L. Dolphin, personal communication, September 7, 1999).

Instead of focusing on the transmission of knowledge as do Gene and Susan, Lambert considers his Web site 'worthwhile' because it 'generates comments'. The 'library' includes materials and articles he has collected and developed for use in his lectures, Bible study groups, and Sunday school programs; many of these materials are eschatological in nature. Over forty links take site visitors to eschatological articles and other materials he has written and created for the library.

One of these library links, which are periodically revised, leads to "Lambert's Chart of the End Times" (Dolphin, 1999). In two large graphic files, it presents a fairly standard Dispensationalist understanding of Endtimes events. However, the *only dates* Lambert places on his time-line are '1997' (in his upper diagram) and '1999' (in the lower); rather than predictive values these represent 'the present', the last times he updated the charts.

Unlike some Dispensationalists, Lambert's understanding of Christian eschatology can offer neither specific dates for events nor concrete descriptions of who will be anti-Christ, and so forth. Thus, neither of his timelines offers any predictive chronology. And, as Lambert says: "In fact, it's probably perfectly acceptable to have equivalent models [of eschatology] and use the one that you feel most comfortable with – or the one that fits best to your circumstances" (L. Dolphin, personal communication, September 7, 1999).

While this makes Lambert an extreme example of an Endtimes debater using heavily negotiative rhetoric, it is still not as cut-and-dried as one might think. Lambert, Gene, and Susan have all had similar conversion experiences which include a strong sensation of euphoric joy brought on by prayer and sometimes lasting for days or weeks afterward. For Lambert, this experience plays a central role in his spiritual belief system. Lambert describes his 're-birth' experience in the following terms: "There was this feeling of being washed, and clean, and guilt going away, and this sense of peace of mind about the future, and hope, and then this new excitement" (L. Dolphin, personal communication, September 7, 1999).

This experience, however, was unlike Gene's in which he believes he has direct aural and/or visual contact with the divine. Nor did Lambert's experience offer him any final or direct Truth from God of anything more than God's grace.

Instead, Lambert insists on replicability of experimental trials: "And then I can go compare notes with other people who have had an experience like mine, and does their experience seem similar – and then I asked, 'Is this the real thing?' " I asked him if he was able to verify his experience 'scientifically'. He responded: "Is it verifiable? Not scientifically verifiable, but it is experientially verifiable" (L. Dolphin, personal communication, September 7, 1999). Even though he is a spiritual pluralist who believes that the divine can be accessed by many different, but potentially equal means, at the level of quiet personal knowledge, Lambert too relies on his direct experience of the divine.

The pairing of Gene and Susan with Lambert offers the extremes of revelatory versus negotiative rhetoric. However, most millennial believers tend toward the center of this continuum. In so doing, they exhibit much more complex rhetorical behaviors. One such case is Marilyn Agee and her Web site, 'Bible Prophecy Corner'.

CASES:

http://www.kiwi.net/~mjagee

Marilyn is a well known Web site builder and author. Her three books have sold more than 90,000 copies. She gained particular notoriety when she was forced to recant her prediction that the Tribulation would begin on Pentecost 1998. In September 1999, I interviewed her and her husband near their home in Riverside,

California. At that time, she contended that the Tribulation will begin on Pentecost 2000 or 2001 (M. Agee, personal communication, September 4, 1999).

While the typical appeals Marilyn uses are experiential and revelatory in nature, overall, her on-line persona contains a strongly negotiative twist. Discussing with me how she claims such powerful knowledge of the divine, she stated that she spent seven years reading "everything man had written about the Bible," but was disappointed with their lack of understanding. "I wanted to know the hard things," she said. "So I just opened my Bible, and put my hands on it, and I said, 'Lord you'll have to show me'. The next seven years I learned so fast I could hardly keep up with it" (M. Agee, personal communication, September 4, 1999).

Based on this divine infusion of understanding, Marilyn commonly makes rhetorical claims to authority based on her personal experience through study. On her biographical page, she states: "I am a Baptist believer who has been studying the Bible as deep as I can go for over 38 years" (Agee, 1998a). This 'depth' comes by way of being 'led by God' in her studies.

Despite this revelatory authority, the bulk of her Web site is bluntly negotiative. The main section, some 13 megabytes in size, is devoted to what she calls the 'Pro and Con Index', and consists of over 400 individual pages. Each page contains her personal debates with an individual who has emailed her with questions or disagreements. She has posted these exchanges for visitors to review and comment upon. Still, she contends that her responses to these debaters are divinely inspired and, therefore, authoritative. In fact, starting with her first publication, all her discourse seems to have been so inspired:

> So I'd been typing all day, and I grabbed my Bible by the back of it and I just pounced down across the bed. And I said: 'Why am I doing all this work for anyway?' The next thing I knew, I'm looking at my Bible – about an inch from my face and Jeremiah 50 verse 2 has rectangle of light on it. Everything else looks gray. I could have read it if I wanted to, it wasn't that dark, but it looked gray – and this verse had light on it, saying: 'Publish and conceal not'. (M. Agee, personal communication, September 4, 1999)

Marilyn often shares this story with people she is debating, and, when she does this, it serves to divinely authorize her arguments.

CASES:

http://www.mt.net/~watcher

In October of 1999, I drove to Helena, Montana and interviewed 'Jane' and 'John' who know Marilyn's claims of inspired authority well. Together, Jane and John comprise the on-line personality know as the 'Watcher'.

Since 1993, they have built and maintained one of the most visually appealing and influential Endtimes Web sites. Featured on the television show *Strange Universe*, an A&E documentary, they even had Ted Koppel comment negatively on their work in the aftermath of the Heaven's Gate suicides. Their case is particularly interesting for this discussion because, as it turns out, 'Watcher' emailed with Marilyn for a long time; in the end, however, their relationship soured.

Like Lambert, Gene, and Susan, Jane and John have both had conversion experiences. They both consider themselves 'born again'. Before they became Christians, John and Jane solidly believed in the UFO phenomenon. John was a lapsed Catholic, and Jane was practicing Wicca.

> The reason we put the Web site up was because we wanted to combat this cognitive dissonance that's set up by the fact that UFOs exist *and* there's a Gospel. Then we wanted to point out that the Bible does clearly define what's exactly happening and what will happen and outlines what UFOs are. Then there's this idea that there's actually monuments on another planet – and that blows most peoples' minds! ('Jane', personal communication, October 17, 1999).

This work has resulted in 4 megabytes of text and images about monuments on Mars, UFO technology, government conspiracy, *The X Files*, and much more.

While I interviewed the 'Watcher' couple, I mentioned a page I found on their Web site where they specifically refute Marilyn Agee's assertion of Two Raptures. Apparently, a few years ago, Marilyn emailed Jane when she found the 'Watcher' site. Soon, Jane, John, and Marilyn were debating Endtimes topics. However, this relationship fizzled over differing interpretations of a passage in Second Thessalonians where it seems to state that Christians will live to see the anti-Christ in power (see Watcher, Rapture on Pentecost?). From Jane and John's perspective, this means that there will be no pre-Tribulation Rapture, but Agee disagrees – arguing, somewhat idiosyncratically, that there will be a two-phased Rapture. Again, this is part of the Pre-, Mid-, or Post-Trib debate, the most common Endtimes exchange issue. Talking about their discussions with Marilyn, Jane said:

> We just tried so hard to say, "Marilyn, what does this passage in scripture mean then? How can you interpret it any other way, because it's in black and white, the Greek means this." And, she won't look at it because it hurts too bad. It's a very painful thing to think ('Jane', personal communication, October 17, 1999).[5]

While Jane was ready to move on or reconsider Marilyn's two Rapture assertion saying, 'what does this passage mean then?', Marilyn refused to continue the debate and negotiation ended. In fact, to this day, Marilyn refuses to return Jane or John's emails. From my analysis, this is not surprising. While the 'Pro and Con Index' seems to present a desire to negotiate, the rhetoric that Marilyn uses is closed because of its basis in the personal authority of experience and revelation.

All this is not to say that 'Watcher' does not also have their own sense of experiential authority. However, both Jane and John do reject most claims to direct aural or visual experience of God – including the account of Agee's high-lighted passage directing her to publish. A psychologist, John called it 'mildly neurotic'. Commenting on Gene and Susan's experiences with demons and possession, both Jane and John agreed that such beliefs are dangerously rooted in 'superstition' and myth. As they describe in their Web pages, such super-stitions are a demonic tactic to lead humans away from Christ. Speaking of Gene's experience of possession by and getting rid of demons, John stated:

> He's tricked! It serves a huge point because all it is is a red herring. The forces that they're playing with are all the same. Their [the demons'] agenda is only one: to get man away from the truth. So, if you can get them to think, ya know – to play good cop/bad cop, that's *super* effective ('John', personal communication, October 17, 1999).

Jane and John limit valid direct experience of deity to conversion experiences similar to those which they themselves have had. As a psychologist, John discounts Agee's experiences as mildly delusional. Gene's experiences are regarded as demonic and dangerous. For 'Watcher', the only valid experience of deity is the entering of the Holy Spirit into their consciousnesses—the 'born again' experience which is neither aural nor visual.

Although this places 'Watcher' in the experiential, if not fully revelatory frame, their interpretations are not divinely guided. They are adept at debating on the Internet, with each other, and with me, even altering their opinions to suit new facts as their Web site develops. Their understanding of the divine is, as John put it, "dynamic." Because they are clearly more negotiative than Marilyn, they are more likely to continue a debate with her long after she has given up on them.

But both Marilyn and 'Watcher' are very popular Internet Endtimes figures. Although Marilyn can successfully interact with people on the Internet, she still maintains the belief that her divine guidance in scriptural study produces funda-mentally superior interpretations. And, although 'Watcher' can reject all divine experiences different from their own, they still engage in negotiative debate almost indefinitely.

CONCLUSION

On the most basic level, I have been arguing that everyday Dispensational discourse is animated and polarized by a recurring tension between truth arrived at through individual revelatory experience and truth pursued through pluralistic negotiation. Further, I have argued that the structure of the Internet itself encourages negotiative rhetorical techniques. While it would be entirely possible for an individual to access and participate only in discourses in which he or she would not find new or challenging ideas, the Internet itself facilitates multi-lateral communication between widely disparate individuals. It seems that, even if some individuals do avoid new ideas and foreign discourses, the appeal of using Internet technologies in one's spare time is to expand one's discourse audience.

Because the basic narrative set which defines competence in Dispensationalist discourse is widely known, easily assimilated, and open-ended enough to mesh new ideas with very old ones, Dispensationalist debate as I have documented it here is very well adapted to Internet expression. At the same time, in a sort of feedback loop, individuals engaging in this debate are encouraged by the medium of the Internet to use negotiative rhetorical techniques.

I still hold this basic hypothesis to be valid – but my understanding of it has deepened and been complicated by the data I am collecting. While Marilyn Agee is unbudgingly certain of her experienced, revealed truths, she argues on the Internet in what, at first, appears to be a highly negotiative manner. However, when faced with an equally certain debater, her ability to communicate seems to cease.

While 'Watcher' is saddened at the loss of their friend, they both asserted to me specifically that "Marilyn is saved." That is, even if she is dogmatic and wrong, she is a real Christian and, though she will go through the Tribulation with every-body else, she will be saved in the end. Of that they have no doubt. For all of these Endtimes debaters, the experience of God's grace through rebirth seems to out-weigh the significance of on-line dogmatism, difference, and disgreement.

For 'Watcher' and Lambert, this experience of grace seems to be the only sort of authorizing divine experience. For Marilyn, it is one of a few. For Gene and Susan, it is one of many.

As the 1990s have come to an end and the new millennium dawns, the Internet has transformed from the realm of obscure technical enthusiasts and researchers into a commercial juggernaut that has pressed individuals into its service at every level. From ready access to information, to wildly multiplying sources for mail-order products, to complex personal debates on cryptic topics, the average North American is becoming more and more wedded to Internet communication.

At the end of 1999, the mainstream press had picked up, disseminated, and blown far out of proportion the possibility of a Y2K computer bug that might bring modern society to a standstill. Long a topic of some concern for American Dispensationalists, the change from 1999 to 2000 precipitated perhaps the greatest single moment of anticipation for the Endtimes which animates contemporary Dispensationalism. As the clock struck midnight, more individuals than ever before in the history of human consciousness stopped to take note of that very moment, of the passage of time itself – and, maybe, of the finitude of that time. And, of course, nothing much happened.

In a way, this fact exemplifies the most surprising result of the research I am conducting on the effect of Internet use on the personal expression of vernacular religious belief. As much as the technophiles and commercial producers of network technologies argue that every aspect of our lives will be improved by the Internet, religious expression seems to remain fundamentally the same. Devout religious believers like Marilyn can master the new rhetorical forms of Internet communication, and yet maintain the self-assurance of a medieval zealot.

At the same time, we must recognize that something has changed. The effects of that change are already far reaching and the extent to which they will continue to change religious expression and experience can only be guessed. The medieval zealot had no access to Native American or Hindu contemporaries who might hold similar or divergent religious views. If the Internet has had any effect on American Dispensationalism, it is the infusion of otherwise foreign or competing belief elements from radically distinct discourses and among individuals vastly removed in space and experience.

Although examples of this syncretism in the above cases abound, maybe the most obvious is found in the 'Watcher'.[6] Not just the most Internet savvy of the individuals I have discussed in this chapter, they are the most syncretic, pulling together strains of UFOlogy, conspiracy theory, world myth, and Christianity, they reject any denominational affiliation or location-bound church community. Instead, they prefer to worship in a 'virtual' way – by debating arcane topics as diverse as demon-built monuments on Mars and the spiritual significance of Grace. When I asked Jane if they thought of any church as their own, she answered, pointing to the obvious, "Yes. We have church every week on the Internet" ('Jane', personal communication, October 17, 1999). And despite their soured relationship with Marilyn, those failed debates were worship. In different ways, they were expressions of their deep spiritual conviction and their reverence for the Almighty.

ACKNOWLEDGMENTS

An earlier version of this chapter was presented in November 1999, at the Center for Millennial Studies Special Conference, 'New World Orders: North American Millennialism' under the title: 'Negotiating Finality: Electro-Folk Rhetoric of Apocalypse'. The text has been archived on the CMS Web site at: www.mille.org/publications/winter2000/howard.pdf.

Thanks to Daniel Wojcik, Camilla Mortensen, and the editors of this volume for their commentary and support. And a special thanks to all those in the on-line community who have contributed their time and passions to my bumbling questions and all too antiseptic analysis.

NOTES

1. My definition of 'vernacular rhetoric' is based on Yoder 's definition of 'folk religion' (and Primiano's useful extension of it). Vernacular rhetoric is comprised of rhetorical techniques which are learned outside of institutionally instilled rhetorical discourses (Primiano, 1995; Yoder, 1974). As Bascom noted in his third and fourth functions of folklore (and Toelken explored further), vernacular rhetoric is learned during informal socialization and social exchange (Bascom, in Dundes, 1965; Bascom, 1965; Toelken, 1996).

2. A discourse community is very similar to what Dundes means in his famous, all-inclusive definition of folk groups: ". . . the term 'folk' can refer to any group of people whatsoever who share at least one common factor" (Dundes, 1965, p. 2). Further, it coincides with Ben-Amos' description of the conditions necessary to a folkloric performance: "For the folkloric act to happen, two social conditions are necessary: Both the performers and the audience have to be in the same situation and be part of the same reference group" (Ben-Amos, 1971, p. 12). Within a discourse community, there may be varying levels of individual knowledge of the discourse and its terms. Participants may more or less actively transmit those terms which they consider to be important to the discourse, and, if they are highly active in transmitting their terms, they may introduce new terms into a discourse based on a disparate influence. For more on active transmission, see von Sydow (1965). For more on discourse communities, see Gage (1991, pp. 1ff). For parallel ideas, see also Geertz (1983) on 'local knowledge,' and Fish (1980) on 'interpretive communities'.

3. To facilitate the interview process, I have, in some cases, changed the names of my respondents. Although I did receive permission to use the full names of the individuals I am citing in this article, I assured all of my respondents that their names would only be used as necessary. In the cases of Agee and Dolphin, however, because they are both high profile individuals with their names are imbedded in their Web site addresses, I have no choice but to use their actual names. In their cases, they both expressed no reservations about being cited by name.

4. For a general discussion of spirit presence associated with fogs and other common forms, see Hufford, 1982, 1995.

5. Agee's version of this exchange appears in 'Pro and Con 223' (Agee, 1998b).

6. For my analysis of the more complex and completely syncretic example of the Heaven's Gate, or H.I.M., religious group, see Howard, 1998a.

REFERENCES

Agee, M. (1998a). My testimony. Retrieved April 19, 1999, from the World Wide Web: http://www.kiwi.net/~mjagee/picture.html

Agee, M. (1998b). Pro and Con 223. Retrieved April 19, 1999, from the World Wide Web: http://www.kiwi.net/~mjagee/procon223.html

Alpha Thru Omega. (N.d.). End Times Bible Study Part IV. Retrieved April 1, 1999, from the World Wide Web: http://www.alphathruomega.com/endtimes/part4.html

Alpha Thru Omega. (N.d.). Hedges. Retrieved April 1, 1999, from the World Wide Web: http://www.alphathruomega.com/warfare/hedges.html

Alpha Thru Omega. (N.d.). Spiritual Warfare Training. Retrieved April 1, 1999, from the World Wide Web: http://www.alphathruomega.com/warlist/contents.html

Bascom, W. (1965). The Forms of Folklore: Prose Narratives. *Journal of American Folklore, 78,* 3–20.

Ben-Amos, D. (1971). Toward a Definition of Folklore in Context. *Journal of American Folklore, 84,* 3–15.

Boyer, P. S. (1992). *When Time Shall Be No More: Prophecy Belief In Modern America.* Cambridge: Harvard University Press.

Dolphin, L. (1996). A Very Brief Resume. Retrieved April 1, 1999, from the World Wide Web: http://ldolphin.org/LTDres.html

Dolphin, L. (1999). Lambert's Eschatology Charts. Retrieved April 1, 1999, from the World Wide Web: http://ldolphin.org/eschat.html

Dolphin, L. (2000). Lambert Dolphin's Library. Retrieved April 1, 1999, from the World Wide Web: http://ldolphin.org/asstbib.shtml

Dundes, A. (Ed.), (1965). *The Study of Folklore.* Englewood Cliffs, NJ: Prentice-Hall, Inc.

Fish, S. (1980). *Is There a Text in this Class? The Authority of Interpretive Communities.* Cambridge: Harvard University Press.

Gage, J. T. (1991). *The Shape of Reason: Argumentative Writing in College.* New York: Macmillan Publishing Company.

Geertz, C. (1973). *The Interpretation of Cultures.* New York: Basic Books.

Geertz, C. (1983). *Local Knowledge: Further Essays in Interpretive Anthropology.* New York: Basic Books.

Hauben, M. (1995). The Vision of Interactive Computing and the Future. Retrieved July 12, 2000, from the World Wide Web: http://www.columbia.edu/~rh120/ch106.x05.

Howard, R. G. (1997). Apocalypse in your In-Box: End-Times Communication on the Internet. *Western Folklore, 56,* 295–315.

Howard, R. G. (1998a). Attitudes Toward the Tragic: a not-so-horribly-biased approach to the Heaven's Gate email campaign. *Journal for Millennial Studies, 1*(1). Retrievable from the World Wide Web: http://www.millie.org/publications/summer98/rghoward.pdf

Howard, R. G. (1998b). Toward a Folk Rhetorical Approach to Emerging Myth: The Case of Apocalyptic Techno-Gaianism on the World-Wide-Web. *Folklore Forum, 29,* 53–73.

Hufford, D. J. (1982). *The Terror That Comes in the Night: An Experience-centered Study of Supernatural Assault Traditions.* Philadelphia: University of Pennsylvania Press.

Hufford, D. J. (1995). Beings Without Bodies: An Experience-Centered Theory of the Belief in Spirits. In: B. Walker (Ed.), *Out of the Ordinary: Folklore and the Supernatural* (pp. 11–45). Logan, UT: Utah State University Press.

Lindsey, H., with Carlson, C. C. (1970). *The Late Great Planet Earth.* Toronto and New York: Bantam Books.

Lindsey, H. (1994). *Planet Earth–2000 AD: Will Mankind Survive?* Palos Verdes, CA: Western Front, Ltd.

McQuail, D. (1994). *Mass Communication Theory: An Introduction.* Thousand Oaks, CA: Sage Publications Ltd.

Primiano, L. N. (1995). Vernacular Religion and the Search for Method in Religious Folklife. *Western Folklore, 54,* 37–56.

Redfield, R. (1930). *Tepoztlan, A Mexican Village: A Study of Folk Life*. Chicago: The University
    of Chicago Press.
Robbins, T., & Palmer, S. J. (Eds), (1997). *Millennium, Messiahs, and Mayhem: Contemporary
    Apocalyptic Movements* . New York and London: Routledge.
Strozier, C. B., & Flynn, M. (Eds), (1997). *The Year 2000: Essays on the End*. New York: New
    York University Press.
Toelken, B. (1996). *The Dynamics of Folklore*. Logan, UT: Utah State University Press.
von Sydow, C. W. (1965). Folktale Studies and Philology: Some Points of View. In: A. Dundes
    (Ed.), *The Study of Folklore* (pp. 219–42). Englewood Cliffs, NJ: Prentice-Hall, Inc.
Watcher. (N.d). *Rapture on Pentecost*. Retrieved April 1, 1999, from the World Wide Web:
    http://www.mt.net/~watcher/pentecost.html
Wojcik, D. (1997). *The End of the World as We Know It: Faith, Fatalism, and Apocalypse in
    America*. New York: New York University Press.
Yoder, D. (1974). Toward a Definition of Folk Religion. *Western Folklore, 33*, 2–15.

4. WEBS OF DECEIT: RELIGIOUS PROPAGANDA ON THE NET

RELIGIOUS MOVEMENTS AND THE INTERNET: THE NEW FRONTIER OF CULT CONTROVERSIES

Jean-François Mayer

ABSTRACT

The development of the Internet has been seen with apprehension by some as a new, powerful proselytizing tool for emergent religious movements. The thesis of this chapter is that the Internet – being a means of communication which even lone individuals are able to use efficiently – has probably up to this point helped critics of religious movements more than the movements themselves. The chapter also defines various types of strategies adopted in relation to the Internet (aggressive counter-attack, strong official presence, multiplication of Web pages by members, delegitimation, refusal). Using the concept of 'cyberspace propaganda wars', it attempts finally to identify some of the new battlegrounds.

INTRODUCTION

For missionary religious movements, the world of cyberspace may appear as offering unparalleled opportunities to spread their messages to far larger audiences than has ever been possible with more conventional means of communication. In juxtaposition to the hope, those movements have occasioned

Religion and the Social Order, Volume 8, pages 249–276.
Copyright © 2000 by Elsevier Science Inc.
All rights of reproduction in any form reserved.
ISBN: 0-623-0535-5

a fear that recruiting on the Internet would pose a great threat to innocent and unsuspecting persons.

This study explores what has already been learned about how the Internet is being used both by religious movements and their adversaries. Several questions are explored. We begin with the question of whether the Internet has proved to be a viable instrument for recruiting new members. The short answer to this question is that there is not much supporting evidence. On the other hand, there appears to be substantial evidence to support the proposition that the Internet has been used effectively by adversaries of controversial religious movements to shake the confidence of a fair number of current members. And it has provided critics with a relatively low-cost tool with potentially wide impact.

What is clear at this early date is that many new religious movements are locked in a conflict with those who would define them to the world in very different terms than they see themselves. The conflict is likely to continue for a protracted period, with little sign that there will be any abatement in the intensity of the struggle. Having explored the dynamics of this struggle to define the heart, soul and character of new religious movements to audiences of the Internet, we have concluded that the concept *cyberspace propaganda wars* is altogether appropriate. The work concludes with a discussion of some of the issues that are likely to emerge and give direction to the propaganda wars as they unfold in the future.

AMAZING GRACE ON-LINE: A LOOK AT THE EVIDENCE FOR CYBER CONVERSIONS

Scientific Pantheism (www.pantheism.net) is a cyber religion founded as an email group in March 1997. Paul Harrison, the founder of the group, claimed 645 members in forty-three countries by mid-1999. There are other examples of new religions either being formed, or bolstered by their presence on-line. What we don't know at this point is whether the Internet has really created or is capable of sustaining a *Virtual Community*. Further, can the Internet really be used to effectively recruit new members and, if so, what level of commitment is possible?

As the Internet became increasingly popular in the mid-1990s, some newspapers began to sound an alarm that it might become a channel for proselytization by a variety of new religious movements (NRMs; see *Der Spiegel*, 1995; Rosenthal, 1995; Wright, 1996). This feeling was substantially reinforced by the death of 39 members of Heaven's Gate in late March 1997.

On the face of things, it seemed to confirm the fears that this might be a dangerous trend. But more sober voices were also heard. Witness, for example, Joshua Quittner writing in the international edition of *Time:*

> Spiritual predators? Give me a break. Better yet, go look at this stuff yourself and tell me if you think it's dangerous. A Web page that has the power to suck people – against their will – into a suicide cult? The whole idea would be laughable if 39 people weren't dead. If you want to find out what killed them, however, you're going to have to click a lot deeper than www.heavensgate.com. (Quittner, 1997).

In fact, Heaven's Gate had proselytized on the Internet, but had little more success than it experienced with other methods of recruiting over almost two decades. Apparently no more than two people were recruited (Perkins & Jackson, 1997, p. 65). One of these persons who died in the March 1997 collective suicide had come in touch with Heaven's Gate over the Internet and left her family in September 1996 in order to join the group, following electronic correspondence (Introvigne, 1997, p. 39).

One might expect that UFO believers, whose doctrinal world predisposes them to a high level of openness toward new technologies, would be comfortable with searching for knowledge on the Internet. But UFO aficionados clearly are not representative of the entire population of religious seekers. While some members of Heaven's Gate were very able technicians who developed Web pages commercially, they could hardly be judged as effective users of the Internet for the purpose of recruiting new followers. And the sample is too small for drawing conclusions about the potential of the Internet for recruitment.

There are several other data sources, albeit mostly anecdotal, that shed further light on the question of whether the Internet has been an effective instrument for recruiting to new religious movements.

Take, for example, The New Apostolic Church International that has been present on the Web since April 1997. The New Apostolic Church in Switzerland (some 38,000 members) has had its own Web page since January 1998. According to the Swiss statistics, the first year of operation brought an average of about 120 site visits daily. The page was accessed mainly for news and addresses of local branches. Email inquiries averaged about six per week. Over this 12-month period, two persons are reported to have become members of the New Apostolic Church following an initial contact made over the Internet (http://nak.ch/news99_1.html).

A survey conducted among several prominent critics of a variety of NRMs produced mixed comments about their experience with recruitment over the Internet. For example, persons working with the American Family Foundation (AFF) and with Spiritual Counterfeits Project (SCP) confirmed that they had been in touch with people "who were originally drawn in through contact with the group Web page" (D. Aguirre, personal communication, May 19, 1999).[1] Or, alternatively had left home to join with a group after contacts over the Internet (C. Giambalvo, personal communication, May 20, 1999).[2]

Other counselors replied that they had seen few cases. The director of Trancenet.org reported no contact with persons claiming to have been converted through the Internet. John Knapp wrote that he had heard of one case – a convert to the Unification Church (J. Knapp, personal communication, May 19, 1999). The director of the Peregrine Foundation wrote that there were 'a few' people who had become fellow travelers of a group in California (Morning Star Ranch/ San Francisco Diggers movement) after discovering materials on the Internet (R. Sender, personal communication, May 18, 1999). Scholars who do field research with various religious movements have yet to report instances of persons who changed their beliefs and joined a new religion through the Internet. It may be that the widespread use of the Internet is just too recent to have recorded systematic observations.

Lorne Dawson has astutely observed that "studies of conversion . . . have found that recruitment to NRMs happens primarily through preexisting social networks and interpersonal bonds" (Dawson, 1998, p. 79). In a later paper with Hennebry, he affirms this point: "It is unlikely that [the Internet] has intrinsically changed the capacity of NRMs to recruit new members" (Dawson & Hennebry, 1999, p. 30).

NRMs, being missionary groups by definition, will quite naturally seek to use new means available to reach more people. However, unless the Internet would succeed in changing radically the ways human beings interact, the process of recruitment can be expected to continue to follow the same pattern. Consequently, we may presume that no more than a minor percentage of future converts will have a first introduction to their newly found beliefs over the Internet. Most of them will continue to be converted through other, 'classical' means.

Still, there are other aspects to consider. As Colin Campbell has noted in a seminal article, "cults must exist within a milieu which, if not conducive to the maintenance of individual cults, is clearly highly conducive to the spawning of cults in general" (Campbell, 1972, pp. 121–122). Thus, we might anticipate that the Internet would act as a powerful tool, not as much for conversion to specific groups, as for spreading and mixing ideas that can then flourish in the 'cultic milieu'. More attention should probably be given in the future to the potential role played by links on Web pages for promoting such a syncretism.

Another possibility to consider is the ease and quickness with which the Internet can move a user from one location to another. A religious seeker is no longer confined to using social networking, community bulletin boards or newspaper ads to discover new and potentially interesting groups. By using search engines, and following the trail of links, a seeker can encounter many groups of possible interest in a very short time. But we know that the sheer and immediate availability of a nearly unlimited number of messages does not necessarily constitute an incentive to a commitment.

Today, seekers can initiate contacts without resorting to traditional means for learning about groups. And they can do so without even leaving home. For example, in 1998, a teenager living in a small city in Switzerland reported to me about schoolmates who were attempting to spread satanic ideas based upon American Satanist literature. When I asked how they gained access to those books – which cannot be found in Swiss bookshops (especially in a small city) – the teenager explained how they had got in touch with the Temple of Set over the Internet. These young people did not become members of the Temple of Set, but borrowed ideas that allowed them to articulate their chosen worldview much more elaborately than they could have without access to such sources of information. This example may better portend the use of the Internet in the future than the hypothesis that the groups will attract large numbers of recruits via the Internet. I will return to this idea later.

Any group that would attempt to recruit exclusively over the Internet would not likely be very successful. When looking at millenarian Web sites, for example, one fairly quickly arrives at the conclusion that there are probably quite a large number operated by lonely prophets, to whom the Internet may give the illusion that they are not just a voice preaching in the desert. Most of them are not getting very many visitors and remain virtual unknowns. But a few break through to a much larger audiences than they had been available to attract by conventional methods. Twenty years ago, we would have heard about few, if any of these prophets of doom. Public meetings are of no avail if they fail to attract an audience; printed material must be paid for and distributed; radio and television are expensive.

In contrast, the Internet is cheap and allows potentially unlimited access – even if the number of 'hits' on some Web sites indicates disappointing results. But a presence on the Internet may have a distorting effect even upon scholars, who might unconsciously come to feel that a message deserves notice because it is preached on a well-designed Web site. A good Web site, of course, may sometimes reflect the technical skills of its author rather than the content of the message or the effectiveness of the real outreach. Meanwhile, groups with hundreds of followers, but without a Web site, might remain virtually unnoticed.

For the first time in history, the Internet has the potential to allow a newly founded religion to go global from its very beginning. This, of course, does not imply that the founder will be making any converts. Still, we can anticipate that virtually every newly launched religious message will want to be on the Internet.

Even if a lonely prophet develops a handsome presence on the Internet, without ever gaining a convert, the psychological satisfaction derived from a virtual audience and the feeling of being able to reach the entire world should not be underestimated. There is probably no way to measure this, since empirical research on this subject would be extremely difficult. Still, there is good reason to suspect that cyber prophets, especially millenarian prophets, with a strong sense of imminence, may be desperate to attract attention. We know also that the desire to make the headlines has played a role in some violent outcomes (Introvigne & Mayer, 2000; Mayer, 1999). Although difficult to prove, it is not impossible that the outlet provided by the Internet may deflect the pressure felt by some minuscule groups to proclaim their message to the world.[3] The Internet does not only affect the ability of an emergent religious movement to reach outsiders, but it may have an impact on the internal life of the movement as well.

EXPOSING THE DARK SIDE OF NEW RELIGIOUS MOVEMENTS

NRMs are like almost every other kind of voluntary organization in several respects. First, joining is a voluntary decision – although like other organizations people may be pressured in varying degrees to join. Second, while many join, only a relatively small proportion of joiners stay long and become 'totally' involved to the point that membership radically transforms how they live their lives. Third, large proportions of all people who join terminate active affiliation after a relatively short time. Fourth, of those who do leave a small percentage leave with a profound sense of disillusionment and anger about their experience in the group.

For those disaffected followers, the Internet is a special interest because it provides a new and different structure to find one another and spread their message. Already before most new religious movements were even aware of the existence of the Internet, former members of numerous groups were becoming active on the World Wide Web.

The case of opponents of the Church of Scientology is well known to virtually everyone who has explored the presence of religious movements on the Internet in any detail at all. As a report on the controversies surrounding Scientology summarized a few years ago, "The Church has lawyers, the critics have computers" (Grossman, 1995).[4] But Scientology is by no means the only group that has been vigorously attacked on the Internet. Let's consider the case of a Sukyo Mahikari, a striking example of a group that appears to have been seriously affected by negative information on the Internet.

Sukyo Mahikari is a Japanese new religion founded by Kotamo Okada in 1959. It is not very well known in the United States, but it is actually active on all the continents and is estimated to have around 700,000 members world-wide (Introvigne, 1999, pp. 38–40). An examination of how it came under serious assault on the Internet is instructive of the dynamics of this process.

The major impulse for this assault came from a report by former Australian Mahikari member Gary Greenwood, *All the Emperor's Men* (1995, revised 1997). Only a few years earlier, Greenwood would likely have printed a few hundred copies of his report and sent them to people he knew and maybe to a few journalists. The impact of this work would have been minimal and it would almost certainly have remained unknown outside Australia.

With the advent of the Internet the book is now freely distributed on Web pages of former members, making it available around the world. Greenwood's report has been criticized for its depiction of Mahikari as a kind of 'yellow peril' (Introvigne, 1999, pp. 95–96). What matters here has nothing to do with its accuracy or lack of accuracy. The fact of interest is that it has made an impact and that the anti-Mahikari activities on the Internet have produced results.

For example, James Wilson is another Australian who used to have a pro-Mahikari Web site until he turned anti-Mahikari in May, 1999.[5] He emphatically asserted that the Internet was a major factor in bringing adverse information to his attention. Interestingly, he had previously attempted to implement a strategy for countering critical pages against Mahikari:

> I learned many tricks regarding search engine rankings solely in the pursuit of attempting to push down the negative pages in the rankings . . . At one time all the pages regarding Mahikari that were immediately accessible were positive, because of my effort. However, this is a massive effort which requires constant attention, and I stopped promoting any Mahikari page upon discovering Okada's [the founder] past. This allowed the negative pages to creep up in the rankings; meanwhile, more adverse information continued to come to light. Now, most of what is there is negative (J. Wilson, personal communication, May 20, 1999).

The full implications of the dynamic of the silent wars conducted on the Internet first became evident to me in 1998 as the result of a chance meeting on a morning commuter train in Switzerland with a member of Sukyo Mahikari whom I happened to know. As I turned our discussion to the Internet and mentioned the critical Australian page, my traveling companion replied that he was aware of the site and, further, volunteered that the critical material had shaken the beliefs of not a few members outside Australia.

This chance encounter set me to thinking more seriously about how negative materials about new religions on the Internet might impact different groups. Suppose someone becomes interested in Sukyo Mahikari, by whatever means and, feeling somewhat attracted by its practices and teachings, decides to search for more information on the Internet. Since more and more people are turning to the Internet for information, this seemed like a reasonable supposition.

To explore this natural curiosity that someone might have, I conducted a simple inquiry utilizing the Alta Vista search engine. The search produced a list of 458 entries.[6] If a hypothetical person who was looking for information that would reinforce his interest in Mahikari had conducted this search, he would have been in for quite a surprise. Here is what I found:

- The first page contained a report from a critical Australian site regarding Mahikari beliefs about the tomb of Jesus in Japan (see Cornille, 1994): definitely teachings which are not usually shared with newcomers at Mahikari centers and would sound rather strange to somebody just acquainted with the movement.
- The second Web page appeared to be a Mahikari site. However, if the visitor had been at all familiar with the group and looked at the addresses, he wouldn't have found any of the Mahikari centers known to him. Further, the picture of the temple in Japan would not have been familiar. Sooner or later, the visitor would have realized mahikari.org is not a Web page of Sukyo Mahikari, but of its main rival, Sekai Mahikari Bunmei Kyodan, which owns the domain name mahikari.org!
- The next two Web pages, under the title 'Crumbling Foundations', would have led the Web-surfer again to the critical Australian site.
- The fifth link was to a critical Belgian site and the following entry to Sekai Mahikari Bunmei Kyodan in Japanese.
- The seventh link opened with a notice informing that the old site (a pro-Mahikari page) had been discontinued on May 14, 1999, and would be "modified to reflect its new purpose: a support group for ex-Mahikari members"!
- The next page was Sekai Mahikari Bunmei Kyodan again.
- The two following pages were finally Sukyo Mahikari ('unofficial home page'). One of them had only a list of addresses and the following notice: 'This page used to be a much better reference for Sukyo Mahikari than it is now . . . but the powers that be have decided that they don't want any reference to Sukyo Mahikari on the Internet'. This was in reference to the fact that Mahikari leaders had discouraged members from creating Web pages.

The author of this page couldn't resist the following: "I consider that to be silly." One has to wonder how long the author of this comment will remain a member. The implication of his comment is certainly correct – discouraging members from developing pages does not mean that Mahikari will not be on the Internet; only that the content of the pages on the Internet will shift decidedly toward negative content.

Not until the third set of ten entries did my Alta Vista Web search find a happy Sukyo Mahikari member, but next to his page was another with the title 'It Is a Mind Controlling Cult', which was followed by 'Sukyo Mahikari and Aum Shinrikyo'.

If a person who began this search predisposed to wanting to participate in Mahikari had pursued the Internet entries this far, one might be inclined to view him or her not so much a truth-seeker as an adventure-seeker![7]

It is fascinating to read comments by former members, explaining how they could just no longer remain members of the organization after reading the information they found on the Internet. Thus was the case of Fabien Cheslet, from Belgium: "In September 1996, I discovered on Internet the book by Gary Greenwood."[8] Cheslet then became the Webmaster of one of the most active anti-Mahikari sites, distributing information in French as well as in English.[9]

Other groups have fared better. Transcendental Meditation (TM), produced no less than 6,565 Web pages with Alta Vista search. Only three negative pages appeared in the first 100 links, and they were all in the fourth quartile (rankings: 76, 81 and 83). Siddha Yoga was less successful, but not too bad. The first negative page was the 18th entry, a critical site named 'Leaving Siddha Yoga'. Ananda Marga also came out quite well with the Alta Vista search, the first negative site appearing in rank 39 out of a total of 760 Web pages.

Among the considerable number of groups I searched, Seicho-No-Ie had one of the more felicitous outcomes on the Internet. Seicho-No-Ie is a Japanese new religion of the 1930s that adapted the New Thought teachings of Fenwicke Holmes (brother of Ernest S. Holmes who founded Religious Science). Of 340 entries, Seicho-No-Ie received no adverse mention among the first hundred. It is true that, at least in the Western world, 'anti-cult' literature rarely (if ever) even mentions Seicho-No-Ie, and the propaganda wars on the Internet seem to be rather an extension of controversies raging at the same time in other settings.

RESPONDING TO THE INTERNET WARRIORS

While this survey has by no means been exhaustive, it seems reasonably clear that small groups of ex-members have been able to create a Web presence that paints a very grim picture of the groups they attack. Again, I would emphasize that the issue that concerns us here is not whether the claims are true or false. What concerns us here is the impact of that material on the groups that have been targeted for attack.

We turn next to an examination of how selected religious movements have responded to the negative propaganda of their adversaries. How seriously do they take this literature as a threat? What is the nature of the threat? What at some of the strategies they have developed to respond? While some groups engage in multiple strategies, five distinct strategies are identified: (1) aggressive counter-attack, (2) development of a strong official Web presence, (3) encourage members to create pages, (4) de-legitimate the Web as a source of information, and (5) ignore the Internet. Each of these approaches is illustrated with a discussion of how particular groups employ the strategy. Finally, we will also show how the harsh realities of the Web finally convince some reluctant groups to change their policy.

1. Aggressive Counter-Attack

Before its presence of the World Wide Web, Scientology was the target of Internet attacks on the newsgroup alt.religion.scientology, created on July 17, 1991. For a good many years it was not unusual for more than a thousand postings to appear on alt.religion.scientology in a single day. In a real sense, this news group was a pioneer spot for the development of nasty, in-your-face communication on the Internet. There continue to be many postings every day, and a useful weekly review summarizing the most important ones is available as well on several sites, allowing one to follow the development of controversies around the movement (www.xenu.net/archive/WIR).

Alt.religion.scientology became one of the most contentious and heavily trafficked news groups, in considerable measure because Scientologists logged on and attempted to defend their movement. But "there was apparently no coordinated action taken by the C[hurch] o[f] S[cientology] against its electronic critics until 1994" (Lippard & Jacobsen, 1995). This was the consequence of the posting of copyrighted Scientology material on the newsgroup. The first copyright suit was filed in February 1995. This led to heated debates which continue to this day. Opponents of Scientology claim that it is an issue of free speech (a very sensitive topic for Internet buffs), while Scientology replies that free speech cannot justify violations of copyrights and 'trade secrets'. One can follow on a number of Web pages about Scientology the various episodes of this ongoing conflict around the world (including police raids in several countries, following complaints by Scientology lawyers). It involves legal issues which certainly go beyond the specific case of Scientology, as the group itself is eager to mention.[10]

But the legal side is only one aspect of the controversies. Clearly aware that the members of a movement putting so much emphasis upon modernity and technology are unlikely to renounce scouting the Web, Scientology developed a strategy allowing it to acquire a massive presence on the Internet and at the same time making access to negative information less easy for its faithful. Scientology decided not to limit itself to the abundant material which it offers on official Web pages. In 1998, a Scientology official announced that every Scientologist would be encouraged to have a personal Web site (see Brown, 1998). Interestingly, there is a listing of all those pages, country by country, accessible from http://on-line.scientology.org/splash.htm. The movement has not been afraid to make the names and email addresses of thousands of its members around the world accessible in such a way, including in countries where the movement is quite controversial. The presentation of each page seems to follow the same pattern, insofar as one can ascertain through consulting a few dozen of them, which creates an impression of uniformity – although the human side of each Scientologist appears clearly in the section where he or she introduces himself or herself. A clear advantage of such a massive presence – Scientology claims to have "over fifteen thousand Scientologists" connected – is the flooding of the Web (especially search engines) with pro-Scientology pages.

Of course, there was a risk: some Scientologists going on the Internet might become avid readers of negative informations on the movement. But a counter-strategy has been implemented from the beginning of that operation and has become strongly decried by anti-Scientology critics: the starter kit provided to Scientologists for building their Web site ('Scientology Web Kit' CD-ROM) includes a filtering program, similar to censorware used by parents who desire to prevent children from accessing obscene material. Users sign a contract – made public on several anti-Scientology sites – by which they agree to use that filter program for surfing "without threat of accessing sites deemed to be using the Marks or Works in an unauthorized fashion or deemed to be improper or discreditable to the Scientology religion." There is a rather long list of forbidden terms and sites, which actually makes more than just critical pages unaccessible to Scientologists using such a device.[11]

In no other case seems the metaphor of a war as appropriate as with Scientology; on the one hand, a number of cyber guerillas around the world, either former members or people who are critical for some other reason; on the other hand, the massive presence of Scientology's cyber army, not only the official Web pages, but also those thousands of personal pages all constructed along the same pattern, exactly like an army in uniform. There are leading figures or especially famous cyber warriors whose names soon become familiar to all those who follow the development of the controversies. At the same time,

Scientology's strategy on the Web cannot just be reduced to the type of "aggressive counter-attack," it obviously incorporates elements from some other strategic approaches which we will now examine. This observation is valid for a number of other groups as well.

2. Develop Strong Official Home Page

A good many religious movements have decided that a solid home page, accurately presenting themselves in an attractive manner, is preferable to attacking adversaries. The Church of Jesus Christ of Latter-day Saints is a good example of this strategy. Elder Jeffrey R. Holland, a member of the Quorum of Twelve Apostles, has played a major role in developing the Mormon's strategy for the creation of an official Web site. In an interview in Lauramaerey Gold's *Mormons on the Internet*, Holland acknowledges that the LDS leadership was aware both of the opportunities for communication and of the presence of negative content about the church on the Internet. He describes the Church's position as 'cautious and measured' (Gold, 2000, p. 28). And cautious they were. In 1996 the Church put up a front page at www.lds.org that contained nothing but a piece of attractive art and the promise of a Web site to follow.

When the official homepage of the LDS finally came on-line it had two foci that reflected a strategy for communicating with: (1) the mass media, and (2) non-members, investigators and other inquiring persons who were interested in learning more about the Church. Notes Holland:

> We were aware that there was a lot of inaccurate information being put out by others. We wanted to share our own story with inquiring people not of our faith who were interested in the Church.

This "reaching out to non-members" is abundantly apparent to anyone who explores the content of the page. As the official Mormon homepage has developed, it has expanded to include content that is more clearly intended for the use of members. Still, a large front-end segment devoted to family life can be viewed as a way of calling visitors' attention to the fact that Mormons are profoundly interested in the family.

What is clear throughout the content of the Web site is a focus on presentation of factual information, content that is likely to be of value to persons wishing to learn more about the Latter-day Saints. One does not find any counter-assault on the many anti-Mormon pages.

There are Web pages created by individuals that take on the adversaries of the Church. Much of this content may be appropriately described as 'contextualizing' a long history of anti-Mormon sentiment. For example, an essay from the *Encyclopedia of Mormonism* leads with a late nineteenth-century cartoon that depicts Mormons as a "despotic, ignorant, adulterous threat to society."[12]

3. In My Fathers' House are many Web pages

Some religious movements seem clearly to have pursued a strategy of developing many pages. The Hare Krishna, for example, encouraged members to develop Web sites. Members responded by creating hundreds of beautifully designed Web pages. The purpose of this was to glorify Krishna, but clearly the anticipated impact of the presence of a large number of member generated pages was to diminish the impact of negative pages.

There appears to be a presumption of Gresham's Law in reverse, i.e., many 'good' Web pages will dilute the impact of negative pages when someone was looking for information about a group with a search engine. Whether this is, in fact, true is not clear. The creators of Web pages are constantly in search of insights that will help them push their own pages higher up on search engine lists. The managers of search engines, in turn, are continually looking for better schemes of organizing information that will increase their market share.

This said, when a religious group has a very large number of sites, or a number of very large sites, it would appear that they will at least improve their odds that persons searching the Web will land on a page that will present the group in a positive light.

Consider, for example, the case of the Mormons. When the first edition of Gold's *Mormons on the Internet* was released in late 1997 there were about 500 Mormon sites on the Internet. In the introduction to the second edition, released in early 2000, she notes there were more than 6000 sites (Gold, 2000, p. xix). A cursory examination of several searches did not suggest that the number of anti-Mormon sites had increased by the same ratio in just a little over two years, i.e., twelve-fold.

The Unification Church is unique in that it has approximately two dozen 'official' Web pages. Most of these pages contain very substantial content. This unusual number of official pages does not include the Web sites of many affiliated organizations. And, in addition, many church members have Web pages.

4. De-legitimate the Web as a Source of Information

The origins of Jehovah's Witness, like Mormons, date to the middle of the nineteenth century. Like Mormons, they have experienced a history of fairly high tension with the broader culture, and both groups remain targets of substantial attack. While the leadership of the Mormon Church has cautiously embraced the Internet as yet another means, among others, for communicating the Gospel, the leadership of the Jehovah's Witnesses is less certain that it is an appropriate tool for evangelization. As a result they have begrudgingly developed a Web presence and, simultaneously admonished members for creating Web pages. George Chryssides (1996) has accurately noted that while Jehovah's Witnesses are not enthusiastic about the Internet as an instrument for propagating their message, this is not because they are adverse to the use of modern technologies. Indeed, they did not hesitate to create radio programs and have even owned radio stations in earlier times. They argue, however, that "the Internet cannot serve as a substitute for the traditional door-to-door ministries."

This emphasis on person-to-person evangelism is reflected in the structure of their official Web site. Under Publications, some Jehovah's Witnesses pamphlets are available on-line, but the emphasis is upon encouraging personal contact. For example, click on a picture of *The Watchtower* or *Awake*, the two standard instruments for evangelization, and the reader is advised that copies may be obtained from the local Kingdom Hall of Jehovah's Witnesses. One is advised to check their local telephone book for an address or contact a branch office (by mail) for information.

If you want more information, the Web site provides a one-way structure for submitting your name, address, telephone number and the "best time to reach you." There is no space for comments or special instructions. Three pictures beside the address form leave little doubt about what one can expect if the form is submitted – two Witnesses will come and knock at the door. There is no email address or other structure for interactive communication. Jehovah's Witnesses have followed the lead of the LDS Church and provided on-line information for the media through a link to the authorized site of the Public Affairs Office. Here one can find telephone and fax numbers, and a contact address, but no email address.

Two things seem fairly evident here. First, the Jehovah's Witnesses do welcome the opportunity to reach out and evangelize. Second, they are firm in their resolve to do it their own way and on their own terms. Part of their cautiousness, including their reluctance to use email on the official Web site would seem to reflect their uncertainty about how to make appropriate use of the new technology without departing from classical patterns of sharing the faith. Consider the following comment in an article entitled "Use of the Internet – Be Alert to the Dangers!" which appeared *Our Kingdom Ministry* (November, 1999). The article does not condemn the Internet in itself, but cautions against indiscriminate use and offers up the alternative of time better spent:

> Time spent in personal and familial Bible study, meeting attendance, and field ministry far outweighs time spent browsing the Internet, expecting to gain benefits . . . Are you not the

happiest when your life is filled with Kingdom pursuits rather than any other activity? [And further:] It is imperative that we stay close to our brothers in the congregation and use the remaining time wisely, thus making ourselves available for the advancing of the Kingdom interests.

One does not have to question the sincerity of the writer to recognize that there may be another rationale behind this counsel. The danger that members may come in touch with 'apostates' over the Internet is seen as a serious one. The risk of contact with 'apostates', knowingly or not, recurs several times, in different ways, throughout the article. This at least suggests that influence by anti-Jehovah's Witness propaganda is the main reason for the unease of the Society toward the Internet (see Penton, 1997, p. 335), even if other dangers (immorality, lack of discernment by young people) are evoked as well.

If the WatchTower Society has not officially banned the use of the Internet, there have been cases of Witnesses being disfellowshipped for 'imprudent use' of computers and the Internet. The impact of the article in *Our Kingdom Ministry* to many Witnesses was to lead them to the conclusion that they had no choice but to close down their Web sites or significantly edit the contents. The modest 'official' presence of the Jehovah's Witnesses on the Internet plus strong admonitions of caution to members about creating Web pages has left the Web free for many critical pages. This point was not missed in discussions on forums for Witnesses following the article in *Our Kingdom Ministry*, who were quick to point out the consequences of the closure of member pages:

... many good sites will disappear ... whereas the bad ones [will] flourish as never before, even rejoicing I suppose that the stage is theirs alone, albeit for the Society's official Web sites (http://discussion.witnesses.net).

And another Witness from Germany wrote: "During the next years the number of Internet users will increase dramatically and if a person is interested in our religion, he also will look on the Internet. Unfortunately he will find a lot of opposing views but only a few positive comments."

Watch Tower Society officials are not unaware of the fact that many persons have created highly critical Internet resources and that these resources may have the impact of disseminating 'distorted views' (M.R. Woernhard, personal communication, May 21, 1999). The Society has not been entirely inactive in trying to counter this threat. It has recently launched a nicely designed "Authorized Site of the Public Affairs Office of the Jehovah's Witnesses" (http://jw-media.org) in order to address issues often raised, like the question of blood, and it has also launched sites dealing with developments in Russia, Germany and France.[13]

In spite of their good intentions to create a positive picture of Jehovah's Witness on official Web pages, it is not clear that they fully understand the implications of discouraging individual members from being on the Internet. Like every other religious movement, the growth of Internet resources is increasing exponentially. A recent check of using several different search engines indicates that the overwhelming proportion of information about Jehovah's Witnesses is highly critical. But they have a long experience with opposition. They may very well view the Internet as merely a continuation of those controversies under new forms.

5. Ignoring the Internet

If Jehovah's Witnesses have had, at best, modest impact in controlling the content of the Internet, there are several groups that have elected to have no Web presence at all. Theirs appears to be an even more difficult situation. Consider the case of The Way International.

The Way International was founded in 1942 by Victor Paul Wierwille as Vesper Chimes, a radio program, in Ohio. Wierwille took his message to the youth counter-culture in the 1960s and his movement became one of the more successful manifestations of the Jesus People phenomenon. Estimates of the group's size run as high as 100,000, but 30,000 is a more generally accepted figure.

The problem of leadership succession following the death of Wierwille in 1985 was tumultuous and the leadership of President Craig Martindale has continued to be a source of controversy. Almost from the death of Wierwille, various allegations have been rampant. The leadership has been charged with personal misconduct. There are continual accusations of brainwashing. And, for a while, there were rumors that the organization had the potential of violence.

The Internet has provided a significant forum for the spread of these claims, and in recent years, TWI has reportedly experienced a sharp decline in membership.[14] As of this writing, The Way International has eschewed any presence on the World Wide Web.[15] There are a few individual pages of persons who have been associated with, and offer praise to, founder Victor Paul Wierwille. None of these pages offers any information about the status of TWI.

There is no way of verifying the role of adverse publicity on the Internet by the organization's defectors, but the content of the Web pages of several adversaries is altogether unflattering. It is difficult to imagine that they have had no impact. It seems more plausible to suspect that adverse publicity on the Internet has contributed substantially to the problems of The Way.

The development of the Internet puts difficult questions indeed to groups that would prefer to remain out of the limelight. As much as The Way International might have preferred to remain low profile, they have not succeeded in doing so. The fact is that the only public information available is that which is found on the pages of apostates on the Internet.

Another fascinating case is provided by the Two-by-Two's, a group known to be quite secretive to the point of not providing any public address (see Parker, 1982). Of course, the Two-by-Two's, who do not want to publish information about their group, don't have a Web page. But former members do: one can visit the site of Veterans of Truth (VOT),[16] RIS (http://workersect.org), or Telling the Truth (TTT; http://home.earthlink.net/~truth). According to the TTT Webmaster, Cherie Kropp, 'countless people' have contacted the three Web sites: people who had left the group years ago and felt guilty all those years; people who discovered the Internet information, questioned and left the group; members who were angry about the Web site (C. Kropp, personal communication, May 24, 1999).

The leadership is not unaware of what is going on the Internet: for instance, when a follower – who actually had not yet seen the material on the Internet – made his decision known to leave the group, someone asked him "if it was the stuff on the Internet." It was unfortunately not possible to ask the Two-by-Two's directly for their comments about the critical Web sites, but, according to well-informed Cherie Kropp, "the preachers are preaching about the evils of the Internet, which causes people to search and find the Internet sites" (C. Kropp, personal communication, May 24, 1999). Obviously, just warning against the Internet is doomed to be a losing fight in the long term. The leadership of the Two-by-Two's is said to "have used the Internet for some time," according to Kevin Daniel (RIS), who helps with maintaining the RIS critical Web site:

> Eventually they may find ways to use it to recruit new members and/or to control members' approach to it so that they can use it to further the solidarity of existing members. Thus far, they have failed in doing either. Their approach to the Internet, as a source of outside information, reflects their attitude to other media (television is denigrated, and until relatively recently radio, newspapers, movies and even books were widely condemned as harmful) (K. Daniel, personal communication, May 26, 1999).

6. Transitions: When a Group Chooses to do an 'Outing'.

Since the Internet can become a real pressure upon some groups, it can also reasonably be assumed that it will contribute to changes inside them (not only regarding their policy about the Internet), as other kinds of external pressure do. Regarding the Two-by-Two's, according to Cherrie Kropp, the Internet is already having an impact on the inner life of the group: "They are loosening up the requirements that the people object to the most" (C. Kropp, personal communication, May 24, 1999).

But for other groups, the change can become first a change of attitude toward the Internet itself. Such is the case of the followers of Guru Maharaji. The youthful Guru Maharaji came to the United States in 1971 and established a considerable following for his organization, the Divine Light Mission. In the early 1980s the movement was reorganized as Elan Vital (still called Divine United Organization in India). For nearly two decades the organization remained active, but kept a low profile in the West.

The Internet changed this. In early 1997, a group of former devotees, describing themselves as "ex-followers of the ex-Lord of the Universe," launched a quite attractive site (available in French beginning in May 1998).[17] Elan Vital initially discouraged Web pages. But, having assessed the possibilities of the Internet, as well as the existence of adverse information, their policy changed in 1999. There are now several elegantly designed Web sites that offer significant information about Maharaji's message, current activities and forthcoming gatherings (www.enjoyinglife.org), a chat room on the official Web site (www.premie.org), and the opportunity to purchase publications and videos (www.visions-intro.org). There is also a substantial Australian Web site (www.inspiration.org).

All of this represents a definite break with the former policy.[18] Again, there is no empirical means to assess this change in policy. From a purely tactical viewpoint, Elan Vital would seem to have made the right decision. Without directly taking on their adversaries, they now offer clear alternatives to the critical information, developed by former members, which once had a virtual monopoly on the Internet. Whether or not it can be said that they are now winning the Internet propaganda wars, they are at least well armed for the battle.

JUBILEE: THE CYBER WARRIORS PERSPECTIVE

In assessing the impact of the Internet on new religious movements, this one thing is clear – they are all aware of the presence of their adversaries on-line. We have seen that their responses range from aggressive battle to effectively being immobilized – for whatever reasons – and doing nothing (or maybe pondering still how to react in an adequate way). Yet another important perspective in trying to assess the impact of the Internet propaganda wars is that that of the persons and groups who have utilized this medium to spread information with the intent of exposing particular religious groups.

The inescapable conclusion is that virtually all individuals who have utilized the Internet to spread their critical perspectives about 'cults' view the World Wide Web as a very positive development. Steven Hassan, one of the most visible 'anti-cultists' in the U.S., has been on the Internet since August 1995 (www.freedo-mofmind.com). Hassan does not hesitate to say that "the Internet is the single best thing to ever happen to fight destructive cults since I left the Moonies in 1976" (S.

Hassan, personal communication, May 18, 1999). He estimates he spends two or three hours every day answering email from people. "A great burden," Hassan says, but he believes he is "helping more people than ever."

Stephan Wolf, a key person in a network of former Jehovah's Witnesses in Germany, is quick to note that "[the] distribution of information has become less of a cost factor" – nothing comparable with the cost of printing and distributing printed information, the need to know addresses to which to send it, etc. (S.E. Wolf, personal communication, May 18, 1999). Danny Aguirre, a representative of Spiritual Counterfeits Projects, a group which was active long before the Internet became popular, comments also on the utility of the Internet. Changes due to the Internet, argues Aguirre, "have brought unbelievable convenience and efficiency" (D. Aguirre, personal communication, May 19, 1999). Ramon Sender believes the Internet is effective because "it is almost impossible for any group to shield themselves from this information stream . . . unless they cut themselves off completely" (R. Sender, personal communication, May 18, 1999).

Hassan also observes the usefulness of the Internet to bring resources to the relatives of a member of a controversial group. Carol Giambalvo makes the same point noting:

> I am now able to direct families who are inquiring about specific groups to the group's own Web site so that they can begin to understand the beliefs/culture their family members have embraced so that they can keep lines of communication open. And I am able to direct the family to Web sites of former members to learn what their experiences were like (C. Giambalvo, personal communication, May 20, 1999).

Janja Lalich counsels persons who are currently in or leaving a religious group. She believes "the Internet is a fabulous venue for open discourse . . . It can be a prod to get a person thinking critically and seeing that there are other points of view, which is what is needed to counteract the deception and cover-ups of some groups" (J. Lalich, personal communication, May 20, 1999).

If the Internet has become a resource for augmenting personal counseling, as suggested by these comments above, it is also clear that quite a number of persons have posted documents of religious organizations on the Internet because they believe this information is intrinsically damaging to the group. Typically, these are 'secret documents' that are intended for official use, or only for the use of persons who have reached higher levels of preparedness.

The most celebrated case is the repeated posting of portions of 'sacred texts' of Scientology. In another instance, Sandra and Jerald Tanner, long-time critics of the Mormon Church (see Foster, 1984), posted a restricted LDS handbook of instructions dealing with church disciplining procedures on their Web site. Both organizations pursued the violators of their secret or restricted documents in courts and achieved at least some measure of success in having the documents removed from the Internet. The fact that both organizations pursued legal action speaks to their perceived threat of the Internet as a repository for documents.

Additional anecdotal testimonies and examples could be offered, but the general level of enthusiasm exhibited by the persons cited here point to the conclusion that the Internet has been an enormously valuable resource for those critical of some movements. The two examples of groups which have responded so vigorously to the violation of copyrighted materials, sacred texts, or 'trade secrets', suggest that they too see the potential effectiveness of unbridled use of the Internet by their adversaries.

IDENTIFYING NEW BATTLEGROUND IN THE INTERNET PROPAGANDA WARS

This study has attempted to assess the impact of the Internet on contemporary religious movements. The great dividends that had been foreseen by some are not materializing quickly. There is little evidence to support the proposition that the Internet is a fertile crescent where recruiting and conversion is likely to be efficient. As systematic studies are pursued, it is possible that we will see patterns that suggest a multiple stage process by which new members are recruited.

At the same time, it would appear that one of the consequences of so much information about so many different religious groups is that potential recruits may be reluctant to 'sign on' to any faith. Recognizing there is still so much spiritual information yet to be explored, commitment may not be viewed as prudent. Alternatively, people may make only tentative commitments – gradually creating there own privatized faith. The Internet, thus, may provide the context for more rapid development of what Peter Berger calls 'privatized religion'.

Along with the uncertainty of benefits to be derived from the Internet, it is also clear that the large majority of new religions find themselves caught up in *propaganda wars* on the Internet.

We have explored some of the strategies that religious movements have employed to defend themselves against adversaries, but this inquiry has not explicitly examined the 'anti-cult' movement. Clearly that is a topic in its own right, deserving more careful examination. We have, instead, taken the adversarial relation as a given and focused on the dynamics of the process.

What we have learned provides a foundation for further reflections regarding how the Internet propaganda wars are likely to unfold. In this final section we will seek to identify and briefly discuss some of the fault lines that we should pay attention to in the future.

Free access to the Internet

As the Internet develops, more and more segments of this vast communications structure will likely become taxed in the form of fees for access. While this may have some impact in shaping the character of the Internet, the underlying structure of free (or very inexpensive) access is not likely to change. The most important implication of this is the democratization of access to information. Not only will the whole world be able to access the Internet, regardless of class or other origins, those who create knowledge (or merely post information) will have the potential for very large global audiences.

It is instructive to compare the size of religious groups and examine the extensiveness and quality of their Web presence. The United Methodist Church, with approximately 10 million members in the U.S., has a creditable but uninspiring Internet presence. By contrast, the Unification Church has perhaps five thousand members in the U.S. and the quality and quantity of materials accessible from their Web pages (they have 25 official pages) dwarfs the Methodists. The Assemblies of God, a rapidly growing Pentecostal denomination with approximately two million members in the U.S., has effectively utilized radio and television as part of their growth strategy. The AG Web site, however, is no match for that of The Family, formerly and better known as the Children of God, with perhaps two thousand U.S. members.

These comparisons do not mean the Unification Church and The Family are about to make great leaps forward and become competitive with larger, established groups. It portends nothing other than the fact that the Internet can level the playing field in terms of potential access to potential adherents. Some established groups may well become pioneers in the utilization of the Internet for church growth, but cursory comparisons suggest smaller religious movements have taken the Internet more seriously and are positioning themselves to use it to achieve their goals and agendas.

This may change in the future. An increasing number of mainline Christians are becoming aware of the prospects of the Internet. As one of the lectures at the 4th Conference of the European Christian Internet Conference (ECIC; www.ecic.org) Network in Budapest in July 1999 noted: "There is no alternative than being also a church on the Internet." This may be a rather prophetic example of the kind of reflection that is currently occurring among mainline Churches about the implications of the Internet.

Freedom of Expression

The Internet currently is, and will likely remain, a forum of free inquiry that is without parallel in the history of free speech. This is a mixed blessing for new religious movements. On the one hand, their free speech is unlikely to be impinged. On the other hand, neither will be the voices of their adversaries.

Any group that expects to succeed will find it essential to develop an effective Web presence – not only to present itself, but also to neutralize or minimize the negative propaganda that will be present on the Internet from its adversaries.

This dilemma will not likely be solved at once but, rather, will be an ever-changing problem. As distasteful as this may seem to some groups, the propaganda wars will remain a part of the cost of doing business.

An article published in the newspaper *The Guardian* (October 27, 1997), strongly critical of the Friends of the Western Buddhist Order (FWBO), and especially of its leader, Sangharakshita (Dennis Lingwood), led to controversies on the Internet, especially after the anonymous, 70 page *FWBO Files* were posted in May 1998.[19] The FWBO called the allegations "silly," but had no other choice than to reply,[20] due to the Internet echo of the document, while stating the dilemma: "to address these issues . . . is to allow our detractors to set the agenda" (Shukman, 1999, p. 67). There is little doubt that before the advent of the Internet, the echo of the article in the *Guardian* would have been more localized and the wide distribution of an anonymous document would have been nearly impossible, sparing the FWBO to have to come so intensely under scrutiny.

The Increasing Pressure Toward Transparency

Many religions shroud aspects of their beliefs and rituals in secrecy. New religious groups are not different in this respect. Indeed, new recruits may be attracted by the unusual, the esoteric, and by beliefs and rituals the general population would find questionable if not down right bizarre or illegal. In addition, every religion, old and new, has skeletons hidden in its closet.

With the Internet, what might formerly have been known only to a limited audience now becomes instant public knowledge – and globally. When ISKCON's Harikesha Swami (Vishnupada) broke with the movement during the Summer of 1998, it was possible to follow the controversy (at least from one side) on Hare Krishna independent Web sites (www.vnn.org; www.chakra.org). Ten or fifteen years ago, it would have been much more difficult for outsiders to know about that before some time (not even mentioning the details of the case), unless having some good connections inside the movement or monitoring very closely its activities.

But the problem is that virtually everyone can become a source. Rumors and allegations can spread virtually unchecked without any accountability for the source of the information. This has two implications. On the one hand, some groups will likely seek isolation and security to try and protect secrets. On the other hand, the transparency of group life may alter the shape and character of many new religions in ways that are scarcely imaginable. I do not have any firm hypotheses as to how transparency might change new religions; I merely offer the suggestion to encourage others to consider.

The Internet as Leverage for the Powerless and Oppressed

For those lonely former members who felt they had to confront and expose international movements they had left, the Internet provided them with an unprecedented venue for voicing their complaints and concerns. But there are also instances where the Internet might well become an instrument for positive propaganda for the promotion of a group. The case of Falun Gong in China unquestionably offers the best example to this point in the short life of the Internet.

Caught between the drive to modernize, and the desire to keep control of the Communist state structure, the PRC banned Falun Gong in China. Even before Falun Gong defied the government's prohibition against public gatherings and staged a large protest in Tiannaman Square, they had developed a substantial Internet communications structure. The Internet infrastructure, which has been used in China to announce the location of public meditations, was quickly able to mobilize for organizing protests, for exporting information abroad, for contacting journalists and otherwise mobilizing world sympathy.

Why the Chinese government viewed Falun Gong as such a threat is beyond the scope of this discussion. It should be noted, however, that the government's creation of an official Chinese site, available in English, for the purpose of "exposing the cult"[21] speaks to the effectiveness of the Falun Gong Web presence. Barend Ter Haar, who regularly posts updates on Falun Gong on a University of Heidelberg site, notes that the government's site provides "a rewarding exercise in PRC propaganda and [for understanding] the increasingly sophisticated state use of the internet" (Ter Haar, 2000).

Beyond this observation, it is interesting to speculate about how the Internet may be utilized by social movement organizations both for the purpose of promoting organization goals, but also as a communication instrument times of crisis management. Imagine, for example, how the siege of the Branch Davidians in Waco, Texas, might have had a different outcome if the Davidians had: (1) a Web page, and (2) the technology to daily upload their story via wireless transmission? The possibilities offered by the Internet have already been well understood and used by some political groups, as the example of the Mexican Zapatistas and others has shown.

CONCLUSION

The challenges posed by the Internet do not only affect NRMs, but potentially all religious groups. The Internet is likely to contribute to the acceleration of globalization in the field of religious studies, making religious material even from little-known traditions available to the general public. It will also likely help diasporas to organize and keep in touch. The potential is amazing. Consider, for instance, how many Zoroastrian Web pages have been available for several years on the Internet, not for the purpose of proselytizing, since Zoroastrianism is not a missionary religion, but for reinforcing community links. Old and new religions alike may reap benefits or suffer damages from the Internet.

Traditional religious authorities can find themselves challenged by competing channels claiming authority in religious matters, and the same already begins to apply to NRMs, as some examples throughout this article have shown.

Religious scholars studying contemporary groups are aware how the Internet has already changed their lives in less than ten years, allowing them to network much more efficiently and to gain access to unprecedented amount of material. Religious groups are increasingly aware too that the rules are changing with the advent of new technologies. But nobody is as yet able to understand precisely how this will affect the future developments.

At a first and very practical level, there are legal issues involved. Disputes regarding the ownership of domain names have led to some picturesque skirmishes, with cyber pirates occupying a domain before a group had even realized the potential consequences. For instance, the German page for the word 'Mormons', www.mormonen.de, was actually bought as late as June 1997 by a critic of Mormonism. After having threatened to sue, the LDS Church finally gave up, but in the meantime LDS-related entities bought all the domain names in several countries which may in some way or another be associated with their religion, obviously in an effort to prevent the repetition of such cases. However, this was really a case on the border, since 'Mormons' has never been claimed as an official name by the LDS Church.

In most cases, developing jurisprudence on domain names leads one to think that, while there will certainly be a constant flow of new cases, the golden days of cybersquatting are behind. Despite the first-come first-served principle, it will become increasingly difficult to occupy a name in .com, .org or .net if it is obviously intended to create confusion. The Jews for Jesus successfully sued the operator of the domain jewsforjesus.org, a Jewish opponent of the organization: the court deemed that the name was used in a deceptive way and the trademark deserved protection.

While abuse of domain names can be expected to become increasingly difficult, there are other dimensions of Internet wars which can be expected to continue, such as the posting of 'secret documents'. Court cases will probably be decided in most cases in favour of those legally holding the trademarks or copyrights. Such decisions are likely to be quite difficult in cases of religious schisms: it is one thing to decide about the legal ownership of a building, a quite different one to decide about the ownership of documents claimed to be 'sacred scriptures'. The spread of the Internet will probably make it possible for people wanting to post controversial material to do it for a short period from exotic places, with mirror sites in rapid succession. And who knows which possibilities future technical developments may still offer? The end of those cyber fights is certainly not in sight.

The sheer abundance of material and sites on the Internet will make it a more difficult task to retrieve some information with search engines. However, there will conceivably be improvements in the possibilities offered by search engines, in addition to those sites which offer information accessible in an organized way. Specialized portals for various topics are developing, and their quality will certainly grow too. They usually will want to offer a variety of viewpoints. This means that flooding the Web with a huge number of pages might finally be of little use: critical voices will still remain accessible.

NRMs themselves too may increasingly learn how to benefit from the Internet, which will allow people to study their messages even in countries where the political or religious climate may make it difficult for them to operate normally. But it will probably become ever more difficult to hide unpleasant facts in the history or life of a group, just as a change of geographical setting will no more allow a group to escape the attention and criticism of inquisitive opponents. There are certainly negative as well as positive aspects in those trends: some groups can be just defamed at a worldwide level without any real recourse if they do not want to fan the controversies. However, considering the increasing proliferation of available religious paths, the Internet might also become one of the tools contributing in fact to a regulation of the religious super-market.

ACKNOWLEDGMENTS

In addition to all those who have helped me through their comments or replies to my email messages and questions, I want especially to thank Jeffrey Hadden, who has a long experience with the Internet, for his major contributions to the in-depth revision of the original version of this chapter and for his insightful suggestions to improve it.

NOTES

1. Aguierre is Access Director for the Spiritual Counterfeits Project.

2. Carol Giambalvo is a   thought reform consultant with the American Family Foundation.

3. Interestingly, some experts in the field of terrorism make a similar hypothesis regarding the possible effects of the Internet on the behavior of extreme political groups, according to a remark by Brian Jenkins, senior advisor to the President of RAND, in his keynote address at the conference Terrorism and Beyond . . . The 21st Century, Oklahoma City, April 17-19, 2000 (proceedings forthcoming).

4. I thank Prof. George Chryssides (University of Wolverhampton) for having provided a copy of this article.

5. Wilson was not an affiliate of Sukyo Mahikari, but of the main competing organization, Sekai Mahikari Bunmei Kyodan.

6. This exercise was conducted on May 19, 1999. The addresses of those pages are not provided in the footnotes, since some changed or disappeared in the meantime.

7. Another search conducted in November 1999 produced similar results. On April 27, 2000, however, there were 827 entries found; the first one was an unofficial, positive Mahikari Web page by an Australian follower who wanted to contribute to dispel adverse information found on the Internet. The presence of critical Web pages remained however massive.

8. See http://www.geocities.com/Tokyo/Flats/1374/fmbr.htm

9. See   http://www.geocities.com/Tokyo/Flats/1374/index_e.htm   The   Web   page remains active, but is no longer updated since April 2000.

10. See a briefing provided to Jeffrey Hadden, The Church of Scientology and the Internet, June 30, 2000. Retrieved July 16, 2000, from the World Wide Web: http://cti.itc.virginia.edu/~jkh8x/soc257/nrms/scientology_briefing.html

11. For more information about the way the filtering program operates (and uninstallation instructions), see : http://www.xenu.net/archive/events/censorship

12. See http://www.mormons.org/response/general/Publications_EOM.htm

13. See http://www.jw-russia.org/, <http://www.jehovaszeugen.de/ http://www.temoinsdejehovah.org

14. See Waydale Document Archives, http://www.waydale.com

15. Rico Margnelli, head of the TWI Public Relations Department, advised Jeffrey K. Hadden on July 30, 1998 (telephone conversation) that they were developing a Web site. As of this writing, a through search found no evidence that a site has been launched.

16. See   http://ourworld.compuserve.com/homepages/2x2info_namelesshousesect/ homepage.htm

17. See http://www.ex-premie.org, http://www.ex-premie.org/french/index-fr.htm

18. Even if the Terms under which this Web site is made available to you at maharaji.org still reflects some caution: "You may not copy, reproduce, imitate, alter, modify, publish, disseminate, distribute, transmit, transfer, create derivative works, post

on any computer, 'frame' or broadcast in any other media, or in any way exploit, any of the content of this Web site, including the Web site Materials." Retrieved from the World Wide Web: http://www.maharaji.org/notices/site_terms.htm

19. They can currently be found on the following Web sites: http://www.bluelotus.com/fwbo/default_last.htm and http://www.fwbo-files.com

20. See http://www.fwbo.org/criticisms.html

21. See http://ppflg.china.com.cn/indexE.html

REFERENCES

Brown, J. (1998). A Web of Their Own. *Salon,* (July 15). Retrieved July 16, 2000, from the World Wide Web: http://www.salon.com/21st/feature/1998/07/15feature.html.

Campbell, C. (1972). The Cult, the Cultic Milieu and Secularization. *A Sociological Yearbook of Religion in Britain, 5,* 119–136.

Chryssides, G. (1996). New Religions and the Internet. *Diskus, 4*(2). Retrieved July 16, 2000, from the World Wide Web: http://www.uni-marburg.de/fb03/religionswissenschaft/journal/diskus/chryssides_3.html

Cornille, C. (1994). Jesus in Japan: Christian Syncretism in Mahikari. In: P. B. Clarke, & J. Somers (Eds), *Japanese New Religions in the West* (pp. 89–103). Folkestone (Kent): Japan Library.

Dawson, L. L. (1998). *Comprehending Cults: The Sociology of New Religious Movements.* Toronto, Oxford, New York: Oxford University Press.

Dawson, L. L., & Hennebry, J. (1999). New Religions and the Internet: Recruiting in a New Public Space. *Journal of Contemporary Religion, 14*(1), 17–39.

Der Spiegel. (1995). Torloses Tor: Das Internet entwickelt sich zum neuen Medium für Kirchen und Sekten, Gurus und Satanisten. No.31, (July 31): 88.

Foster, L. (1984). Career Apostates: Reflections on the Works of Jerald and Sandra Tanner. *Dialogue: A Journal of Mormon Thought, 17*(2), 35–60.

Gold, L. (2000). *Mormons on the Internet.* Rev. ed. Rocklin, CA: Prima Publishing.

Grossman, W. (1995). War of Words. *Wired,* (July-August): 4–7.

Introvigne, M. (1997). *Heaven's Gate: Il paradiso non può attendere.* Leumann (Torino): Editrice Elle Di Ci.

Introvigne, M. (1999). *Sukyo Mahikari.* Leumann (Torino): Editrice Elle Di Ci.

Introvigne, M., & Mayer, J-F. (2000). Occult Masters and the Temple of Doom: The Fiery End of the Solar Temple. Forthcoming in D. G. Bromley (Ed.), *Dramatic Confrontations: Religion and Violence in Contemporary Society.* New York: Cambridge University Press.

Lippard, J., & Jacobsen, J. (1995). Scientology v. the Internet: Free Speech and Copyright Infringement on the Information Super-Highway. *The Skeptic, 3*(3), 35–41. Retrieved July 16, 2000, from the World Wide Web: http://www.skeptic.com/03.3.jl-jj-scientology.html.

Mayer, J-F. (1999). 'Our Terrestrial Journey is Coming to an End': The Last Voyage of the Solar Temple. *Nova Religio: The Journal of Alternative and Emergent Religions, 2*(2), 172–196.

Mayer, J-F. (2000). Les nouveaux mouvements religieux à l'heure d'Internet. *Cahiers de Littérature Orale,* 47, 127–146.

Parker, D. & H. (1982). *The Secret Sect.* Pendle Hill (N.S.W., Australia): The Authors.

Penton, M. J. (1997). *Apocalypse Delayed: The Story of Jehovah's Witnesses.* 2nd ed. Toronto: University of Toronto Press.

Perkins, R., & Forrest, J. (1997). *Cosmic Suicide: The Tragedy and Transcendence of Heaven's Gate.* Dallas: Pentaradial Press.

Quittner, J. (1997). Life and Death on the Web. *Time* (International Edition), *14*, (April 7): 39.

Rosenthal, D. (1995). Sekten setzen die Datenautobahn für ihre Zwecke ein. *Die Weltwoche* (Zurich), *27*, (July 6): 25.

Shukman, H. (1999). Friends of the Western Buddhist Order. *Tricycle: The Buddhist Review, 8*(4), 66–68, 112–118.

Sturcke, H. (1998). Das Jahr 2000 und das Ende der Welt auf Internet. Retrieved July 16, 2000, from the World Wide Web: http://www.unizh.ch/theol/publ/weltende/index.html

Ter Haar, B. (2000; originally 1999, regularly updated). Falun Gong: Evaluation and further references. Retrieved July 16, 2000, from the World Wide Web: http://sun.sino.uni-heidelberg.de/staff/bth/falun.htm.

Wright, R. (1996). Can Thor Make a Comeback? *Time* (International Edition), *51*, (December 16): 50–51.

'SO MANY EVIL THINGS': ANTI-CULT TERRORISM VIA THE INTERNET

Massimo Introvigne

ABSTRACT

After the Heaven's Gate suicide in 1997 the media worried about cults recruiting via the Internet, but opponents of new religious movements appear to have been more aggressively active in cyberspace than the movements themselves. This chapter discusses some theoretical models of cyberspace, and of violence and terrorism via the Internet. It then applies the models, after a methodological discussion, to the extreme fringe of anti-cultism (not to be confused with the more moderate cult awareness community) whose hate propaganda is carried out primarily via the Internet. The activities of this lunatic fringe, whose impact is discussed in the conclusions, focus on demonizing and dehumanizing the 'cults' and their alleged supporters; in promoting increasingly wild conspiracy theories; and in targeting scholars of new religious movements singled out as 'cult apologists' and targeted with personal attacks.

INTRODUCTION

Following the mass suicide of Heaven's Gate in March 1997 the media openly expressed concern that naive Internet surfers might be easily recruited into

Religion on the Internet, Volume 8, pages 277–306.
2000 by Elsevier Science Inc.
ISBN: 0-7623-0535-5

suicidal cults through well-crafted Web sites. While the Internet is still very new and, hence, this concern has not been studied extensively, the available scholarship does not support this view. The limited evidence available suggests that Internet conversions to new religious movements are rare (Kellner, 1996; O'Leary, 1996) and almost certainly do not contribute significantly to their growth (Dawson & Hennebry, 1999; Mayer, 1999).

The thesis argued in this chapter is that the source of such concern is to be found in the aggressive proselytization of a group of persons who are known to the scholarly community as 'anti-cultists' because of the adamant opposition to virtually all new religious movements. Even a cursory examination of mass media coverage of crisis events involving religious movements reveals that the anti-cultists are highly visible on television and as sources for newspaper articles. They are also abundantly present on the Internet, where they enjoy a substantially unchallenged forum to spread their views.

These anti-cultists not only present themselves as 'experts', but they also seek to discredit scholars, and other persons, who challenge their perspective. A small group has become quite aggressive on the Internet, disrupting list-servers, bulletin boards and chat rooms so that civil discourse becomes impossible. On their Web sites they publish slanderous comments about individual scholars. Whenever the targets of their hate propaganda seek to fight back, the anti-cultists portray themselves as victims of heavy-handedness and censorship.

This study concentrates on the most aggressive Internet anti-cultists, detailing how they have systematically sought to disrupt civil discourse and turn persons who disagree with them – especially scholars – into enemies and 'traitors of truth'.

The study is divided into five parts:

- First, to establish context, I begin with a review of social scientific theories that explain how cyberspace is constructed.
- Second, drawing from social science literature on how events are socially constructed, I will explore the emergence of the anti-cult movement in cyberspace as a discrete form of information warfare and terrorism.
- Third, some comments will be offered on the background and development of the extreme anti-cult fringe, particularly in Europe, as well as a brief examination of its differences (and relationships) with the mainline anti-cult community.
- Fourth, examples will be given of how this fringe is particularly (if not exclusively) active through the Internet, and its problems in obtaining off-line results from its on-line activism.

- Fifth, the main body of the study concludes with an application of scholarship about the Internet and violence in general to the activities of the anti-cultists. Attention will be focused on how their efforts have affected both new religious movements and their more moderate critics.

CYBERSPACE AS A SOCIAL CONSTRUCTION

The very concept of cyberspace is a fairly obvious example of what Berger and Luckmann (1966, pp. 76–79) would characterize as the social construction of a symbolic universe. The process of social construction occurs through a three-fold process of externalization, objectivation, and internalization.

The term 'cyberspace' comes from fiction, and was originally defined by cyberpunk novelist William Gibson (1984, p. 67) as "a consensual hallucination experienced together by billions of legitimate operators." In his novel *Neuromancer*, Gibson invented the notion of cyberspace as a computer-accessible location where all the existing information in the world was collected. Later, John P. Barlow described the real world of connected computers using the same term as Gibson. Some claim, therefore, that cyberspace, as it exists today, should be called 'Barlovian cyberspace' in order to distinguish it from the fictional 'Gibsonian cyberspace' of cyberpunk literature (Jordan, 1999, pp. 20–21).

Interestingly enough, two of the best known social scientific textbooks on cyberspace, divide their discussion of cyberspace into three parallel parts. Jordan (1999) whose work is strictly sociological, is primarily interested in power and social politics in cyberspace, and sees three layers of the virtual space: individual, social, and imaginary. Gackenbach (1998), who writes from a more social-psychological perspective, also divided her textbook into three parts devoted respectively to the intrapersonal (or personal), interpersonal, and transpersonal dimensions of cyberspace.

The three dimensions in the two textbooks (personal-individual, interpersonal-social, and transpersonal-imaginary) are obviously parallel. And a cursory examination will reveal that they parallel Berger and Luckmann's social construction model to a certain extent. In the personal-individual stage, human actions, through a process of externalization, create cyberspace as a new form of social institution. When cyberspace appears, through objectivation, as a given 'objective' reality, new forms of interpersonal-social relations develop. Subjective understanding of the objectified cyberspace, obtained through internalization, gives rise to transpersonal-imaginary experiences, a virtual imaginary in which both 'visions of heaven' and 'fears of hell' develop (Jordan, 1999, p. 185).

A significant literature now exists on all three stages of this process. For our purposes, it is important to note that the main social and psychological problem in cyberspace has been discussed under the name of 'information overload'. Sociologists have explored the paradoxical notion of receiving too much information, more than even the most gifted individual is able to absorb.

Shenk (1997, p. 15) states that information overload "threatens our ability to educate ourselves, and leaves us more vulnerable as consumers and less cohesive as a society." Kraut and Attewell (1997, p. 325), in their study of transnational corporations, note that 'communication is a resource-consuming process . . . As a result, one would expect that as the volume of communication increases, so will the problems of feeling rushed and overloaded." Jordan (1999, p. 117) points to the problem of having "so much information that the ability to understand it is impaired: the important cannot be distinguished from the unimportant, and too large amounts of information simply cannot be absorbed."

Jordan (1999, p. 128) also mentions a related phenomenon, the "spiral of technopower', generated when information overload is confronted by introducing new technological tools for information management. If these tools are good enough, however, they in turn increase the amount of information available in cyberspace, and 'simply return users, after varying lengths of time, to the first step because new forms of information overload emerge."

The whole concept of information overload is, in turn, politically negotiated and conditioned. Ultimately, the evaluation of information overload is connected with the transpersonal-imaginary level of cyberspace. People make political evaluations as to whether so much information is liberating or threatening. The political issue, here, is that the overload may threaten our normal ability to internalize an information hierarchy.

When dealing with the printed media, we realize that *The New York Times* is not infallible, but is in any case more reliable than the *Weekly World News*. A similar information hierarchy is much more difficult to reconstruct in cyberspace, although it is slowly emerging in specialized areas such as financial information.

Libertarians may celebrate the subversion of off-line hierarchies as the greatest achievement of cyberspace, and some early scholarly studies agreed with them (see Rheingold, 1993). It is true that any attempt to censor parts of cyberspace may sooner or later be bypassed.

However, as Jordan (1999, p. 79) notes, claiming that subverting off-line hierarchies automatically creates an anti-hierarchical, and truly democratic, communication may be an example of the logical fallacy known as *technological determinism*. The latter mistakenly implies that a certain technology necessarily determines a certain social outcome. "Such pure or strong forms of technological determinism are always weak because they define causes of society through non-social systems, technologies, that appear social as soon as they are themselves investigated" (Jordan, 1999, p. 79). Jordan suggests that cyber-political issues are much more complicated, and that "off-line hierarchies are subverted by cyberspace but are also reconstituted in cyberspace ... The subversion of hierarchy does not mean that cyberspace is devoid of hierarchy. Rather, new and different hierarchies emerge" (Jordan, 1999, p. 83).

Arguing from a social psychological perspective, and studying newsgroups and other sub-Web on-line communities, Reid concludes that "virtual communities are not the agora; they are not a place of open and free public discourse. It is a mistake to think that the Internet is an inherently democratic institution, or that it will necessarily lead to increased personal freedoms and increased understanding between people" (Reid, 1998, p. 33). The technology allows those who have the best equipment, or technical capabilities, to claim that their information is also inherently better, "creating social hierarchies that can be every bit as restrictive and oppressive as some in the corporeal world."

MALICIOUS USE OF THE INFORMATION OVERLOAD AND INTERNET TERRORISM

In the early 1990s, social science pessimism about the information overload regarded it as an entirely spontaneous phenomenon. In the second half of the decade a new scholarly literature emerged, suggesting that the overload may be manipulated and, moreover, it may be manipulated for the purpose of damaging specific organizations, governments or groups (Denning & Denning, 1998; Denning, 1999).

This new way of thinking about Internet terrorism almost certainly contributed to the phenomenon becoming an increasingly well researched issue, even though the concept itself was variously defined. Terrorism is generally conceptualized as the symbolic use of actual violence, for political reasons, against non-military targets. By symbolic use, scholars of terrorism suggest that terrorism is successful when its message reaches a large public, much larger than the circle of those actually harmed by it (Thornton, 1964; Wilkinson, 1975). But if terrorism is a socially constructed notion that is continuously renegotiated at the political level, it is essentially a truism that one person's terrorist is another person's freedom fighter.

In the context, violence too becomes a controversial concept. In the area of religion-related terrorism, particularly, the impact of verbal violence has been regarded as tantamount to terrorism. *Verbal violence* is defined by Sprinzak as:

... the use of extreme language against an individual or a group that either implies a direct threat that physical force will be used against them, or is seen as an indirect call for others to use it. Verbal violence is often a substitute for real violence, for it helps excited leaders to vent their frustration in less than a physically violent manner. The problem of verbal violence is that it may incite followers who are incapable of distinguishing between real and verbal violence to engage in actual violence (Sprinzak, 1999, p. 316).

In turn, terrorism against transnational corporations has often been studied in the shape of 'information terrorism'. This is usually defined as the systematic spreading of information aimed at damaging or destroying the business of a corporation. Corporations have employed various strategies in order to persuade legal authorities that *information terrorism* is not a 'cleaner' form of terrorism and, thus, deserves no added indulgence. While it is true that information terrorism does not normally involve the loss of human life, it may inflict damage far greater than other non-lethal terrorist activities. An ecoterrorist group targeting a transnational corporation, for instance, may cause comparatively little damage by blowing up one or more warehouses. Additionally, after the first terrorist acts, security will inevitably be increased, as also the risk for the terrorists themselves. Successfully spreading 'information' that a key product of the same corporation causes cancer, or other lethal diseases, is much more effective. In fact, in 1998, ecoterrorists targeting a transnational food corporation in Europe simply shipped to an Italian news agency a poisoned and potentially lethal Christmas cake manufactured by that corporation, claiming that many more had actually been poisoned and were on the shelves of unsuspecting stores. When caught, their defense was that they had, in fact, poisoned only the single cake sent to the news agency, without endangering anybody's health since it was clearly marked as 'poisoned' with plenty of warning labels. The incident prompted a number of corporations in Italy to request that the law be amended to deal with this new information terrorism.

Another interesting feature of the 1998 Christmas cake incident, was that any attempt by the printed media not to carry the news would have been ineffective, since the letter claiming that a number of cakes had been poisoned was widely circulated via the Internet. This was a case both of information terrorism and of terrorism via the Internet.

The latter category needs to be elaborated. 'Internet terrorism', as used in the relevant literature, seems to cover different and not necessarily related activities. First, a large part of the literature discusses *cyberterrorism*, i.e. the manipulation of an information system through the alteration, or theft, of data. Authors agree that the most dangerous form of cyberterrorism is that which attacks vital infrastructures, such as hacking an air traffic control system, thereby threatening the actual collision planes. Whether this is actually possible is debated among many counter-terrorism specialists, with some contending that cyberterrorism risks are often overestimated in popular literature and by politicians (Pollitt, 1997).

There is little doubt, however, that cyberterrorism is a daily event on a scale somewhat less than that of attacking infrastructures: computer systems are damaged, viruses are spread, and Web sites are hacked. Other authors include in their concept of 'Internet terrorism' the simple propaganda distributed on the Web by groups they regard as terrorist. Destouche (1999) provides a large list, from Islamic fundamentalists to followers of the late Rabbi Meher Kahane.

Regrettably Destouche's book, which is otherwise informative, is significantly conditioned by the anti-cult climate currently prevailing in France. His list of 'subversive' and, thus, potentially Internet terrorist groups includes what he calls 'degenerate sects'. Accordingly, the very fact that such degenerate and subversive groups have a Web site is an 'Internet risk' and they should be part of any terrorism survey. Together with Aum Shinrikyo, Destouche lists the Church of Scientology, the Jehovah's Witnesses, Transcendental Meditation, Soka Gakkai, the Raelians, New Acropolis and the Church of Satan (1999, pp. 38–143, pp. 238– 239). This list clearly shows how socially held prejudices can easily become grist for the social construction of subversion.

A third category of Internet terrorism is *information terrorism via the Internet.* Here, the Internet is the privileged source used to spread information politically aimed at damaging or destroying a particular organization. Legal literature discusses cases in which the target is a corporation ('Legal Wars on the Web: A Checklist', 1999).

Categorizing these activities as 'terrorist' seems to be more appropriate when they are perpetrated in furtherance of a political (as opposed to a merely economical) aim. The Internet, in this sense, may be particularly attractive for information terrorism as a way of circumventing possible censorship by the mainline media, and of making legal counter-attacks more difficult. This has been particularly true of 'single issue terrorism' in fields such as animal rights, environmentalism, and abortion (Smith, 1998). In these fields, a preferred strategy, whereby the Internet has played a key role, has been the publication of 'hit lists' of both individuals and corporations allegedly associated with extra-ordinary evil.

Perhaps the most famous legal case, evidencing the problems in defining the boundaries between verbal and non-verbal violence, concerns the anti-abortion Web sites publishing the so-called Nuremberg Files. This list includes names and other personal information concerning a number of doctors performing abortions, and qualifies them as 'baby butchers'.

Notwithstanding the inflammatory language, the main site publishing the Nuremberg Files argued that it did not promote actual (as opposed to verbal) violence, and that the information was available, anyway, to a determined searcher through other public sources. In fact, the name implied the call for a future Nuremberg trial established by a government outlawing abortion as homicide. These arguments did not satisfy a U.S. federal court in Portland, however, when three doctors on the list had actually been killed.

Planned Parenthood and a group of doctors sued, claiming that this was a matter of 'domestic terrorism', and on February 2, 1999, were awarded a record $107 million in damages (Verhovek, 1999). The original provider immediately removed the site from the Web. It was mirrored, however, by other providers, encouraged by a ruling of the Portland judge that he had no jurisdiction over new defendants not included in his original case (Green, 1999). Eventually, most U.S. providers were scared by the threat of legal liability, and by the amount of damages awarded in the Portland decision.

On February 22, 1999, however, Internet libertarian activist Karin Spaink of Amsterdam, Holland, published a manifesto claiming that "while I strongly hold that every woman should have an abortion if she needs one," "there is a distinct difference between words and deeds." As a libertarian, Spaink explained, she 'decided to put up a mirror of the Nuremberg Files' (Spaink, 1999), and the Files are to date still available through her controversial provider www.xs4all.nl, at the address http://www.xs4all.nl/~oracle/nuremberg/aborts.html. Spaink's organization, as we shall see, also plays a role in the anti-cult Internet wars.

Information wars on the Internet are no longer entirely in private hands. Several national intelligence services have become quite active both in preventing cyberterrorism and in monitoring foreign activities against key national corporations (Guisnel, 1997). In France, according to Destouche (1999, pp. 215–216), a number of intelligence agencies watch both the Web and the newsgroups. (In fact, one intelligence agency seems to be "mostly interested in newsgroups"). There is little doubt that similar activities are being carried out by intelligence agencies also outside of France.

ANTI-CULT TERRORISM

The development of the 'anti-cult' movement has been documented in scholarly literature on new religious movements since the early 1980s (see Beckford, 1985; Shupe & Bromley, 1980, 1985; Shupe, Bromley & Oliver, 1984). More recently, these studies have been both updated (see Melton, 1999) and re-examined in a cross-cultural perspective (Chryssides 1999; Shupe & Bromley, 1994; Usarski, 1999).

The demise of the largest American anti-cult organization, the Cult Awareness Network, occurred in 1996 because of its involvement in a violent and illegal activity, i.e. forcible deprogramming. In addition to their engagement in politics and direct action, most mainline anti-cult groups in the United States have maintained an interest in researching and arguing their position. Anti-cult movements in Europe have, from the very beginning, been less research-oriented and more proactive.

Following the Order of the Solar Temple suicides and homicides in 1994–1997, in particular, some European anti-cult movements experienced an unprecedented degree of public support. Parliamentary reports generated immediately after the Solar Temple incidents, inter alia in France (Assemblée, 1996) and Belgium (Chambre des Représentants de Belgique, 1997), simply mirrored the approach of the anti-cult organizations, explicitly distancing themselves from the work of legitimate scholars.

Beginning in 1998, a 'second generation' of European parliamentary and administrative reports, somewhat more moderate (Introvigne & Richardson, 1999), followed. Countries such as France maintained their earlier attitudes, and ultimately came under heavy criticism from the U.S. State Department and a number of international bodies. In 1998, France established a governmental Mission to Fight Cults and published a second report in 1999 (Assemblée Nationale, 1999), devoted to cult finances. In 2000, the French National Assembly approved a draconian anti-cult law.

Both the Belgian and the French reports included lengthy lists of groups investigated as possible cults, and the French report of 1999 even included the names of several individuals. The 'second generation' (or Type II) reports, while maintaining some elements of the anti-cult perspective agreed with international scholars that France and other countries had probably gone too far.

The Swedish report ('In Good Faith', 1998) lamented that "in France the state has on the whole made common cause with the anti-cult movement," ignoring the fact that "the great majority of members of the new religious movements derive positive experience from their membership."

The 1998 report issued by the Swiss Canton of Ticino (Dipartimento delle Istituzioni, 1998, pp. 17, 39) claimed that, while co-operating with anti-cult movements may occasionally be appropriate, governments "should avoid becoming accomplices in the work of spreading generalized prejudices," or even in promoting an 'anti-cult terrorism'.

While in this Swiss document the expression 'anti-cult terrorism' was used metaphorically, acts of terrorism in the strictest sense of the word were indeed perpetrated in France in 1996 and later (see Introvigne, 2000). Premises of both the Unification Church and New Acropolis (a movement founded in Argentina) were bombed in Paris. Nobody has suggested that the largest anti-cult organizations were actually involved in the bombings. On the other hand, as noted by Usarski (1999) with reference to Germany, the publication of inflammatory documents by both private organizations sponsored by government, and by the government itself, proclaiming that literally hundreds of cults are pure evil, and that the country is at war with them, is dangerous. It may inadvertently create a background favorable to extreme (and occasionally violent) manifestations of discrimination and hate.

This danger is not purely theoretical in Europe, where the anti-cult fight has been picked up by fringe movements whose language (and, occasionally, deeds) already had a violent edge to them. At least four such movements can be identified in this context.

- First, an extreme form of anti-Catholic and anti-religious language expressed in a fringe of the secular humanist movement in French-speaking Europe (David, 1997).
- Second, a left-wing anti-globalization discourse sees cults, as well as transnational corporations (and McDonald's franchises too perhaps), as agents of an evil plan to destroy Europe's socialist identity in the name of the American free-market economy.[1]
- Third, right-wing groups at the other end of the political spectrum propose the same anti-globalization discourse. What we may call European Identity Movement attacks, with similar arguments, U.S.-led globalization plans. The difference between right-wing and left-wing anti-globalization discourses is that, while both claim to fight for European identity against Americanization, they adopt opposite definitions of this identity. European Identity is regarded as intrinsically spiritual and religious, based on Europe's Christian history, by the right-wing discourse, while the left-wing anti-globalists would insist on socialism as an intrinsic part of European cultural and political history.
- Fourth, some Islamic fundamentalist groups have also welcomed a violent anti-cult discourse. This results as a tactical maneuver to avoid inclusion in the anti-cult public repression, and because cults often target Moslems for proselytization.

Although very different from each other, these groups occasionally cross-fertilize. An exemplary case is the Italian magazine *Orion,* published since 1984 as "an anti-globalist monthly . . . against the planetary *homologation* of the New World Order" (see its Web site at http://space.tin.it/lettura/vileonar/orion.html). It publishes both right wing and left wing anti-globalization tirades, promotes a 'national communism' as well as authors connected with Nazism and anti-Semitism (including Holocaust negationist Robert Faurisson).[2] *Orion* has, in fact, been quite active in the anti-cult fight, seeing cults as one of the most dangerous agents of U.S.-led globalization projects.[3]

INTERNET TERRORISM AND CULT WARS

Wars between new religious movements and their opponents have found a battleground on the Internet since at least the Web's early beginnings. Very few groups, however, have actually been accused of cyberterrorism. Aum Shinrikyo was accused by a Christian Web site in Japan of preparing a cyber-attack against national infrastructures, but no evidence of this has emerged.

Cult wars are much more related to *information* terrorism via the Internet. Authoritative scholars of information terrorism via the Internet, such as Denning (1999, pp. 101–129), include 'perception management' in their studies. These may take the form of "offensive operations [which] reach the minds of a population by injecting content into the population's information space." Denning lists systematic 'lies and distortions', fabrications, hoaxes, social engineering, 'denouncement' ("messages that discredit, defame, demonize, or dehumanize an opponent'), and – strictly related to the latter – 'conspiracy theories."

Denning also includes harassment through hate mail or 'spamming', and even systematic copyright infringement (1999, pp. 90–94). The latter, she argues, may in fact become part of a terrorist 'offensive information warfare'. Activities aimed at destroying an organization or corporation through the destruction of copyright can be one the most valuable assets of information terrorists. In each of these instances we can see, and need to stress that information terrorism is a politically constructed category. What for one is verbal terrorism is for another free speech.

The whole notion of 'copyright terrorism' is a good example of how language in this field is politically negotiated. The Church of Scientology (which has obtained quite a few court orders against Internet opponents on the basis of copyright infringement) and its critics have liberally traded accusations of 'copyright terrorism'. For the Church of Scientology, terrorism is the systematic copyright infringement, while for its opponents the real 'terrorism' lies in Scientology's use of the copyright law for the purpose of silencing its critics (Holeton, 1998, p. 353).

Apart from copyright issues, other kinds of information terrorism and offensive information warfare listed by Denning are well represented in the cult wars on the Internet. Unlike in the United States, the largest anti-cult organizations in Europe have but a limited presence on the Internet. They probably see no reason for diverting resources from other successful strategies. On the other hand, fringe groups, and (particularly) single individuals in the anti-cult camp, operate large Web sites.

What differentiates anti-cult information terrorism and offensive information warfare via the Internet from less extreme forms of anti-cult activity in cyberspace, is the presence of one or more of the criteria outlined by Denning: "messages that . . . demonize, or dehumanize an opponent', 'conspiracy theories', and the systematic 'publication of false statements."

A fourth element is the publication of 'hit lists' of individuals (other than the founders and leaders of the targeted movements), thus inviting – if not extreme measures, as in the tragic case of the Nuremberg Files – at least discrimination, and boycotts of 'cult-related' businesses.

Although a few dozen similar anti-cult enterprises exist on the Web, I will examine only a few specific examples and then discuss counter-terrorism retaliatory measures used by some new religions movements, focusing on the special case of the Usenet.

Three elements are present, in different degrees, in extremist anti-cult Web sites.

- First, attempts at dehumanizing or demonizing the target (normally a single new religious movement, although other groups are also mentioned, and links to other 'specialized' anti-cult sites are offered).
- Second, extreme conspiracy theories.
- Third, attempts at immunizing the anti-cult movement from its principal problem, which has been defined as its "almost unanimous lack of support from academics" (Chryssides. 1999, p. 263), or "lack of any convincing scientific evidence" for its theories (Usarski, 1999, p. 238).

To deal with this latter problem, academics and other scholarly researchers are systematically discredited through ad hominem attacks as 'cult apologists', or 'hired guns' for 'cults'.

One of the three elements is normally prevalent, and gives to each individual Web site its distinctive flavor. Mayer (1999) has studied the impact of the Web assault against Sûkyô Mahikari, a Japanese new religious movement, by Australian ex-member Garry A. Greenwood. Now self-published (Greenwood, 1997), his book *All the Emperor's Men* has been available via the Web since 1995 (see now http://www.geocities.com/Tokyo/Shrine/5712/copy.htm).

Greenwood begins with facts well known among scholars of Sûkyô Mahikari (although perhaps not among its members). For example, its founder was associated in his early life with other Japanese new religious movements. From these kinds of innocuous observations, the text, and the Web site, quickly degenerate. Kotama Okada (1901–1974), the founder of Mahikari, is first dehumanized by associating him with a number of war crimes committed by the Japanese Army, in which he was an officer, during World War II. Although Okada was undoubtedly a fervent nationalist, allegations of atrocities are unsubstantiated (see Introvigne, 1999).

Second, associating it with Nazism and anti-Semitism dehumanizes the movement. Again, as in other Japanese movements, an anti-Semitic element was present in Mahikari's early texts. Greenwood's allegations elevate this not so unique element of Mahikari's early life to a completely different order of magnitude. Mahikari, he writes, is "promoting the same notorious ideals as those enforced by Adolf Hitler" (Greenwood, 1997, p. 76).

Finally, Mahikari is further dehumanized through an association with Aum Shinrikyo. Here, Greenwood is repeating the common Japanese anti-cult theme, namely that the sins of Aum Shinrikyo are the sins of new religious movements in general. But Greenwood adds a distinct conspiratorial emphasis. This conspiracy, Greenwood states, is called 'The Black Hand', and the fingers are Aum Shinrikyo, Sûkyô Mahikari, the Unification Church, Agonshu, and Soka Gakkai. Writes Greenwood:

> Now that one of the hand's fingers (Aum Shinrikyo) has been severed, the remaining four must now strive even harder until it can regrow, or be replaced with something different, presumably under a different disguise (Greenwood, 1997, p. 91).

Ultimately, within the framework of a 'yellow danger' rhetoric, Japan itself becomes demonized as the 'author' of a national conspiracy aimed at enforcing a 'global theocracy' under the Japanese emperor, through cults no matter how criminal, international terrorism, and violence. Anti-cultism, therefore, ultimately becomes a form of racism.

Greenwood's Web page is an example of how some actual (and actually objectionable) features of new religious movements, or the careers of their leaders, are so distorted through gross exaggeration, that the rhetoric of controversy mutates into character assassination, demonization, and racism.

A similar Web site aimed at demonizing a single target, Opus Dei, is www.mond.at/opus.dei, managed in Vienna, Austria by Franz Schaefer, who owns his own Internet service provider, mond.at. The similarities to Greenwood's anti-Mahikari site are worth noting.

First, although continuously claiming to offer a balanced perspective, Schaefer in fact uses inflammatory language ("A friend of mine," he starts, "got sucked into this cult"), and repeats in an almost obsessive way the word 'evil' ('evil ideology', 'evil character of the founder', 'so many evil things', etc.). Brainwashed 'victims' can be brought 'back to real life' only by causing them to leave Opus Dei.

Second, Schaefer demonizes Opus Dei by associating it with fascism and Nazism. The founder of Opus Dei 'is the perfect fascist', Opus Dei spreads 'the evil of the Fascistic ideology', and 'Hitler would have loved' their books. Opus Dei's conservative theology may be controversial in several quarters, but Schaefer's denouncement goes far beyond political and theological criticism, and ends up describing Opus Dei as the embodiment of an extraordinary evil.

The Church of Scientology is the subject of the largest number of such assaults. It is almost a truism that Scientology is surrounded by controversy. It has been particularly unpopular among Web libertarians since its use of vigorous legal strategies against copyright infringement and defamation.

The demonization of Scientology in some Web sites goes, however, far beyond normal controversy. One of the largest, and certainly most typical Web pages demonizing Scientology is the Tilman Hausherr Home Page in Berlin, Germany (http://www.snafu.de/~tilman). Although Hausherr's page includes links to pages against a variety of other 'cults' – from Jehovah's Witnesses to Opus Dei – most of this large-scale Web site is devoted purely to disparaging Scientology.

The first welcome on Hausherr's Web page is a quote from an early parliamentary report in Australia that reads:

> Scientology is evil; its techniques evil; its practice a serious danger to the community, medically, morally and socially; and its adherents are sadly deluded and often mentally ill.

Among hundreds of pages on this site, one looks in vain to learn anything about Scientology's beliefs, philosophy, theology, or critique of contemporary culture. Instead, Hausherr offers a lengthy list of previously published anti-Scientology articles, decisions unfavorable to Scientology in courts of law, personal recollections by apostate ex-members, and governmental reports against Scientology.

If there is a redeeming feature to Hausherr's page, it is a sense of humor normally lacking among the extreme fringes of anti-cultism. It is difficult to be amused, however, when reading Hausherr's Web page laundry lists of individual Scientologists and of 'companies and organizations owned or managed by people listed as Scientologists'. Some are well known Scientologists such as Kristie Alley or John Travolta. Most, however, are private individuals unknown to the general public. Companies 'owned or managed by people listed as Scientologists' (an ambiguous concept) range from law firms to architects, computer businesses, and to Elvis Presley Enterprises (Priscilla Presley is a Scientologist).

Finally, there is a list of 'miscellaneous support for Scientology', including both academics and other scholarly 'cult apologists' (Hausherr maintains an encyclopedia of cult apologists in the form of a FAQ, and posts it regularly to Usenet groups), as well as others accused of being 'soft' on Scientology. The latter include the CNN (accused of having "a long record of supporting Scientology"), the IRS (because of the 1993 settlement), the Los Angeles Police Department, and even a lawyer who actually fought against Scientology but settled for terms Hausherr did not approve of.

It is unlikely that CNN or Elvis Presley Enterprises will really suffer from being listed in Hausherr's Web page. A doctor, dentist, or architect in a small town, or a small business, on the other hand, may be easily discriminated against. If 'Scientology is evil', nobody should associate with an 'evil' business. And who would want a Scientologist as a doctor or architect if Scientologists are 'often mentally ill'? Although no actual violence is advocated, the list, a main feature of Hausherr's site, becomes in fact a 'hit list'.

There are other Web sites devoted to attacking Scientology in Europe. Most have the character of national versions, in the local language, of Hausherr's enterprise. They tend to be very much the same, from Roger Gonnet (a former Scientologist) in France (http://home.worldnet.fr/gonnet/index.htm#hp1) to the pseudonymous 'Harry' and 'Martini' in Italy (http://xenu.com-it.net/).

To illustrate a different kind of anti-cult terrorism via the Internet, let us consider Web sites that are primarily *conspiratorial*. Watch Unto Prayer (http://watch.pair.com/pray.html) is a large American-based site that is frequently quoted in European controversies. This is an Evangelical fundamentalist site, although non-Christian anti-cultists such as Miguel Martinez (whose own Web site will be mentioned later) have co-operated with it and expressed support.

Most Christian fundamentalists of conspiratorial persuasion identify the Roman Catholic Church and the Pope with either the Antichrist or the Antichrist's closest ally. Not so, claims Watch Unto Prayer. A closer reading of Revelation, they claim, will reveal that at the end of time a pseudo-Antichrist will be the first to appear. The evil of this pseudo-Antichrist will be extreme but not final. The Roman Catholic Church is only the penultimate evil. The Church of Rome, the 'Mother of Harlots and Abominations of the Earth', is not a Christian denomination. Rather, the Catholic Church is a renewed pagan 'cult of Mithra'. The Church of Rome is not the real Antichrist: it is only the 'pseudo-Antichrist' – even if "the masses have been led to believe that a Revived Roman Empire, controlled by the Roman Church, will be the final Antichrist system."

This 'deception' that will play into the hands of the real Antichrist. The latter is a 'Revived British Empire' led by a character called 'Michael'. By vanquishing "the Pope and his Roman religious system' (the pseudo-Antichrist), 'Michael' (the real Antichrist) will deceive many, including a number of Christians, and 'will be crowned upon the throne of the [rebuilt] Temple of Jerusalem as 'the Christ."

'Michael' will be "the first of many demons to be manifest physically," but his spirit will be embodied in a prince of the Merovingian dynasty. Although the Merovingian lineage of the kings of France is believed by historians to have disappeared well before the year 1000, there are persons who today claim to be descendants of the Merovingians.

Watch Unto Prayer identifies this as the bloodline that will eventually produce the demonic 'Michael' and also connects it with the Stuart dynasty. Although spelled differently, we learn, they are related to the Stewart clan in Scotland. Everybody called Stewart (including rock star Rod Stewart and Star Trek actor Patrick Stewart) is part of this conspiracy, aimed at ultimately promoting Prince Michael Stewart of Albany (a popular author of occult lore) as 'the Michael', a name which would in fact hide the Antichrist.

Both the Roman pseudo-Antichrist and the British real Antichrist need armies. These include Jews (the Web site is distinctly anti-Jewish), Freemasons, Rosicrucians, Theosophists, and cults such as Scientology. While most Jewish organizations (including the State of Israel) secretly co-operate with the Vatican, most cults are ultimately controlled by the Stuart/Stewart conspiracy, which also controls key institutions in the United States.

This explains why Watch Unto Prayer provides links against Scientology and the 'international cult apology network' (through which scholars co-operate with the Stewart-controlled institutions of the American 'Fourth Reich', such as the State Department or the Helsinki Commission).

Watch Unto Prayer may appear so bizarre that no one could possibly take it seriously. Conspiracy theories, however, are part and parcel of Internet terrorism, and they dehumanize opponents as demonic figures (here, as agents of a conspiracy led by 'Michael', who is in fact the embodiment of a literal demon). This is why Watch Unto Prayer has been able to enlist the co-operation and support of other extreme anti-cult Web operations,[4] although the latter are normally not engaged in such wild conspiracy speculations.

A third type of extreme anti-cult Web site is devoted primarily to *assaulting* '*cult apologists*', i.e. scholars who criticize the anti-cult movement. A primary, although extreme, example is Kelebek (http://www.ummah.net/kelebek or www.kelebekler.com) originally operated out of Imola, Italy by Miguel Martinez (an ex-member of New Acropolis) and Banu Sarper (in 2000, Martinez and Sarper parted company, and the site is now operated by Martinez alone).

Kelebek is primarily devoted to ad hominem attacks against scholars associated with CESNUR, the Center for Studies on New Religions, whose managing director is the author of this chapter. While it would be both tasteless and inappropriate to elaborate on character assassination and conspiracy theories directly involving the undersigned and his closest associates, some general remarks about the rhetoric, legal strategy, and international connections of the site, are relevant for the purpose of this work.

The style and rhetoric of Kelebek appears to be an extreme version of what I have discussed elsewhere as a common fallacy in the controversies surrounding 'cult apologists' (Introvigne, 1998). Imre Lakatos, an influential philosopher of science, proposed the distinction between the *external* and *internal* histories of scientific theories.

Internal history deals with how theories are proposed, accepted, or rejected within the community of scholars and how they contribute to the advancement of knowledge. *External history* deals with the private lives, motivations, and religious or other affiliations of scholars who propose theories (Lakatos, 1971).

External history of scientific theories, Lakatos claims, may be occasionally entertaining, but is largely irrelevant. While disclosing the source of funding for each research is generally regarded as ethically necessary in all fields of science, funding is by no means the only possible influence on a paper. Religious and political affiliations, sexual preferences, academic or publishing connections, and many other factors may also play a role, and it is extremely unlikely that even the most astute reviewer (or opponent) will acquire total knowledge of all these factors.

This is the reason why scholarly criticism usually focuses on the internal history, and evaluates papers and books on the basis of their specific intrinsic value, rather than carrying out extensive detective-like investigations of the authors.

While the scholars it attacks have written literally thousands of published and easily accessible pages, a Web site such as Kelebek hardly contains any substantive discussion of such published works (as a bitter academic reviewer would). The focus, rather, is almost exclusively on sources of funding, political affiliations, or religious affiliations, of the scholars themselves.

The aim is to discover 'secret histories' and 'hidden documents', rather than to discuss the intrinsic quality of scholarly works. Ultimately, and not surprisingly, scholars are dismissed as the 'hired guns' of the cults, or as non-persons of dubious credentials[5] whose personal lives, when carefully scrutinized, reveal a pattern of association with religious or political 'cults'.

Moving from the internal to the external history is a typical tool in offensive information warfare. If the scholars so attacked fail to answer, this is claimed as evidence that the allegations are true. On the other hand, if the targets do respond, they quickly find themselves discussing their own political opinions or places of worship on Sunday rather than new religious movements.

It makes no difference whether the allegations are true or false. By the very act of replying, they have moved to the precise battlefield selected by the attacker. A similar win-win strategy is pursued by these Web sites in the legal field as well. If the target does not file a lawsuit, it is claimed that he or she falls under the logic of 'sue or it's true', well illustrated by the 'legal note' posted by Tilman Hausherr when dealing with particularly extreme allegations. Notes Hausherr:

> These are collections of allegations, about which I have not verified the accuracy, but it has never been challenged in court!

If the target sues, he or she is exposed, additionally, as an enemy of the freedom of the Net, the effect being to immediately mobilize Internet libertarian solidarity. Karin Spaink of the Dutch provider xs4all, for instance, is a folk hero in the anti-cult community, and is herself active in the fight against Scientology.

The scholars under attack ignored Kelebek for months. Later this failure to respond was offered as evidence that all the allegations were true ("otherwise, they would have sued us"). Lawyers for CESNUR wrote to the Italian provider and settled with no money changing hands. The provider simply agreed to pull the offending site off the Web and write a letter of apology. Kelebek immediately mobilized Internet libertarians and the site was mirrored outside of Italy, including by the ubiquitous xs4all.

Kelebek's first new home (before Franz Schaefer's provider hosted it in Austria, enabling it again to use the domain name kelebekler.com) was, on the other hand, interesting. Kelebek was hosted (and is still mirrored) at www.ummah.net, a London-based megasite associated with the neo-traditionalist Islamic Brotherhood Movement. Although ummah.net hosts a variety of Islamic organizations, most of them are neo-traditionalist or fundamentalist.

Anti-cultism was welcome on the basis that "the agents of Shaytan (Satan) are many. Many efforts are put forth to mislead masses into darkness via Satanic philosophies, ideologies, and schisms brought forth to divide and keep humanity divided" (http://www.ummah.net/moa-on-line/conspiracies). Although ummah.net also hosts organizations that are not anti-Semitic, you could download until recently (at http://www.ummah.net/moa-on-line/conspiracies/zionism.html) the infamous Protocols of the Elders of Zion, with the caveat that they are "currently being forced upon Western society," concluding in red lettering: "Now, you determine who is the real terrorist!"

Nobody, of course, should be regarded as guilty by association, and certainly not all groups whose pages appear on ummah.net are anti-Semitic. On the other hand, ummah.net's association with fundamentalist groups is quite well known. While Kelebek is primarily devoted to assaulting 'cult apologists', it also tries to explain its motivation through an anti-globalization, anti-American rhetoric, in addition to protesting against 'the desert' where "McDonalds open, while minds shut tight."

At the beginning of his anti-cult career (after having left New Acropolis), Martinez wrote for *Orion*, and *Orion* is frequently quoted by Kelebek. His former partner, Banu Sarper, claimed in a militant Islamic style, that the Catholic Church:

> originally a movement ... became an ideology with expansion as its goal ... Peter's followers, we could say, registered a firm ... an industry whose managers had power over life and death, heaven and hell. With an incredible weapon, the key to eternal life. The company has grown into a transnational ... religious monopoly, right until the Crusades.

"Then, quite unexpectedly, this certainty was cast into jeopardy. Another power had appeared on the scene. The Church cried out for help against this new power, Islam . . . an ideology which had nothing in common with the advertising strategy of the Catholic Church . . . [During the Crusades] the commanders counted on the ignorance of their followers [and] the majority was unable either to read or to write . . . now things are more difficult." "It would be much harder today for a NATO general to jump on horseback to drive the Muslims out from somewhere . . . in the name of God. [Accordingly] today, the Church/company is forced to use a more softer strategy . . . it has to launch its crusades using other weapons, those of the media." [In fact], "the Church tries to take advantage here too of 'spiritual searching' . . . as do so many companies."

Sarper claims that the Catholic Church, in its centuries-old fight against Islam, now claims for itself the power of defining words such as 'sect' and 'cults'. "The word 'sect' becomes a weapon. A weapon which can be employed against a little-loved religion, Islam" (downloaded from the address:http://www.kelebekler.com/satrancgb.htm on August 1, 1999; the article has since disappeared from the site).

The aim of Kelebek, in this perspective, is to break the alleged Christian monopoly on the definition of 'sects', 'cults' and 'new religious movements', by exposing both 'cult apologists' and mainline cult critics as motivated by a hidden religious and political agenda.

The main features of offensive information warfare, or even plain information terrorism via the Internet, are present in this fringe of anti-cultism: 'denouncement', in the sense of Denning (1999, p. 112); distortions; conspiracy theories; lists of individuals; and – occasionally – copyright infringement.

It would be wrong to conclude that only fringe anti-cultists use extreme strategies in the Internet cult wars. They are also pursued by new religious movements, or at least by individuals or entities promoting the interests of new religious movements.

Not all groups act like Sûkyô Mahikari which, when challenged by Greenwood's Web page, did basically nothing (and lost some membership in different countries as a consequence). Scientology, by contrast, reacts vigorously in the legal arena. There are also pro-Scientology Web sites devoted mostly to personal attacks against the most active on-line and off-line opponents (such as http://www.parishioners.org). There have also been more technical cyber-attacks, minor forms of cyber-terrorism, used against Scientology critics.

The most famous counter-attack is the so-called 'attack of the robotic poets' (Poulsen, 1999). A 'poetry machine' generates and sends thousands of unsolicited messages to Usenet groups, re-using headers of frequent contributors.

Newsgroups are thus flooded by a deluge of riddles reminiscent of the 'cut-up' experiments of the Beat generation poets, such as: "Why is another horseman either cytoplasm enchantingly?"

Although other newsgroups have also been targeted, the 'most consistent target' is alt.religion.scientology, a newsgroup in which some Scientologists are also active, but which in fact is dominated by Scientology critics (Poulsen, 1999). Tilman Hausherr, a daily contributor to alt.religion.scientology, coined the word 'sporgeries' (spam-forgeries), and is promoting software to kill the unwelcome messages. Hausherr also claims that anonymous friends of Scientology have perpetrated other cyber-attacks against the hostile newsgroup, and does not exclude a class action suit. To this prospect, Poulsen (1999) comments: "inviting law enforcement to protect free speech brings to mind roosters and hen houses."

In discussing alt.religion.scientology, we have moved from the Web to the Usenet. This is a collection of discussion groups covering very different areas of interest that have been in existence since before the Web itself. They have been the objects of considerable sociological interest (see, for example: Dery 1994; Holeton 1998; Jones 1994, 1997; Rheingold, 1993; Smith & Kollock, 1999). Other communities in cyberspace, such as synchronous chat lines, MUDs (multi-user dungeons), and email lists have also been studied (Dibbell, 1994; Kiesler, 1997; Macduff, 1994).

The Usenet is particularly relevant for the cult wars. Robotic poets notwithstanding, alt.religion.scientology is one of the best known and successful groups on the Usenet. Smaller groups for anti-cultists are alt.support.ex-cult and (in France) fr.soc.sectes.

The fight between the Church of Scientology and alt.religion.scientology is one of the best known Usenet sagas. In some instances, at least, Scientology has managed to scare Usenet posters into maintaining anonymity as far as possible. Donath quotes a participant encountered on a newsgroup that is about as unrelated as possible (misc.fitness.weights), who also happens to be an opponent of Scientology. This individual was so scared by all kinds of wild rumors, that he categorically refused to give his name: Writes the anonymous contact:

> There is more going on in this net than just misc.fitness.weights . . . I'm involved in the net war in alt.religion.scientology. Those cultists have so far raided four of their net critics on bogus copyright violation charges, and in one case they placed a large amount of LSD on the toothbrush of a person who was raided . . . In my city they have been convicted of several crimes, including infiltrating the municipal, provincial, and federal police forces. So, I will not give out my name just to satisfy your curiosity. Deal with it (Donath, 1999, pp. 52–53).

From a certain point of view, alt.religion.scientology may be considered, as a useful resource. Almost certainly, any item of news, rumor, claim – true or false – of, on, or about Scientology from anywhere in the world will surface on this news-group. Most likely, sooner rather than later. On the other hand, it is far from being user-friendly for the outsider, since what may be classified as real information is submerged by endless tirades, occasional flame wars (the Usenet name for fight-ing with an increasingly loud tone), and simple four-letter word sequences.

Although some Scientologists participate in the newsgroup, most participants are rabid opponents of Scientology. One 'Bernie', who claims to be a moderate critic of Scientologists, manages an impressive Web site collecting examples of flames, insults, and racist remarks against Scientology that, in his opinion, have now far exceeded any measure of what might be considered tolerable (http://www.bernie.cncfamily.com/ars.htm). It is true that four-letter word sequels and insults, against both Scientologists and academic 'cult apologists', are often posted in the newsgroup and occasionally, in case they don't read alt.religion.scientology, are emailed to the individual targets, sometimes with an invitation to file a lawsuit.[6]

On the other hand, notwithstanding the concerns of 'Bernie', or the Church of Scientology, and the folk hero status of the anti-cult cyber-warriors among the Internet libertarian community, they are mostly preaching to the converted. The overwhelming majority of messages on alt.religion.scientology are posted by fellow anti-cultists. The same is also true of fr.soc.sectes and alt.support.ex-cults.

Extreme anti-cultists have sought to infiltrate other newsgroups with a larger scope, and dealing with religion in general, New Age, and the occult. In these newsgroups, however, they have rarely found people interested in sustaining a continued discussion. Posting in the newsgroups has, in consequence, become just a way of advertising Web sites (particularly those aimed at discrediting 'cult apologists', who may be known as scholars in a larger field). This is part of what many see as Usenet decadence. An insider, quoted by Poulsen (1999), claims that "many Usenet groups that were once full of spirited discussion are now ghost towns," where 'only solicitations' and advertising thrive.

Anonymity once regarded as an advantage of Usenet (Turkle, 1995), is being made increasingly difficult by sophisticated services and software able to trace the origin of the postings. Smith (1999, p. 212) claims "these services do create a dramatic change in the balance between self-exposure and self-disclosure." Anonymity, however, may survive technology as pseudonymity, since (as the 'robotic poets' incident shows) it is now possible to replicate a header, and extremely difficult (particularly for the average user) to identify whether a message really comes from its alleged source.

A 'troll' (a message intended to deceive users as to its origin) may, in some groups, be "admired for its cleverness," while "undermining the trust of the com-munity" in others (Donath, 1999, p. 47). Technology is now so sophisticated, however, that Internet terrorism scholars such as Denning (1999, pp. 241–246) have described the evolution of more or less inoffensive deceptions into full-scale 'masquerades', aimed at a terrorist strategy of 'identify theft'.

Optimistic evaluations of Usenet's potential for creating real and useful communities are still proposed nonetheless (see Wellman & Gulia, 1999). Some contributors to the collection edited by Dery in 1994 also argued that flame wars may have an occasionally therapeutic effect. Others, however, notice a certain decline in the quality and audience of 'cultural' newsgroups, while those in which computer experts exchange technical information remain extremely successful.

When used by extreme anti-cultists slandering 'cult apologists', the Usenet magnifies the obsessive attempt by extreme anti-cultists to switch from the internal to the external history of scholarly theories. Here, the widely discussed, and often exaggerated phenomenon of 'Internet disinhibition' is also more apparent (see Joinson, 1998).

Findings about anti-cultism on the Usenet confirm conclusions drawn by Mitra (1997) on newsgroups on the subject of Indian politics and religion and by Zickmund (1997) on interaction with white supremacy 'cyber-haters'.

The typical Internet myth of the 'crucial document' appeared to be even more pervasive on the Usenet. Extreme anti-cultists are constantly looking for 'smoking guns' – a message, a letter, or a document that would conclusively prove their point and 'expose' the opponent.

When the 'crucial document' is, in turn, analyzed or exposed as being less than vital, the search for a new 'crucial document' begins. The concepts of both 'document' and 'information' are naively constructed as anything existing in print or electronic form, leaving serious difficulties with regards to reconstructing a hierarchy of sources. The 'crucial document' could be a private memorandum, an article from a tabloid or extremist publication, or a court decision.

Heated comments by extreme anti-cultists also confirm Reid's conclusion on the crucial 'lack of flexibility' in Internet identities, that prevents negotiation and escalates conflicts. "In the normal course of daily life," Reid argued:

> . . . we often speak with imprecision. We assert certainty where we have only hunches, appeal to authority when what we truly have is a vague memory of an old magazine article, assert rank when we have only opinion. We rephrase and repudiate our own arguments, relying on force or character and the vagaries of our interlocutors' memories to allow us an attitude to redefine our position to suit the emerging argumentative terrain (Reid, 1998, pp. 37–40).

In on-line dialogues, on the other hand, "frequent calls are made in flame wars for combatants to produce documentation and references, and very often the prior words of a combatant are quoted to the detriment of their author." As a result, "we cannot be flexible when easily referenced documentation of our words makes flexibility look like hypocrisy. The resultant illogicalities necessitated by this lack of flexibility compound the hostility of combatants as they are forced to eat their own words."

Flexibility, therefore, is sought by multiplying identities, and leads to disintegration of the self and of communication itself. Or, in the words of Duval Smith (1999), "the computer interface, the anarchy of the Net structure, and the power asymmetry of most virtual communities, make the task of conflict management especially difficult."

It is also the case that, outside such specialized groups as alt.religion.scientology, only a limited number of users are really interested in participating in discussions of 'cults' on the Usenet. An analysis of postings against 'cult apologists' in alt.religion.scientology and other newsgroups show that more than 90% of them are posted by three individuals only: extreme anti-cultists Roger Gonnet and Tilman Hausherr, and Dutch counter-cultist Anton Hein. The anti-cult flame wars, therefore, look more like a tempest in a teacup.

SOME CONCLUSIONS

Cult wars have found a new battleground on the Internet. Mainline anti-cult organizations are more active on the Internet in the United States than in Europe, where extreme anti-cultism and a lunatic fringe have a more dominant Internet presence.

Cyber-terrorism, in its technical sense, is almost completely absent in the Internet cult wars. On the other hand, offensive information warfare, or information terrorism, as defined by mainline scholars, includes what the most extreme anti-cultists do on the Web as well as on the Usenet.

The most effective tool used by extreme anti-cultists has been perhaps, the systematic copyright infringement perpetrated against the Church of Scientology. It has also elicited the most vigorous legal reactions. Outside of the copyright field, lists of private individuals identified as 'cultists', 'cult apologists', or 'cult supporters', may have a discriminating effect and eventually cause violence (as evidenced by another case of single-issue Internet terrorism, i.e. abortion and the Nuremberg Files).

'Victories' scored on the Internet are largely symbolic. Only a very limited number of people interested in, or members of, new religious movements actually care about the Web, and probably even less about the Usenet. The claims made by Mayer (1999) that a certain number of persons have left new religious movements because of opposition propaganda read on the Internet are interesting, but need to be verified by more systematic quantitative studies.

If fast-growing international movements such as the Jehovah's Witnesses lose ten or twenty people per year because of the Internet, they are probably right in their decision not to divert too much energy to the Web but to expend their energies instead on regular proselytization activities. The damage inflicted by Greenwood on Sûkyô Mahikari may have been more extensive, but one wonders whether this is equally true outside of Europe and Australia (in Japan or even in Africa, a remarkably unwired continent), and whether Mahikari is perhaps the exception rather than the rule.

Carrying on-line crusades off-line is a notoriously difficult exercise. There are also a number of counter-effects for the anti-cult movement as a whole. Initially enthused by the unexpected support from extreme Internet anti-cultists, mainline anti-cult organizations, particularly in the U.S., are now increasingly embarrassed by the extreme tactics, wild conspiracy theories, and association with political and religious extremism of the most extreme Internet anti-cult combatants.

While European anti-cult organizations use information obtained from the Internet fringe quite liberally (and reciprocate by offering links from their Web sites, together with promotion in their printed newsletters), the U.S. anti-cult community is increasingly suspicious and wary of potential embarrassment. After all, association with the extreme Internet fringe may well become, in the next decade, what the association with deprogrammers was in the 1980s and early 1990s for larger anti-cult organizations.

It is even more embarrassing when European governments include unchecked information, picked up on the Web and the Usenet, in their official documents. This practice caused at least two diplomatic incidents in 1999. The first incident involved the French Mission to Fight Cults 'exposing' a member of an official U.S. fact-finding delegation investigating religious intolerance in France as an "activist of one of the most dangerous international transnational cults." The delegate was, in fact, a member of a small Christian charismatic congregation. In the same year, again acting on information picked up on the Internet, the French delegation at an international diplomatic conference on religious pluralism wrongly accused three speakers of being Scientologists or representatives of the Church of Scientology. The meeting, held in Vienna, was organized by the Organization for Security and Co-Operation in Europe (OSCE). One of the wrongly accused was an official rapporteur on religious intolerance designated by the OSCE.[7]

Governments may carry a heavy responsibility in generating violence both against, and by, assaulted minorities. The extreme discourse of the most lunatic Internet anti-cult fringe may claim legitimization by the similar rhetoric used in French and Belgian official documents. Violence, as Sprinzak (1999, pp. 311–312, 317) comments, "does not just originate from below, from individuals who do not respect the law. Governments and government agencies are responsible for the generation of large amounts of violence." "The deeper the sense of delegitimation" experienced by a minority "vis-à-vis the government or another political rival, the higher its readiness to use physical force against the perceived foe. Intense delegitimation has in fact a double effect on the likelihood of violence. Not only does it increase the chances of violence against the object of delegitimation, but that object, sensing the imminent threat, is likely to consider counterviolence." In other words, and even apart from such deviance amplification scenarios, political and religious "violence is not a product of inherently violent people but of social and political circumstances."

Diplomatic incidents confirm, on the other hand, that in order to take advantage of Internet as a resource, and thus avoid the trappings of Internet terrorism, a hierarchy of sources must be recreated. There is no reason why this should not happen, even in the limited field of religious information or new religious movements.

While celebrations of the Internet as a new and more democratic approach to information were probably premature, despotic perspectives of manipulated Internet hierarchies subverting off-line hierarchies, destroying responsibility and accountability in the process, need not necessarily prevail. Students educated in the use of the Internet since primary school (Garner & Gillingham, 1996), religious leaders, reporters, and perhaps in the long run even French government officials, will learn to distinguish between the Web equivalents of tabloids and *The New York Times*.

Gackenbach and Ellerman (1998) invite us to avoid the easy comparison with television, and "take a lesson from radio" instead. Before the 1920s, and in some countries up to World War II, radio was dominated by thousands of small, independent local stations. Almost everybody was able to air literally anything from radio stations, originally with little or no control, and widespread fears were expressed that people would believe anything coming from them – perhaps originating from foreign spies and other subversives.

"The exponential growth of the Internet," Gackenbach and Ellerman (1998, p. 11) note, "has happened before," with radio. Although some secret services did use radio stations for pre-war propaganda, ultimately the worst doom scenarios were never realized. Slowly but surely, technological evolutions and governmental regulations limited the number of stations and created more accountability. This is a development we may, or may not, see on the Internet in the near future. In the case of radio, and later television, information hierarchy frames had to be reconstructed and re-internalized. But the ordinary citizen was soon able to reconstruct and internalize a new hierarchy of information sources, including radio.

Today we face the Internet. It is important to recall that technologies are also social constructs. Technological determinism has been largely debunked as a positivistic fallacy. While vigilance against information terrorism via the Internet is in order, the best weapon against any form of information terrorism will ultimately be the integration of new sources into the already existing and internalized hierarchy of information sources. Education, social science, and courts of law will each have a major role to play in this eminently human enterprise. Reconstructing new meanings to deal with concerns such as copyright infringement and defamation, that seems so prevalent in cyberspace today, will emerge in due time and, most likely, before any great harm is done.

NOTES

1. In Latin America, left-wing guerrillas have targeted Mormon chapels and missionaries as quintessential U.S. cultural agents.

2. *Orion*, like several similar publications, also cares little for copyright. It reproduced an interview with Swiss scholar Jean-François Mayer from a Belgian magazine without his knowledge or permission (J-F. Mayer, personal communication, June 1999).

3. Another interesting Italian case concerns a small political organization known as Forza Nuova ('The New Force'; http://www.forzanuova.org), that participated in the 1999 European Parliament elections in association with the controversial Southern League. The latter should not be confused with the larger Northern League, and is led by a former mayor of Taranto and charged in June 1999 with racketeering and co-operation with organized crime. Forza Nuova calls for the promotion of a 'European identity' with extreme anti-American and anti-Jewish undertones. Terrorism in Italy is attributed by Forza Nuova to the covert operations of U.S. and Israeli intelligence services. On May 15, 1999, Forza Nuova launched its electoral campaign in Milan with a conference on 'Lodges, lobbies, and cults', calling for laws to ban cults, freemasonry, and 'New Age anti-national forces'. Although it was able to enlist some mainline anti-cultists (including an anthropology professor associated with both mainline and fringe anti-cult movements in Italy), they had to share the podium with anti-Jewish activists and Holocaust negationists such as Jürgen Graf, sentenced to 18 months imprisonment in Switzerland in 1998 for racial discrimination. In turn, Graf is promoted by www.radioislam.org, the Stockholm-based Web site of Moroccan Islamic fundamentalist Ahmed Rami, well known for his rabid anti-Semitism and occasionally mentioning 'cults' and 'brainwashing'. Several anti-cultists whose articles are reproduced, or quoted, on the Kelebek Web site attended the Forza Nuova electoral meeting in Milan.

4. Miguel Martinez of kelebekler.com writes about Watch Unto Prayer: "I do not share their theology, but the editors of watch.pair.com have had the courage to challenge some of the most powerful and least lovely people in the world. Perhaps in certain cases they tilt against windmills, but this only shows they are like Don Quixote. Maybe the Priory of Sion does not exist, but they have had the guts to face all the 'New Right', to say the names of those who intend to launch new wars of religion around the world. I do not know the editors of watch.pair.com personally, but they are honest people, something that cannot be said of everybody" (www.kelebekler.com/cesnur/txt/mig2.htm).

5. Not that scholarly credentials are accepted as such. According to Tilman Hausherr, "sociologists of religion who study 'new religions' are mostly cult apologists. Logic is not one of their skills" (message posted on alt.religion.scientology on May 29, 1999).

6. Hate email occasionally includes threats of physical violence. For example, Zenon Panoussis (a well-known anti-cult cyberwarrior on alt.religion.scientology) emailed to me (and copied to a number of colleagues) on July 5, 1999, a message threatening, inter alia, that: "If you want to be the donkey, we'll be happy to use the cane on you."

7. I.e. the undersigned. Given the keen interest of French intelligence services in the Internet and the Usenet (Destouche, 1999), and the fact that they currently regard the fight against cults as a top priority, one may wonder whether these services are simply picking up 'information' from the Internet, or whether they are also actively contributing to its propagation.

REFERENCES

Assemblée Nationale. (1996). *Les Sectes en France. Rapport fait au nom de la Commission d'Enquête sur les sectes* (document n. 2468). Paris: Les Documents d'Information de l'Assemblée Nationale.

Assemblée Nationale. (1999). *Rapport fait au nom de la Commission d'Enquête sur la situation financière, patrimoniale et fiscale des sectes, ainsi que sur leurs activités économiques et leurs relations avec les milieux économiques et financiers* (document n. 1687). Paris: Les Documents d'Information de l'Assemblée Nationale.

Beckford, James A. (1985). *Cult Controversies: The Social Response to New Religious Movements.* London: Tavistock Publications.

Berger, P., & Luckmann, T. (1966). *The Social Construction of Reality.* Harmondsworth: Penguin Books.

Chambre des Représentants de Belgique. (1997). *Enquête parlementaire visant à élaborer une politique en vue de lutter contre les pratiques illégales des sectes et les dangers qu'elles représentent pour la société et pour les personnes, particulièrement les mineurs d'âge.* Rapport fait au nom de la Commission d'Enquête. 2 vol. Bruxelles: Chambre des Représentants de Belgique.

Chryssides, G. D. (1999). Britain's Anti-Cult Movement. In: B. Wilson, & J. Cresswell (Eds), *New Religious Movements: Challenge and Response* (pp. 257–273). London and New York: Routledge.

Clarke, R. (1994). The Digital Persona and Its Application to Data Surveillance. *The Information Society, 10*(2), 77–92.

David, F. (1997). *Les Réseaux de l'anticléricalisme en France.* Chartres: Bartillat.

Dawson, L. L., & Hennebry, J. (1999). New Religions and the Internet: Recruiting in New Public Space. *Journal of Contemporary Religion, 14*(1), 17–39.

Denning, D. E. (1999). *Information Warfare and Security.* Reading, MA: Addison-Wesley.

Denning, D. E., & Denning, P. J. (Eds), (1998). *Internet Besieged: Countering Cyberspace Scofflaws.* New York: ACM Press.

Dery, M. (Ed.), (1994). *Flame Wars: The Discourse of Cyberculture.* Durham and London: Duke University Press.

Destouche, G. (1999). *Ménace sur Internet: Des groupes subversifs et terroristes sur le Net.* Paris: Éditions Michalon.

Dibbell, J. (1994). A Rape in Cyberspace; or, How an Evil Clown, a Haitian Trickster Spirit, Two Wizards, and a Cast of Dozens Turned a Database into a Society. In: M. Dery (Ed.), *Flame Wars: The Discourse of Cyberculture* (pp. 237–261). Durham and London: Duke University Press.

Dipartimento delle Istituzioni, Repubblica e Cantone del Ticino. (1998). *Interrogazioni sulle sette religiose*. Bellinzona: Dipartimento delle Istituzioni, Repubblica e Cantone del Ticino.

Donath, J. S. (1999). Identity and Deception in the Virtual Community. In: M. A. Smith, & P. Kollock, (Eds), *Communities in Cyberspace* (pp. 29–59). London and New York: Routledge.

Gackenbach, J. (Ed.), (1998). *Psychology and the Internet: Intrapersonal, Interpersonal, and Transpersonal Implications*. San Diego and London: Academic Press.

Gackenbach, J., & Ellerman, E. (1998). Introduction to Psychological Aspects of Internet Use. In: J. Gackenbach, (Ed.), *Psychology and the Internet: Intrapersonal, Interpersonal, and Transpersonal Implications* (pp. 1–26). San Diego and London: Academic Press.

Garner, R., & Gillingham, M. G. (1996). *Internet Communication in Six Classrooms: Conversations Across Time, Space, and Culture*. Mahwah, NJ: Lawrence Erlbaum Associates.

Gibson, W. (1984). *Neuromancer*. London: Grafton Books.

Green, A. S. (1999). Judge Won't Pull Abortion Web Site off Internet. *The Oregonian*, February 5.

Greenwood, G. A. (1997). *All the Emperor's Men*. Rev. ed. Alstonville, NSW, Australia.

Guisnel, J. (1997). *Cyberwars: Espionage on the Internet*. New York and London: Plenum.

Holeton, R. (1998). *Composing Cyberspace: Identity, Community, and Knowledge in the Electronic Age*. Boston: McGraw-Hill.

In Good Faith: Society and New Religious Movements. [Official summary in English of the Swedish Government Commission's report on new religious movements]. (1998). Stockholm: Norstedts Tryckeri AB.

Introvigne, M. (1998). Blacklisting or Greenlisting? A European Perspective on the New Cult Wars. *Nova Religio: The Journal of Alternative and Emergent Religions, 1*(3), 16–23.

Introvigne, M. (1999). *Sûkyô Mahikari*. Leumann (Torino): Elle Di Ci.

Introvigne, M. (2000). Moral Panics and Anti-Cult Terrorism in Western Europe. *Terrorism and Political Violence, 12*(1), 47–59.

Introvigne, M., & Richardson, J. T. (1999). European Parliamentary and Administrative Reports on Cults and the Brainwashing Argument. Paper presented at the International Conference of the International Society for the Sociology of Religions. Louvain (Belgium), 26–30 July 1999.

Joinson, A. (1998). Causes and Implications of Disinhibited Behaviour on the Internet. In: J. Gackenbach, (Ed.), *Psychology and the Internet: Intrapersonal, Interpersonal, and Transpersonal Implications* (pp. 43–60). San Diego and London: Academic Press.

Jones, S. G., (Ed.), (1994). *Cybersociety: Computer-Mediated Communication and Community*. London and Thousand Oaks, CA: Sage Publications.

Jones, S. G. (1997). *Virtual Culture: Identity and Communication in Cybersociety*. London and Thousand Oaks, CA: Sage Publications.

Jordan, T. (1999). *Cyberpower: The Culture and Politics of Cyberspace in the Internet*. London and New York: Routledge.

Kellner, M. A. (1996). *God on the Internet*. Foster City, CA: IDG Books Worldwide.

Kiesler, S. (Ed.), (1997). *Culture of the Internet*. Mahwah, NJ: Lawrence Erlbaum Associates.

Kraut, R. E., & Attewell, P. (1997). Media Use in a Global Corporation: Electronic Mail and Organizational Knowledge. In: S. Kiesler, (Ed.), *Culture of the Internet* (pp. 323–342). Mahwah, NJ: Lawrence Erlbaum Associates.

Lakatos, I. (1971). History of Science and Its Rational Reconstructions. In: R. C. Buck, & R. S. Cohen, (Eds), *In Memory of Rudolf Carnap. Proceedings of the 1970 Biennial Meeting of the Philosophy of Science Association* (pp. 91–124). Dordrecht: D. Reidel.

Legal Wars on the Web: A Checklist. (1999). *Horizon*, 5, 1–3.

Macduff, I. (1994). Flames on the wires: mediating from an electronic cottage. *Negotiation Journal*, *10*(1) 5–11.

Mayer, J-F. (2000). Les nouveaux mouvements religieux à l'heure d'Internet. *Cahiers de Littérature Orale*, 47, 127–146.

Mayer, J-F. (1999). New Religious Movements: Facing the Challenge of the Internet. Unpublished paper presented at the 13th International Conference of CESNUR (Center for Studies on New Religions), Bryn Athyn (Pennsylvania) June 2, 1999.

Melton, J. G. (1999). Anti-Cultists in the United States: An Historical Perspective. In: B. Wilson, & J. Cresswell, (Eds), *New Religious Movements: Challenge and Response* (pp. 213–233). London and New York: Routledge.

Mitra, A. (1997. 'Virtual Commonality: Looking for India on the Internet'. In: S. G. Jones, (Ed.), *Virtual Culture: Identity and Communication in Cybersociety* (pp. 55–79). London and Thousand Oaks, CA: Sage Publications.

O'Leary, S. D. (1996). Cyberspace as Sacred Space: Communicating Religion on Computer Networks. *Journal of the American Academy of Religion, 64*(4), 781–808.

Pollit, M. M. (1997). *Cyberterrorism – Fact or Fancy?* (Unpublished paper available on the World Wide Web: http://www.cs.georgetown.edu/~denning/infosec/pollitt.html.)

Poulsen, K. (1999). *Attack of the Robotic Poets*. Retrieved August 1, 1999, from the World Wide Web: http://www.zdnet.com/zdtv/cybercrime/chaostheory/story/0,3700,22 54578,00.html); no longer available at this address.

Reid, E. (1998). The Self and the Internet: Variations on the Illusion of One Self. In: J. Gackenbach, (Ed.), *Psychology and the Internet: Intrapersonal, Interpersonal, and Transpersonal Implications* (pp. 29–42). San Diego and London: Academic Press.

Rheingold, H. (1993). *The Virtual Community: Homesteading on the Electronic Frontier*. Reading, MA: Addison-Wesley.

Shenk, D. (1997). *Data Smog: Surviving the Information Age*. San Francisco: HarperSanFrancisco.

Shupe, A. D., Jr., & Bromley, D. G. (1980). *The New Vigilantes: Deprogrammers, Anti-Cultists, and the New Religions*. Beverly Hills, CA: Sage Publications.

Shupe, A. D., Jr., & Bromley, D. G. (1985). *A Documentary History of the Anti-Cult Movement*. Arlington, TX: Center for Social Research, University of Texas.

Shupe, A. D., Jr., & Bromley, D. G., (Eds), (1994). *Anti-Cult Movements in Cross-Cultural Perspective*. New York: Garland.

Shupe, A. D., Jr., Bromley, D. G., & Oliver, D. L. (1984). *The Anti-Cult Movement in America: A Bibliography and Historical Survey*. New York: Garland.

Smith, A. (1999). Problems of Conflict Management in Virtual Communities. In: M. A. Smith, & P. Kollock,. (Eds), *Communities in Cyberspace* (pp. 134–163). London and New York: Routledge.

Smith, G. D. (1998). Single Issue Terrorism (Commentary No. 74 of Canadian Security Intelligence Service). Ottawa: Canadian Security Intelligence Service.

Smith, M. A. (1999). Invisible Crowds in Cyberspace: Mapping the Social Structure of the Usenet. In: M. A. Smith, & P. Kollock (Eds). 1999. *Communities in Cyberspace* (pp. 195–219). London and New York: Routledge.

Smith, M. A. & Kollock, P. (Eds), (1999). *Communities in Cyberspace*. London and New York: Routledge.

Spaink, K. (1999). The Nuremberg Files: Motivation and Introduction. Available from the World Wide Web: http://www.xs4all.nl/~oracle/nuremberg/index.html.

Sprinzak, E. (1999). *Brother against Brother: Violence and Extremism in Israeli Politics from Altalena to the Rabin Assassination.* New York: The Free Press.

Thornton, T. P. (1964). Terror as a Weapon of Political Agitation. In: H. Eckstein, (Ed.), *Internal War* (pp. 22–42). New York: Collier and Macmillan.

Turkle, S. (1995). *Life on the Screen: Identity in the Age of the Internet.* New York: Simon and Schuster.

Usarski, F. (1999). The Response to New Religious Movements in East Germany after Reunification. In: B. Wilson, & J. Cresswell (Eds), *New Religious Movements: Challenge and Response* (pp. 237–254). London and New York: Routledge.

Verhovek, S. H. (1999). Creators of Anti-Abortion Web Site Told to Pay Millions. *The New York Times,* February 3.

Wellman, B., & Gulia, M. (1999). Virtual Communities as Communities: Net Surfers Don't Ride Alone. In: M. Smith, & P. Kollock (Eds), *Communities in Cyberspace* (pp. 167–194). London and New York: Routledge.

Wilkinson, P. (1975). *Political Terrorism.* London: Macmillan.

Wilson, B., & Cresswell, J. (Eds) (1999). *New Religious Movements: Challenge and Response.* London and New York: Routledge.

Zickmund, S. (1997). Approaching the Radical Other: The Discursive Culture of Cyberhate. In: S. G. Jones (Ed.), *Virtual Culture: Identity and Communication in Cybersociety* (pp. 185–205). London and Thousand Oaks, CA: Sage Publications.

5. INTERNET TEACHING: PEDAGOGY AND THE WORLD WIDE WEB

EVOLUTION OF A RELIGIOUS WEB SITE DEVOTED TO TOLERANCE

Bruce A. Robinson

ABSTRACT

This chapter details the genesis and development of the Ontario Consultants on Religious Tolerance Web site. This is an Internet site devoted to the reduction of religious tension and discrimination, the dissemination of religious information, and the promotion of religious tolerance and respect.

INTRODUCTION

In Pakistan, members of the Ahmadiyya sect of Islam are subject to three years imprisonment and heavy fines if they identify themselves as 'Muslims'. In Nepal, Greece and a growing number of other countries, Christians risk arrest if they seek to evangelize or proselytize. New religious movements are under attack in France and Germany. A Texas pastor calls for the U.S. Army to napalm Wiccans. Can the WWW be a mitigating force in the clashes among religions, the state and secular groups? Can a web presence promote tolerance in an intolerant world? This essay explores one attempt to say 'Yes' to those questions. Using the tools of cyberspace, this is a personal journey down a road as old as human religious consciousness.

Religion on the Internet, Volume 8, pages 309–323.
ISBN: 0–7623-0535-5

INITIATING EVENTS

Three events in my life triggered the idea of an Internet site about religious tolerance:

When I was born, my parents were Baptists. A few years later, my family joined the United Church, Canada's largest (and perhaps most liberal) Protestant denomination. In my late teens, I experienced a religious conversion and joined the First Unitarian congregation in Toronto. Unitarians (now Unitarian Universalists) are one of the most liberal religious organizations in North America. Some might describe this personal pilgrimage of faith as a gradual slide towards an eternity roasting in the fires of Hell. Only time will tell. However, my personal journey effected a heightened concern for human rights, and for issues of tolerance and personal freedom.

In 1995, then nearing 60, I was approaching the end of my professional career as an electronics and software engineer. I recalled my father's experience at this age. As a bank executive, he watched as many of his co-workers retired, seemingly to a life of leisure, only to die within a very few months. Retirement can be a life-threatening transition. It seemed that those who kept their minds active and challenged lived the longest. This motivated me to look for some type of intellectually stimulating retirement project. Since I had been fascinated with both religion and spirituality since my mid-teens, this seemed an interesting area to explore.

Finally, there was the civil war in Bosnia-Herzegovina. Each day during the spring of 1995, it seemed that the evening's television news reported at least one new atrocity from that part of the former Yugoslavia. No matter which network we watched, the war was described as an 'ethnic conflict'. I was angered at this because I believed it to be a religious conflict, driven primarily by intolerance of other faiths. Located within the Roman Catholic and the Eastern Orthodox spheres of influence, the former Yugoslavia is also caught in the tension between Christianity and Islam. I believe that during the 1990s various political leaders capitalized on these religious frictions to pursue their own nationalist aims. The result was horrendous suffering for the survivors and death for the rest.

Conversely, I believe that the prevention of similar situations in the future requires *both* the active promotion of religious tolerance, and a broader understanding of the violence that religious beliefs often engender. One project that held promise was a World Wide Web (WWW) site devoted to the promotion of religious tolerance. Because inter-religious friction is among the root causes in many conflict situations around the world (e.g. Bosnia, Cyprus, India, the Middle East, Northern Ireland, Pakistan, Philippines, Sri Lanka, Sudan, and the former Yugoslavia), the importance of such a project could hardly be overstated. The equation seemed simple. If people achieved greater tolerance of other religions, there would be significantly less violence around the world. And, over time, perhaps humanity could move beyond mere tolerance and more openly embrace religious diversity.

While the WWW was still in its infancy in early 1995, it was growing at a furious pace. Between mid-1993 and mid-1995, it increased from approximately 130 Web sites to 20,000 (Gray, 1996; O'Reilly & Associates, 1997). A search of the WWW with the Lycos search engine in May, 1995, generated only four hits for the phrase *religious tolerance*: two were essays by members of the Baha'i faith; another was a sermon by a Baptist minister; the fourth was an article about religious tolerance in ancient Egypt. A new site dedicated to promoting religious tolerance seemed an ideal project to help fill a near vacuum on the Internet. The Ontario Consultants on Religious Tolerance (OCRT; www.religioustolerance.org) is the result.

ONTARIO CONSULTANTS ON RELIGIOUS TOLERANCE: BEGINNINGS

I felt that the OCRT should be a multi-faith organization, whose members followed as broad a sampling of religious faiths and theological positions as possible. Our group would be one more example that persons from a wide range of beliefs can cooperate on a religiously oriented project. Four members comprise the OCRT: I am an agnostic; another member is an atheist. Two other staff members, a Christian and a Wiccan, complete the group. We decided at the outset not to publish the names of the staff, other than that of the coordinator. This is due to the high level of animosity in North America directed towards Wicca by some devout, intelligent, but misinformed religious folk. Most Wiccans prefer to keep a low profile (Robinson, 2000e). We felt that nominal confidentiality would afford our Wiccan member some degree of protection. Our next task was to select a name for the organization. We felt that the 'Ontario *Centre* for Religious Tolerance' (OCRT) expressed our purpose well. Being a Canadian group, we used the British spelling, *Centre*.

Our original goals were small. We expected to incur no significant expenses and to generate little or no revenue. Because we treated the Web site more as a personal hobby of its coordinator than as an actual agency, we felt no need to register our name with either municipal or provincial authorities. However, in the event that we might chose to register the OCRT at a later date, we conducted a search of all business and agency names in Ontario. Only one organization's name contained the word 'tolerance', a high-quality machine shop that manufactured precision metal parts.

In 1996, a year after the web site was placed on-line, a representative of Lucent Technologies, the former Bell Laboratories, sent us an email. They asked if we gave lectures on religious diversity and tolerance. Further discussions led to a visit of their facility in Columbus, Ohio, where I delivered a lecture on religious tolerance in the workplace. Since they offered to pay for our out-of-pocket traveling expenses, some financial transactions would be involved. The OCRT would require a bank account to cash Lucent's check. We discovered, though, that we could only open a business bank account if the group had been first registered with the Government of Ontario. Because the creation of a not-for-profit organization is an arduous and involved process in this province, we decided to register the OCRT as a sole proprietorship – an organization that could theoretically generate a profit. This takes only a few minutes, and requires only a modest licensing fee. Unfortunately, the government rejected our proposed name; they reserve the word 'Centre' for not-for-profit organizations. So, the *Ontario Centre for Religious Tolerance* became the *Ontario Consultants on Religious Tolerance.* In retrospect, a much shorter name would have been preferable. It would be easier to remember, to enter into forms, and to write on checks. We are now gradually adopting *ReligiousTolerance.org* as our web site's informal nickname.

DEVELOPING THE OCRT MANDATE, GOALS AND PRINCIPLES OF OPERATION

The mandate of the OCRT derived from our own beliefs about organized religion. According to the homepage on our site:

> Religion is a unique force in society. It promotes both good and evil. Historically, it has helped to abolish slavery. It has promoted racial integration, equal rights for women, and equal rights for gays and lesbians. It has motivated individuals to create massive support services for the poor, the sick, the hurting, and the broken. Conversely, it has also been used to justify slavery, racial segregation, oppression of women, discrimination against homosexuals, genocide, massive crimes against humanity, extermination of minorities, and other horrendous evils.

> Religion drives some to dedicate their lives to help the poor and needy (e.g. Gandhi, Albert Schweitzer, Mother Teresa). It drives others to exterminate as many 'heretics' as they can. Consider the mass murders and genocides from the Armenians in Turkey to the Muslims in Kosovo.

> Religion has the capability to generate unselfish love in some people, and vicious, raw hatred in others (Robinson, 2000a).

As a result of our early discussions, we identified three main areas of religious intolerance.

- Intolerance directed from one faith group against another (e.g. a conservative Protestant group against Roman Catholicism: see Chick, N.d.);
- Intolerance directed from persons of one faith group against a secular group (e.g. conservative religious groups against gays and lesbians: http://www.godhatesfags.com/);
- Intolerance directed from persons in a secular group against a faith group (e.g. secularists against fundamentalist Christians: http://landoverbaptist.org)

Having identified these different variations of religious intolerance, we decided to concentrate our creative efforts in four major ways: exposing religious tolerance; providing information on 'hot' religious topics; supplying accurate religious information; and exposing fraud, hatred, and religious misinformation.

EXPOSING RELIGIOUS INTOLERANCE

Two of our members have worked in professions where the precise use of language is of great concern; one was a professional engineer, the other a registered nurse. Misunderstandings in these fields can be disastrous: bridges or buildings may collapse; patients may sicken or die from incorrect medication. With these personal backgrounds, we were surprised at the ambiguity of many religious terms. Words such as 'Christian' or 'Witch', 'God', 'Cult', and 'messiah', have been defined very differently by different religious groups. Often these definitions are mutually exclusive. The concept 'religious tolerance' is no exception.

Some believe that a person is only religiously tolerant when they regard all religions as equally valid (e.g. McDowell & Hostetler, 1998). Others define a person as religiously tolerant when he or she considers that all religions and faith groups are equally 'good'. Again, this makes little sense, because some religions teach their followers to hate minorities (e.g. World Church of the Creator), while others stress inclusiveness, love, and acceptance (e.g. the Unitarian Universalist Association).

The OCRT defines the concept of tolerance differently. We view it as a civil liberty issue. Religious tolerance requires that a person *value freedom of expression, assembly, and belief for followers of all religious traditions – especially those beliefs and practices that differ from one's own faith.*

While religious tolerance is guaranteed by Articles 13–15 of the United Nations *Universal Declaration of Human Rights* (United Nations, N.d.), few of the signatory countries have implemented it fully. Violence produced by religious intolerance is occurring with alarming frequency. As described in essays linked to our religious hatred menu (Robinson, 2000c), lynching, stoning, fire-bombing, shootings, physical assaults and economic attacks by devout followers of one faith have victimized followers of another – and that is in the United States! Outbreaks of antisemitism continue to plague both the United States and Canada, and appear to be increasing around the world.

Islam is seriously misrepresented in many media accounts, the most egregious the misinterpretation of the word jihad. Rather than 'holy war', as is often reported, it means a personal, internal struggle with one's own imperfections. Some conservative Christians are discriminated against in employment hiring and promotion. Children of some controversial religious groups have been seized from their homes on the basis of misinformation about the parents' faith (e.g. Palmer, 1999). Because of a judge's religious bias, parents have been prohibited from visiting their children. In parts of the rest of the world, government oppression, crimes against humanity and genocide have occurred. Injustices such as these need to be exposed.

DISSEMINATING INFORMATION ON 'HOT' RELIGIOUS TOPICS

While hardly a new phenomenon, these are issues over which various religious groups are in conflict either with each other, or with secular forces in society, or both. Currently active debates deal mainly with sex and violence. They include: access to abortion; equal rights and treatment for women in society; equal rights and legal protection for gay men and lesbians; the debate between creation science and evolution; corporal punishment of children, and capital punishment of adults. Our goal is to provide background information in a fair and balanced manner. We seek to explain the beliefs of all groups involved in a particular debate. If the disputants include Christians, for example, we cite applicable Biblical passages and describe how the groups involved have interpreted them. Where statements by professional organizations are available and germane, we list these as well. It is our hope that our visitors will gain insight into beliefs that oppose their own. Hopefully, they will begin to view their opponents as dedicated, thoughtful advocates, rather than as demonically inspired, evil fanatics.

DISSEMINATING ACCURATE RELIGIOUS INFORMATION

The OCRT tries to provide users with clear, balanced, and complete descriptions of the beliefs, rituals, symbols, and political goals (if any) of many different faith traditions – 84 as of mid-2000. Information is obtained from books on new religious movements, from the Internet, newsgroups, the media, etc. Before we publish any information about a particular faith group on our Web site, we attempt to have it reviewed by at least three adherents of that group. Most of these volunteer editors are webmasters of religious sites. We continually receive emails that contain documentation of errors and suggestions to improve these essays. We never regard any of our essays as complete. All are gradually refined over time.

Since approximately 87% of Americans and Canadians identify themselves as 'Christian' (Reeves, 1996), our site concentrates largely on the Christian religion. Notwithstanding this, we also give priority to those minority faith groups that have been the target of misinformation and/or disinformation campaigns in North America. Among others, these include: the Church of Scientology, The Family, Jehovah's Witnesses, the Church of Jesus Christ of Latter-day Saints, the Unification Church, and Wicca. By informing people about various religions (and counteracting misinformation spread by others), we hope that understanding and tolerance will increase, while bigotry and intolerance will decrease. We also hope that visitors to our Web site will better identify the positive and negative practices in their own faith traditions, maximizing the former while actively opposing the latter.

EXPOSING RELIGIOUS FRAUD, HATRED AND MISINFORMATION

As described in essays linked to our religious hatred menu, there is an enormous amount of misinformation found in textbooks, reference books, on the Internet, and in the media about religion. Some is intentional religious propaganda; much is simply repetition of entrenched stereotypes.

OCRT'S 'RULES OF ENGAGEMENT'

Four caveats govern the generation of information for the OCRT Web site: a neutral stance towards religious, spiritual and secular beliefs; criticism and opposition; respect for privacy; and coverage of all points of view.

A Neutral Stance Towards Religious and Secular Belief

Unlike most religious WWW sites, the OCRT does not promote any particular religion or religious position. Neither do we argue for secularism as superior to religion, or vice versa. We adopt a neutral stance towards religious and secular points of view. Our position is not unlike that of U.S. public schools and other governmental organizations.

Criticism and Opposition

Our policy is not to criticize a person or faith group for their theological beliefs. However, we do expose individual and group actions that harm people, limit personal freedoms, or otherwise restrict their spiritual, mental, religious, or emotional growth. For example, our section on homosexuality and bisexuality compares the conservative Christian understanding of sexual orientation with the beliefs of religious liberals, professional mental-health associations and gay/lesbian groups and individuals. We simply explain all sides to the issue. However, we are critical when these beliefs lead to actions that promote discrimination against sexual minorities.

Respect for Privacy

Many faith groups (e.g. the Church of Jesus Christ of Latter-day Saints, the Church of Scientology, and some groups within Ceremonial Magick, Wicca, and Satanism) prefer to keep some of their beliefs and rituals secret from the public. Such knowledge is only passed on to adherents and initiates gradually, as they advance in their involvement and/or training. Although some copyrighted and esoteric information has been published on the WWW (in some cases in breach of copyright), the OCRT does not contribute to that practice.

Coverage of All Points of View

We try to describe religion and religious ideas from as many different points of view as possible. When describing a Christian belief, we try to include both conservative and liberal positions. Statements from the early Christian movements are often added.

THE OCRT WEB SITE

In early May 1995, I signed up for Internet access through a local Internet Service Provider (ISP) in Kingston, Ontario. The initial home page and a few essays were placed on-line later that month. The Web site was assigned a directory on one of their servers; the URL prefix, however, was quite complex: http://www.kosone.com/people/ocrt/. Because I anticipated relatively little traffic on our Web site, I accepted a server directory normally reserved for individuals rather than companies. Being rather naive concerning Internet technology and orthography, I selected *ocrt_hp.htm* as the filename for the OCRT homepage; thus, the site's full address grew to: *http://www.kosone.com/people/ocrt/ ocrt_hp.htm.*

In retrospect, a standard default filename such as *index.htm* or *welcome.htm* would have simplified our visitors' navigation. When these are used, the index filename need not be included in the home page URL. This would have shortened our original URL considerably, thus significantly reducing the risk of misspelling and thereby minimizing missing hits to the site.

Inexperience also led to a second error. At the start-up of the Web site, I did not consider renting a full domain name, such as the one we eventually selected: http://www.religioustolerance.org. A full domain name has several advantages. It is easier for visitors to remember. It is transferable from one ISP to another. It conveys more information to potential visitors. When we had to switch to a different ISP, our URL became *http://web.canlink.com/ocrt/ocrt_hp.htm.* This left hundreds of *kosone.com* links orphaned and broken in various Internet search engines. A full domain name would have avoided this problem. We strongly urge people who are starting a Web site to rent one before starting up.

Recent versions of Internet browsers do not require the user to enter the complete URL. By entering just the center part of a URL, (like 'ibm'), the browser attempts to connect to a '.com' web site (http://www.ibm.com, in this case). We rented a second full domain name: (http://religioustolerance.com). This URL is automatically forwarded to our '.org' home page. Thus, when a person enters 'religioustolerance' in their browser, they will connect to our site.

We designed our homepage in a traditional format. A graphic – a dove with a white ribbon in its beak, a symbol of peace and tolerance – welcomes visitors, while underneath, a few words of introduction explain what the OCRT is. Down the left side of the screen, a table of contents provides hyperlinks to various main content menus: Christianity; other religions; spiritual topics; religious hatred; religious legislation; 'hot' topics, etc.

The OCRT site uses a standard pyramid structure. Although the homepage does allow visitors to select one of a few important essays, its main purpose is to guide them to the content menus. In turn, these menus are hyperlinked to individual essays on specific topics. We generally use a three-layered page structure: homepage, topic menus, and topic essays. In some complex cases, we insert a fourth layer: sub-topic menus. Although we expected that this would allow our visitors to navigate the site with the greatest ease, we have since found that many of our visitors bypass the menu structure altogether. Because they have come to our site through an Internet search engine, they are taken directly to the particular essay of interest to them. Our hit counters indicate that relatively few visit the homepage itself.

Within a few years, the Web site grew to more than five hundred menus and essays. Our readers found increasing difficulty locating specific material. To alleviate this problem we added an internal search engine. This also resulted in two extra benefits. First, the commercial search engine to which we link internally pays us a few cents whenever a visitor performs a search using that engine. Second, because we can obtain a list of the most common search terms and strings used by visitors, we can prioritize essay upgrades, the creation of new essays, and generally tailor the site to meet the needs of our clientele.

By February 2000, we added other special features to the site. A *message board* provides a discussion forum for our visitors. We feel it helps to build a community spirit among site readers and site builders. Visitors are free to post any thoughts they wish, and to respond to the thoughts of others. Because it is an unmoderated list, no one vets the posts before they appear on the message board. We have also added a hyperlink to *The Hunger Site*; our visitors can click on this and make arrangements to donate food through the *United Nations World Food Programme. The Hunger Site*'s sponsors pay the bill for this. We have included banners from paying advertisers, such as *The Religious Freedom Page* and the *WorldPeace Peace Page*. A graphic linked to *Hitbox.com* tracks our visitor traffic at our home page and a few main essays. This provides the OCRT with various statistical data about our site, its traffic and popularity. Another hyperlinked graphic allows a visitor to email a friend and recommend that he or she surf our site. In May 2000, we added a chat connection so that a visitor can exchange messages via keyboard with an OCRT staff member.

TRAFFIC ON THE OCRT WEB SITE

It took a few months until we received our 10,000th visitor. We suspect, but cannot prove, that a number of factors contributed to the subsequent sustained growth of traffic to the web site: increasing numbers of people with access to the Internet, additional essays and menus on our site, a general increase in interest in religion and spirituality, and perhaps an increasing concern for religiously-motivated conflicts in the world. Starting in late 1999, *Hitbox.com* listed our site as the most-visited religious site on the Internet.

As of late 2000, our site now has one thousand essays and menus. About 450,000 unique visitors each month generate in excess of 8 million 'hits', 2 million 'page loads' and 60 Gigabytes of data flow. A 'page load' represents one visitor requesting the home page, an essay or menu. A 'hit' is generated every time that a visitor's browser reads a file from our web site. Since a typical essay will have a text file, background file, banner file, and some navigation button files, the number of hits is much greater than the number of page loads. Most webmasters prefer to quote their hit count for this reason. Our number of page loads is growing about 75% per year. Many of our visitors are high school, college and university students. They generate a surge in our site metrics during September and a decline during May and June.

We have received 60 awards to date. However, we have a chronic battle with Web censorship software companies like *Cyberpatrol,* and *NetNanny.* Their programs find trigger words on our site (like Witch, Satan, abortion, and homosexuality) and often block their users from gaining access to our entire site. Censorship companies often talk about preventing access to pornographic sites and bomb-making instructions. However, some of them have a hidden agenda and ban access to sites dealing with human sexuality, Neopaganism, feminist issues, etc. We have had good success in negotiating the unblocking of our site with these companies.

Our most visited menus and essays typically deal with abortion, physician assisted suicide, naturism, religions of the world, Wicca, Buddhism, capital punishment, Islam, cloning of humans and Christianity. Occasionally a seasonal day of celebration (e.g. Easter, winter solstice) or a news item (e.g. partial birth abortion) will cause an essay to surge in popularity for a week or two.

FUNDING THE OCRT

Originally, the OCRT received no outside funding. It was run as a hobby. However, when the number of hits skyrocketed, and our Internet Service Provider began to charge large throughput penalties, we began to seek other sources of funding. Currently, we receive donations by cash, check, and money orders; they may also be charged to a U.S. visitor's telephone bill via a 900 number or a major credit card. Recently, the OCRT created a '100 Club' for visitors to our site who are willing to donate US$5.00 or more per month on their credit card. This is a major source of funding. We also sell commercial banner space on our homepage and 'Religions' menu. Revenue is also generated by advertisements placed on our Web site by banner ad companies. We also receive commissions from book sales at *Amazon.com* that are referred from our site.

Our major expense is the monthly bill for Web hosting, paid to the Internet Service Provider. Depending on the traffic volume, this amounts to many hundred dollars each month. Office and computer supplies, as well as reference books for the OCRT library, add to the cost of the operation. Although the OCRT is staffed by volunteers, the organization has run a deficit since its inception in 1995 through to early 1999. Sufficient revenue was generated in the latter part of 1999 and early 2000 to offset the losses incurred in previous years.

Our goal is to see the OCRT on a firm financial footing, so that it will survive beyond the involvement of the current members. Since the current volunteer effort invested in its operation amounts to the equivalent of two full-time positions, and this burden is borne by four volunteers, we would like to be able to hire additional staff in the future. Writing and editing essays, responding to email requests for information, and providing general maintenance and upkeep of the site, would need a staff of about three full-time employees.

Finally, we would like to see the OCRT reorganized as a not-for-profit agency. This would enable us to apply for grants from various foundations and religious denominations. Unfortunately, this would present our organization with conflict of interest issues that are not easily addressed. If we accepted money from government sources, our writers may be influenced to not be as critical of government policies. If we obtained a grant from a religious organization, we might pull our punches when preparing an essay on that group. We will probably have to separate completely the Web site from the accounting activities within the OCRT so that our authors remain unaware of external funding sources.

EMAIL GENERATED BY THE OCRT

Webmasters of religiously oriented sites can expect to receive a great amount of unsolicited email from their readers. We receive about two negative emails each day; some could even be considered as hate mail. We publish small excerpts from some of the more amusing of these emails on our site (www.religioustolerance.org/comments.htm).

For example, a conservative Sikh complained that we had misrepresented the source of his religion. Our essay stated that most historians believe that Sikhism is a syncretistic religion, containing elements of Hinduism and Islam. We also explained that many traditional Sikhs believe that their religion is not related to any other, but was revealed to them by God. The visitor threatened to lodge a formal complaint against us with a Canadian human rights body unless we deleted the first statement. We refused.

On another occasion, a conservative Muslim was very distressed and angry at what he felt were errors in our essay. He demanded that we travel to a city many hours away from our office, and attend a public meeting to discuss the matter. His concerns involved our descriptions of events in Muhammad's life, the origin of Islam, and the precise meaning of the term *Jihad*. We were able to resolve most of his concerns via emails.

Similarly, we received three letters from Satanists angry that we included a section on Satanic Ritual Abuse (SRA). When we pointed out that each of our essays concluded that SRA is a hoax, two writers responded, apologizing for their original emails.

Almost all of the remaining negative email comes from conservative Christians. To date we have received approximately three thousand. Some examples are listed in our 'Comments' page.

- "it is a load of s—t and if u ask me u should be killed."
- "YOU ARE SO DICUSTING, [sic] YOU LIE AT EVERY PAGE YOU SCUMMY PEICES [sic] OF COW DUNG."
- "You and your children will rot in Hell for all eternity because of what you have put on the Internet."
- "My God, JESUS CHRIST . . . will use me to execute His wrath upon you . . . I'll knock you down and cut your heads off!"
- "The Bible condemns those who trifle with it's [sic] sacred contents. You guys are toast!"

However, each negative E-mail is, on average, outnumbered by about 3.5 positive responses. Among the most moving are letters from gays and lesbians who had been taught as children to hate homosexuals. Passing puberty, they had realized that they were themselves homosexual. Some of these letters tell us that reading our site has been a life-changing experience for them; they have been able to recapture some of their self-esteem. Far more common are letters remarking how a particular essay has helped them personally:

- understand their partner in an inter-faith marriage;
- deal with religious conflicts in a friendship with a member of another faith;
- realize that their child is not a member of a harmful doomsday cult;
- handle religious conflicts in a business setting by making allowances for a member of a minority faith;
- obtain objective information for a course paper or debate.

Many letters question our theological credentials. We explain that we are not theological innovators; we are simply reporters on religions, spirituality, and ethics. We believe that a formal theological degree or Bible school diploma would be counter-productive, because it would tend to bias us in either a liberal or conservative direction. Our post-secondary education trained us in the skills we require as reporters: analytical thinking and the ability to express our thoughts clearly. One of us is a retired professional engineer; another is a registered nurse; a third has a PhD in urban planning.

THE FUTURE OF THE OCRT WEB SITE

The OCRT began as little more than a hobby for an engineer in retirement. It has grown into a full-time occupation for one of our volunteers, and a part-time job for the remaining three. Our original goal was to write 2,000 essays on topics that were linked in some way with religious tolerance. We completed our 1,000th essay in mid-2000. We still feel that we have another 2,000 to go before the topic is reasonably covered.

We hope that the number of visitors to our site will continue to expand in the future. There are some indicators that we are in a growth business: the Internet itself is expanding. Polls seem to indicate an increasing interest in spirituality throughout North America. The population is aging, and people tend to become more religiously active as they grow older (Robinson, 2000b, 2000d). The size of our Web site is continually increasing. All of these factors should attract more visitors.

CONCLUDING REMARKS

We have no way of measuring the impact that our site has on our visitors. It is a simple task to measure the numbers of visitors. But we have no idea on how we are affecting their attitudes, relationships, and actions. We have even less idea whether we are having any significant impact on society itself.

When I started the Web site in 1995, I was uncertain whether organized religion has had an overall positive or negative influence on the world. Five years later, I am still not certain. Religion inspires people to achieve greatness. It gives to billions of people a feeling of security and a personal relationship with a variety of deities. It motivates people to pursue spiritual matters, to love their neighbor as themselves, and to help the broken, hurting and suffering. But it has also promoted intense hatred of people who differ in faith, race, gender, sexual orientation, and other apects. It has become obvious to us that many of the world's conflicts involve religious, ethnic, economic, political and other factors. Organized religions may not be the only contributor to crimes against humanity. However, they may offer the principal solution – but only if they can be convinced to promote tolerance.

REFERENCES

Chick, J. (N.d.) *A Special Gatefold: The Satanic Roots of the Roman Catholic Church.* Retrieved July 13, 2000, from the World Wide Web: http://www.revolting.com/1.2/chick/vatican.html

Gray, M. (1996). *Web Growth Summary*. Retrieved July 13, 2000, from the World Wide Web: http://www.mit.edu/people/mkgray/net/web-growth-summary.html

McDowell, J., & Hostetler, B. (1998). *The New Tolerance: How a Cultural Movement Threatens to Destroy You, Your Faith, and Your Children*. Wheaton, IL: Tyndale House Publishers.

O'Reilly & Associates, (Eds), (1997). *The Harvard Conference on the Internet and Society*. Sebastopol, CA: O'Reilly and Associates, Inc.

Palmer, S. J. (1999). Frontiers and Families: The Children of Island Pond. In: S. J. Palmer, & C. E. Hardman (Eds), *Children in New Religions* (pp. 153–171). New Brunswick, NJ: Rutgers University Press.

Reeves, T. C. (1996). *The Empty Church: Does Organized Religion Matter Anymore?* New York: Simon & Schuster, Touchstone Books.

Robinson, B. A. (2000a). Ontario Consultants on Religious Tolerance. Retrieved July 13, 2000, from the World Wide Web: http://www.religioustolerance.org

Robinson, B. A. (2000b). Religious Beliefs in the U.S. Retrieved July 13, 2000, from the World Wide Web: http://www.religioustolerance.org/chr_poll.htm

Robinson, B. A. (2000c). Religious Hatred, Intolerance, and Other 'Not So Spiritual' Topics. Retrieved July 13, 2000, from the World Wide Web: http://www.religioustolerance.org/negative.htm

Robinson, B. A. (2000d). Religious Practice in the U.S. Retrieved July 13, 2000, from the World Wide Web: http://www.religioustolerance.org/chr_prac.htm

Robinson, B. A. (2000e). Witchcraft and Wicca. Retrieved July 13, 2000, from the World Wide Web: http://www.religioustolerance.org/witchcra.htm

United Nations. (N.d.) Universal Declaration of Human Rights. Retrieved July 13, 2000, from the World Wide Web: http://www.un.org/Overview/rights.html

MAPPING A 'CYBERLIMEN': A TEST CASE FOR THE USE OF ELECTRONIC DISCUSSION BOARDS IN RELIGIOUS STUDIES CLASSES

Joanne Maguire Robinson

ABSTRACT

What happens when student discussion outside of class is 'captured' electronically, when it moves from the controlled arena of the classroom into the protean realm of cyberspace? This central question guides this chapter, which explores the benefits and limitations of integrating electronic class discussion boards into religious studies classes. This technological teaching tool, which is both easy to administer and easily accessible, has been used to great effect in the 'hard' sciences but has been relatively neglected in the humanities. This test case involves the use of one such board in a class devoted to examining contentious theological, political, and ethical issues from the perspective of one religious tradition.

INTRODUCTION

Generations of students have lingered in hallways to extend class discussions beyond class time. They have continued those discussions with friends in cafeterias and dormitories, and some have brought conversations home to their

Religion on the Internet, Volume 8, pages 325–344.

families. While their effect is not quantifiable nor are they always 'academic', such discussions are an integral part of each student's education. Yet what happens – for both student and teacher – when such discussions are 'captured' electronically, when they move from the realm of in-person contact to the realm of cyberspace?

As our colleagues in the so-called 'hard' sciences work to integrate technology into their classrooms (Cavalier, 1992; Collins, 1995, 1998; Coombs, 1992; Grassie, 1997; O'Keefe, 1996; Zack, 1995), this question is becoming increasingly important for teachers and researchers in religious studies and other humanities disciplines as well (Burr, Clark & Wyschogrod, 1995; Barnette, 1998; Clarke, 1997; O'Leary & Brasher, 1996; Roberts, 1998). In the secular marketplace, any number of specialized discussion groups and *listservs* cater to individual interests, creating what some have termed a 'virtual university' (Strangelove, 1993); in the marketplace of faith, worshippers can find 'cyber-churches' and participate in on-line rituals. This chapter is one account of the electronically mediated discursive 'maps' which can be made by teachers and students in religious studies classes.

This study contributes to the emerging discussion over the use of electronic learning technologies in the field of religious studies. It is concerned with several core issues, such as whether this technology changes when, how, and why students ask and answer questions. More importantly, perhaps, does it change *what* students ask and *what kind* of answers they provide for themselves and others? Does the relatively impersonal medium of the electronic bulletin board result in a lowering of academic discourse? Or do students provide more measured and tolerant thought in writing than they might in class? And, finally, can an electronic discussion medium extend the classroom in a useful way that contributes to student learning?

This experiment shows that an electronic discussion board is not simply a 'virtual hallway', where students talk with each other about issues and ideas presented in the classroom and in class readings. I found that an electronic class discussion board could become a dynamic boundary space (what I will call a cyberlimen), that exists neither wholly within the classroom nor wholly without it. As this work will show, students in this experiment were continually faced with the imprecision of definitions and ideas that guided their lives. They were challenged to find ways to understand each other's arguments, even if they were not working specifically with the particular arguments and texts I put before them. Students found their own way and made their own 'maps' through this new territory in ways they did not in papers or class discussions. This experiment shows that, while the territory might be the same, the maps we all draw through that territory often differ. It seems true, then, as Jonathan Z. Smith reminds his colleagues in religious studies, that " 'Map is not territory' – but maps are all we possess" (Smith, 1978, p. 309). This experiment made students' maps clearer to me.

A common set of pedagogical and institutional problems contributed to the need for this discussion board. Pressures at our state university have resulted in overenrollment in classes that lend themselves better to smaller numbers. Many of my students are working commuters who find arranging and attending study groups extremely inconvenient, if not impossible. Indeed, the prevailing student culture does not always encourage learning for learning's sake. My classes generally rely on discussion for clarification and application of ideas, methods, and issues, and the pressures I have just outlined make this far more difficult. Small group work in class has remedied this problem somewhat, yet my students and I still find that we often run out of time for discussion of sufficient breadth and depth. On many days, students lingered after class to continue a discussion, and many reported that they talked about class readings with others not in the class. Students seemed hungry for an alternate forum for the exchange of ideas, and I embraced the challenge.

This test case is quite specific to one particular class and one particular set of students. Thus, it speaks of a single example under a certain set of rules and circumstances. It is certainly possible that the relatively familiar topic of this particular course – debates within Christianity throughout its history – combined with the somewhat undefined forum of the electronic discussion board, fostered an idiosyncratic kind of discussion. Yet I believe this experiment is representative of what electronic communication does and does not accomplish from a pedagogical perspective. It speaks to the complexities inherent in teaching religious studies as the boundaries of discourse stretch beyond the relatively controlled interaction in the classroom and the quantifiable measure of tests and papers.

It must be noted that I continually reiterated to all of my classes that any understanding of any religion is culturally, socially, and historically located. This new mode of eliciting ideas and thoughts from students proved to illustrate precisely that point, although in a way I did not expect. Indeed, one of the most delightful and yet problematic results of this project is that students defined the space for themselves, in ways I could anticipate, in ways I could not have imagined, and in ways I would never have chosen. In my naivete, I imagined an electronic discussion board would prove to be a relatively 'neutral' medium, like the hallway after class. I imagined that I would be able to read student comments on the board as if I were overhearing just such a conversation in the hallway.

I was wrong.

GOALS OF THIS EXPERIMENT

Let me state at the outset that I am not a rhetorician, nor do I claim to analyze what some have called a developing 'postmodern pedagogy' (Enstrom & Fedderson, 1995; Hogsette, 1995; Zappen, Gurak & Doheny-Farina, 1997). This project arose not from a desire to understand postmodernity with its "decentered authority, destabilized selves, or commodified subjectivity" nor from an interest in parsing students' syntax; rather, it arose from a common set of acute pedagogical frustrations. It was, quite simply, the act of a teacher wanting to patch certain holes in instruction. And the class in which I conducted the experiment was itself the child of frustration and curiosity.

Too often, I have found, students resisted learning about a religion (in this case, Christianity) they felt they lived and, therefore, understood. While this is, in part, a resistance to history, it is also a resistance to challenging 'truths' long held and a resistance to doing the hard work of critical thinking. This class was designed explicitly to introduce disjuncture and conflict into what many students seemed to see as a monolithic, ahistorical tradition. Students too often yearn for simplicities, for definitions that are straightforward and easily comprehended. They want 'Christianity', for instance, to mean X, Y, Z, and nothing else.

In this course I explicitly sought to highlight the changing response of this particular tradition to a changing world, one tradition's continuing redefinition as it moved through time. Thus, the primary goal of this particular course was to show these students that there is no one 'correct' Christian response to any theological, political, or ethical issue. I wanted them to see that individuals and groups who call themselves Christian make and justify certain truth claims even though those claims might contradict those of others who call themselves Christian. I am the first to argue – and to show with texts – that "There is no Christianity in itself; there are only christianities" (Webb, 1997, p. 767). I hoped that the board would give students a space to continue discussions in this vein.

Entitled 'Christian Controversies' and taught in Spring 1999, this course focused on a series of theological, ethical, and political issues, such as the death penalty; reproductive technologies and abortion; euthanasia; the role of women in the church; free will and predestination; faith and works; slavery, poverty, and human rights; and the authority of the Bible. All class readings came from primary source materials representing a range of Christian perspectives, both historical and modern. Students were required to enter into some contentious and problematic historical and contemporary territory, some of which they responded to on very personal levels.

I chose this class for the e-board experiment because of these complexities, and because the class was small enough to manage. Twenty-seven students were enrolled in the class, the majority of whom were religious studies majors or minors. Slightly more than a third were women. From my experience, the students appeared to reflect the demographics of the University of North Carolina at Charlotte campus. Most notably, a vocal minority defined themselves as 'Christian' in a form they considered uniquely 'right'. I know this not because I asked students about themselves, but because such information was freely offered, either in class or, more often, on the discussion board. The e-board became the liminal space in which some students chose to establish identities other than those they felt required to assume within the classroom.

RULES OF ENGAGEMENT

Students were not required to use the board as part of their grade, although they were strongly encouraged to participate, and they did – in larger numbers than I initially expected. Most students reported reading the board fairly often, although only a handful (about seven) actually contributed regularly. Students were evaluated on their preparation for and participation in class, for writing a series of shorter papers, and for writing a substantial research paper on a topic of their choice.

Overall, the system is quite simple to use. The board is appended to a web site and can be read (and responded to) by anyone who has access to the site. Except on an individual basis, it does not rely on passwords for security. To use the system, students log-in with a username and password, and they have the option of starting a new discussion or participating in an ongoing debate. The result is a collection of conversations of varying sizes. Some discussions begin from one root message and flower into a multi-layered web of conversation; others begin from one root and go in several directions of different length; and some queries and comments sit alone as students move on to other issues. In other words, students might pick up on one aspect of one conversation and follow it for as many as a dozen entries; other comments might solicit only one or two shorter responses. Any level of any conversation can be read on screen or printed off with the click of a mouse.

In addition, any user's identity can be discovered just as easily.[1] The site is not secure and usernames do not veil true identities. In this case, students who called themselves 'Isaiah' and 'Man of the Book' (hereinafter MOB) regularly sparred against 'Friedrich' (as in Nietzsche). Others chose names that highlighted their heritage and loyalties ('GoIrish'), favorite television shows ('Boomhauer') or other, more enigmatic connections, such as 'Buzzing Like A Fridge'. It is most important to note that those who did not know who Man of the Book 'really' was from the content and tone of his postings could discover his identity with another click of the mouse. It is likely that this helped control potential inflammatory attacks and rhetoric for which an individual student would be reluctant to take responsibility. In short, a student could not 'hide' behind a username (although it is worth considering whether such apparent role-playing does change the ways students interact. I do not yet have the data to begin answering that question.).

I set up the board at the beginning of the semester by outlining simple rules. All postings were to be modeled on classroom rules: avoid *ad hominem* and *ad feminam* attacks; beware of uninformed oversimplification; use concrete examples from the texts we read for class in making arguments; beware of anachronism; and use standard grammar. Any lapse into email and chat room irregularities or shortened forms would not be tolerated. And I asked that students stick to academic discourse and rely on the texts we read for class as the basis for their discussion. One student had a particularly memorable way of stating this requirement: "base your arguments on solid things, not on the incomplete knowledge of what Satan knows and thinks" (RP, 96).

Ideally, while I wanted the board to emulate class discussion by focusing on assigned texts and issues, I also wanted it to differ by muting my voice in order to see what students would do with a space they considered their own. I participated in the discussion occasionally, and students knew I was 'listening in'. Nevertheless, I 'shaped' the discussion only at the outset in asking for religious studies majors to describe the field as they understood it (see below). My only other contributions were brief factual clarifications.

On the whole, contributors were polite to one another, engaging only occasionally in personal criticism, as in describing another student's viewpoint as 'scroogelike'. The few exceptions to a sense of civility were caught and swiftly dealt with, as apparent in the following response:

> You often like to talk about leaving things in the realm of academia ... Then you go and respond to others with attacks. Attacks are not an argument, nor evidence for your point. They are simply attacks. And as such they have no business in the realm of academia ... We are not interested in what you have to say against someone [e.g. calling another student's stance 'uneducated and trifling'] but what you have to say about the topics (RP, 97).

Although students were generally quite civil, respect for other's views was sometimes limited. This kind of bias was implicit, for instance, when a student urged another to act in a more 'Christian' manner:

> ... you need to settle down and quit alienating your fellow Christians. If you truly are as versed in scripture as you state, then you should know that if you are going to correct a brother or sister Christian, you need to do it with love. Call me crazy but I saw none of that in your post (DC, 15).

Reminders among students about the rules of academic discourse became part of an ongoing discussion about what was appropriate and inappropriate from the standpoint of the academic study of religion, as described below. I knew from experience that some of them had to learn or be reminded of the standards and rules of such study, an issue made more acute by the relatively familiar subject at hand. As I wrote on the board early in the semester:

> We all must respect personal faith convictions while recognizing that we are explicitly NOT in the classroom to learn 'how' to be Christian. We are there to learn how Christians with many different viewpoints have constructed their own interpretations and worldviews over 2,000 years of history; how they've responded to political, social, and ethical issues; and how particular arguments are built on certain presuppositions and supported by a complex hierarchy of authorities (textual, traditional, conciliar, individual, etc.).

To get students to think about this approach, and to fend off (I hoped) some of the more polemical apologetics, I opened the discussion board with a request that religious studies majors clarify what other students might need to know about the methods and approaches used in the discipline. Those who responded gave some very straightforward guidelines: "Students in this class should keep personal opinions and beliefs OUT of this academic study of Christian controversies" (Sunshine, 7) or, more bluntly, "you should listen and leave your faith in the hall" (Friedrich, 8).

Not surprisingly, more than one student took offense at this 'requirement'. Throughout the semester, students continually used the board to assert their own 'correct' interpretation of Christianity and 'the Christian'. Here is one example:

> Christians are to say what they believe, why they believe it, and live that belief no matter where they are or what they are doing. So I will never leave my Christianity in the hall or anywhere else for that matter, and take the words of the Bible to heart: "But whoever shall deny Me before men, I will also deny him before My Father who is in heaven" (Mt. 10: 33). If the idea of a believer who will not relinquish his/her beliefs to the will of the secular bothers anyone, then they can take it up with God on judgement day, but as for me, I will never let God or His word be discredited or invalidated (MOB, 1).

Interestingly, other students responded in a similar vein, and several of those also invoked the 'ultimate' lesson that might be awaiting us all. For instance, one noted that:

> I find interesting this enormous push for students (Christians specifically) to leave their personal beliefs outside. I'm curious as to how you can have a discussion when people are not permitted to voice what they believe about a certain issue. A belief in essence is one's interpretation of things ... Bring your opinions and beliefs into class with you, but realize that not everyone shares those views. That doesn't make one right and the other wrong. That just means you believe what you believe and one day we'll ALL find out the truth of whether there is a Heaven or a Hell, or if we all just rot after death (DC, 2).

Even students who clearly understood the formal class requirements addressed
Christian students directly as somehow separate from the others:

> I do not believe that the classroom is the appropriate place for sermons and bible thumping.
> That kind of thing only makes people look foolish. I do believe, however, that we [Christians]
> can give an argument for our case that is more effective, and just as compelling, if we play
> by the rules of academic endeavor ... This has nothing to do with betraying our moral
> obligations or our personal beliefs, but everything to do with treating opposing viewpoints
> with fairness and respect (Lee, 41).

What is most interesting to me about this particular set of postings is that I
never set "leaving your beliefs in the hall" as a requirement of the class; rather,
I insisted over and over again on academic discourse and critical thinking in
both the classroom and in student papers. As I will show below, this ideal was
extremely difficult to achieve, not in the classroom or in student papers, but on
the board itself. It was clear to me that students learned to "play the critical-
thinking game" for those parts of the course for which they were being graded.
Nevertheless, self-identified Christian students continued to 'preach' on the
discussion board, even toward the end of the semester when such rhetoric was
rare in the classroom. This often took the form of identifying 'Christianity' or
'the Christian' with a student-defined set of standards or authorities. In essence,
the divides between Christian and non-Christian, and between 'the academic
perspective' and one's 'faith commitment', was never fully resolved.

Before I illustrate that claim, I must note that students did use the board in
ways that I officially sanctioned as constructive. On the simplest level, for
instance, they used it to restate something they felt they had misstated in class
or to note a related interest. For instance, "What I was trying to say in class
regarding ... " and "something intrigued me in our discussion yesterday ... "
(DC, 114); or "The discussion today brought up a thought" (GoIrish, 102).

At times the students were very open and welcomed criticism, along the lines
of "If you think I am totally off or just want to respond, please do" (Boomhauer,
81). Others wrote that they were simply trying out new ideas, and they were
willing to admit that they did not have the answers. Said Friedrich on the topic
of free will and grace, "The fact is that I am not sure" (Friedrich, 86). Still
others posed pivotal questions that required reading into the sources. For
instance, one student asked a fine question about Pelagius' optimistic anthropology: "Does the ascetic background of Pelagius promote an unjustified bias
in his assumptions about the sufficiency of human nature to fulfill the word of
God?" (Lee, 64). He then went on to examine the possible effects an individual's particular circumstances can have on that individual's theological ideas.

In my opinion, the board worked best when students invoked evidence from
the readings to support their point (something I insist on in class discussions).

The following passage illustrates this mode of arguing:

> I must disagree with you on one point in your post. Augustine would not say that God controls whether we sin or not. Rather he says in our in-class reading that "A person becomes an evil tree when he makes himself evil, when he turns from the unchangeable good." This indicates that [for Augustine] God does not choose whether we sin or not (RP, 85).

Or, in another post, a student refers to a specific line in the reading and goes on to give his own interpretation:

> I tend to disagree with the last sentence, "Thus, it is the mood of the contemporary society that judges what is held to be suitable and, therefore, perhaps authoritative." While I see what he is saying and I do agree ... [yet] the question must be asked (Isaiah, 5).

This is how I thought the board would function: as a place to work out ideas sparked by the sources we read for class, enhanced by the help and criticism of others. Some students regularly modeled the kind of analysis that I hoped they would learn to do both collaboratively and alone.

Sometimes they surprised me. I was quite pleased to see the following posting on the board late in the semester: "Christians are as divided on this issue [abortion] as they are on every other issue we've covered all semester. There is no one Christian response for anything, as we have seen" (Sunshine, 123). This comment closely mirrored my own ideals. Yet the board disclosed another 'subtext' that seemed to have been squelched within the classroom after the first few weeks.

'MAPPING' CHRISTIANITY
AND 'MAPPING' RELIGIOUS STUDIES

Despite my insistence on critical standards of thought and argumentation, an 'ideal' Christianity took on a life of its own on the discussion board, particularly under the umbrella of topics such as christology, biblical authority, and abortion. On these issues, in particular, discussion on the board and in the classroom was heated and intense, yet the quality of the postings on the board seemed much more emotional and certainly more personal. Students wrote lengthy excurses on the topics, goading their classmates into responses or aiming to shut down any further argument with "and that's how it is" statements. These topics sparked a quality of debate that I did not see in the classroom, perhaps both because the 'official' map through the material was largely absent and because the professor was a negligible presence.

The board apparently freed students up for more extensive consideration of topics than they gave (or I gave them) in class. If learning is done through active thinking and writing, then the board accomplished a great deal pedagogically.

Yet it also accomplished quite a bit in showing the maps students make of the disciplines we present them. I do not approve of much of the rhetoric on the board, yet I found myself intrigued by the ways students understand the academic enterprise and their own, personal experience of it.

On the issue of whether Jesus was capable of sin, for instance, one student dismissed all interpretations but his own, remarking that "Any conclusions drawn to the contrary are therefore not biblical, and not worthy of debate under Christian understanding" (MOB, 90). Other comments were more general yet equally certain in defining 'Christianity': "Leading a good life is not what gets you to heaven. Salvation comes through Jesus Christ and only Jesus Christ . . . As to what happens to those who have never heard about Christ, I can't say. That is a question I don't have the ability to answer" (DC, 77).

MAP ONE: BIBLICAL AUTHORITY

One particularly energetic discussion focused on the nature of biblical authority. We read two essays on this topic, one of which argues that the Bible ought to be the sole inerrant guide for faith and practice for the evangelical Christian. This author sees the Bible as a static, unquestionably valid guide throughout time and circumstance. His 'opponent' in this debate argues that the Bible is not always suitable or sufficient for answering contemporary questions. Rather, he says, contemporary perspectives are most authoritative, arguing in part that people by necessity pick and choose relevant parts of scripture. He calls this the "canon within the canon" and argues that the authority choosing a passage is ultimately more authoritative than the text being chosen.

Several students found this latter notion compelling, noting that throughout history particular groups of people gain power by means of having what is perceived to be a 'correct' interpretation. One student spelled out an understanding of the hierarchy of authorities chosen by Protestant and Roman Catholics:

> Generally, and I do mean generally, Protestants regard the Bible as ultimate authority. As we discussed, Catholics do not necessarily hold to that same sentiment . . . This does not mean that Catholics disregard the teachings of the Bible, but some do feel that all answers cannot be found in it. Maybe this is the impasse that no matter how hard we try, we can't understand each other's view. I guess tolerance and patience are the keys to this process. It's a lot easier to debate politics, that is for sure (GoIrish, 120).

On the other hand, this idea that a 'Christian' might not take the Bible as the supreme authority was simply unpalatable to several students who considered the Bible beyond critique and even interpretation. The following passage illustrates this point of view.

> The Bible is what it is simply because that is the book that Christians hold to be the Word of God, infallible and Holy. For those who do not believe that, simply put they are not Christians. Logic, according to the text, would tell one that if there were any need of new inspiration it wouldn't be new at all; the inspiration would already be in there (the Bible) ... To the believer, it is not important who said it, but what is being said in scripture. Consequently, holding 'truth' to be found in scripture as 'True', and claiming it to be divinely inspired has nothing to do with being Protestant, it has to do with being Christian (MOB, 108).

For this student, then, divine inspiration is captured in the text of the Bible; indeed, any apparently 'new' inspiration would also be found there, because the Bible encompasses all inspiration ever possible. This book defines the only possible 'Christian' life. Still another student took issue with that idea:

> Nice try, but once again the notion that biblical text, written by humans, can be the only thing divinely inspired is short-sighted. This notion only points to the fact that the apostles during and right after Christ's time on earth could be divinely inspired ... People were divinely inspired prior to Christ's time on earth. Therefore, it would stand to reason that people would be divinely inspired even in today's society. Who is to say that the clergy of the Catholic Church are not divinely inspired? Mainly, Protestant thinkers who do not wish to look beyond their own personal beliefs (Golrish, 104).

A related debate swirled around the issue of textual criticism and interpretation. One felt that "If the Bible is the word of God it should withstand all criticism" (Isaiah, 5), while another insisted that "The Bible is a good book, but if you leave it on a pedestal you will never learn much about it" (Friedrich, 9). Yet what of interpretation? One student insisted that the Bible is to be read in one way only: "But I warn you, do not put your own spin on scripture, it can only hurt you and other believers in the long run" (MOB, 92). This same student argued later in the semester that misinterpretation of the scripture – not scripture itself – is to blame for bad human ideas and behavior:

> A small political commentary, if you all don't mind. The discussion in class that ended up leaning toward, in my opinion, a discussion of oppressed people blaming their lives on the concept of a perceived 'white male God', brought out many misconceptions. There have been throughout all of history in the past 2000 years gross mistranslations, serious misuses of scripture, and terrible monstrosities in the name of Christianity. That I am not going to deny, but for one to claim to be a Christian, the only way to go about changing the way things are/have been is not to complain about the obvious errors or humanity, but rather take steps in each and every life to correct his/her own misconceptions of scripture and not blame the faults of humanity on the Bible (MOB, 112).

The problems of interpretation lingered for many students as, at best, problematic if not impossible to resolve:

> If I remember correctly we had this discussion at the beginning of the term, and I believe that the problem didn't lie in the quoting of scripture, the problem was in people using scripture

to attack and also stating it as though their interpretation was the only correct one . . . No matter how many sects of Christianity there are, every one is at least some way based on the Bible. After all, Christianity equals Christ—ianity . . . see my point (DC, 118).

Another student related this divide to the atmosphere in class later in the semester:

> Today's class was definitely filled with some hostility towards each side's position. This class is not intended to show preference to one side or the other in regards to issues. No one in this class should feel they are being railroaded by one side. This leads in to my point. I have heard numerous times in this class, "If you read your Bible, it says . . ." or "The Bible says this . . . " I believe everyone should keep in mind that statements such as these only promote your own personal agenda and interpretation of scripture. Unless you are God himself, don't think for a minute that your interpretation is the absolutely correct one. There would be no need for this class if you were infallible and we should believe every word you say. If this were the case there would not be all the various denominations within Christianity. I do, however, believe that this class is for discussion of topics, not for the conversion of people who follow a different path (GoIrish, 117).

MAP TWO: ABORTION AND THE ROLE OF WOMEN

Similar divisions were apparent in many of the texts we read, not least on the topic of abortion. We read several essays on the subject, each of which presented a reasoned position from a Christian point of view. As with certain other issues, students tended to avoid the assigned sources in favor of a 'truth-centered' debate. Consequently, a certain smugness and moral superiority prevailed. One student's postings are representative of this point of view.

This student, vocally against abortion under any circumstances, wrote that "In a Christian context, it should be extremely rare that a woman need to even consider getting an abortion. It should not be an issue . . . to the Christian who is not married, [premarital sex] is not an issue, for the Christian should not fornicate" (Isaiah, 124). The same student concluded, "for the Christian, to disregard [my] arguments is to compromise, to some degree, your faith. I understand minor variances on extreme cases, that is fine, but on the whole the Christian must to some extent agree with these statements" (Isaiah, 124). For this student, the biblical text answers all such questions and puts humans – and particularly women – in their proper place:

> I realize people may disagree with me. That is fine. Just realize the standpoint that I take this from. It is coming from someone who sees the Bible as the Holy Word of God, without errors. That God is personal, and He is concerned for each of us. If you do not hold these positions (in other words, if you're not a Christian), then I do not expect you to agree with me necessarily . . . While some women may see [pregnancy] as a curse, it is the way that God has designed reproduction. If you do not like the system, then you only have Adam and Eve to blame . . . For the Christian [a woman's] body is not her own. It is also her husband's and

> Christ's. And does not Christ have more sway than one's husband? . . . If a 'Biblical Christian' holds the Bible with supreme authority in their life then look for the verses that support abortion. You will not find one! (Isaiah, 124).

This passage, written by a male student, seemed to be an appropriate follow-up to an earlier posting by another male student. Again, the authority of the Bible prevails:

> So it is true that women have not been fairly treated in the past, and some would say even now they are unfairly treated. I say to the Christian, is it fair to question the ordainment of God in the scriptures, which tell believers very clearly the roles of men and women? If one claims to be a believer, then fairness is not a question that he/she should ask – EVER! For those of you who are not believers, this does not apply to you . . . The ordainment of gender roles is as God justified it, and not to be disobeyed or altered just because we are in the 90s. The Bible still says the same things today as it did when written, and for a believer there is no reason to think that should change just because time has passed (MOB, 112).

It is worth noting here that this student was far more reticent to express his views so definitively during class discussion. The e-board provided him an alternative space, still connected to the class, but not bound by the same strictures. Discussions with other students that he might not otherwise have had were made possible in this environment.

MAP THREE: RELIGIOUS STUDIES

'Christianity' was not the only target for continued redefinition. Students also tried to work out what religious studies is and what this particular class was designed to do. Student musings on the academic endeavor are fascinating. One student, for instance, described the class this way:

> [This class] is here for us to broaden our knowledge of beliefs across the lands, and within our own land. Each person in the class should feel free to let their beliefs be known, but the key is this: Do not attempt to change someone's view just because you think you are 'right' . . . the more and more I think about why I am in this class, I continue to arrive at this conclusion: we [Christians in the class] must understand that we believe what we do because we feel it 'right' for US; and that our beliefs may not be 'right' for others. Religious studies is just that . . . the STUDY OF RELIGIONS, not solely the study of Christianity (Cltqtpi, 10).

Yet even such apparently measured explanations sparked debate. Certain students questioned the whole endeavor of religious studies as an academic discipline, as summed up in the following remark: "Unfortunately, religious studies is not looking for the truth in the matters of validity in Christianity, but would rather scrutinize the smallest of HUMAN errors in a God-breathed endeavor" and described religious studies as 'dissecting faith' (MOB, 4).

Another student immediately countered that "Fortunately, religious studies is not looking for the 'Truth' in anything" (Friedrich, 8). This divide, it seems, caused much of the ongoing tension on the board between Christian and non-Christian, and between 'faith' and 'academia'. Once again, rather than sublimate the tension by disallowing such argument in class (i.e. with no other course-related outlet), the e-board allowed this discussion to take place, as it were, out in the electronic open.

It is not surprising that one student examined the situation at the university from what he perceived to be the perspective of Jesus Christ:

> I am left with the position of common Christian marketing: W.W.J.D? ... Without delving into scripture for reference (heaven forbid I take it out of context – serious sarcasm in that sentence), I would ask the simple question as a believer what Jesus would do in the university setting, and try to make a play from there. Jesus was thought to be anti-religious to the leaders of Judaism in his day, but history shows us quite the contrary. Learning does not merely come from understanding facts about something, but rather is achieved through the knowledge of what to do with the facts presented. If we downplay the faith aspect in Christianity, then we are not truly studying it (MOB, 19).

To this student, the academic study of religion "leaves half of Christianity out" and in doing so creates a situation much like that in which Jesus found himself. "He knew [his contemporaries] would not listen, they were too busy trying to dispute his authority (much like a university classroom) ... The goal of this class it to look at the way people in history have interpreted Christianity. Well, I intend to do just that" (MOB, 42).

In the post below, this student perhaps unwittingly reiterated precisely what I was trying to convey in the class, and brought up questions about the status of a discussion board within an academic setting:

> You cannot debate Truth in religion academically. Believe me, I have tried and failed. What you believe must stay out of the classroom as it applies to faith. This message board is not the forum for Sunday School dialogue. There are chat rooms for that which I, for one, frequent ... The only responsibility a Christian has is to themselves and God. I am not held in regard for the deeds of others ... I for one am willing to talk about faith issues outside of the classroom but have found that bringing them into the classroom only caused problems (MOB, 65).

ASSESSMENT

As is likely clear by now, I never intended (or imagined) that students would use the board to 'debate Truth'. Yet I am forced to conclude that this discussion board was a more valuable tool in the students' hands than in my own, who directed the discussion in class away from issues that students were apparently aching to discuss. To their credit, students themselves were generally aware when their discourse wandered into issues that were not strictly academic.

> It is not my impression that this board is solely confined to academic discussion. 'Red' has every right to ask whatever questions she comes up with after reading a post. The initial post was academic, but she chose to ask a different type of question. She has that right. If you don't wish to be a part of the discussion, that is your right . . . Although I don't believe this board is solely confined to academic discussion, I can see why things of a spiritual nature would want to be discussed with caution . . . I don't mean to take the discussions away from academic discussion, though I feel when I'm asked my opinion, I should be able to give it with the proper backing (DC, 79–80).

In student opinion, it seems, the board worked best when they explored issues of concern to them and with a set of authorities that they established for themselves. For some, faith was the arbiter of value; for others, critical thinking; for still others, pleasing the professor. None of these is mutually exclusive.

So what did this board accomplish that brought the discussion beyond the more traditional boundary walls of the classroom? It proved to be, in a way, both less and more than the class as a whole. I aimed at a voluntary, egalitarian space that was not as teacher-centered as the classroom, hoping for the meeting of ideas to which all could contribute informed and critical discussion. I expected to see the students use the materials I had given them as springboards for the discussion, yet they most often left those behind in favor of personal issues and witnessing. This was due, at least in part, to my plan to leave the students on their own on the board, and it would have been more successful from my point of view had it been: (a) more restricted, and (b) required for student evaluation. In that case, I imagine, students would be more likely to think and act in 'academic' mode. Yet the board was more than this for the students who created an alternative discussion medium that they sometimes chose to use for personal (sometimes trenchant and critical) reflection.

Unlike a hallway and unlike a 'real-time' chatroom, an electronic bulletin board is an asynchronous forum for posting messages, which means that the medium itself has limitations beyond merely those common in cyberspace (e.g. server crashes). Yet it also has benefits. For instance, I was concerned in advance that the built-in delay might stifle 'hot' debate and that the lack of face-to-face interaction might increase instances of miscommunication. I could not have been more wrong and more right. The discussion on the board was, at times, as dynamic as that taking place in the classroom, yet miscommunication also happened more often than it did in class. One of the most critical questions I had going in to this project was whether the level of academic discourse would suffer in such an impersonal medium and whether such a medium would encourage the silent to speak up. It seems that students did provide more thoughtful comments on the board than they might have in class, although those who spoke up in class and lingered after class to continue the discussion were also those who contributed most to the board. It is my impression, though, that while written responses seemed more measured on the board, students also felt freer to be intolerant than they might have face-to-face.

This board certainly reveals some of the problems inherent in distance learning. For instance, it is clear that students are likely to establish their own agendas and paths through the class material (or outside it). I can only imagine that this would be compounded in a true distance-learning course, where the map employed is by necessity less distinct. Without in-person discussion and direction, students are much more likely to establish and/or maintain their own agendas. Yet this test case also shows that such a space is not necessarily more inclusive than the traditional classroom, in which shy students and women often feel shut out. Those with computer access from home were not only more frequent contributors but spent more time at each session, writing longer responses. And men outnumbered women on the board by quite a margin.

These more practical issues are important and worth considering. Nevertheless, the most critical question I had at the end of the semester was how such technology changes the boundaries of what we tend to emphasize in this discipline and what we (and those in other disciplines) tend to overlook.

Ideally, of course, the content of electronic discussion boards should enhance and complement – not replace – in-class, in-person discussion. Yet it must be remembered that technological go-betweens are neither class discussions nor exclusively personal space. They exist in a sometimes awkward boundary status, a 'cyberlimen' where a student might not let 'everything go' but might feel freer than in the classroom. I did want the board to encourage students to engage with students knowing that it should, like any class discussion, be controlled and focused. Yet I realized that control takes away from the educational possibilities of the board from the students' point of view. On the whole, the discussions that took place on the board could not have happened in the classroom, in large part because I would have controlled them myself. I mapped the discussion as I saw fit, yet the students continually redrew the boundaries. We were all looking at the same territory, yet the maps we drew differed enormously.

Most importantly, perhaps, this board in this particular class illustrated what is perhaps best called 'living Christianity'. Students, both Christian and non-Christian, saw Christianity defined from different perspectives over and over again on the e-board. For example, one student, early in the semester, wrote to another "I must admit that you are right, there is no one Christian response. But is it possible that some responses are more correct than others? I think there are," and the student went on to defend that perspective. The 'living

Christianity' presented by several of the students serves as its own valuable topic for exploration. After all, students must deal with issues of 'faith', 'belief', 'reason', and 'science' every day.

While this medium can be used to directly mimic the controlled arena of the classroom, I now see the value in capturing students' sometimes tangential, perhaps not always academic, perspectives. While adopting technology as another medium for teaching religious studies requires students to engage with the subject in a different way, it also informs teaching in a way papers and class discussions cannot.

The feedback from this medium has allowed me to maintain a valuable archive of comments from students for when I next teach this class. This record is, in a way, more valuable in reshaping the course than the standard student evaluations. Rather than rely on often sketchy student evaluations written at the end of the semester, the e-board discussions track the students' interest throughout the course. What their questions were about particular issues, which readings generated more discussion, which parts of the course left them stranded – all are available for review. In revising the syllabus to teach this course again, I have regularly referred to these postings and I find them a gold mine of memories, far more valuable than my impressions of what a 'good' or 'bad' topic or reading was from the evidence of class discussion. And students rarely give detailed advice in their end-of-semester evaluations. Now I have an incomparable method of tracking class history.

I will repeat this experiment in future courses, although there is much I will consider changing. In the future I will have to strike a balance between insisting on course content and allowing students to explore more tangential issues that inform their lives as students and citizens. Perhaps I chose to be too 'hands-off' in this experiment, and perhaps I made a mistake in choosing to make the board a voluntary (and therefore, to some students, irrelevant) part of the course. It would be most helpful, I think, to provide two discussion boards: one would be for class content and announcements, and the other would be available for students who want to reflect on the issues in a student-defined space. In this case, one board would be graded and the other would be for more personal reflection. I would require students to lead queries on the board as part of their grade, and I would require regular, substantive contributions as a requirement of the course.

After this experiment, I am more willing to recognize that critical reflection which more closely mirrors the students' own concerns can be equally – or far more – valuable to their education than what the discipline requires. And yet I still insist (and always will) that students engage the texts before stepping off into other realms. I am now more open to the reality that some students will openly struggle with such issues outside of the assigned readings. I know that if I require contributions to such a board as part of the grading for the course, my own standards would require me to grade off for excessive personal statements. And yet that seems to belie my message that there is no such thing as *objectivity*: there are only *objectivities*. Doesn't this same logic apply of necessity to the way that I design a course such as 'Christian Controversies'?

This project brought to mind an article I read when I was still in graduate school. The article described what the authors called 'rhetorical teaching'. By this was meant a method whose primary aim is "neither to improve technique nor simply to make students more knowledgeable, but to empower student voices and to provide a space for practicing critical skills and reflective inquiry about matters of personal and public importance" (Miller et al., 1994, p. 820). When I first read that article, having very little experience teaching, I found myself wondering about the value of students' personal growth; in fact, I tended to feel it would be entirely irrelevant to whatever I meant to accomplish in the classroom. Now, after nearly four years of teaching, I see the tremendous value in "the stories [students] tell about themselves and their worlds" (Miller et al., 1994, p. 842).

It took this cyberlimen to help me outline the maps my students and I tended to draw around the subject matter, and to become aware of the sometimes vast differences between them. As all of those who teach religious studies can attest, one avoids the problems inherent in students' commitments and loyalties only at great risk.

I close with a brief interaction on the board, which was prompted by an extremely aggressive argument made by one of the regular apologists for Christianity. I read the posting, considered the attitude behind it, and responded with a request for the student to ask himself, "Are you alone wise?" The student responded with "To quote the great thinker, 'Here I stand, I cannot do otherwise. God help me. Amen' " (MOB, 99). The response is not original, but I believe the sentiment must be respected. Above all, it is important to note that this interaction would not have happened within the confines of the classroom. It happened in a space that allowed the student to assert his own convictions more clearly than he would face-to-face. It happened within the cyberlimen, a space that is not quite the classroom and not quite the 'real' world. On the evidence of this experiment, it could become a space where the boundaries of learning might well be redrawn in coming years.

NOTE

1. In this chapter, I will refer to students by their usernames, accompanied by the particular number of their post. I have regularized spelling and made a few grammatical changes to aid in reading. No such changes alter the substance of any posting.

REFERENCES

Barnette, R. (1998). Using Computer Technology for Teaching Philosophy: An APA Report. *Metaphilosophy*, pp. 323–332.

Burr, E. S., Clark, M. A., & Wyschogrod, E. (1995). Integrating the Net into the Religion Classroom: Some Notes from the Field. *Religious Studies News, 10*(2), 23–24.

Cavalier, R. J. (1992). Course Processing and the Electronic AGORA: Redesigning the Classroom. EDUCOM *Review, 2*, 32–37.

Clarke, K. (1997). Surfing the Sacred: Meeting God for Lunch @ the Global Ethics Café. *Sojourners, 26*, 63–64.

Collins, M. (1995). Using Electronic Bulletin Boards with College Biology Classes. *American Biology Teache*r, *57*, 188–189.

Collins, M. (1998). The Use of Email and Electronic Bulletin Boards in College-Level Biology. *Journal of Computers in Mathematics and Science Technology, 17*(1), 75–94.

Coombs, N. (1992). Teaching in the Information Age. *EDUCOM Review, 27*, 28–31.

Enstrom, E., & Fedderson, K. (1995). Culture and Anarchy in Cyberspace. *Works and Days, 25*(26), 91–104.

Grassie, W. (1997). Powerful Pedagogy in the Science-and-Religion Classroom. *Zygon, 33*(3), 415–421.

Hogsette, D. (1995). Unstable Conditions: Dynamics of Dissent in Electronic Discursive Communities. *Works and Days, 25*(26), 63–80

Kellner, M. (1996). *God on the Internet*. Foster City, CA: IDG Books Worldwide.

Kinney, J. (1995). Religion, Cyberspace and the Future. *Futures, 27*(7), 763–776.

Miller, R., Patton, L., & Webb, S. (1994). Rhetoric, Pedagogy, and the Study of Religion. *Journal of the American Academy of Religion, 62*(3), 819–850.

Mitcham, C. (1986). Computers: From Ethos and Ethics to Mythos and Religion: Notes on the New Frontier Between Computers and Philosophy. *Technology and Society, 8*, 171–201.

O'Keefe, J. J. (1996). The Virtual Classroom: Using an Electronic Discussion Group to Teach Theology. *Horizons, 23*, 296–305.

O'Leary, S. (1996). Cyberspace as Sacred Space: Communicating Religion on Computer Networks. *Journal of the American Academy of Religion, 64*(4), 781–808.

O'Leary, S., & Brasher, B. (1996). The Unknown God of the Internet: Religious Communications from the Ancient Agora to the Virtual Forum. In: C. Ess (Ed.), *Philosophical Perspectives on Computer-Mediated Communications* (pp. 233–269). Albany, NY: State University of New York Press.

Roberts, E. (1998). Strategies for Using Technology in the Teaching of Ethics. *SIGCSE Bulletin, 30*(3), 209–212.

Smith, Jonathan Z. (1978). *Map is Not Territory: Studies in the History of Religions*. Leiden: E.J. Brill.

Strangelove, M. (1993). Electronic Discussion Groups: A Virtual University. *ARC, 21*(2), 123–147.

Webb, S. H. (1997). The Voice of Theology: Rethinking the Personal and the Objective in Christian Pedagogy. *Journal of the American Academy of Religion, 65*(4), 763–781.

Works and Days (1995). CyberSpaces: Pedagogy and Performance on the Electronic Frontier, *25*(26), 131–132.

Zack, M. H. (1995). Using Electronic Messaging to Improve the Quality of Instruction. *Journal of Education for Business, 70,* 202–206.

Zappen, J. P., Gurak, L .J., & Doheny-Farina, S. (1997). Rhetoric, Community, and Cyberspace. *Rhetoric Review, 15*(2), 400–419.

CONFESSIONS OF A RECOVERING TECHNOPHOBE: A BRIEF HISTORY OF THE RELIGIOUS MOVEMENTS HOMEPAGE PROJECT

Jeffrey K. Hadden

ABSTRACT

The Religious Movements Homepage was a serendipitous by-product of my effort to learn how better to utilize multimedia resources in the class-room. The account that I offer tells the personal story of how problems encountered became challenges to tackle yet bigger opportunities. Initiated as a class project to organize Internet resources for future students in my course at the University of Virginia, The Religious Movements Homepage has become a global classroom with visitors from over a hundred nations each month.

INTRODUCTION

I recognized many years ago that multi-media technologies can be very effective tools in the classroom, but it has taken me many years to overcome my fear of technology so that I could explore the full potential electronic technologies offer.

Religion on the Internet, Volume 8, pages 345–362.
2000 by Elsevier Science Inc.
ISBN: 0-7623-0535-5

I began to overcome my discomfort as the result of a teaching technology initiative my university inaugurated in 1995. While I'll probably never learn enough about computers to be called a 'techie', during the past several years I have made significant strides in controlling the fear and exploiting the potential I long believed technology could offer for effective teaching.

This contribution is presented in two parts. First, I offer a plea to my colleagues in the sociology of religion to explore the benefits of using technology in the classroom. Second, I present some guidelines for utilizing the Internet for both in-class and out-of-class instruction

CONFESSIONS OF A RECOVERING TECHNOPHOBE

Technology has never come easy to me. When I was younger, I called on friends to set up and show me how to work almost every electronic or mechanical product I ever carried home. When I got a little older, I called upon technicians for help. In this era that medicalizes virtually every human shortcoming, I guess it is appropriate to identify myself as a recovering technophobe. And, in my case, the antidote has been massive exposure to the source of the disease.

My journey into the world of high tech began rather innocently in 1995 when my university announced a new program designed to encourage the use of technology in the classroom. I reasoned that my life might be easier and my classroom presentations more effective if I had a little time to organize and edit my bulging videotape library. A few months earlier I had seen a presentation using Power Point slides. I had no idea how those slides were created, but the presenter told me after his lecture that it wasn't difficult. I reasoned that creating lectures in this manner would force me to do a better job in organizing my presentations.

With little consideration of the implications of what I was doing, I wrote a proposal and became one of the first dozen Teaching Technology Initiative Fellows at the University of Virginia. So, there I was, ignorant as sin about technology and very uncertain of my ability to learn what I needed to know if I was to achieve my stated project goals. Nevertheless, as one among a dozen elite selected to lead one of the nation's fine public universities to the next level of technology utilization in the classroom, there was no turning back. Had I known the road ahead, I might well have never taken the first step.

My project was somewhat ambiguous in its formulation and not particularly ambitious in conception. As I began to master the most rudimentary rules for using the gadgets, my sights soared. I recall the morning I walked into the multi-media laboratory with a box of materials to create a lecture on Shakers. I imagined a seamless presentation with Power Point lecture notes illustrated with pictures scanned from several books in my library and photos I had taken on a visit to

Mount Pleasant Village in Ohio. All of this would be accompanied with an overlay of excerpts of Shaker music. And for good measure, I would digitize a piece of videotape I had captured from a human interest news story about two Shaker survivors who still resided in the Shaker Village in New Hampshire. It took the better part of the day for me to see, with my level of skills, I had set up about three weeks of work. The Shaker presentation was a marvelous idea, and I'm thinking that I might go back and work on it some at some future date. But in the summer of 1995, I wasn't ready for such an undertaking.

I spent a fair amount of time that first summer finding the proper balance between my increasingly ambitious presentation ideas, on the one hand, and my limited skills and time on the other. As the fall term approached, I had scanned hundreds of images from books, magazines, slides, pamphlets, and newspaper headlines in preparation for insertion into my lecture notes. I had learned Adobe PhotoShop editing and some of the materials I had created were, frankly, pretty good. But I had only a few lectures that were ready for presentation. Had the fellowship not provided for a teaching reduction to a single course, I would never have made it through that first semester.

I wish I could say that I soon became comfortable with my high tech classroom. After eight semesters teaching in a high tech classroom, I still get a little nervous at almost every transitional step along with way. In the beginning I often didn't know the difference between a technology failure and my ineptitude in working the technology properly. In the beginning, a technology failure, self-inflicted or otherwise, left me feeling utterly helpless and humiliated. I wanted to curse or cry out in anguish.

I still get frustrated when technology fails, but I no longer experience anxiety or a sense of rage. I have come to recognize that technology failures or glitches are part of life (at least for now). I joke about technology, and have learned a self-effacing comment can go a long way toward smoothing over the disruption of a presentation caused by failed technology. Students readily understand jokes about failed technology. Contrary to the myth that today's students are all techies, most of them are not. They too are struggling to apply the exploding technologies of the late twentieth century to their learning. So, when something doesn't work, I try to make light of the occurrence and then move on as smoothly as possible to a different mode or presentation.

UNANTICIPATED PROBLEMS ALWAYS PRESENT NEW OPPORTUNITIES

As I reflect back upon all the years I spent watching televangelists for my research, I have to confess that Robert Schuller's positive thinking, or possibility thinking as he calls it, has impacted my consciousness. In moderation, there probably really is a place for bumper sticker theology in all of our lives. "Inch by inch, anything's a cinch," is probably not a bad attitude to bring to the world of technology.

As my first year of instructing with technology progressed, I faced seemingly unending problems. Some were of such a nature that I would go home at night and contemplate as to whether there might be some graceful way to bail out. Each time, when faced with solving a problem, I came to realize that the crisis had generated an opportunity. Recognizing, and then acting upon, the opportunity created by problems has unquestionably had a greater impact on the direction of my teaching than anything that was structured into the teaching technology proposal.

Two examples of unanticipated problems I encountered may be helpful in understanding how my New Religious Movements Home Page came to be, and how this experience has impacted my teaching of other courses. The first really big crisis I encountered was the realization that students had become slaves to copying everything in my lecture slides to the point that they were not paying the slightest bit of attention to what I was saying. The second problem arose from my attempt to draw upon Internet resources to help students understand the fierce war between religious movements and their adversaries. When I began this exercise, anti-cult materials so overwhelmed everything else on the Internet that I feared I was going to end up with a whole classroom of anti-cultists.

The creation of a class Web page seemed to point the way to the solution of both of these, as well as other, problems.

THE POWER OF POWER POINT LECTURES

Eventually, I got the hang of efficient creation of Power Point slides. Most of my lecture presentations involve pretty detailed notes; typically 40–60 slides for a seventy-five minute class. My slides have additional lecture points that are hidden from the students' view, and I have hidden slides that I can pull up on screen if students ask questions about subjects that are not in the lecture. For example, I don't cover 'revitalization movements' in my lecture on fundamentalism, but over the years I learned that bright anthropology students often see the parallels in the two kinds of movements. When this happens, I have a hidden slide that can be pulled up in responding to the question. By anticipating the question, I have a crisp answer to the student's query and, at the same time, the information on the slide makes the issue accessible to the rest of the class who have probably never heard of revitalization movements.

The first benefit of creating slide presentations was a heightened awareness that my lecture notes were not nearly as well organized as I had imagined.

Getting materials better organized proved to be a time consuming task, but I have no doubt that this was a very important step in improving the quality of my lecture presentations.

What I did not anticipate was the degree of intensity that students exhibited in getting the content of every slide into their notes. My efforts to get students to put their pencils down were to no avail. Early that first term I expressed my concerns in a meeting of the TTI Fellows. "Put your notes up on the Internet after each lecture," one colleague urged. "If he did that, why would anyone ever come to class?" replied another. That problem could be solved with required attendance another suggested. I rather appreciated the reply of a chemistry colleague who said, "they'll come to class because Jeff knows a whole lot more interesting things about religious movements than is contained in those slides." At least I hoped he might be right.

At that point, I didn't have a Web page, nor did I have the slightest idea how one might go about creating one. Thus, distributing my lecture notes on the Web didn't seem like a viable solution. So I continued to struggle with the problem. I was leaning toward making the notes available, but the thought that this might impact attendance was, frankly, a bit scary.

During the intercession between the fall and spring terms, I created a modest Web page with a syllabus and a few readings that were accessible with a password. Early in the spring term, I took the plunge and made my notes available to my students on the Web site. This happened only after I staged a precipitating event that was calculated to move me off dead center. I carefully planned a presentation in which I would talk about one subject while popping slides on another. The Power Point slide presentation was my lecture on social science explanations for why people leave religious movements. My oral presentation was on the anti-cultists take on the same subject. As I spoke, the students dutifully copied every word they could write down from the slides. I was even interrupted once and asked to go back to the previous slide. I don't know how long I proceeded with this charade before I stopped to test my hunch. (It was probably only a few minutes, but it seemed like an interminable exercise at that time). When I finally paused and asked a question, my deepest suspicions were confirmed. No one had any idea that I was talking about a different subject.

So, with considerable trepidation, the lecture notes were made available to students on the class Web site. Initially I just put up the Power Point slides with their highly variable font sizes. They weren't very pretty, but they got the job done. That attendance didn't seem to be impacted by this move was not really surprising, but it was certainly gratifying. The following summer I restructured the notes so students would have a somewhat condensed version of my lectures.

I don't have a before and after control, so I don't know that students are doing better on exams. I do know that the notes are popular with students. I encourage students to read the notes before class. Many arrive to class with a copy of the notes and some come to class early and print a copy. Now, instead of cramping their fingers trying to get everything written down, I often observe that students use highlighters, and add marginal or in-text notes. Occasionally a student will arrive to class early and ask if I would expand in more detail on some particular point in a lecture.

The lecture note crisis probably would not have happened if my Power Point slides had only been the bare bones outline. But as it turns out, students now have a much better set of notes from which to study than most would have had if they had taken the notes themselves. Further, if I had created only brief outlines, I probably would not have had the experience of working through the development of a set of notes that are now clearly better organized. I believe that my own lecture notes in student's hands assure that they will have a better chance to master material I believe to be important.

UNEXPECTED GUESTS

Another unanticipated consequence of putting the notes on the class Web page was that I began to receive communications from people who had found them while searching the Internet. While I knew in the abstract that the class Web site was accessible to anyone in the world, it never really occurred to me that anyone outside my class would actually find and read them.

In the beginning, I didn't receive a lot of correspondence, but enough to heighten my consciousness to the fact that my notes and thoughts were available to anyone who might wish to check out the site. Most of the correspondence was positive and complimentary of my efforts. Some came from people who wished to express their disagreement with my perspective. And, there were also some that challenged my information and provided documentation to back up their challenge. Needless to say, these communications had profoundly important implications for how the Web page and my approach to teaching would unfold.

The awareness of a global audience, however small, heightened my awareness of the necessity of presenting factual information. This knowledge would figure very prominently when students started creating Web pages that would become a part of the class page. It gave me leverage to demand that they carefully document their research. Equally important, awareness that people from around the world visit the site has helped instill a sense of professionalism on the part of my students.

DISCOVERING THE WORLD WIDE WEB

I had never heard of the big WWW or Netscape, which had not yet gone public, when I began my teaching technology fellowship. It didn't take long to discover that in its infancy, the World Wide Web was a virtual war zone for many new religious movements. Since an important part of the study of cults and sects is to understand their conflict with adversaries, the prospect of being able to observe this on-line struggle seemed to me very exciting.

Beyond the recognition that this movement/counter-movement struggle was raging on the Internet, it didn't take much longer to see that the war zone was not a level playing field. Nowhere was this more evident than the case of Scientology and its adversaries. For all their wealth, lawyers, and commitment to aggressively pursue their enemies, the Scientologists were no match for the guerrilla tactics of their adversaries on the Net. I found literally scores of anti-Scientology sites and Scientology didn't even have an official home page. The 'unofficial' Scientology site, under the name Leisa Goodman's Home Page, contained lots of material, but good luck trying to find it on a search engine with all the registered anti-Scientology pages. A few Scientologists sought to defend their faith on "alt.religion.scientology," the Internet's most notorious brawl room, but it was a hopeless battle.

Few new religions fared much better than Scientology. Like Scientology, they either didn't have an official Web site or, if they did, they were not particularly effective instruments for presenting themselves. And, with few exceptions, neither official pages nor sites created by members viewed the Internet as the place to do battle with adversaries. Most of the cults and sects were reluctant to participate in the war. As a result, the Internet cult wars turned out to be pretty much one-sided ambushes. The more fortunate New Religious Movements (NRMs) were smaller groups who, by virtue of their smallness, did not have many apostates.

From my own searching, I was convinced that it was possible to locate enough different types of sites to provide a balanced perspective of most groups. But it was also clear that the disproportionate amount of negative materials made this a challenge for students. While I could quickly determine whether a page was the product of a friend or adversary of any group, it also was clear to me why this capacity to discern was not intuitive or self-evident to the novice student.

To facilitate students' using the Internet to learn about religious movements, I determined that I would produce a listing of hyperlinks for each of several groups that would be divided into four categories:

- official (and 'unofficial') home pages;
- friendly pages (typically created by members of the group);
- anti/counter pages (pages intended to undermine the credibility of a group); and
- scholarly/analytical pages.

While this didn't seem to me to be a very difficult task, with everything else (including learning how to efficiently create Web-page content), searching for sites and getting them up on my own page was going to be a time consuming task.

I believed the Internet had rich potential as a learning resource. The task, as I saw it, was to locate and then organize materials so students could use them. I created a prototype for a series of pages about different groups. Each page would have a common presentational format beginning with a Profile. This Profile would cover the essential information about the group: name, when created, by whom, why, how, etc. The Profile would conclude with a succinct statement of the unique features of the group's beliefs. This would be followed with a set of abstracted hyperlinks. The final feature of the presentation would be a print bibliography. I didn't envision these presentations as being comprehensive, but rather an effective means for gaining a good overview of many religious movements. And for those who were interested, the site would provide a gateway to far more comprehensive Internet and print resources.

I identified about twenty-five new religious groups as candidates for this task. In the fall term of 1996 I offered students an opportunity to create a Web page as a term project. I strongly urged participation in this undertaking and offered incentives for those who would participate. A little more than half of the class signed up to work on a group, but several did not complete the assignment. At the end of the term, those who had participated were highly laudatory of the exercise. For them, the reward was both the creation of a Web page of their own and discovering how the Internet can be an effective instrument for learning. In the course evaluations, two students wrote nearly identical comments to the effect "don't let the wimps off the hook; make the Web page development a requirement."

As I considered this counsel, I realized that making the assignment a requirement would fairly quickly organize an abundance of materials that students in subsequent semesters could use to enrich their learning. It would also address a latent embarrassment that I had lived with from the first day I walked into this 34 seat high tech classroom – rows of computers that students were only using when they came to class early to do email.

Proceeding with making the Web page development a course requirement, I now had a use for the computers. But once again, I had created new problems

I had not fully considered. The optional assignment to develop a Web page came with the expectation of attending training sessions outside of class time. By making the assignment a requirement, I was pretty much committed to taking regular class time for instruction. I was reluctant to take any class time away from the theoretical and substantive content, as there is never adequate time to cover everything I would like to do in a term anyway. But I really didn't have a choice. The second problem was more serious. I was still struggling to learn HTML and Web page construction myself. I was certainly not qualified to offer this technical instruction. The thought of doing so was nothing short of terrifying.

While I was pondering how to deal with this, I picked up the materials of a second year student named Craig Hirsh who it turned out had developed an astonishingly fine Web page. There were some 25–30 in-text hyperlinks, a navigation bar to guide the reader through the page, detailed abstracts to the off-site links, and even a search engine to explore the Internet. Wow! I was impressed. I hastened to write Craig a note of congratulations for earning an A+ for the course. I paused for a moment and then proceeded to invite him to help me with the course the next term in the role of technology instructor. He was on-line when I sent the message and immediately sent his one word acceptance 'absolutely'. I've learned a lot from this undergraduate student and he deserves a good bit of the credit for what the site has become. When Craig Hirsh graduated in 1999, I declared him Webmaster Emeritus.

FROM CLASS RESOURCE TO GLOBAL RESOURCE

Over a period of five years, the Religious Movements Home Page evolved from a simple page designed to service the learning needs of my students at the University of Virginia to a resource that is accessed from all over the world. As the page developed, the increasing volume of mail gave some hint of the fact that people all over were accessing the page. But creating a page that would become a leading site for accessing information on religious movements was not something I self-consciously set out to achieve. It just sort of happened.

A turning point of my own consciousness of a considerable readership occurred with the Heaven's Gate tragedy. I awoke the morning of March 27, 1997, as I normally do when the clock radio connects me to National Public Radio's *Morning Edition.* The voice was familiar, but it was not one of the program's regulars. "What do we know about this group," the reporter asked. 'Not much', the voice replied. "We're in the process of finding out right now."

Unlike my usual slow pace of waking, I came straight up out of bed. The voice was that of Gordon Melton, a friend of more than two decades and perhaps the world's leading authority on religious movements. For years I had sought to find a cult or sectarian movement that Gordon didn't know about. And every time I thought I had found one, I was disappointed to learn that he was way out in front of me. I didn't yet know that sleepy morning that there had been a mass suicide, but I knew if there was a group that Gordon didn't know about the group, it must be esoteric indeed.

I arose quickly, popped a tape in my video recorder, and managed to get maybe fifteen minutes of news coverage from three networks before I had to leave for school. I brought the tape to class and prefaced our viewing with the comment that neither Gordon Melton nor anyone else seemed to know anything about the group. Before we began viewing the videotape, I posed the following question to my students: "If you want to try and figure out the identity of this group, how would you go about it?"

Before we got very far into viewing the tape, I noted that several students had opened their computers to the Profile on UFO Cults on the class page. A few minutes later a student called me to her computer and pointed to the Heaven's Gate link. In the early morning news coverage, the media had identified the group as Higher Source which, of course, turned out to be the name of their business. But one of the videotapes we listened to also used the name 'Ti' as one of the group leaders. The student who had created the UFO Cult page had noted in the Heaven's Gate annotation that the leaders of the group sometimes went by the names of Doe and Ti, but they formerly had been known as Bo and Peep.

Bingo! I recognized immediately that my student had identified the group. It was not surprising, however, that neither the experts nor the media were able to identify the group for the better part of a day. The initial information with respect to the age (18–24) and gender (all male) was so off base that even Rob Balch, a sociologist who had studied the group in its formative years did not recognize it as 'his group'.

The Heaven's Gate Web site was almost immediately unplugged by the authorities and then reloaded on a 'secret' URL later that day. Thanks to some crafty sleuthing by Bill Bainbridge, we learned the identity of the new location and had the site mirrored on the class page late in the evening of that same day. Our curiosity to know whether we were getting some action led to the quick installation of an access counter that we had been considering for some weeks. Immediately upon installation, and for several days to follow, our access was bouncing in the range of 5,000–10,000 accesses. (Access refers to the number of times another computer comes to a site; 'hits' refers to how many locations on the site are visited. On average, we get about four hits per access.)

To our astonishment, it wasn't the Heaven's Gate mirror that was attracting attention. There were quickly lots of Heaven's Gate mirrors on the Internet as almost every major newspaper in the country put one on-line. There were also thousands of UFO sites, but we learned later that only a few of these sites bear the identity of a 'UFO cult' page. The Web spiders of several leading search engines had earlier found our profile page, which is thus titled. Thus, when people searched on 'UFO Cults' – and a lot of people did those days – our page was on the top, or near the top, of sites identified by the search engines.

Once Heaven's Gate had dropped out of the news, we were surprised to see that we were still getting a steady access in the range of 1,000 to 2,000 virtually every day. By commercial standards, and the fads of popular culture, the New Religious Movements Home Page was not dealing with large numbers. But as an academic site that had been designed to service the students in a single course, with an enrollment restricted to 34, the cumulative numbers were impressive.

Without our even recognizing it, the site was becoming a gateway to access information about religious movements for people from all over the world. From the beginning of our tracking of access statistics, the large majority of all visitors came from outside of the University of Virginia domain (>95%). And when we created a convenient structure for people to send us email, the messages started coming from all over the world. From the first month we tracked nation statistics we had visitors from more than 85 countries, with persons from somewhere between fifteen and twenty countries accessing the site daily.

WHERE WE ARE AND WHERE WE HOPE TO GO

The mail box and the access counter have changed a lot of things since March of 1997 when thirty-nine souls, who belonged to a group named Heaven's Gate, left their 'physical containers' behind to join a space ship they believed to be trailing in the shadow of the Hale-Bopp comet. The awareness that people from all over the world were watching in on our class exercises changed the agenda for my students and for me.

The classroom in Wilson 308 was no longer just an instructional laboratory for students at the University of Virginia, it was Control Central for information about religious groups that was going out to the whole world.

The stark realization that the world was watching changed how I approached the teaching of the course. I realized that I needed to raise the bar so that all students were striving toward excellence. My rising expectations needed to be communicated to the students in ways that would motivate them to want to achieve excellence. I'll readily confess that I have employed a variety of techniques, not all successful. I sometimes feel like I am practising sports psychology without a license. Fortunately, the University of Virginia has an outstanding student body and a large proportion of them are substantially self-motivated already. It is a matter of making clear the course requirements and my expectations, focusing their attention on the rewards of excellence, and then being available to prove support and reassurance.

Term papers, read by the professors, seldom see the light of day again. And only infrequently are students required to hand in multiple drafts that are critically reviewed and sent back for rewrites. Papers produced by the students of Soc 257, New Religious Movements have to be able to stand up to the scrutiny of anyone, from anywhere, who might drop in at anytime.

So, one of the things I try to instil in the consciousness of my students early on is that the product they are expected to produce for this course is not an ordinary term paper Many students understand and respond to this challenge early. I employ a variety of carrot and stick techniques that I hope will catch their attention and challenge them to strive to achieve. For example, every term there is some religious group that receives a fair amount of media attention, and this leads to significant traffic on our profile page of the group. The Branch Davidians were back in the news in the Spring of 2000, and our page received many thousands of hits.

When a group we have previously profiled is in the news, I like to open up the access statistics to show students how much action the particular page is receiving. This provides a transition to show them it is not unusual to have several individual student pages that are receiving several hundred hits a week. When I show the class how many hits some student pages receive, I like to point out that the number of hits received in a single month exceeds the total number of students I have taught in the classroom over more than forty years. And I also point out that this can be a positive or a negative motivator depending on their perspective. If they produce a quality page they can expect to receive email messages of praise which will be good for their self-esteem and, perhaps, suggest to them that they should list their page on their resumé when they enter the job market. On the other hand, I note, a page with inaccurate information is almost certain to produce mail from persons who may not exactly be polite in notifying you of your page's deficiencies. And, I am candid in telling them that poor work on their part reflects negatively on the University of Virginia and on me.

Not everyone in the class achieves excellence, but each term about four out of five students produce a profile page that I judge of sufficient quality to be uploaded to the permanent class collection of Web pages.

The project began as an exercise in learning the technology to produce a Web page and create content that would hopefully be useful for students in future semesters of the course. When we commenced, I was not very confident about what I was doing, so my expectations of students were, to be perfectly candid, not particularly high. In addition, the amount of material available on the Internet for any given group was only a fraction of what is now available. As a result of these factors, we accumulated several semesters of pages that do not measure up to the quality of pages students have produced over the last several semesters. We are now in the process of going back and upgrading pages produced in the early terms of the project.

The content of The Religious Movements Homepage has grown in many directions that could not have been anticipated at the onset. Most of this work has been done during summer months, a sabbatical leave in the Fall of 1999, and in spare moments during the term when I get a break from assisting students with the construction of their pages. About a half-a-dozen students, having taken the New Religious Movements course, have signed up for independent research credits and produced some most valuable components to the site.

For the more than twenty years that I have been teaching the New Religious Movement course, I have tried to find ways to build more content on religious freedom into the course. In the spring of 1998 we launched a companion Web page on Religious Freedom (www.relfreedom.org).1 This site contains substantially more material than is available on The Religious Movements Homepage, yet it remains underdeveloped in terms of the master plan.

At the same time we were designing The Religious Freedom Page, we launched a third component on Religious Broadcasting (www.religiousbroadcasting.org).[2] This segment reflects my on personal research interests in televangelism and the history of religious broadcasting. Eventually, I anticipate that this will also be a major Web site. It will contain profiles of significant religious broadcasters (paralleling the profiles of religious movements), short video clips of broadcasters, and a lot of historical material on the development of religious broadcasting. Religious broadcasting played a major role in the development of Fundamentalism and Pentecostalism during most of the twentieth century. In my view, these are the two most important religious movements of the century just past and I hope to develop resources that will show why this is so.

At the present time, the major content of the Religious Broadcasting page consists of most of my own writings on the subject, including both of my books: *Prime Time Preachers* (with Charles E. Swann) and *Televangelism, Power and Politics on God's Frontier* (with Anson Shupe).

I view these three components as part of an integrated religious movements Web site, with The Religious Movements Homepage the main entrance. Each component can be accessed from the other. At the present time, the student generated profile pages remain the most accessed part of the site.

Access has continued to grow at a level far beyond any expectation that I might have hoped for. During the Spring Term of 1999 the site received an average of a quarter-of-a-millions hits a month. In late May Craig Hirsh's final contribution to the project before graduating from the University of Virginia with honors was a new homepage for the religious movements segment. His new design not only gave the page a much more professional look, it significantly improved the navigability of the site. The results showed almost immediately. During the summer months, traffic on the site tripled to nearly a million. By the end of 1999 we were exceeding a million-and-a-half hits per month, and growth continued at a brisk pace during the first six months of 2000.

I spent the Fall Term of 1999 on sabbatical leave. My major goal was to develop a master site development plan. Still, the sense of urgency to tidy up a site that had grown rapidly, running off in many directions, was compelling. And, as traffic on the site increased, so too did my email. Much to my surprise and delight, the mail I received was mostly a combination of praise and encouragement, along with enormously helpful criticisms and information that could help improve the site. Assistance offered out of respect and appreciation for what we were doing was hard to ignore. As the weeks of my sabbatical leave passed all too quickly, it became increasingly clear to me that a master list of things to be done was not a master plan. Still, all those good suggestions kept coming in my email box. The list of tasks undone continued to grow.

Mid-way through the sabbatical period, I decided that the master plan would have to remain a nascent construction of my mind while I worked on improving many features of the page that seemed to cry out for attention. By the end of the sabbatical I felt a sense of pride and confidence that the Web site had moved a long way toward achieving the excellence that I strive to achieve. Six months later, we have added another forty pages in our religious movements profile section and I am once again aware of so many tasks that need to be done.

Is this any way to run a Web site? Probably not. Were I more disciplined and focused, the site might bear more visible evidence of systemic development. But this is the way it has happened, and the development of The Religious Movements Homepages has been one of the most felicitous experiences of my life. I confess to feeling just a little bit jealous when I read in the *Washington Post* reported that iBelieve.com and Beliefnet.com, two commercial Web pages, have been bankrolled to the tune of $30 million and $5 million respectively.[3]

So far, *The Religious Movement Homepage* has spent about $200 for some software that was not available from the university. I sometimes imagine a *deus ex machina* appearing with a bundle of resources that would permit me to hire some paid helpers. But most of the time when I'm in this mood, I think of Bruce Robinson who has created *The Religious Tolerance Page* (www.religioustolerance.org), probably the most magnificent religious Web page on the

Internet, with nothing but sweat labor. And his reward for this success is that he gets to spend a significant proportion of his retirement check to pay for server access.

I am delighted to have been the principal in the creation of The Religious Movements Home Page. I am inspired by its success and aspire to create a page that will have even greater impact, and a page that will have utility for all who seek to understand religion from the perspective of sociology. This requires both a critical assessment of what I have attempted to accomplish to this point, as well as sober reflection on the specific question of how the site might be useful to colleagues who teach sociology of religion courses. I turn to these matters in the final section of this chapter.

Without my students, this page would never have been possible. It is their page every bit as much as it is mine. As the shepherd of their labor, my possession of detailed knowledge of some groups falls short of what it should be. The result is that not every bit of information on the page is completely accurate. My students will attest to the fact that I push them hard to 'get it right' but sometimes their resources, and/or interest, are lacking. When this happens, the responsibility is mine, both to discover and correct errors.

If I was a little apprehensive when I first invited readers to communicate with me if they found errors in our work, I have come to recognize my correspondents as another tremendously valuable resource. Each time I enter a correction, or follow up on a suggestion offer by a reader, I am mindful that yet another person has become a collaborator in this enterprise.

The possibilities for Web-based learning seem to me to be all around us. Those of us who are teachers need to become self-conscious of these possibilities, and active participants in shaping this new learning environment. If we fail to do so, others who do not share the universal goals of free inquiry, critical reflection, tolerance for diverse views, and respect for cultural and religious pluralism will step in and organize Internet resources for pernicious purposes. And if we fail to do so, others who know much less about our subject of inquiry, will step in and organize information in ways that do not realize the potential of the electronic communications revolution we are currently experiencing.

My course on new religious movements, and the instructional content of The Religious Movements Homepage, stress the importance of studying new religious as the pathway to understanding all religions and developing sociological theory about religion. I also argue that the 'virtual reality' of the Internet is no substitute for experiencing religious movements in the flesh. Still, the Internet does provide unique possibilities to get closer to movements than is generally possible with textbooks and journals on the one hand, or mass media coverage on the other. As more and more religious groups go on-line with official home pages, we have the opportunity to access significant bodies of information about them, and how they see themselves.

I have encountered a lot of academics that don't want their students using the Internet because so much information 'out there' is unreliable. Whenever I hear this complaint, I always respond that this is one of the best reasons I can think of for sending students to the Internet for information. If our goal is to teach students to think for themselves, then we should want to expose them to situations where they know that they have to be able to discern the difference between facts, half-truths and irresponsible lies. Similarly, I want them to develop the capacity to discern the difference between a carefully documented argument and an opinion. In short, I think it is good that we send them out to encounter the world as they will find it when they leave the protected halls of academia.

The Internet is a wonderful place for students to encounter the world and develop the skills of critical thinking and discernment. The study of religious movements is a particularly valuable subject of inquiry to hone the skills of discernment precisely because the content is so highly volatile. Most of the students I have taught over the past two decades come to my course with the presuppositions of the anti-cultists. This is not surprising. Why would we not expect students to mirror the dominant perspective communicated in the mass media?

Most of my students readily grasp my theoretical perspective that views religious movements as a vital source for invigorating both faith and the broader culture. But once they leave my classroom, they will again be exposed to a steady diet of media coverage that views 'cults' as a menace to culture. If I expect my students to carry what I teach them into life, it is critical that the menacing intolerance of anti-cultists be observed and analyzed.

This comes to the very heart of what I have tried to do in developing The Religious Movements Home Page – to create a total learning environment. This characterization is, of course, an exaggeration, but it speaks to the goal of making accessible a wide array of learning resources at a single location.

At the present time, students can access detailed lecture notes on approximately thirty religious movement subjects. Each lecture comes with on-line readings that are integrated with the lectures and a select bibliography for further exploration of the topic. These lectures cover a general theory of religion that includes the growth and development of new religions, historical assessment of important religious movements, and an examination of the most important religious movements of the 20th century. The opportunity to learn about specific religious groups is enhanced by more than 200 profiles of religious movements (and the number grows each semester). Each profile includes a discussion of the group's distinctive beliefs and, when appropriate, a discussion of issues that have placed the group in tension with society.

Another important feature of this learning environment is the structure of links that connect this site to literally thousands of pages on the Internet that deal with religious movement subjects. For each group profiled, we have attempted to identify the most important sites about the group. These links provide a gateway to literally thousands of pages of valuable reading material. For each hyperlink, students have developed annotations about the content of the site at the other end. This helps the reader move more efficiently to explore his or her own interests and to determine whether it is useful to wait when a site is slow in downloading.

Through a combination of official Web sites and pages of members, students who feel brave can reach out through email and enter into conversation with group members. They can also access sign onto *listservs,* enter chat rooms and in many other ways develop contact with both group members and those who are self appointed adversaries.

Finally, for each group, we offer a select bibliography of both print and electronic resources.

The typical lower-division university level course is taught with a textbook; upper-division courses often utilize several books and/or a series of articles. Articles are typically selected by the instructor and then either sold by a local vendor or placed on reserve in the library. Custom tailored readings, available for less than a generation, significantly augment the resources an instructor can place in students' hands. But the Internet significantly enhances the opportunity to expand easy access to vast resources. This is what we are seeking to do.

The concept of total learning environment is a goal toward which we strive. Examination of the New Religious Movements site will verify the fact that we are making significant strides toward this goal. But it is also clear that our goal will never be fully attainable because knowledge keeps expanding, and the possibilities for delivery of new knowledge expand as well. Each new piece of material on the site and each new link increase the learning resources available to students and push us a little closer to the goal of a total learning environment.

Viewed from another perspective, the total learning environment concept speaks to a way of reinventing the library as the repository of knowledge. Card catalogues have already given way to electronic databases of resources available through a library. Increasingly, these resources are not on a shelf in the library stacks, but are residing on a server half-a-world away, and accessible with the click of a mouse. Much that is worth knowing has not yet found its way into textbooks or even journal articles. Web-based learning can open the world of knowledge and ideas to everyone, not simply that knowledge which has achieved legitimacy by appearing in journals and books, but literally all knowledge.

Some of us bristle when we consider the fact that anyone can publish on the Internet on any subject with no regard whatsoever as to the wisdom or validity of their thoughts. The capacity of the Internet to spread rumors, conspiracy theories and what most of us would consider just plain rubbish is astonishing. In the area of religious movements, this is no small concern. Religious intolerance, bigotry and hatred abound on the Internet and there is little we can do to unplug the computers of those who put it up. We can expose religious hatred for what it is, but more importantly, we can provide alternative perspectives.

We are only beginning to understand how the Internet can become a global classroom, accessible to all at any moment. I can think of no higher priority than trying to understand how it works and how we who are committed to expanding and transmitting knowledge can use it effectively. I view the Web site I have created with my students as one experiment in this learning process. I encourage teachers and students to utilize the considerable resources we have organized. I also encourage others to join in creating Web-based environments that will open new vistas for instruction and learning

NOTES

1. The Religious Freedom Page was designed by Young Woo. At this writing, Mr. Woo has completed his second year of Law School at the University of Virginia.

2. The structure for the Religious Freedom page was designed by Kuan Cho. Mr. Cho was graduated from the University of Virginia and has returned to his homeland of Korea.

3. See Bill Broadway, 'Prophets of Profit', *Washington Post*, Feb 5, 2000: B9.

4. In a sense, that is what happened when anti-cultists moved quickly into cyberspace to attack many religious movements.

ABOUT THE CONTRIBUTORS

Matt Bahr is a Research Associate for the American Religion Data Archive and a Ph.D. candidate in sociology at Purdue University. His areas of specialization include political sociology and sociology of religion. His current research in religion focuses on financial giving in American congregations

William Sims Bainbridge, Ph.D., is Director of the Sociology Program at the National Science Foundation. His many books and articles in the sociology of religion, including The Sociology of Religious Movements (1997), are well know to scholars of religion. He is also a cutting edge author of works dealing with culture, science and technology including Goals in Space (1991), Dimensions of Science Fiction (1986) and The Spaceflight Revolution (1976).

Kenneth B. Bedell, Ph.D., Kenneth B. Bedell, Ph.D., is Vice President of the Forum Foundation and in Seattle. Editor of the Yearbook of American and Canadian Churches from 1991–96, Bedell's current research and writing interests focus on the utilization of communication technologies by religious organizations.

Gary R. Bunt, Ph.D., is a Lecturer in Islamic Studies at the University of Wales, Lampeter, United Kingdom. He has a particular interest in contemporary Muslim expression, and has published a book on how Islam and the Internet combine and interact, entitled Virtually Islamic: Computer-mediated Communication and Cyber Islamic Environments (Cardiff: University of Wales Press, 2000).

Douglas E. Cowan, Ph.D., is an Assistant Professor of Sociology and Religious Studies at the University of Missouri-Kansas City. He is the author of A Nakid Entent unto God: A Source Commentary on The Cloud of Unknowing

Religion on the Internet, Volume 8, pages 363–365.
Copyright © 2000 by Elsevier Science Inc.
All rights of reproduction in any form reserved.
ISBN: 0-7623-0535-5

(Longwood Academic Press, 1991), and other scholarly articles. He has a particular interest in method and theory in the study of religion.

Lorne L. Dawson, Ph.D., is an Associate Professor of Sociology and Chair of the Department of Religious Studies at the University of Waterloo. He is the author of Comprehending Cults: The Sociology of New Religious Movements (Oxford University Press, 1998) and many scholarly articles on new religious movements and other aspects of the study of religion.

Roger Finke, Ph.D., is Professor of Sociology and Director of the American Religion Data Archive (www.thearda.com) at the Pennsylvania State University. He is co-author with Rodney Stark of The Churching of America 1776–1990 (Rutgers University Press, 1992) and has recently published another book with Stark entitled Acts of Faith: Explaining the Human Side of Religion (University of California Press, 2000).

Jeffrey K. Hadden, Ph.D., is Professor of Sociology at the University of Virginia. He founded The Religious Movements Homepage(www.religious-movements.org) in 1996 in conjunction with his undergraduate course on New Religious Movements. He is author and editor of more than twenty-five books and monographs including the two volume work The Handbook of Cults and Sects in America (with David Bromley) in this JAI series.

Christopher Helland is a Ph.D., is a doctorate student in sociology of religion at the University of Toronto, Centre for the Study of Religion. His research focuses upon religious accommodation and innovation in relation to the scientific and technological developments of the twentieth century.

Sara Horsfall, Ph.D., is Assistant Professor of Sociology, Texas Wesleyan University, Fort Worth, Texas. She graduated from Texas A&M University December 1996. Her publications include Chaos, Complexity and Sociology: Myths, Models and Theories (Sage Publications, 1997).

Robert Glenn Howard is a Ph.D. candidate in English at the University of Oregon. His research interests range from Native American thought to Christian Internet communication. He has published on Internet religious behavior, New Age millennialism, revelatory personal narratives, and the role of technology in education.

Massimo Introvigne, Dr.Jur., is managing director of CESNUR, the Center for Studies on New Religions, in Torino, Italy (www.cesnur.org) and a partner in a large international law firm. He is the author of thirty books in Italian (several have been translated into German, Spanish, and French), one book on the Unification Church in English, and more than 100 articles and chapters in scholarly journals and collected works.

Jean-François Mayer

Jennifer McKinney is a Research Associate for the American Religion Data Archive and a Ph.D. candidate in sociology at Purdue University. Her areas of specialization include the sociology of religion, social psychology and networks.

Bruce A. Robinson is founder and coordinator of the Ontario Consultants on Religious Tolerance (www.religioustolerance.com). He graduated with a BaSc degree from the University of Toronto in 1959. He recently retired as a Professional Engineer who developed textile instruments and process computer software for a multi-national chemical company.

Joanne Maguire Robinson, Ph.D., is Assistant Professor of Religious Studies at the University of North Carolina at Charlotte. She received her Ph.D. in the History of Christianity from the University of Chicago Divinity School in 1996.